CINEMA AND THE SANDINISTAS

Texas Film and Media Studies Series
Thomas Schatz, Editor

Cinema and the Sandinistas

FILMMAKING IN REVOLUTIONARY NICARAGUA

Jonathan Buchsbaum

UNIVERSITY OF TEXAS PRESS

AUSTIN

Some of the material in Chapter 10 was published as "A Closer Look at Third Cinema" in the *Historical Journal of Film, Radio, and Television* vol. 21, no. 2 (June 2001): 153–166.

First edition, 2003

Requests for permission to reproduce material from this work should be sent to Permissions, University of Texas Press, Box 7819, Austin, TX 78713-7819.

⊛ The paper used in this book meets the minimum requirements of ANSI/NISO Z39.48-1992 (R1997) (Permanence of Paper).

Library of Congress Cataloging-in-Publication Data

Buchsbaum, Jonathan, 1946–
Cinema and the Sandinistas : filmmaking in revolutionary Nicaragua / Jonathan Buchsbaum.
        p.   cm. — (Texas film and media studies series)
Includes bibliographical references and index.
ISBN 0-292-70523-9 (cloth : alk. paper) —
ISBN 0-292-70524-7 (pbk. : alk. paper)
1. Motion pictures—Nicaragua—History.   2. Motion pictures—Political aspects—Nicaragua.   I. Title.   II. Series.
PN1993.5.N537 B87   2003
791.43'097285—dc21

                                                    2003005000

For Layla Sacasa

Contents

List of Acronyms

AMNLAE—Association of Nicaraguan Women "Luisa Amanda Espinosa"

AMPRONAC—Association of Women Confronting the National Problematic

ANCI—Nicaraguan Association of Cinema

ANCINE—Association of Nicaraguan Cinematography

APP—Area of People's Property

ARDE—Revolutionary Democratic Alliance

ASTC—Sandinista Association of Cultural Workers

ATC—Association of Rural Workers

CAS—Sandinista Agricultural Cooperative

CCS—Credit and Service Cooperative

Cine RAP—State Cinema Theaters

COCULTURA—Cultural Corporation of the People

COIP—Industrial Corporation of the People

CORCOP—Commercial Corporation of the People

COSEP—Superior Council of Private Business

COSIP—Superior Council of Private Initiative

CST—Sandinista Central of Workers

DEPEP—Department of Propaganda and Political Education

DN—National Direction (of the FSLN)

ENABAS—Nicaraguan Company of Basic Foods

ENCI—Cinema Company of Nicaragua

ENIDIEC—Nicaraguan Company of Cinematic Distribution and Exhibition

EPS—Popular Sandinista Army

FDN—Nicaraguan Democratic Force

FMLN—Farabundo Martí Front for National Liberation (El Salvador)

FSLN—Sandinista Front for National Liberation

GPP—Prolonged Popular War

ICAIC—Cuban Institute of Cinematographic Art and Industry

INCINE—Nicaraguan Institute of Cinema

JGRN—Governmental Junta of National Reconstruction

MDN—Nicaraguan Democratic Movement

MICOIN—Ministry of Interior Commerce

MIDINRA—Ministry of Agricultural Development and Agrarian Reform

MIPLAN—Ministry of Planning

MISATAN—Organization of Nicaraguan Miskitos

MISURA—Miskitos, Sumos, Ramas

MISURASATA—Miskitos, Sumos, Ramas, Sandinistas Together

PCD—Conservative Democratic Party

TP—Proletarian Tendency

UNAG—National Union of Farmers and Cattlemen

UNO—National Opposition Union

Acknowledgments

In a project on such recent history, I benefited enormously from the information and memories shared with me by many of the people who worked at INCINE. I would like to thank all those who generously granted interviews; they are listed at the end of the book. In particular, I would like to thank the filmmakers who extended their warm hospitality and friendship to me and offered help in innumerable ways: Frank Pineda, Florence Jaugey, María José Alvarez, Martha Clarissa Hernández, Fernando Somarriba, Mariano Marín, Bolívar González, and Johnny Henderson.

In the course of my research, I learned from many others who worked at INCINE. Though I did not conduct formal interviews with them, the following people passed on valuable information in informal conversations or allowed me access to archival sources: Rodolfo Alegría, Ronald Porras, Eddy Meléndez, Wilmor López, Lucho Fuentes, Roberto Zepeda, and Eduardo Guadamuz.

When I first arrived in Nicaragua I depended heavily on the kindness of strangers. Those who went out of their way to ease my transition to a new culture included the late Roberto Porrales, Dolores Torres, and Layla Sacasa and her family.

For many years, Eric Holt and Kaki Rusmore (and Gabo and Eva) accepted me into their family and home and shared their deep appreciation of and commitment to Nicaraguan culture with me. They were endlessly instructive, helpful, and diverting.

In an economically poor country like Nicaragua, a weak infrastructure poses challenges for many tasks, both small and large—and often makes it difficult to distinguish between the two. I would like to express my appreciation to the following people for their help in navigating those challenges: Rubén Abreu, Daniel Alegría, Amy Banks, Abbie Fields, Suzanne Gasiglia,

Galio Gurdián, Barbara Kritt, Martha Juárez, Maricela Kauffman, Ariana Linger, Claudia Oquel, Trish O'Kane Adriana Ortíz, Carlos Powell, Mayra Luz Pérez, Karen Ranucci, Luis Serra, Silvia Serra, and Hessel and Teresa Weersma-Haworth.

For help in various stages of preparation of the book, Kate White offered invaluable advice and unquenchable enthusiasm (particularly for anecdotes tucked away in footnotes, even as prudence and space limitations sometimes forced their removal). Frankie Westbrook intervened at a crucial moment with incisive editorial recommendations. Thomas Schatz provided many helpful comments and suggestions and constant encouragement during the long march toward publication. Robert Sklar was kind enough to read the manuscript and bring his considerable writing and editing skills to bear in passing on suggestions. Other scholars who helped in a number of ways and deserve my thanks are Julianne Burton, Ana Lopez, Margaret Randall, the late Michael Rogin, and Susan Ryan.

I thank Barbara Bowen and Charles Molesworth—colleagues and comrades at Queens College—for their support.

The Research Foundation of the City University of New York provided generous support from the earliest stages of the project.

In gathering and processing the photographs—all of which are frame enlargements taken from the films—Pedro Linger was a solid pillar of support. Thanks also to David Bordwell for his helpful advice about the photos.

At the University of Texas Press, Jim Burr shepherded the book through to completion. Lynne Chapman devoted considerable time and demonstrated skilled professional care and patience throughout the final editing process.

I thank the following friends for their professional and personal support, which are always—or at least usually—delightfully intertwined: Henry Bean, Giuliana Bruno, Mark Jacobson, Doris Lee, Stuart Liebman, Patricia Meoño Picado, Uday Mohan, and Laura Mulvey. Joel Haycock, as always, offered constant wise counsel that I often associate with the advice of Carl Zumbach to Michel Poiccard: "D'accord, mais alors pas de Tweed."

While I didn't understand it immediately, Layla Sacasa offered revolutionary inspiration from my first days in Nicaragua.

Introduction

While working on an earlier book about progressive filmmaking in France during the 1930s, I interviewed as many survivors of that period as I could locate. They recalled those days as the most exciting ones of their careers, and I could sense that enthusiasm in the films, so often filled with the images and sounds of workers, artists, and intellectuals linking arms in their struggle against Fascism.

I had also studied other progressive filmmaking experiments in various countries, including the great "heroic" era of Soviet filmmaking of the 1920s; almost 50 years after that, following the success of the Cuban revolution in 1959, another creative explosion in filmmaking occurred in Latin America in, among other places, Argentina, Brazil, Chile, and Bolivia. Those latter experiments were snuffed out by repressive military regimes.

In 1979 the people of Nicaragua—workers, artists, and intellectuals— were struggling to transform their country after 50 years of dictatorship under the Somoza dynasty. With my interest in revolutionary filmmaking, I was eager to see what they had done in film. I went to live, work, and study in Nicaragua during a year-long sabbatical from Queens College, part of the City University of New York.

In 1989, when I first traveled to Nicaragua, the revolutionary Sandinista government was still in power. The only person I knew in Nicaragua, a man I had met one day for lunch in Washington, D.C., met me at the airport in his battered BMW. He invited me to eat at Los Ranchos, a fancy restaurant in Managua. The day, August 1, happened to be a holiday, and throughout the meal old Somocista friends of his passed by the table greeting Roberto, himself a member of the old bourgeoisie. Clad in expensive riding gear, the friends urged him to join them in the private room where they were celebrat- ing, but he refused, explaining to me with evident disgust that they had come back to Managua from Miami, to which they had fled after the triumph of the revolution in 1979. Roberto had worked for the Sandinista government in the early days of the revolution but eventually resigned. Only later did I learn that Roberto, though infinitely generous in extending his hospitality to me—an obvious Sandinista sympathizer—hated the Sandinistas.

By that time, the contra war had ended, and the second elections of the revolutionary period were scheduled for February 1990. Everyone I got to know assumed that the Sandinistas would win the elections, as they had in 1984. Once installed in a house in Colonia Centroamérica, and having begun teaching at the Jesuit Universidad Centroamericana, I had the good fortune to meet several filmmakers who had worked throughout the 1980s at the Nicaraguan Institute of Cinema (INCINE), the government filmmaking institute.

I knew very little of the work of INCINE, so I was eager to speak with the filmmakers and hear firsthand the excitement of revolutionary filmmaking. I found myself in the midst of a loose faction of former INCINE filmmakers; as I spent long hours with this group, I began to learn of the history of INCINE not in terms of some master narrative soldered by the fervor of revolutionary political commitment, but through a thick sediment of anecdotes, gossip, jokes, backbiting, rivalries, and bitter resentments. I was not exposed to a forum on revolutionary aesthetics, but rather to a primer on the institutional stresses and tensions of a revolutionary governmental institution.

Once my Spanish improved, I began to haunt the premises of INCINE to conduct more serious research. The principals had either left or been dismissed by this time, and the few people remaining evidenced little interest in the history of INCINE. Nonetheless, they helped me intermittently with screenings of films, but they were understandably more concerned with the difficult task of preserving the institution, now that it had fallen on hard times.

Actual archival research at first was virtually impossible for a number of reasons. I had heard many stories about incompetence and even malfeasance at INCINE, and the personnel were not eager to share internal materials. I believe most of the workers did not quite understand what I was looking for, and I do not believe they knew where the relevant material might be. Over time, as the institution became increasingly moribund, I was given greater access, to the point that I was poring through dust-covered file cabinets and crumbling boxes in forgotten corners, turning up assorted documentation in a largely random fashion. For example, I had heard a great deal about the innovation of the *talleres* in the mid-1980s, but I had seen no documentation. One day I happened to notice some pages from an official document on the *talleres* on the floor in INCINE's men's room. Later that day I discovered that, at least at INCINE, the need for toilet paper took precedence over historical preservation.

My research, then, began with fragments of the written record and a mass of contradictory and often incredible accounts from disaffected filmmakers. Though all were apparently pro-Sandinista while working at INCINE, they hardly sounded like Sandinista militants by 1989. I recall one evening in one filmmaker's backyard watching reel after reel of INCINE shorts made by the two filmmakers watching with me; they roared with rum-enhanced laughter at their own Sandinista follies, what they identified as pure Sandinista propaganda. The projector light blazed through the mosquitoes to the screen tucked among the mango trees as I peered unsuccessfully to find the humor.

When I lived in Nicaragua teaching at the Universidad Centroamericana in Managua from 1989 to 1990, and during subsequent extended visits of one to three months, I spoke repeatedly with, and recorded over a hundred hours of interviews with, former directors and other INCINE personnel. In addition to conducting formal interviews, I also spent countless hours socializing with the filmmakers, and I have drawn on those informal discussions. I tried to balance conflicting accounts and perspectives with the written and filmed archival evidence.

Most important, I have based my research on the films themselves. INCINE made some 70 films, for the most part shorts, during the Popular Sandinista Revolution from July 1979 to 1990. I have seen all of the films produced by Nicaraguans at INCINE and managed to copy most of them. As INCINE understood its function as mainly political, many films addressed political issues, and I have approached them on such terms. I have intentionally not discussed the many films made in Nicaragua by foreigners. While these films would undoubtedly illuminate the complementary perspectives of foreign observers, they would at the same time divert attention from INCINE's stated goal of constructing the first *Nicaraguan* national cinema project in its history. The extended published debate on the coproduction of *Alsino and the Condor*, however, will reveal the reservations expressed by Nicaraguans about one such film.

In July 1979 the Sandinistas suddenly faced the task of governing a poor country devastated by war. The Sandinistas quickly established a new army, the Sandinista Army, and a new police force, the Sandinista Police, in addition to other government institutions. However, the names of these two institutions indicate a collapse between the "national" and the "political/military organization" of the Sandinista Front for National Liberation (FSLN, Frente Sandinista de Liberación Nacional). This confusion between country and party was a constant source of tension in the ensuing years.

In fact, that tension runs as a thread throughout this book. The newly formed Ministry of Culture did not bear the Sandinista name, but like most institutions, it was run by Sandinistas, whether formal militants (full members) or not. On the other hand, neither the Sandinistas nor the Ministry of Culture ever promulgated an official state or party cultural policy. Internal divisions that eventually cracked the Ministry of Culture did not follow clearly ideological fault lines imposed by the Sandinistas. But the Ministry personnel certainly tried to develop revolutionary policies.

INCINE was established two months after the victory. As in most small, poor, third-world countries, Nicaragua had no previous filmmaking history. In 1979 that history began with the victory of the revolution. As part of a state institution, the debutant filmmakers wanted to contribute to the revolution. But what forms should their films take? What was their function? Who was the audience? They wanted to make *Nicaraguan* films, but would they also be *Sandinista* films? These questions have guided my work.

In fact, INCINE's distance from the central priorities of the Sandinista Front makes its films interesting: they provide a unique vision of the Popular Sandinista Revolution. The images and sounds they chose to represent the revolution reveal a Nicaraguan portrait of the revolution drawn not from official directives, but from the filmmakers' own interpretations of the Revolution as they were living it.

INCINE quite specifically identified one of its goals as "the recovery of national identity." In recent years, national identity has become a terrain of scholarly debate. Rather than an intervention, per se, in that debate, this book offers some observations on how INCINE's work might be construed as a project of constructing or recovering national identity. In many popular revolutions, particularly in small countries emerging from years of colonialism or neocolonialism, recovering national identity has been a central theme. On the one hand, this idea refers to achieving some degree of economic independence. But cultural production assumes a central role, too, for identity is often projected through a country's cultural production, paradigmatically through literature, but more popularly, through widely distributed forms such as cinema. Hence, INCINE's films reveal something about how Nicaraguans themselves perceived the new project of retrieving national identity in Sandinista Nicaragua. While INCINE was officially part of the governmental apparatus, it was located in a cultural institution with artists, not political directors.

On another level, INCINE's output belongs in the context of Latin American filmmaking. Historic changes in the media landscape over the past several decades, specifically since the establishment of the Cuban Cinema Institute (ICAIC) in 1959, have threatened the viability of national cinema projects. Though Cuba serves as one reference point, I have tried to think through a sustained and new interpretation of the meaning of "third cinema," another subject of renewed attention in recent years.

The INCINE films tried to make sense of a complex reality and contribute in their own ways to consolidating the revolution. Viewed retrospectively, the films perhaps did not penetrate deeply into that reality, with analyses of class factions, price inequalities, negative interest rates, population transfers, and so on. Naturally, the polemics of those years often clouded and skewed clearer perspectives. I have used those analyses to examine evolving discrepancies among the visions of the revolution promoted by the Sandinista Front, the revolution presented by the films, and the revolution on the ground.

In the end, while the Popular Sandinista Revolution was heralded and theorized about as a new form of revolution, its filmmaking experiment ultimately wrote the epitaph to a long tradition of militant, revolutionary filmmaking. This book seeks to rescue that national experiment in film—once the popular art par excellence—from historical oblivion as accelerating globalization and technological change threaten to engulf such efforts of national cultural expression.

CINEMA AND THE SANDINISTAS

One   THE CREATION
OF INCINE

In 1979 the people of Nicaragua, led by the Sandinista Front for National Liberation (FSLN), overthrew Anastasio Somoza, the last ruler in a dynasty that
had controlled Nicaragua since 1936. In April of that year, as the struggle
against Somoza was nearing victory, the FSLN, seeing the need for international publicity, organized a photography and film unit, the Leonel Rugama
Brigade.[1] Though the Nicaraguan militants in this group had no film experience, some foreign filmmakers shot footage, on the Northern Front
in the mountains and on the Southern Front on the Costa Rican border.
When the victorious Sandinista guerrillas streamed into Managua on July 19,
some filmmakers and militants rushed to a Somoza-owned film company,
PRODUCINE (Productora Cinematográfica Nicaragüense Especializada), and
occupied the premises.[2] Meanwhile the company's head, Mexican filmmaker and producer Felipe Hernández, had fled with much of the equipment, but a wild chase to the port of Corinto and back to Managua located
the boxes at the airport. They were seized and returned to the film company
headquarters at the Villa Panama, behind the Universidad Centroamericana.

A few days later, veterans of the Leonel Rugama Brigade congregated at
this same site. With no formal organization and no institutional affiliation,
the foreign filmmakers and Nicaraguan aspirants discussed how to proceed.
A Cuban journalist, Manuel Pereira, reported on these events two weeks
after the triumph:

> The widely known concept of "the camera is a gun" loses
> here its metaphoric aspect to be materialized every
> moment. An automatic rifle resting on a Moviola, a Colt
> 45 next to a can of film, a Galil machine gun hanging
> beside a lighting fixture, all images which, extraordinary

as they are—in these days of jubilation and popular vigilance—appear the most natural thing in the world.[3]

From the beginning, the future personnel of INCINE were debating how to retrieve a Nicaraguan cultural identity. Rafael Vargas, the only Nicaraguan with actual filmmaking experience, commented

> We have not been able to be authentically Nicaraguan.
> Thus, right now, we face having to recover our true identity as Nicaraguans. . . . It's like having to return to the house from which they chased us. They never let us enter the house, which is our Nicaraguan-ness [nicaragüensidad]. Now that we are going to enter the house, we are finally going to know ourselves.[4]

Javier Argüello disagreed, asserting that artists pursue art as individuals, not as representatives of nations. As a Nicaraguan, "I have never stopped being Nicaraguan, even during the dictatorship. Thus, my cinema is going to be necessarily Nicaraguan."[5]

Throughout the history of what would eventually be named the Nicaraguan Institute of Cinema (INCINE), this tension would remain unresolved, but not because shackles were placed on personal expression. The real tension, implicit in the early name change from *Sandinista* Institute of Cinema to *Nicaraguan* Institute of Cinema, involved the congruence between Nicaraguan and Sandinista. Would Sandinista filmmaking be Nicaraguan? Or, perhaps more saliently, would Nicaraguan filmmaking be Sandinista?

In a special section of *Cine Cubano* on Nicaraguan cinema in 1980, Pereira included the "Declaration of Principles and Goals of the Nicaraguan Institute of Cinema."[6] It asserts that the formation of INCINE is a response to the commitment to recover and develop a national identity:

> Our [cinema] will be a Nicaraguan cinema, launched in search of a cinematic language that must arise from our concrete realities and the specific experiences of our culture.
> It will begin with a careful investigation into the roots of our culture, for only thus can it reflect the essence of our historical being and contribute to the development of the revolutionary process and its protagonist: the Nicaraguan people.

The document closes with a "fraternal appeal" to the world's cinemas and filmmakers that "united with the spirit of the General of Free Men, Augusto César Sandino, they support our initiative."

The name Sandinista Front derived from Augusto César Sandino, the Nicaraguan leader who struggled to drive U.S. marines from Nicaraguan soil in the late 1920s and early 1930s. With the departure of those marines, Sandino signed a truce with the Nicaraguan government. The following year he was assassinated by members of the U.S.-trained Guardia Nacional on the orders of Anastasio Somoza. Somoza seized power in 1936, and with massive U.S. support, his family remained in power until 1979.

While Sandino's name disappeared from official Nicaraguan history after his assassination, a young university student, Carlos Fonseca, revived Sandino's memory and anti-imperialist struggle when he and two friends founded the Sandinista Liberation Front in 1961. The Sandinistas called themselves "the children of Sandino." Sandino's writings were a highly idiosyncratic mix of many sources, with considerable doses of mysticism thrown in: Freemasonry, Gnosticism, Rosicrucianism, Spiritism, Kabbalism, and the Magnetic-Spiritual School.[7] Consequently, Sandino's struggle and legacy provided a highly labile body of thought that heirs used in a variety of ways. The Nicaraguan people waged a long and difficult struggle against the Somoza regime. In the 1970s, with the last Somoza ruler bombing Nicaraguan cities, a broad Nicaraguan opposition finally forced his removal from power.

On September 22, 1979, two months after the triumph, the Junta of the Government of National Reconstruction (Junta de Gobierno de Construcción Nacional) issued the following decree:

> Article 1. Creation of the Nicaraguan Institute of Cinema (INCINE), with the appropriate goals and powers which the law establishes.[8]

Using Nicaraguan instead of Sandinista in the Institute's name was now official, but didn't eliminate a troubling confusion over identity and loyalty between the state and the Front throughout the following decade. What was the allegiance of Front members who served in the government, and what was the role of the filmmaking institute, whose leaders, after all, would be named by the Front?

The decree placed INCINE within the Ministry of Culture, headed by Ernesto Cardenal, a member of one "tendency" within the FSLN, the terceristas. By placing INCINE in the Ministry of Culture, the FSLN distinguished cinema from other Nicaraguan mass media. Like INCINE, the Ministry of Culture was supposed to promote Nicaraguan culture. The FSLN did not dictate what Nicaraguan culture should be, but the Ministry of Culture struggled over this issue, most prominently and publicly as it concerned the poetry workshops. At the same time, the Front gathered the press, radio, and television in the Department of Propaganda and Political Education (DEPEP) (though private newspapers and radio stations continued to operate). The state television expressed the FSLN viewpoint, as did the Sandinista daily newspaper, *Barricada*. Evidently, just as the Front recognized cinema's potential only at the end of the struggle against the dictatorship, the Front did not rate Nicaraguan cinema as a political medium of mass diffusion. Thus, in assuming control over the two Nicaraguan television stations, the FSLN named them the Sandinista Television System. Cinema was Nicaraguan Cinema, representing Nicaraguan culture.

INCINE experienced both advantages and disadvantages from its relative autonomy. It benefited from its distance from the party and central elements of the government apparatus. Since economic and political tasks of the revolution were paramount at the beginning, Nicaraguan cinema, which was not considered by the FSLN to be significant economically or politically, attracted little notice. Within the Ministry of Culture itself, intellectuals and writers did not flock to INCINE as the vanguard of the cultural front. On the other hand, the relative isolation indicated that INCINE could anticipate limited resources. Furthermore, the Front blocked INCINE's access to revenue by giving it only administrative control over state distribution and exhibition of films; however, at the same time there existed private distributors and private theater owners.

The Front appointed three INCINE directors. Ramiro Lacayo, scion of a wealthy Nicaraguan sugar family, who had served on the Southern Front in the Leonel Rugama Brigade, took charge of production. Carlos Vicente (Quincho) Ibarra, an older, longtime Front member, who had concentrated on ideological work, primarily in radio, assumed administrative responsibility for distribution and exhibition. The third head, Franklin Caldera, was *the* Nicaraguan film critic and published a book on film, *Cinema Lists,* in 1979. Caldera, however, had little interest in production, was not a Front member, had not fought in the revolution, and soon departed for Miami; he ultimately wrote for a pro-contra newspaper.[9]

For Pereira, the Cuban reporter, this nascent Nicaraguan cinema,

> with a clear revolutionary, anti-imperialist and Latin American vocation, . . . can be nothing other than the New Latin American Cinema.[10]

Pereira is claiming this future Nicaraguan cinema, then, for the Latin American filmmaking tradition that was effectively anchored by the work of the Cuban Institute of Cinematographic Art and Industry, ICAIC (Instituto Cubano de Arte e Industria Cinematográficos). The Cubans emphasized the importance of cinema in their own revolution and inspired filmmakers throughout Latin America. The Cuban example in the 1960s catalyzed filmmaking efforts in countries engaged in revolutionary struggles. When Pereira reported on his visit, Cuba was about to host the first Festival of New Latin American Cinema in December 1979.

A new cinema in Latin America had burst on the scene artistically and institutionally in the late 1960s. With popular movements surging throughout the region, festivals at Viña del Mar (Chile, 1967 and 1969) and Mérida (Venezuela, 1968) marked a creative outpouring of militant cinema, with powerful films screened from Brazil, Argentina, Bolivia, Chile, Cuba, and elsewhere. These were the days of the great successes of Cinema Novo in Brazil, of Miguel Littín, Raúl Ruiz, Aldo Francia in Chile, of Cine Liberación's *Hour of the Furnaces* by Fernando Solanas and Octavio Getino, of Jorge Sanjinés in Bolivia, of the Cuban films by Tomás Guitiérrez Alea, Humberto Solás, Julio García Espinosa. The Cuban journalist Pereira was invoking this heady time when he referred to the literalization of the "cinema is a gun" metaphor.

As these cinemas took shape in their respective countries, the filmmakers began to see themselves as part of a continental project, building and consolidating a *Latin American* cinema. Throughout the early years of this movement, however, the filmmakers chose *national* topics for the films, and the pan–Latin American thrust found expression only in the festivals themselves, for the filmmakers did not make "Latin American" films.

The tension between the national and the continental has generated considerable discussion. In the first festivals, neither filmmakers nor critics spoke of a new Latin American cinema. The only integrative rubric was a still inchoate "New Cinema."[11] In the enthusiasm of these first Latin American meetings, the filmmakers offered many theoretical statements. Understandably, these statements reflected distinct national and personal experiences. The filmmakers shared concerns about national identity and imperialism, but they couldn't articulate a single vision of the New Cinema, let alone a New Latin American Cinema.

The excitement waned during the 1970s, as military rule and repression crushed revolutionary movements and forced revolutionary filmmakers into exile: Littín, Soto, Ruiz, Solanas, Getino, Rocha, Sanjinés. Only Cuba consolidated itself and resisted counterrevolution. ICAIC became an institutional beacon for cinema, but even ICAIC encountered difficulties that led to a major reorganization in 1976. Nonetheless, in 1979, in an attempt to reanimate the New Cinema, Cuba held the first festival of New Latin American Cinema, in Havana, where it has been a December event ever since. The festival programs since 1979 attest that New Latin American Cinema existed after 1979, but stripped of the New Cinema's militant, anti-imperialist animus. Since 1979 virtually any film made in Latin America has qualified as part of New Latin American Cinema.[12]

The search for a renewal at the 1979 Havana festival coincided with the victory of the Nicaraguan revolution and the founding of INCINE. In fact, the Nicaraguan entry in 1979, *Primer Noticiero* INCINE (*Newsreel 1*), was one of the few that carried the original banner of New Cinema at the first festival.[13] Argentina and El Salvador were represented by guerrilla filmmaking groups, but these countries still suffered repressive military rule, whereas the first Nicaraguan noticiero hailed from the newly victorious Sandinista revolution. Awash in unforced exuberance, the Nicaraguan film echoed the militant optimism of the 1960s. In recognition of this promise, the festival awarded the Nicaraguan film a special prize (Saúl Yelín).

More specifically, INCINE was embarking, although perhaps not consciously, on a route mapped by a particular filmmaking practice in the late 1960s, that of Third Cinema. Third Cinema was a concrete proposal for revolutionary filmmaking that grew out of a specific political movement in Argentina; its meaning and relevance cannot be separated from the unique production, distribution, and exhibition of a remarkable film made in Argentina in 1968 by Fernando Solanas and Octavio Getino, the epic *Hour of the Furnaces*. The "cinema is a gun" expression quoted by Pereira became widely known from the diffusion of the 1969 Third Cinema manifesto "Towards a Third Cinema." Of all the historical antecedents and theoretical interventions by Latin American filmmakers in those more militant years, the concept and practice of Third Cinema might have helped INCINE confront its problems during the course of the decade. Unfortunately, critics and filmmakers have not served Third Cinema well. Just as the New Cinema lost its sting in the institutionalization of the New Latin American Cinema, Third Cinema suffered an analogous domestication, blurring critical boundaries, blending historical particularities into one another, and robbing the political and cinematic projects of their distinctiveness, a process examined in chapter 10.

After the triumph, just as the FSLN had disseminated Sandino's thought and practice for its *Nicaraguan* revolution, the INCINE filmmakers did not rush to adopt foreign models. INCINE proceeded empirically and reacted somewhat xenophobically to the foreigners' suggestions.[14]

Some students at exclusive high schools had seen film "classics"—Italian neorealism, the French New Wave—but these were presented as cultural and aesthetic expressions, linked philosophically perhaps to existentialism, not as catalysts for political activism. Ramiro Lacayo, INCINE's principal head in the 1980s, admits that though he had seen various Latin American films, he hadn't heard of the New Latin American Cinema, and this was more than ten years after the Viña del Mar conferences at which the New Cinema first captured the imaginations of Latin American filmmakers.[15] Needless to say, Cuban films were not distributed in Somoza's virulently anticommunist Nicaragua.

INCINE administrative heads had no clear vision of how to proceed. None had formal film training, and retrieving a national identity through film was an oxymoron. Nicaragua had no history, or tradition, of filmmaking. With the exception of Rafael Vargas, all experienced filmmakers on the scene were foreigners, and Lacayo claimed that many foreigners counseled immediate production of fiction films, an absurdly premature proposal. Like the revolution itself, the future filmmakers followed no single historical model. They planned to proceed pragmatically, soliciting and accepting counsel from experienced comrades in Latin America but concentrating on discovering and expressing Nicaraguan identity.

Cuba, without question, has exerted the greatest influence on progressive artists throughout Latin America since 1959, though only Nicaragua welcomed Cuban advisers. Cuba placed a high priority on cinema. In addition to maintaining a large number of theaters (500), Cuba built an extensive infrastructure of mobile cinemas to screen films in the countryside, with 325 different units and some 100,000 projections per year.[16] As a socialist country, Cuba nationalized all the theaters and did not have private distributors and exhibitors controlling competing screens. Cuba created ICAIC as an autonomous entity directly under Castro (though it did become part of the newly formed Ministry of Culture in 1977).

Most of the founders of INCINE, however, were only in their twenties (Lacayo was only 27), only slightly younger than the Sandinista leaders themselves, and knew nothing of this context. The Nicaraguans not only had no filmmaking background, they also had little cinematic culture. In this "country of poets," the cinema occupied a marginal place in national cultural discourse. As in most Latin American countries, U.S. and Mexican films dominated the local market, and there was no national tradition of film criticism, though Nicaraguans attended the cinema regularly.[17] Censorship had previously blocked the exhibition of Latin American militant or revolutionary cinema hailed throughout the world, and the lack of *any* Nicaraguan film production prevented pursuing political work prior to the triumph through clandestine filmmaking as in Argentina, Chile, and Bolivia. Some FSLN leaders were film aficionados, but none saw filmmaking as a political weapon.

During the anti-Somoza struggle, Cuba supported the FSLN in many ways, offering refuge from Somoza repression, medical treatment for wounded fighters, and military training. After the triumph, Cuban advisers helped the FSLN implement the Sandinista revolution, including its dissemination through film. Just as the Cuban revolution inspired the founding of the Front in 1961, the reputation and longevity of ICAIC had no equal in the New Latin American Cinema. Other progressive national filmmaking projects in Latin America flared and faded, though not always because of political repression. The Popular Unity government in Chile failed to establish a national film institute, and the Argentine experience suffered from the paradox of Peronism. Cinema Novo's institutional existence in Brazil was ephemeral at best and promoted no political program. But Cuba had maintained a functioning film industry for 20 years.

After the Sandinista triumph, Cuba established bilateral conventions between ICAIC and INCINE. Cuba provided raw stock, laboratory services, postproduction facilities, and advisers for the planned production of monthly 35-mm black-and-white newsreels, or noticieros, and a smaller annual number of primarily 16-mm color documentaries. In addition, the Cubans offered extensive technical training for Nicaraguans in Cuba. Essentially, ICAIC proposed the construction of a Nicaraguan film project closely modeled on its own system, including a tandem plan for an extensive mobile cinema system to bring film to the countryside.

Unlike the Cuban government's decree establishing ICAIC in 1959, which began with the bold assertion that "The Cinema is an Art," the terse Nicaraguan announcement of the creation of INCINE (cited above) offers no indication of cinema's role in the revolution. In fact, this curious laconism, in retrospect, provides a suggestive guide to INCINE's future, and many of the filmmakers view INCINE's subsequent path as symptomatic of the revolution itself. Unsure of how to proceed, enthusiasm buoyed their beginnings. Once the inevitable setbacks struck, INCINE lost its moorings and struggled to survive.

A comparison with the Cuban decree reveals significant differences. The Cuban document creating ICAIC was the first cultural law enacted;[18] in Nicaragua, Decree No. 6 announced formation of the Ministry of Culture on July 20, one day after the triumph, but did not mention cinema. In Cuba, cinema was privileged among the arts, and its institutional placement underlined that status. The Cuban law directly addresses industrial issues; the name ICAIC included "Cinematic Art" and "Industry." And the Cuban revolution succeeded in a country with a relatively developed industrial formation and an organized working class.

In Nicaragua, industrial development was limited, the working population was not organized and had a small proletariat, and the agricultural economy was not dominated by large landholders. The Sandinista revolution was antioligarchic, not clearly anticapitalist. Thus, the FSLN did not nationalize property of the bourgeoisie. The first decree of the Junta declared the nationalization of the Somoza family holdings and its closest collaborators. Yet Somoza's wealth was concentrated in agro-industry, the processing of materials, more than in land per se. Thus, the initial nationalizations affected only some 20 percent of the land. Though FSLN leaders sometimes spoke of increasing land nationalizations, the state actually reduced its holdings over time as it discovered the difficulty of administering them.

An analogous process took place with cinema, which hardly qualified as an industry. Not only did the government not nationalize all prerevolutionary vestiges of film distribution and exhibition, it also scattered disparate units of a nascent Nicaraguan film apparatus in distant administrative areas. INCINE, assigned to the Ministry of Culture, had responsibility for film production and for Mobile Cinema. The government nationalized one theater chain belonging to a Somoza associate. These theaters, known as Cine RAP (after the name of its former owner, *Ricardo Argüello Pravia*), constituted about 20 percent of the 125 theaters in the country, roughly the same percentage as that for nationalized land. But INCINE had only administrative, not financial, control over Cine RAP. Financial control was located in COIP (Corporación Industrial del Pueblo/People's Industrial Corporation), within MICOIN (Ministerio de Comercio Interior/ Ministry of Internal Commerce). All other theaters remained in private hands throughout the decade. The government took no action against any of the four private distributors. In the first years, the state had no distribution entity, though it formed ENIDIEC (Empresa Nicaragüense de Distribución y Exhibición Cinematográfica) in 1981, within yet another administrative area of the Ministry of Culture, COCULTURA (Corporación Cultural del Pueblo). In other words, unlike Cuba, the government did not plan an integrated film industry with adequate material and administrative resources to constitute a self-sustaining enterprise. No doubt the government was not about to allow INCINE control over a source of revenue that was desperately needed elsewhere.

At the same time, the government did not dictate what INCINE should do. Taking their cues from the Cubans, the heads of INCINE drew up preliminary plans for production, distribution, exhibition, and a mobile cinema. Production would begin with short noticieros that covered the rapid changes taking place. All of the filmmakers claim that the topics for the noticieros were conjunctural. That is, the subjects were the most significant activities of the moment, such as the literacy campaign, the building of the army, the agrarian reform, economic reconstruction, and so forth, what Frank Pineda called "unrepeatable events that were part of our history."[19] The filmmakers selected topics from a list of possibilities. The initial plan to produce monthly noticieros required about five days for research and preproduction, about a week to ten days for filming, and a similar period for editing and printing in Cuba.

The filmmakers did not participate in compiling the list of possible subjects, but none of them questioned the appropriateness of the choices. As head of production, Ramiro Lacayo prepared the list of topics. The earliest noticieros dealt with issues important to the Front, but there is no evidence that the Front imposed subjects on Lacayo. The choices were perfectly consonant with broad national goals articulated by the Front and supported by the people.

Nor is there evidence that the filmmakers were told how to approach the subjects. The filmmakers would screen their films at INCINE before final approval was granted, and Lacayo and others would express their opinions of the films. At the same time, many filmmakers acknowledge in retrospect that they adopted their own forms of self-censorship. Even Rafael Vargas, who has commented bitterly on INCINE's censorship, admitted that he succumbed to self-censorship himself. The filmmakers have complained about the enigmatic critical pronouncements sometimes voiced at the internal screenings, but they have been unable to identify calls for specifically political changes. Furthermore, the INCINE archives, though incomplete, do not contain references either to political guidelines or to memos detailing politically motivated emendations.[20]

INCINE faced a difficult, perhaps insuperable, challenge: how to develop a Nicaraguan cinematic idiom while honoring its self-imposed commitment to the FSLN. With no tradition of cinematic culture, INCINE could practice with and adapt foreign models, but Hollywood filmmaking, and to a lesser extent Mexican melodramas, were the most familiar models. However, the life illustrated in Hollywood films represented the materialistic antithesis of the aspirations of the Nicaraguan revolution. On the other hand, however appreciative the filmmakers were of Cuban support, few embraced what they saw as an overly restrictive and politicized model. INCINE, then, had no obvious historical model. With no experience making, or even seeing, oppositional cinema from Latin America, the filmmakers worked within the vision of a Sandinista Nicaragua. Though INCINE was not part of the FSLN political education and propaganda structure, the new filmmakers were Sandinista filmmakers, if that meant committing themselves to the Sandinista revolution. In the excitement of the time, virtually everyone called themselves Sandinistas though few were actually militants or formal members of the Front.

What the filmmakers and administrators at INCINE did not, and perhaps could not, have realized, were changes in the media landscape throughout Latin America since ICAIC's creation in 1959. At that time, Cuba installed cinema as a favored ideological medium, officially decreeing, "Cinema is an art." Weekly newsreels, documentaries, and fictional feature films projected the revolution to the Cuban people and abroad; the Cuban decree maintained that cinema was "the most direct and extended vehicle for the education and popularization of ideas." Filmmakers in other countries tried to follow the Cuban example, but none of them succeeded, and the Cubans themselves achieved only limited success. Military repression crushed those experiments, but the reverses obscured a more ominous development.

Though it happened gradually, throughout Latin America, television and video replaced cinema in many ways. INCINE took shape in the midst of this change, which did not sink in for other Latin American filmmakers until the 1980s. The Havana festival, for example, did not include video until 1986. In Nicaragua, the disarticulation of cinema functions reflected both FSLN ambivalence about the role and cost of cinema and the centrifugal tensions of bureaucratic feudalism in the new state. But it also traced the competition of alternative media practices. The three most important Ministries—Defense, Interior, and Agriculture—ran video projects primarily, but not exclusively, for internal use, and some political activists championed the advantages of small-scale grassroots media production over the costly demands and dubious political value of a national cinema project. The final chapter will consider the impact and implications of these developments.

However, these changes were not obvious in 1979 when the Sandinistas triumphed and established INCINE; to the contrary: the Sandinistas were only the latest of the anti-imperialist revolutionary movements in Latin America dedicated to restoring national identity. INCINE followed as the latest episode in a distinguished history of militant filmmaking in Latin America. In a time of crisis for revolutions and revolutionary cinema, would the Sandinistas, and INCINE, succeed where the other experiments had failed?

Two   THE FIRST
             NOTICIEROS

The war against Somoza devastated the country. Out of three million Nicaraguans, some 50,000 died. Agricultural production had been seriously affected in a country dependent on export crops for hard currency. Through almost five decades of rule, the Somoza family had extended its power throughout state and private institutions, a process that accelerated after the earthquake in 1972, as the last Somoza ruler diverted relief aid to enrich himself, gutting the economy and running up a huge national debt. When Somoza fell, the state institutions that were so imbricated with his family's interests had to be entirely rebuilt. The new governing Junta of National Reconstruction, named only a month before the triumph, released Decree No. 6 establishing 16 new ministries, including the Ministry of Culture, to be followed five months later by an extensive reconstitution of ministries. The size of the government quadrupled.

In this convulsive first year, INCINE concentrated exclusively on producing noticieros, most shot in 35-mm black and white. In the early years, INCINE finished a noticiero about once a month, from preproduction through release, with postproduction, including editing, completed in Cuba. The eight- to ten-minute noticieros were shown in regular movie theaters, and later, through the Mobile Cinema project in traveling venues. Unfortunately, there is little documentation on the exhibition of the noticieros. The newspapers did not review them, for they reviewed few films. In fact, there was little coverage of cultural events in the newspapers before the appearance of a cultural supplement to the FSLN paper *Barricada* late in 1980. Anecdotal reports from the filmmakers indicate that the state-owned theaters showed the noticieros regularly before the regular feature, but private theater owners screened them more randomly, such as when audiences were arriving or leaving. While television was a natural

place to screen INCINE films, bureaucratic feudalism and personal problems between Ramiro Lacayo and the head of the Sandinista Television System (SSTV) blocked that outlet. In later years, once the economic situation deteriorated, few people had disposable income, and theater attendance
dropped. One editor noted ruefully that INCINE was making films exclusively for foreign festivals.[1] Noticiero production, which continued on a
fairly regular basis for four years and ended in early 1985, provided a training
ground for young filmmakers. The noticieros went through several phases
as the institute and the filmmakers acquired experience, eventually moving
on to documentaries and fiction. In the first year, INCINE concentrated on
establishing a regular noticiero production schedule and completed 11 noticieros during its first year.

INCINE organized the first noticiero, *Nacionalización de las minas* (*Nationalization of the Mines*, Dec. 1979), around the historic nationalist hero,
Augusto César Sandino. This first noticiero combines two basic, and fundamental, themes: Sandino's heroic struggle and the recent nationalization
of the mines, from which came the title of the film. The film is structured
around a former fighter in Sandino's army and links his words to the 1979 triumph and to the challenges of national reconstruction. A long opening shot
features an old Sandino soldier walking down a dirt road. The camera zooms
out to show a small village, then rises to a slow pan sweeping across the
mountains, in Nicaragua's north, an area associated with Sandino's army.
The old combatant José del Carmen Meza, wearing a large hat like Sandino's,
appears in close shot speaking about joining Sandino's army at 20. Several stills of Sandino are inserted, the camera glides slowly over the photographs, then the mountain landscape returns as del Carmen Meza describes
a Guardia massacre of over three hundred people, including women and children. The survivors fled to the mountains, where, says del Carmen Meza, "I
spent then 27 years, 27 years of life." Suddenly there is a cut to shots of coal
mines, with turbulent sounds of machinery covering the transition. As del
Carmen Meza describes the U.S. ownership of the mines, various shots of
workers rinsing ore and women washing clothes illustrate the miserable conditions. Del Carmen Meza returns to speak of his constant desire for victory,
"because what I wanted was triumph, not defeat."

Folkloric music then begins as the camera zooms out quickly from two
large posters of Sandino and FSLN founder Carlos Fonseca to show a group
marching in a small village. Junta member Daniel Ortega appears, rifle over
his shoulder, walking with other armed compañeros to a public presentation
in Siuna, a mining town in which Sandino fought. Comandante René Vivas,
head of the Sandinista Police, announces that they will read an important
decree by the Junta, a law on the nationalization of the mines. During his

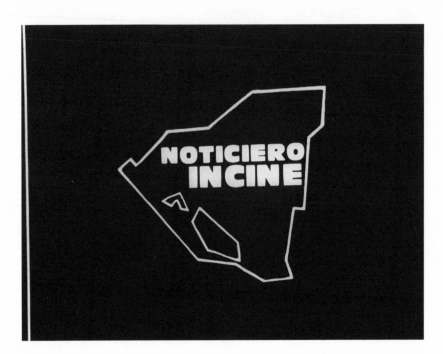

First INCINE logo

Second INCINE logo

speech, there are shots of coal being mined, and when his speech refers to nationalization, a dynamite explosion punctuates this historic event and is followed by the crowd's shouting, "Patria libre o morir! Obreros y campesinos al poder!" [Free homeland or death! Workers and campesinos in power!] Ortega follows and, just before he finishes his speech, there is a long take of children marching with wooden guns resting on their shoulders. Before this shot ends, del Carmen Meza's voice notes that he wasn't dreaming. He knew one day they would accomplish what Sandino was fighting for, and he said, "I feel completely content, and I want to dedicate my last years in the service of my country." As the FSLN hymn comes on, del Carmen Meza walks toward the old cathedral in Managua's Plaza of July 19, the cathedral just an empty shell since the 1972 earthquake, as the camera zooms out slowly to display a huge poster of Sandino gracing the cathedral's entrance.

The Front obviously was inspired by Sandino, whose image with hat and boots was everywhere in Nicaragua after 1979. The Sandino veteran del Carmen Meza provides the historic link with Sandino. The mines' nationalization completes one of Sandino's demands, the elimination of foreign exploitation in Nicaragua. The explosion captures the people's power, or more specifically, the power of the workers and campesinos in the worker-peasant alliance, for unlike much of the population of Nicaragua, the mine workers were salaried workers. This audiovisual punctuation places a rhetorical stress on this alliance, a classical Marxist tenet, despite the numerical weakness of a Nicaraguan working class. Though the film makes no verbal reference to this, the mines were located on the Atlantic Coast, traditionally inhabited by indigenous peoples, and Miskito Indians were the dominant group working in the mines. Throughout Nicaragua's history, there has been a deep division between Nicaragua's Pacific and Atlantic regions, physically and culturally. The Pacific region's population is predominantly mestizo, or people with Spanish blood. Indians and black Creoles lived in the Atlantic region, often ignored by the central government, and they viewed the mestizos as Spaniards. In recent decades this ethnic distribution on the Atlantic Coast has changed in favor of the mestizos, but the cleavages persisted, to the point of armed conflict in 1981. In any event, including Siuna in the first noticiero indicates an attempt to address this problem through a unifying association with Sandino.[2]

When Ortega says the future of the country is in the hands of the children, he means that the youth are the source and guardians of power, and also that the youth will be armed. Nicaragua will not neglect military defense. The militarization of the society, and the degree to which youth would participate in national defense, would become sources of tension in the years to come, though this might have been difficult to imagine in 1979.

*Militarization of society, in first noticiero (*Nacionalización de las minas*)*

*Veteran of Sandino's army providing the link to the victorious FSLN in the first noticiero (*Nacionalización de las minas*)*

In fact, Frank Pineda, the filmmaker credited with directing the film, objected to including the shot of armed children, but wanted to avoid friction with the Cubans, who were contributing personnel, equipment, and post-production facilities to INCINE.[3] Pineda worked on the film, but all of the Nicaraguan filmmakers consider this noticiero, and the second one, Cuban films.[4] Expertly shot by Cuban cinematographer Alvaro Jimenez, the film is constructed effectively, with its sweeping pans suggesting the sweep of history, its use of del Carmen Meza framing the coverage of the nationalization of the mines, and its choice of popular music furnishing a Nicaraguan pedigree. Pineda and others also recall a certain fascination with arms and guerilla clothing in the early years. Many INCINE people carried weapons even though not engaged in fighting.

With the first noticiero establishing the historical link between Sandino and the FSLN, the second offers an overview of 1979 and a glimpse of the revolution's agenda. This second noticiero, *1979: Año de la liberación* (*1979: Year of the Liberation*, Jan. 1980), begins with television footage of Somoza's new year's speech to the country. Titles are superimposed over Somoza:

Nombre [Name]:	Somoza
Edad [Age]:	53 años [years]
Ocupación [Occupation]:	Dictador [Dictator]
Misión [Mission]:	Exterminar a un pueblo [Exterminate a people]

As Somoza speaks of national reconciliation, archival images from the insurrection replace him on screen: planes bombing cities, dead bodies lying in the street, Guardia Nacional pouring gasoline on a pile of bodies to incinerate them. After television footage of demonstrations, FSLN Dirección Nacional (DN) members issue a statement from "somewhere in Nicaragua." After more insurrection footage, Sergio Ramírez (future Junta member) speaks at a famous 1977 news conference of Los Doce [The Twelve], refusing any accommodation with Somoza's regime. Realizing that Somoza's power was crumbling, the United States promoted forming a new government, derisively referred to by the Nicaraguan opposition as "Somocismo without Somoza" because the proposal did not call for the dissolution of the Guardia Nacional. Los Doce, formed specifically to deflect this tactic, represented a broad alliance of opposition groups.

After a map shows FSLN forces converging on Managua, a freeze-frame of a young guerrilla rhetorically transforms the earlier image of Somoza with a new set of superimposed titles:

Nombre [Name]:	FSLN
Origen [Origin]:	Augusto Sandino
Fuerza [Strength]:	Militar todo un pueblo
	[A whole people under arms]
Misión [Mission]:	Liberar a su patria
	[Liberate his homeland]

A church bell rings and the camera tilts down to reveal a guerrilla pulling the bell cord as an automatic weapon dangles from his shoulder. The bell intro-duces the victorious march of guerrilla columns into Managua on July 19.

The film's second half articulates the FSLN program. Jaime Wheelock, head of the Agrarian Reform, explains to some peasants that the land is theirs; they have fought for it. *Barricada* headlines precede speeches from a series of comandantes. The Comités de Defensa Sandinista (CDS; block com-mittees) are "the eyes and ears of the revolution." The Sandinista Workers Federation (Central Sandinista de Trabajadores, or CST) represents the "work-ers' unity with the revolution." In footage from the first noticiero, Daniel Ortega arrives in Siuna to announce the nationalization of the mines. After a large poster refers to the Atlantic Coast, stating "The Giant Awakens," the famous poet Ernesto Cardenal, Minister of Culture, addresses some women and children on the reconstruction of national culture. Tomás Borge, Minis-ter of the Interior, informs the newly formed Sandinista Police that its own work in defense of the Sandinista revolution is part of the Latin American revolutionary struggle. Finally, Henry Ruíz, Minister of Economic Planning, addresses the first National Assembly of the Association of Rural Workers (Asociación de Trabajadores del Campo, or ATC), stressing the importance of reactivating production. As women operate machinery in a factory, hands pick coffee beans and pour them into a basket, and Ruíz declaims, "Viva the worker-peasant unity." The film concludes with children waving Sandinista Army flags.

However quickly this noticiero was assembled, *1979: Año de la libera-ción* accurately delineates broad themes that would dominate Nicaragua: agrarian reform, popular participation (CDSs), industrial production (CST), the Atlantic Coast, the worker-peasant alliance, and military defense. The formal mechanism of governing the country receives no mention, though the most important mass organizations are represented in the film: CDS, CST, ATC.

To organize the people before the victory, the FSLN encouraged forming large groups of supporters into diverse "mass organizations" of neighborhood residents, Sandinista youth, women, industrial workers, and rural workers.

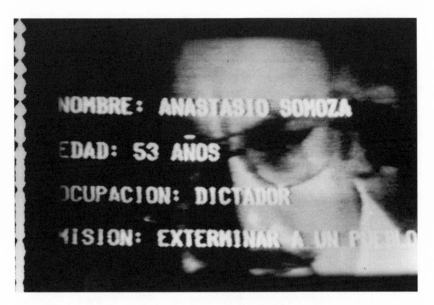

*Mission: Exterminate a people (*1979: Año de la liberación*)*

*Mission: Liberate his homeland (*1979: Año de la liberación*)*

The First Noticieros

These groups gave institutional voice to their constituencies in a two-way communication with the small FSLN. Until 1984 the mass organizations had seats on the Council of State, which advised the highest governing body, the Junta. In the early years, the FSLN justifiably claimed that the mass organizations were a cornerstone of popular, participatory democracy and guaranteed a voice for the popular classes in national decision making. However, as pressures from the contra war and economic hardship mounted, these mass organizations lost independence. For the most part, the Front depended on them to execute policies instead of incorporating their input to form policies. In the film, the individual FSLN comandantes form the armature, not the programs of the mass organizations; the FSLN comandantes speak, but the heads of the mass organizations do not. And the CDSs are represented only by a headline from *Barricada*.

In this second noticiero that, at 20 minutes, was twice as long as most later noticieros, one can detect tensions that would emerge more dramatically later. The mass organizations have no independent voice; comandantes speak for them. Only members of the Dirección Nacional, the FSLN's nine-member supreme decision-making body, are shown. The head of the CDSs, Carlos Nuñez (also a member of the DN), is not shown, and the film omits the mass organization of women, Asociación de Mujeres Nicaragüenses Luisa Amanda Espinosa (AMNLAE), named after the first Sandinista woman to die in battle.

After the first two noticieros, Nicaraguans began their real apprenticeship. The Cubans acted more strictly as advisers, although postproduction was still done in Cuba. Despite the presence of so many foreigners, and some veterans of the Leonel Rugama Brigade, INCINE mainly stayed with Nicaraguan personnel. For the third noticiero, *Economic Plan of 1980* (Feb. 1980), Lacayo assigned María José Alvarez. Lacayo had known Alvarez for years, for they shared a similar upper-class background. Alvarez had left Nicaragua in 1975 to study photography in Boston but had remained in contact with Lacayo and had returned to Nicaragua from time to time to take photographs for the Front. After the triumph, Lacayo called her in Boston and asked her to work at INCINE.

With little experience in government and little reliable information, the FSLN needed time to articulate an economic plan. The presumed centerpiece would be the Agrarian Reform, but the first task was reactivating the economy. Somoza and many Somocistas had fled, taking cash, and many business interests had been hoarding money in Miami since the insurrection started two years earlier. Other business interests remained but withheld investing in production. Many technical personnel left the country, depleting an already weak pool of technical expertise. Meanwhile, peasants and workers,

Agroindustrial machinery dwarfing workers (Plan económico 1980)

flush with the victory, occupied abandoned lands and factories, but without supervision or administrative experience. In short, the economy was reeling.

This modest film illustrates some early problems of the noticieros. First, the comandantes dominate the images and sounds. Although some shots show Ruíz and Wheelock standing amidst groups of workers, the FSLN leaders, in military dress, do the talking. Not a single worker is heard. Comandantes exhort the listeners to work hard. As a song in the film puts it, "If we reap the harvest, we raise the nation." Second, the film effectively gathers the images to turn the comandantes' words into an illustrated speech, a filmed pamphlet. All the filmmakers look back on these early efforts as too "panfletario," too much like a propaganda pamphlet, hammering at audiences with the same rhetoric delivered in rallies and on the radio and television daily nationwide.

In addition, the film unintentionally reveals some future FSLN problems. In the first images, the camera glides over shells of large buildings, evidently factories. Industrial production precedes agricultural production, and both Ruíz and a poster refer to the working class, a tiny proportion of the economically active population. But the film, like the Front, gives priority to this industrial working class, an orthodox Marxist perspective that overlooked the composition of Nicaragua's productive forces and the relative participation and importance of the working class in the war. Similarly, the agricultural section introduces the agricultural discussion with the large machinery of agro-industry, and Wheelock refers to his listeners as "workers," not peasants. Wheelock groups workers in coffee, sugar, tobacco, rice, and meat, all export crops. Only later does he mention basic grains, calling on those workers to work harder to guarantee the supplies of basic food. Throughout, the images and sounds relegate the listeners, the workers, to secondary status. They are silent, and in the images, machinery dwarfs them: They are barely visible in the shots of the factories. Mechanization pervades the film, in industry and in agriculture. In a country highly dependent on agriculture, campesinos are almost invisible. The FSLN later realized the complexity of the agricultural situation, but their initial policies favored the city over the countryside, and the agricultural proletariat over the campesinos.

The next noticiero, *Patriotic Day of Sandino* (Mar. 1980), commemorates another public event, the birthday of Sandino. In this noticiero there is a clear stylistic discrepancy between the first and second parts. The first part privileges popular images and sounds: Ordinary people speak in unrehearsed scenes of everyday life. Nicaraguans would have immediately recognized these images and sounds as Nicaraguan, unmediated by FSLN messages. The filmmakers understood that they were making FSLN films, even without specific directives. In the early months, the FSLN was perceived as the revolution. There was no separation between the two. On the other hand, Alvarez, perhaps intuitively, included ordinary people, speaking colloquially and anecdotally, a contrast to the comandantes' standardized rhetoric. Although the filmmakers did not see themselves as strict propagandists for the Front, they wanted to communicate fundamental ideas of popular power and to empower audiences to believe in their own revolutionary potential. The second part of the film, however, covers the official speeches of the comandantes speaking from a podium.

The most renowned demonstration of popular participation in the revolution was the Literacy Campaign. In 1979 fewer than half of the population could read or write. Organized into literacy brigades, teachers, predominantly urban high school and university students, fanned out, often discovering their own country for the first time. The exchanges between brigadistas and campesinos bridged traditional barriers of understanding between the city and the countryside. The Literacy Campaign won international approbation when UNESCO awarded Nicaragua its literacy prize in 1980.

INCINE devoted the fifth noticiero to the Literacy Campaign, and Alvarez oversaw the work. Camera crews traveled throughout the country, filming the brigadista training, the rally kicking off the campaign in Managua, the departure for the countryside, and some initial encounters with campesinos.

The government announced the literacy crusade in August 1979, less than a month after the victory, and two weeks before the formation of the

A proud mother with daughter at beginning of the Literacy Crusade
(Inicio cruzada nacional de alfabetización)

new Sandinista army. The announcement declared 1980 the Year of Literacy.[5] Months of preparation preceded the campaign's official beginning on March 23, 1980. *The Opening of the Literacy Campaign* (Apr. 1980) opens with young brigadistas exercising in a field, while the campaign's official song plays. Interviews with parents and brigadistas fill the first part of the film. One brigadista explains, "Now we are going to engage in a battle, not with rifles, Fals, little pistols or a .22 rifle. This time it is going to be with a pencil and a notebook." Another reports that her mother objected to her leaving home, fearing "we will come back pregnant." These interviews take place in the large plaza by the old Managua cathedral. In each interview, the subjects are surrounded by others: mothers ringed by their children or brigadistas flush with excitement. With the microphone jutting into the frame, and questions posed offscreen by Alvarez, the images confer a powerful authenticity on the interviews. These spontaneous testimonies by the muchachos and muchachas capture their enthusiasm, seriousness, and commitment.

As usual, FSLN leaders spoke at the rally, from the rostrum.[6] However similar, the FSLN leaders' exhortations came from a different place, a place with the people, but simultaneously above them. This spatial disparity, per-

Learning to write (Inicio cruzada nacional de alfabetización)

haps inevitably, prefigured a growing ideological distance. As buses and trucks of young people glide across the screen in the collapsed space of a long lens, DN member Bayardo Arce speaks of the utility of an educated citizenry for production:

> The problem of the revolutionaries now is to look at what and how much we produce in this country. How can we succeed . . . if we find that 52% of Nicaraguans do not know how to read and write? This is the fundamental importance of the Literacy Crusade.

This highly functional characterization of literacy's value contrasts vividly with the idealistic visions evoked by the participants and their mothers. In a sense, like the war of liberation itself, the people's energy, once released, overtook the FSLN's political-military plans. The FSLN found itself following the people. During its years in power, the Front began to corral and direct this energy more efficiently; but with pressure from the contra war and economic hardship, the bond between the Front and the Nicaraguan people frayed. In the film, the shot of Arce bridges the brigadistas' departure from Managua and the campesinos' anticipation of their arrival. Squatting in a row, campesinos, identifiable by their clothing and speech, comment on

Tomás Borge and Edén Pastora saluting together
*(*Inicio cruzada nacional de alfabetización*)*

Effacement of Pastora after Pastora's defection to the contras (Mobile Cinema print
of Inicio cruzada nacional de alfabetización*)*

what they look forward to reading. One campesino mentions seeding, farming, and agriculture, but above all, he wants to write his name. When Alvarez asks what they can teach the brigadistas, another campesino says, "We can teach them about agriculture, how to make charcoal, how to use the machete; they can learn from us all that we know."

Fernando Cardenal, the leader of the Literacy Campaign, then speaks from the rostrum. Cardenal, Minister of Education and a priest like his brother Ernesto, Minister of Culture, declares, "We have demonstrated to the entire world, and especially to imperialism, that the Nicaraguan people neither sell out nor surrender," repeating the words from the FSLN hymn. The film concludes with a montage of shots of campesinos and children painstakingly learning to write the alphabet. Young brigadistas raise their arms in unison in a freeze-frame at the end.

None of the first noticieros dealt with the FSLN's political strategy. That strategy entailed creating a modus vivendi with the patriotic bourgeoisie under FSLN hegemony. Of course the situation was not static. Some of the bourgeoisie adopted a wait-and-see attitude; others simply left for Miami.

The next noticiero, *Acto del primero de mayo* (May 1980), however, shot during the May Day rally in Managua, addresses the resignation of two non-FSLN members of the Junta. Violeta Barrios Chamorro was the widow of the assassinated anti-Somoza editor of *La Prensa*, and Alfonso Robelo was a wealthy businessman who had opposed Somoza. With Lacayo directing, the film opens in the Mercado Oriental, the large popular market near what was once downtown Managua, leveled by the earthquake of 1972, never to be rebuilt; many shells of buildings still bear witness to the vast damage. The Mercado Oriental is Nicaragua's popular retail market par excellence, selling any consumer item available in the country, with vendors, transient and permanent, crammed together in a labyrinth of small and large shops.

The setting, then, connotes a truly popular ambience, the antithesis of any programmed party line. When asked about Robelo, a middle-aged woman responds, "Señor Robelo, as he wants nothing to do with us Nicaraguans, naturally didn't send his children on the literacy campaign, for he didn't want them to mix with the campesinos." A teenage girl believes Robelo has acted "because he wants to go backward, instead of calling on his brothers to go steadfastly forward with the revolution, demonstrating that he is a true revolutionary and that he is rising up." Another man says, "It seems to me that we are living a revolutionary process, and that it is the revolution that is defending the interests of the people, not Robelo, so I don't agree with him, and if he has resigned, it's because it didn't benefit him." According to these Nicaraguans, Robelo is not one of them. His nonparticipation in the Literacy Campaign surely proves his opposition to the revolution, for the Literacy

Campaign was the revolution's first great success.[7] The voices of the people themselves, not the official spokespeople of the FSLN, brand Robelo's stance as anti-popular.

After the interviews, officials again take over and the remainder of the film is speeches. As in most of the early noticieros, the FSLN rhetoric overwhelms the simple but powerful words of ordinary people. Standing before Sandino's portrait on a podium and shot from below, Junta member Sergio Ramírez links the resignation of Barrios Chamorro, who "has explained with characteristic honesty her support for the revolutionary process," with Robelo's actions and statements in an effort "to create a climate of instability and challenge to the popular revolutionary process which is supported by the immense majorities of the Nicaraguan people." Bayardo Arce, FSLN political director, indicts Robelo and others for breaking "the unity which was the determinant factor in our triumph over the dictatorship." After a high-angle panning shot capturing the huge crowd, Ramírez mocks Nicaraguans who have fled to Miami and now want to return. A cartoon then shows Robelo in an MDN (Movimiento Democrático Nicaragüense, Robelo's party) airplane next to a caricature of Uncle Sam. After a pan of the Council of State, Arce explains, "It is the people who will be in the Council of State. The Council of State, for the first time in our history, institutionalizes the participation of the workers, the campesinos, and other sectors of the nation in the determination of its historical destiny." Members of AMNLAE walk to the head of the chamber in the Council of Deputies to receive credentials.

As in earlier noticieros, *Acto del primero de mayo* combines interviews and official speeches. The title suggests a single event, rather than a larger theme, such as the economic plan or the Literacy Campaign. The film also mixes demonstration footage with sounds of popular celebration and repeated references to Sandino, with his huge portrait overlooking the speakers' platform and his quotes sprinkled throughout the film. In the tension between the voices and images of the people and those of the FSLN, the FSLN dominates. Clearly, the filmmakers are helping institutionalize Sandino as a national hero and martyr. Like the other films, *Acto del primero de mayo* insists that the people sacrifice to escape backwardness and underdevelopment.

With calls to rally behind the nationalist Sandino, the FSLN stresses unity and working together toward their "revolutionary destiny," for the forces of history do not go backward. However, despite its being May Day, there are no portraits or allusions to Marx and Engels, the theoreticians of the international workers movement and the laws of historical materialism, or to their most famous revolutionary heir, Lenin. No foreign revolution serves as a model, not the Soviet Union, not Cuba, key sources of material and financial support. The FSLN is the vanguard, but the leaders do not mention the working class; instead they speak of workers [trabajadores, obreros] and peasants [campesinos]. And the early interviews take place not in the countryside or in a factory, but in the Mercado Oriental, heart of the so-called informal sector of unorganized and unsalaried workers who would be key players in the success or failure of the Sandinista reconstruction.

The May Day commemoration, divested of associations with International Workers Day or any foreign antecedents, reflects the FSLN's anomalous ideological strategy. Upper estimates of FSLN membership at the triumph run to 1,500 militants. As the insurrection gained momentum, many joined the insurrection, led by the FSLN; but in many ways the FSLN was overtaken by the popular movement. The FSLN formed an alliance of national unity, promising a commitment to the poor and trying to reassure the patriotic bourgeoisie. However, after years of Somoza's anticommunist rhetoric, the FSLN saw the danger of appeals to foreign models. They chose Sandino for his nationalism: He named his army the Army of Defense of National Sovereignty and promised peace as soon as U.S. marines vacated Nicaraguan soil. The FSLN wanted to create itself as a national movement with deep roots in Nicaraguan history, not as a traditional political party led by one or another faction of the Nicaraguan bourgeoisie vying for power in a minuet of political maneuvering.

Until the 1990 elections, the FSLN struggled to weld Sandinismo to Nicaragua. The new army became the Sandinista Army; the police force, the Sandinista Police. INCINE was initially the Sandinista Institute of Cinema, but changed its name to the Nicaraguan Institute of Cinema. However, every early noticiero began with the FSLN hymn. Legally, the Junta was the supreme governing body, but even Robelo stated in 1979, "The FSLN Directorate is the head of the revolution. The vanguard."[8] Effectively, the FSLN's Dirección Nacional set policy, and the Junta, in coordination with the Council of State, drafted the laws. Despite its name change, INCINE did not question the FSLN's identification with Nicaragua. INCINE identified with the FSLN, and INCINE personnel considered themselves Sandinistas. The tension between the voices of the people and the FSLN leaders was not necessarily antagonistic. At first, the FSLN leaders were unfamiliar in Nicaragua, so the films introduced these young newcomers on the national political stage.[9] Interviews complemented official speeches, providing a visual vernacular and translating FSLN discourse into popular language. Equally, if not more significant, were the marches, chants, and songs used as transitions or caesuras between speeches. Songwriters were constantly composing FSLN songs for pro-FSLN musical groups to sing at rallies. The literacy crusade had a hymn, as did Carlos Fonseca, other martyrs, and so on. Young people quickly learned these songs, which formed part of the aural ambience of the FSLN identity, preserving FSLN uniqueness as a popular movement, not a traditional political party.

The greatest challenge for the revolution's transformation of Nicaragua was agricultural policy. As in many twentieth-century revolutions, the Sandinistas planned an agrarian reform immediately after the triumph. Somoza had begun modernizing agriculture in the 1950s, when high cotton prices worldwide fuelled a Nicaraguan cotton boom. With rising exports of coffee, sugar, and meat in the 1960s, Nicaragua's agriculture prospered and the exports generated hard currency. With the Sandinista triumph of 1979, the FSLN knew it needed to export crops for hard currency to finance industrial development. Because land used for export crops was largely held by the rural bourgeoisie and because attempts to expropriate that land would threaten export earnings, the FSLN halted unauthorized land confiscations of Somocista lands, many abandoned by Somocistas fleeing the country. At the same time, the Ministry of Agricultural Reform, under Jaime Wheelock, wanted production on expropriated land to be organized in large state farms and cooperatives.

To finance industrialization, a state needs a surplus in the economy. In agricultural societies, the state looks to agriculture for the surplus. In Nicaragua, the FSLN hoped to attract the peasantry with land, and by supporting prices, offering credit, and improving machinery and production methods. In exchange, they expected higher yields and a higher standard of living, with the provision of health care, education, and other non-wage goods. Following the war's devastation and a severe drop in agricultural production, the highest priority was restoring prewar production levels. As the FSLN studied the situation, it limited planning to stopgap measures establishing criteria for state land takeovers and resource allocation. Though the FSLN planned to announce the Agrarian Reform in 1980, the difficulties both of the problem and of reaching a policy consensus forced a postponement until 1981.

In June 1980, when INCINE made its first noticiero on the Agrarian Reform, also directed by Alvarez, there was no formal agrarian reform program in place. Not surprisingly, *The Agrarian Reform* avoids discussing specific plans for agriculture. In the opening sequence, over aerial shots of fields, the voice-over summarizes:

> Nicaragua enjoys a favorable climate and fertile lands
> that permit the development of diverse and important
> products to satisfy national consumption and to gain
> exportable surplus. The peasantry was harshly exploited

and even displaced from its lands to benefit the minority Somocista landholders.

María José Alvarez, again with microphone, asks some peasants about past exploitation. After these interviews, enter the FSLN. A younger man in military dress, clearly FSLN, stands alone beside a field and rattles off a clipped litany of changes introduced within "a revolutionary panorama." The changes include control over blight, a technical improvement, and a reorganization of the "relations of production." All this is possible with the "unity of the participation of the organized labor force brought about by the association of workers," or the ATC. After the FSLN speaks of these plans, peasants return to extol the cooperatives: "The advantages are that the work proceeds better together than separated, because before I could not resolve the problems alone, but now one of us represents a group and it's easier, for they give us loans and credits."

Under an ATC banner, Wheelock summarizes the Agrarian Reform, avoiding specifics but indicating the positive role the agricultural bourgeoisie can still play. After enumerating products being developed on state farming units, he explains that the reforms are quantitative but also that "social relations are changing," the formerly exploited now occupy positions of power, and

> whereas in the past your sweat went toward filling the
> pockets of Somoza, today this sweat is transformed into
> schools, is transformed into houses, is transformed
> into health, is transformed into guns, is transformed
> into bullets for the defense of the Sandinista Revolution.

After speaking of workers' needs, Wheelock turns to the landowners and says, "All who wish to reconstruct Nicaragua and are engaged honestly and patriotically in this, even if they belong to private property, we are going to protect them and welcome them also." (In FSLN discourse, "private property" as used here normally referred to owners of private property, normally powerful.) A private cotton producer demonstrates the willingness of the private sector, especially the export sector, to work within the revolutionary system.

The film says that the peasants are pleased with the revolution. The Agrarian Reform gives them seeds, loans, credits, and equipment. In addition, their standard of living is improved with non-monetary benefits of health clinics, education, and housing, often referred to as the "social wage." The law protects their working conditions, recognizes their human dignity, and encourages their participation in peasant organizations. The film does not speak of land ownership, however. State policy emphasized industrialized agricultural production, particularly export crops, in state farms and cooperatives, passing over individual ownership of land. It also omitted any mention of spontaneous land takeovers and the FSLN's banning of further seizures. Policies such as these met with significant dissatisfaction in the ensuing years, as the discussion of *Nuestra Reforma Agraria* will show (chapter 7).

If the Agrarian Reform specialists had difficulty formulating a clear strategy for agriculture, so dependent as well on unpredictable exogenous factors (international prices, U.S. trade, weather, etc.), one could hardly expect INCINE's young, middle-class filmmakers to provide more than a general outline of agricultural policy. Under the circumstances, INCINE did an adequate, perhaps even admirable, job. The inclusion of two private cotton producers departed from the earlier reliance on the two FSLN voices, one provided by ordinary people's pro-FSLN interviews, the other by DN members' speeches. Perhaps the family backgrounds of Lacayo and Alvarez, both from wealthy agricultural interests, allowed them access to the agricultural bourgeoisie at a time when the FSLN was courting its support.

The next noticiero called for little deliberation: *Primer aniversario de la revolución popular Sandinista* (First Anniversary of the Popular Sandinista Revolution, July 1980). It also calls for little comment. Instead of listing credits for one director and one realizador, this noticiero lists nine people.[10] The balance between official and unofficial speech tilts completely to official discourses, all pronounced at the mass celebration in the Plaza of July 19. Popular festivities and preparations unroll on the screen at the beginning, replete with traditional masks and costumes. Once the ceremony commences, however, FSLN speeches from the podium take over: Daniel Ortega, Humberto Ortega, Tomás Borge—arguably the most powerful Dirección Nacional members. Perhaps inspired by the attendance of so many dignitaries from the third world—Fidel Castro (Cuba), Carlos Andrés Pérez (Peru), Michael Manley (Jamaica), Maurice Bishop (Granada), Yasir Arafat (Palestine)—Humberto Ortega delivers a defiant tiermondista speech:

> This struggle is difficult. It is the struggle of the peoples of the third world who remain subject to the injustices of the developed capitalist countries, which have converted us into its suppliers of raw materials, imposing low prices for our products and selling dear its industrial products. Today the peoples of the third world are rising in the movement of the non-aligned countries, a battle that is

> forging a new international order in the world, one that
> is ending the exploitation of the powerful countries over
> our countries.

The only surviving founding member of the FSLN, Borge, generally acknowledged to be the Dirección Nacional's most charismatic speaker, manages few sentences in the film, but even the brief excerpts convey some of his popular appeal: "We pledge to continue planting the seed, with greater force and sacrifices and works today, so that future generations can benefit from the rivers of milk and honey that our heroes and martyrs have promised them." Aside from familiar chants and slogans from the huge crowd, only FSLN leaders on the platform speak.

Humberto Ortega does, however, introduce a new topic. Since the victory, the FSLN had used the term participatory democracy in discussions of their political system, a democracy based on popular participation in the mass organizations represented in the Council of State. The Nicaraguan experiences with elections under Somoza did not generate faith in elections, and the FSLN viewed past elections as a charade. In the past, Somoza ran Nicaragua whether he occupied the presidency or not, hence Ortega's derision in announcing "our decision to hold elections which will correspond to the spirit of this new non-aligned democracy. We are sure that the people have rejected forever the crafty elections, the dirty elections, the nacatamale elections."[11]

If the FSLN did not equate elections with democracy, neither did they reject elections. The Sandinistas sought a form of democracy consistent with the broad goals of popular democracy and the "logic of the majority." Though the FSLN bristled at U.S. calls for elections, ultimately, the FSLN held two of the most "observed" elections in history, in which they were victorious in 1984 but defeated in 1990.

Even when popular support was high, *Primer anniversario* exhibits a problem found in INCINE's early films. As cultural/ideological workers, INCINE filmmakers wanted to strengthen popular support for the revolution. But when the FSLN leadership displaced the voice of the people, INCINE films became illustrated lectures, diluting their persuasive and mobilizing potential.

For the next noticiero, INCINE completed the diptych of the Literacy Campaign with *Clausura de la cruzada nacional de alfatibetización* (*Closing of the Literacy Campaign,* Aug. 1980). After five months in the countryside, thousands of brigadistas gathered in Managua to conclude the campaign, having reduced illiteracy from 50 percent to 13 percent. However, as if the pendulum had swung back from the oppressive FSLN presence in the previ-

ous film, *Clausura* devotes ten minutes of the 15-minute film to the brigadistas' return from the remote corners of Nicaragua. No FSLN leader is seen
or heard until the end of the film. A precredit sequence shows a radio operator communicating with a fishing boat loaded with festive youths, the literacy anthem on the sound track. Subsequently, helicopters pick up young
teachers, and other brigadistas climb aboard trucks. An older man strains to
read "illiteracy is a cruel heritage left us by Somocismo." A soft flute plays
over shots of newly literate elderly people, then younger children, writing
their names on blackboards. Groups of brigadistas walk buoyantly through
rain and mud. One young brigadista remarks:

> Regarding the experiences I had, to know, to live, to feel
> in the flesh the miseries of the campesino, to feel hunger
> at the same time that he felt hunger, to feel happiness at
> the same time that he felt happiness, to feel sadness
> when he was sad. This gave me a consciousness of class
> that I did not have before, really, or rather that I saw only
> theoretically. The campesino suffers, but that's all. Now I
> felt it in the flesh, and I think I have come away a little
> different, a little, so to speak, to try to struggle more, to
> try to struggle a little more.

This long, slow, expansive treatment of the brigadistas' departure and
return, edited in a limpid logic, without bombast or partisan interruption,
represents a significant step forward for the noticieros. Young Nicaraguans
have braved the adversity of campesino life, not in a paternalistic mission of
mercy to the poor, but to teach an important skill and to experience firsthand the misery of the "legacy of Somocismo." The images of these young
revolutionaries embody the "poder popular" invoked so often by the FSLN.

Even at the plaza, at the campaign's official closing, the comandantes take
a back seat to the campaign. Fernando Cardenal, official head of the Literacy Campaign and Minister of Education, reports: "We have fulfilled our
task. What are the next assignments?" One of the campaign's beneficiaries,
a middle-aged woman, speaks next, reading:

> In the name of all the literate people in Nicaragua,
> because I also am literate, we thank the Governmental
> Junta, the Dirección Nacional of the Sandinista Front, all
> the literacy teachers who taught us to read. Because they
> truly succeeded in fighting ignorance as their goal with
> heart and soul, to the point of giving even their lives for

this liberation. Now I bid farewell, with all my heart and certainly with thanks, because now in Nicaragua we have conquered ignorance forever.

During her speech, an inserted headline about a literacy worker's assassination demonstrates that "giving even their lives" is not rhetorical.

Finally, a comandante takes the floor. Humberto Ortega also emphasizes what the brigadistas have learned from the campesinos:

You have not only taught literacy to our people, but you have learned from our people what is exploitation, what is oppression, and with this great campaign you have strengthened the anti-imperialist spirit, the class spirit, the popular spirit of this revolution, because you have realized how terrible is the whole system of exploitation and oppression over our poor Latin American peoples.

But he returns to the issue of elections, broached at the end of *Primer aniversario:*

Democracy neither begins nor ends with elections.
That is a myth, to reduce democracy to this condition.
It begins in the economic sphere when the social inequalities begin to weaken, when the workers and the campesinos improve their levels of life. There begins the true democracy. You are in accord with this process. Continue with the unity of the whole nation, with the honest and patriotic businesses, and not with the shameless exploiters who want us to return to the past. This, then, is voting, a popular election; this is Sandinista democracy.

Despite the defiant speech, the FSLN announced at the ceremony that elections would be held in 1985, and President Carazo Odio, from Costa Rica, in a speech not shown in the film, noted that "a man can represent and enjoy the confidence of the people only if this people have chosen him in a free and open election."[12]

The film does not include this announcement, but the next film, *La democracia* (Sept. 1980), clarifies the Sandinista formulation of democracy. Alberto Legall, who shared credit for the previous noticiero with María José Alvarez, received sole credit for *La democracia*. Legall leaped into prominence at INCINE, soon assuming responsibility for noticiero production, and his aggressive personality is evident throughout his active career at INCINE. *La democracia* uses irony to adumbrate the FSLN view of elections. Guitar music dramatizes the arduousness of a barefoot laborer pulling from his waist large bunches of bananas suspended from a cable running above a rickety bridge. A Council of State speaker reports on conditions facing banana workers; a sequence then follows depicting ragged children walking into slum housing, contrasting with the spacious residence of the plantation manager atop a hill, ringed by a high fence. Back in the chamber of the Council of State, the speaker concludes, and the president of the council, DN member Carlos Nuñez, endorses the report. A voice-over explains the functioning of the council, calling it "a democratic and pluralist expression of the Sandinista revolutionary process, based on the policy of national unity." A title repeats the words heard in the preceding noticiero of Humberto Ortega: "Democracy neither begins nor ends with elections."

To illustrate the contrary view, the filmmakers introduce Adolfo Calero, leader of the Conservative Democratic party (Partido Conservador Demócrata, PCD). He claims that democracy does not exist without elections, which haven't taken place under the new government. As he speaks, the camera pans over the PCD's insignia, a triangle with a triad of principles— God, Order, Justice; the filmmakers have placed a photograph of a Coke bottle next to the insignia. Another title asks, "What elections has Nicaragua known?" The camera pans down a photo of Somoza, with solemn church music on the sound track. Archival footage of Somoza shows the dictator encouraging Nicaraguans to vote for his National Liberal party, followed by inserts of well-dressed audiences applauding deliriously. The next shots are taken from archival footage of a swimsuit competition for Miss Nicaragua, another "election," for the most part featuring low-angle shots of the contestants parading down the ramp.

Next, images from the insurrection appear, including the one seen in the second noticiero, with "Nombre: FSLN" superimposed on a young FSLN combatant's face. Another title offers: "Democracy begins in the economic sphere." After workers load cotton and other products, another title ("Thus begins true democracy") follows Ortega's agenda of first improving the lives of the campesinos, illustrated by a following shot from *Clausura* of a woman struggling to write her name on a blackboard. Title: A shot of children carrying wooden guns links this democracy to military defense. Finally, after a newspaper headline reporting Somoza's assassination and shots of his corpse, Legall repeats a shot of Somoza shown earlier in the film, but now riddles it with (bullet) holes, while a fusillade of gunshots is heard on the sound track.

*Election speech of Somoza (*La democracia*)*

*"Machine-gunning" of Somoza (*La democracia*)*

At the time of this film, U.S. pressure was mounting on the Sandinistas to hold elections. The Carter administration had vacillated in its Nicaragua policy. The United States had hoped to convince Somoza to step down, but when he refused and unleashed his military might on his own people, including having U.S.-supplied planes bomb Nicaraguan cities, the United States withdrew support. When it became clear that the FSLN had no intention of ceding power to U.S.-backed business interests, the United States applied economic pressure to force elections. The FSLN eventually agreed, but the films indicate that many FSLN supporters resisted U.S.-imposed elections as an unacceptable intrusion into Nicaragua's internal affairs.

The discrepancy between the official FSLN position and the INCINE film implies that INCINE was pursuing a more intransigent political line than the FSLN on this issue. The FSLN had already announced a timetable for elections, yet *La democracia* ignores this. In all likelihood, Alberto Legall arrived with a background as a political radical and a talent for self-promotion.[13] With the "veteran" filmmakers traveling between Managua and the countryside to shoot film, and then to and from Cuba for postproduction, Legall occupied an administrative vacuum. Ramiro Lacayo, original director and head of production, welcomed Legall to help with details of noticiero production. As combination opportunist/militant, Legall presumably saw no reason to report the FSLN announcement of elections, and the FSLN didn't monitor the noticieros so closely that it would object to the omission. Finally, according to INCINE personnel, so long as the comandantes continued to appear on screen, the FSLN did not interfere with INCINE productions. This is not to say that they interfered when they did not see themselves; rather, they were less interested.[14]

Perhaps the revolution's most vexing problem was the situation on the Atlantic Coast. This area had been a virtually autonomous region during a long succession of Nicaraguan governments, all located in the Pacific region's major cities. The remaining indigenous peoples lived in their traditional lands, most along the northern coast, especially along the Coco River, on the (present-day) border with Honduras. Mestizo campesinos from the Pacific region had increasingly settled on the Atlantic Coast as the expansion of industrial agriculture in the Pacific region forced them to seek land further east. In addition to the indigenous peoples, many English-speaking Africans migrated to the Atlantic Coast to escape slave plantations in British colonies like Jamaica. This population, concentrated further south in Bluefields, certainly felt no allegiance to the distant government in the Pacific region. The Atlantic Coast peoples either practiced their traditional economic activities or worked within the enclave economy run by U.S. mining and lumber interests.

The only significant disruption of this arrangement occurred during Sandino's struggle in the late 1920s and early 1930s. Operating in the mountains in which the major mining towns were located, Sandino's army attracted many Indians. Sandino's assassination closed this episode, but for the FSLN, the earlier struggle installed the resistance of the indigenous peoples in the panoply of heroic antecedents to the Sandinista struggle, hence the importance of announcing the nationalization of the mines in the very first noticiero as a sign of geographical and ethnic inclusiveness. In 1979, though, the war against Somoza had not affected the coastal populations, and few cared about changes in the distant mestizo government.

All of this changed dramatically, rapidly, and disastrously after 1979. Eager to embrace the coastal peoples, the FSLN embarked on an ambitious development program. The FSLN began to construct the first road connecting the coast to the Pacific region. FSLN representatives from the Pacific region, mestizos, traveled to the coast to direct these programs. Unfortunately, many local inhabitants did not identify with the revolution. Even more unfortunately, FSLN cadres, with little knowledge or experience of the coast, exhibited a presumptuous and condescending attitude in the eyes of the coastal people, Indians and blacks alike. The FSLN coastal representative was a mestizo who spoke neither Miskito nor English. The great Literacy Campaign was brought to the Atlantic Coast—in Spanish! Confused by the indifference, and then hostility, of these unappreciative "Nicaraguans," the FSLN reacted defensively, seriously alienating the Miskitos and, to a lesser extent, the blacks.

The tensions began almost immediately after the triumph, and the situation deteriorated quickly (though it did not careen into actual armed resistance until early 1982). In the fall of 1980, INCINE devoted a noticiero to the Atlantic Coast. Lacayo and Alvarez traveled to Bluefields, center of the urban black population (the Miskitos and other Indian groups lived for the most part in small fishing and farming communities concentrated to the north of Bluefields). The film reflects both the FSLN's naïve idealism and their tragic incomprehension of the coastal population's concerns. Once those concerns erupted into full-scale war, INCINE would not venture back to the coast for several years.

Though conforming to the standard 10–11 minute length of the noticieros, La costa Atlántica (Nov. 1980) tries to cover enormous ground. A precredit sequence traces the history of the Atlantic Coast region up to Sandino. Joining early drawings, shots from fiction films, and maps, the sequence begins with the Spanish conquest, the arrival at Gracias a Diós, Indians carrying off heavy strongboxes of gold, and the British intervention in 1760 to "halt the Spanish colonial expansion in the Caribbean" that was later replaced by U.S. expansionism in 1850. As the film depicts signs of U.S. compa-

*Graphic of Spanish Conquest (*La costa Atlántica)

nies such as Standard Fruit Company, the voice-over describes the 1910 landing of U.S. troops on the Atlantic Coast "supporting the oligarchies which
were protecting the interests of the gringo companies." Sandino's seizure of
the North American mines in 1928 begins his anti-imperialist campaign.
Photographs of Sandino conclude this introduction, which segues into the
(new) noticiero logo, while the FSLN hymn is sung *in Miskito.*

Repeating an idea used in the third noticiero, a series of stills document
idle machinery abandoned by the U.S. companies; a locomotive is heard
wheezing fitfully as it strains to reach full speed. A woman's voice observes
that workers were treated like "mules." Another voice introduces the woman
as Hazel Lau of MISURASATA. The FSLN formed MISURASATA, an acronym
for the organization of MIskito, SUmo, RAma, and Sandinistas, "working
together."[15] As a Miskito and Sandinista militant, Lau explains that, under
Somoza,

> the coast population was marginalized almost totally, to
> the extent that the costeños, until the moment of the
> triumph, we felt like second-class citizens. Furthermore,
> the population was marginalized, repressed politically
> and culturally, its language was sneered at, the cultural
> values unappreciated, to the point that education in

Spanish was imposed to try to eradicate the culture
through the loss of the mother tongue.

Several titles provide demographic data about the coast; Palo de Mayo, a popular black music from the coast, accompanies shots of blacks performing the erotic dance, known by the same name. These scenes are intercut with those of handicrafts, turtle fishing, and basketball. A Miskito man describes transportation problems, the excessive time required to travel by boat, the difficulty of getting flights, the unreliability of the roads, and the bad condition of the bridges: "We need wood for these bridges, and in the long run, concrete." Another Miskito testifies to the difficulty of getting news.

These few minutes supply a glut of information about the coast. Hazel Lau conveys the plight of the workers and highlights the *cultural* discrimination against the Miskitos under Somoza with a description of his efforts to stamp out their language. Blacks dance, weave, and play basketball, but never speak. Despite the rapid flow of images and sounds, some significant distinctions can be discerned. The blacks never complain. They dance and work contentedly, even joyfully. The dance and music anchor the representation of blacks, the other shots interpolated as if suggesting porous boundaries between work and leisure. The Miskitos do speak, first about cultural oppression, second about material want and infrastructural deficiencies.

A uniformed official offers the FSLN interpretation, and it is a revealing one. Interviewed by the diminutive Alvarez, seen at the edge of the screen holding the microphone, FSLN coastal representative William Ramírez, speaking in Spanish, asserts that the Atlantic Coast "is an important population sector that we have to integrate in the revolutionary activity, the revolutionary idea." There is little to argue with in his formulation. However, Ramírez speaks exclusively to the question of development. His discourse sounds like the standard developmentalist scenario so often proposed for underdeveloped countries. He ignores the *cultural* issues introduced by Hazel Lau. The FSLN, backed by popular support in the Pacific region, assumed it could apply the same developmental policies on the Atlantic Coast, not recognizing the inextricability of culture and economy in the latter region.

For example, the Agrarian Reform paid careful attention to land ownership, a key issue in the Pacific region for landowners and landless peasants alike. The FSLN understood the needs of these competing groups and deliberated before unveiling its plans. But the Miskitos saw their land as property of the Miskito nation. They had no category for individual land titles. Yet the FSLN had devised its Agrarian Reform for the entire country, including the Atlantic Coast. The FSLN could have revised its plans to accommo-

*María José Alvarez interviewing William Ramírez (*La costa Atlántica*)*

date the Miskitos' cultural traditions, but the wheels of the planning mechanism were not so easily disengaged.

After Ramírez, a series of titles accompanies shots of each natural resource: mines, wood, fishing. One shot from the fishing group shows a package of "Maya Brand Frozen Seafood," whose label is in English. Soon, Jaime Wheelock appears, speaking informally to some blacks while a man translates his words into English, also heard on the sound track. The blacks listen impassively as Wheelock lists the FSLN projects initiated on the coast, including

> a series of works of real progress, transportation, telephone, television, and the reactivation of production here; the road coming here, the road on the Atlantic coast which is already being laid. All these things are important, for we are working in the interests of the people fundamentally.

Several shots attest to these claims: a bulldozer clearing a road, masons laying bricks for the road, and a television transmitter and television set inside a home.

Again, developmentalism drives the discourse. The film doesn't address the blacks' special needs nor does it distinguish them from the Miskitos. The

*Comandante and Dirección Nacional member Jaime Wheelock speaking Spanish to the Anglophone Creoles (*La costa Atlántica*)*

blacks would benefit from infrastructural improvements; but with scant participation in the anti-Somoza struggle, they did not identify with the Sandinistas, or with any mestizos. They spoke English, and their traditional trading partners were the United States and English-speaking Caribbean islands. The flip side of the Sandinista vision of development was the central government's interference in the blacks' affairs and the threat to their established foreign trade, for the FSLN nationalized foreign trade in order to capture hard currency and stop export earnings from pouring out of the country.

Shifting back to the Miskitos, Hazel Lau notes factors that could lead to "a true integration which our country has lacked for so long." She doesn't dwell on material development, but stresses "mutual understanding." Ramírez explains official FSLN history of the Miskitos in Sandino's army, and he projects that history onto the revolutionary present, a wish transparently inapplicable to current reality:

> You have to recall that the first guerrillas which General Sandino took were precisely the Miskitos. So there is a tradition. In addition, it is a people historically combative and we have visited almost all of the communities of the Coco River and we have found great revolutionary potential. They believe in the revolution, and we are trying not to disillusion them as a revolutionary organization.

CINEMA AND THE SANDINISTAS

As usual, INCINE privileges the FSLN view. The filmmakers allot time to Miskito speakers, one a Sandinista activist, others with no apparent FSLN ties. The FSLN mestizo leader on the coast describes the development (and by implication, the integration) of the coast as a "challenge" and concedes that the project may not succeed without sufficient investment. But Ramírez and Wheelock harp on what the revolution is doing *for* the coastal peoples, not what is being done *by* these peoples. No FSLN official suggests what the revolution might learn *from* the coast, a theme heard repeatedly in the literacy films, even from a DN member.

The film could have demonstrated such a learning process. The FSLN started the Literacy Campaign on the coast using *Spanish*-language materials, proceeding according to the pattern of previous mestizo governments, which Hazel Lau deplores in the film as a strategy of "cultural elimination." This error provoked a furor among Miskitos, and the FSLN rectified it, replacing the teaching materials with Miskito booklets and primers. And the film, after the Ramírez paean to the Miskitos' combativeness, shows Miskitos writing in Miskito on blackboards. Inevitably, as with challenges in the Pacific region, the FSLN would make mistakes. But in the Pacific region the FSLN could draw on a deep reservoir of support and goodwill from the popular classes.

On the coast, the FSLN had no predisposition of support from the local populations. The FSLN had to convert them to the revolution. In reality, the FSLN's commitment to coastal development was viewed by the costeños as yet another scheme cooked up in Managua to be inflicted upon the coastal peoples. However beneficial the plans, the people affected were not included in the planning. The film's failure to note the extreme importance of cultural factors in the Literacy Campaign reflects with tragic irony the discomfort, anxiety, presumptuousness, and condescension of the FSLN on the Atlantic Coast.[16]

Reading the film symptomatically, the blind spots shared by the FSLN and the film vis à vis the Atlantic Coast are obvious. First, the developmentalist rhetoric ignores basic distinctions between the two regions' economic realities. Modernization initiatives in the Pacific region had generated high rates of economic growth and aggravated contradictions between capitalist development and political stagnation. On the coast, modernization had taken place decades earlier, in the 1920s and 1930s, followed by continual decline. With the economic stagnation, objective conditions did not lead to popular opposition. Second, various cultural factors inhibited resistance. The Moravian Church doctrines promoted resignation and passivity, unlike the Catholic liberation theology that had challenged traditional Latin American hierarchies. Third, the film ignores tremors within the Miskito community, and among the MISURASATA leadership, represented in the film by the inexperienced, moderate Hazel Lau, rather than the intemperate, more powerful and popular Steadman Fagoth. Fourth, the film grafts a brief episode of Miskito militance in the 1930s to the present, when the militance had evaporated. Finally, the film is without any black voice, or discussion of interethnic differences and tensions, specifically between blacks and Indians, as the film aims to fold ethnic differences seamlessly into the revolutionary project.

What makes these flaws particularly poignant is the coincidence between the film's completion and the outbreak of coastal discontent. INCINE released the film in November 1980 as thousands of blacks marched in Bluefields to protest the presence of Cuban schoolteachers. Through a series of misunderstandings, the demonstrations turned violent, and the government sent troops to quell the disturbances. The reasons behind the confrontation remain murky, but the mutual distrust exposed by these incidents is not described in the film.[17]

In several ways, this eleventh noticiero, *The Atlantic Coast*, concludes INCINE's first phase. With Ronald Reagan's election in November, the U.S. position toward Nicaragua hardened and quickly turned into active support for the counterrevolution. INCINE reacted by producing noticieros related to the counterrevolution. After filming *The Atlantic Coast*, María José Alvarez left noticiero production to work on short documentaries, eventually leaving INCINE to work at the television station in Bluefields near her compañero (and future husband), Lumberto Campbell, FSLN political comandante on the coast. Lacayo and Alvarez had directed most of the first 11 noticieros, so with Alvarez's departure, Alberto Legall assumed responsibility for noticiero production. Lacayo still headed production, but INCINE began preparing to produce short documentaries. During Legall's tenure, new directors began working at INCINE, first as assistants on the noticieros, and soon after as directors. These new directors became the nucleus of INCINE production, significantly changed the direction of the noticieros, and ultimately propelled INCINE into the giddy world of fiction.

Over its first year, INCINE established a successful production schedule of one film per month. Except for the first noticiero, shot in color, all were filmed in 35-mm black and white, and developed, edited, and printed in Cuba at ICAIC. The films tended to be monothematic, structured around FSLN discourses. Apparently without instructions, the filmmakers neither questioned FSLN policies nor established critical distance from the FSLN. With little preproduction time, they focused on generalities about the economic plan, the Literacy Campaign, or the Atlantic Coast. María José Alvarez interviewed ordinary Nicaraguans to balance the comandantes' official rhetoric, but these voices of "the people" are never identified by name, nor do their remarks significantly diverge from those of the comandantes. Rather, they supply a vernacular scaffold for FSLN abstractions. Optical effects—stills, titles, freeze-frames—give rhetorical emphasis.

Despite Cuban support, the Nicaraguan noticieros differed from the Cuban ones in two ways. The Cubans, beginning in 1959, released their noticieros weekly and saw them as newsreels. In an era before television news (and television was not common in Latin America until the late 1960s and 1970s), spectators attended movie theaters to see films of current events (the Cuban decree establishing ICAIC described the cinema as the most powerful means of "diffusion"). The weekly noticieros covered multiple topics. By 1979 in Nicaragua, 20 years of television penetration had changed the media landscape. Although most people in Nicaragua, still an agricultural society with a low literacy rate, received their news by radio, increasing numbers relied on television. INCINE, then, did not structure the *monthly* noticieros as multithematic newsreels covering a week's news. INCINE noticieros were essentially monothematic, as the early titles demonstrate: *The Economic Plan of 1980* (Noticiero 3), *The Opening of the Literacy Campaign* (Noticiero 5), *The Agrarian Reform* (Noticiero 7), *The Atlantic Coast* (Noticiero 11), and so on.

The Cuban influence was less evident, then, in function and structure, but more apparent in style. Titles, freeze-frames, rostrum work (shooting stills with a frequently moving camera to crop the pictures for desired effect) are staples of the Cuban noticieros used for rhetorical emphasis.[18] ICAIC also documented Fidel Castro's public appearances; similarly, the early INCINE noticieros often focused on public appearances of FSLN comandantes, such as Daniel Ortega and his visit to Siuna to announce the nationalization of the mines. The reason for this type of coverage was that FSLN comandantes, or, more precisely, Comandantes de la Revolución (for there were other, lower ranks of Comandante), as the DN members were called, occupied the most important ministerial posts: the Sandinista Army (Humberto Ortega); the Interior (Tomás Borge); Agrarian Reform (Jaime Wheelock); and Economic Planning (Henry Ruíz).

In the rush to meet production schedules and create a Nicaraguan filmmaking apparatus, the few actual filmmakers—as opposed to administrators, technicians, and support staff—spent little time articulating aesthetics. The tragedy and chaos of the preceding years necessitated restoring order, reactivating economic activity, and channeling popular participation. Despite its shortcomings, INCINE could report to the Dirección Nacional, as Fernando Cardenal did at the Literacy Campaign's closing ceremony: "We have completed our duty. What are our next assignments?"

Three   THE SECOND YEAR

Ronald Reagan's election as president of the United States had grave consequences for the new Nicaraguan government. The Reagan administration mounted a vicious propaganda campaign against the Sandinistas, approved financial support to encourage the opposition to break ranks with the government, and provided secret resources to arm several counterrevolutionary groups. Under these pressures, the balance between the Nicaraguan government and the progressive or patriotic wing of capital eroded, polarizing the country, shrinking the ground of dialogue, and expanding the need for militarization of the society. In this atmosphere, the noticieros took on a more militarist cast, though a personnel change contributed to this development.

At the same time, the first documentaries opened a new path. By the beginning of 1981, after barely a year, INCINE had produced eleven noticieros. However, the two directors responsible for most of them, Ramiro Lacayo and María José Alvarez, withdrew from noticiero production. Alvarez left Managua for personal and professional reasons, while Lacayo concentrated on administrative matters and prepared to expand production into documentaries, a provision of the agreements with the Cuban Film Institute. Both Lacayo and Alvarez directed documentaries during the year. Thus, while INCINE continued producing monthly noticieros for three more years, as new directors joined the noticiero program, INCINE sought more supple forms of expression in the first documentaries, an ambition which would eventually lead to fiction.

During the first year or so, the administrative organization had Lacayo as head of production and Ibarra in charge of the state-run exhibition and distribution. In 1981, Lacayo split the production responsibilities into Noticiero Production and Popular Documentaries Production, naming Brenda Martínez and Lilia Alfaro respectively to run each operation, with Lacayo retaining authority over Production. The Consejo Directivo, composed of the heads of each department, met regularly to oversee the functioning of INCINE. INCINE employed about fifty people.[1] Though part of INCINE, Mobile Cinema operated out of separate premises, with about 20 employees, most of whom were projectionists.

Once INCINE had established a stable production schedule of noticieros, it also branched out in an even more challenging direction. The noticeros provided a revolutionary perspective on the convulsive changes taking place in the country, but they could have little effect on attitudes toward the foreign feature films still filling the theaters. To combat this cultural "invasion," INCINE took advantage of a new cultural publication distributed by the FSLN with *Barricada* to essay a new revolutionary criticism.

Responding to the War

Toward the end of the first year, a new director began working at INCINE. Alberto Legall, fascinated by the military, responded to the growing threat of war by metaphorically placing noticiero production on a war footing, as the titles *El Salvador vencerá, La defensa militar, La defensa económica, La defensa política, La contrarevolución, Unidad frente a la agresión* show. During Legall's rise to the head of noticiero production in early 1982, two new directors started making noticieros, though they did not share Legall's view of the noticieros as a military redoubt. By the time Legall left INCINE, the noticieros were markedly different from those of the first year; some would eventually shed the trappings of nonfiction altogether during the leap into fiction.

Among the many charges made against the Sandinistas by the Reagan administration, exporting revolution was a particularly attractive one. The FSLN endorsed anti-imperialist popular revolution and expressed solidarity with other revolutionary movements. In particular, the FSLN publicly supported El Salvador's guerrilla coalition, Frente Farabundo Martí para la Liberación Nacional (FMLN). The Reagan administration extracted hundreds of millions of dollars for military aid from Congress to prop up the murderous right-wing regime in El Salvador but caviled incessantly at the sympathetic words expressed by Nicaragua for that country's revolutionary movement. With the Monroe Doctrine for historical support and ample U.S. precedents for overthrowing Latin American regimes (Guatemala, Dominican Republic, Chile), Reagan justified funding the contras by at one point drawing a picture of Nicaraguan-fomented revolution spreading through Central America to Mexico and to the banks of the Rio Grande, finally threatening the United States itself.[2] But even granting the doctrine's legitimacy in the logic of *realpolitik*, the Reagan administration could never document any significant Nicaraguan material aid to the guerrillas in El Salvador.[3]

As readers of Latin American history, the FSLN took U.S. military threats seriously. The national unity strategy attempted to wean the private sector from relying on U.S. protection. The FSLN leaders also kept their support for the revolutionaries in El Salvador primarily verbal. Albert Legall showed no such reticence and made a rare INCINE foray into foreign policy with *El Salvador vencerá* (Jan. 1981).

Typically, Legall emphasizes the FMLN's military force, not its popular base or political goals. In the first images, Salvadorans rush about on the streets with their hands clasped behind their heads, trying to escape a military sweep; a still shows a refugee center named for the assassinated archbishop, Oscar Romero; a cartoon shows Uncle Sam with a broom sweeping the road into El Salvador for the troops of the Salvadoran army. A voice-over describes El Salvador's high illiteracy rate, paucity of medical care, and high infant-mortality rate and observes, "The Salvadoran people have been a people traditionally rebellious and combative." In clear parallel to the Sandinista movement, rooted in Sandino's army of the 1920s and 1930s, the film's commentary traces the FMLN's beginnings to 1932, when

> the Salvadoran patriot Agustín Farabundo Martí was shot. Martí had joined with General Sandino fighting to expel the invading Yankees from Nicaragua the same year that the dictatorship of Maximiliano Hernández assassinated 30,000 campesinos. Today, the Christian democratic military junta, headed by Napoleón Duarte, is repressing the Salvadoran people. The people of Farabundo Martí are preparing tenaciously to end the more than 48 years of military dictatorships.

The film discreetly omits the split between Sandino and Martí. Martí, a committed Marxist, followed the Comintern leadership. Sandino, like his followers decades later, favored a less doctrinaire nationalist ideology, viewing Marxism with some indigenist suspicion.[4]

Carter's ambassador to El Salvador, Robert White, a moderate in comparison to the Reagan hard-liners, publicly criticized the heavy infusions of aid to the military junta and asserted in an interview excerpted in the film, "Our policy is to support the reform process of this government with considerable economic support and very little military aid." In his flamboyant, ironic style, Legall cuts to two men carrying a corpse and then quickly moves the camera closer and closer to the photograph in a staccato rhythm reminiscent of his "machine gun" spray of bullet holes in Somoza's portrait at the end of *La democracia.*

The rest of the film shows rallies in Nicaragua supporting the FMLN, first showing Nicaraguans at the Salvadoran embassy outside Managua, then depicting U.S. citizens outside the heavily fortified U.S. embassy in Managua, where participants chant slogans such as "U.S. guns killed U.S. nuns." In what was to become a ritual, the U.S. embassy crowd burns an effigy of Uncle Sam. In a long concluding montage, Legall intercuts stills and moving images of armed combatants and street fighting in El Salvador, repeatedly stopping the camera over the weapons, emphasizing the FMLN's military struggle, with no mention of the political organizing that ensured the resilience of the armed struggle.

To judge by the diplomatic maneuvering that took place in 1981 when Reagan took office, Legall entirely misread the FSLN's Dirección Nacional. Like the rest of the world, with the exception of the Reagan administration, Nicaraguans recognized the brutality of the El Salvadoran regime and the terrible inequities of Salvadoran society. But after the new U.S. government indicated that it would not tolerate a Nicaraguan role in shipping arms to the FMLN, and after the defeat of the 1980 FMLN offensive, the FSLN agreed to back off. Probably, Legall took upon himself the mission of producing crude but rousing calls to action. Few other INCINE filmmakers took that path. Frank Pineda, for the first noticiero made in the flush of victory, objected to including children marching with wooden guns. María José Alvarez had a horror of violence. None of the filmmakers had fired arms in battle. Most approved of maintaining a strong national defense, but they had chosen filmmaking as an instrument of reconstruction, not a stage for militant posturing.

After *El Salvador vencerá*, Legall conceived of a national defense trilogy: *La defensa militar*, *La defensa económica*, and *La defensa política*. He directed the first two, but a new filmmaker, Mariano Marín, completed the last one, and the latter's contributions reveal the limits of Legall's vision. Before the credits in *La defensa militar* (Feb. 1981), a soldier in a trench sends an urgent message over his radio: "Listen, compa [compañero], the orders are not to retreat, but to defend the patria to the last drop of blood, over." The film, which preceded the institution of a military draft in 1983, calls for people to join the militia. Women and men, young and old, undergo training with guns. Following the training footage and songs, the comandantes, in this case Tomás Borge and Humberto Ortega, speak. Both call listeners to prepare for future sacrifices. Before and after each speech, Legall inserts shots of loading a gun, making the speeches a metaphor for loading a weapon. A long coda shows the soldiers firing guns and launching grenades and shows artillery and tanks as a Soviet MIG passes overhead. After a tank advances toward the camera and continues over it into a foxhole below, Legall cuts to

*Alberto Legall and the perils of filmmaking (*La defensa militar*)*

still shots of young boys with fists raised, and the last one freezes during the superimposition of yet another quotation from Sandino: "The sovereignty of a people is not debated. It is defended with weapons in the hands."[5]

Legall evidently saw the film as a recruitment tool. However, there was little need to publicize the militias, for the army and mass organizations, such as the CDSs, recruited more effectively. The film presents no argument for defense and merely repeats slogans. In fact, the film does not convey the camaraderie of militia service, so effective in the Literacy Campaign films. And despite invocations of fallen "heroes and martyrs" and references to the historical combativeness of the Nicaraguan people, many Nicaraguans opposed the law of compulsory military service when it was passed in late 1983.

Substituting the idea of making economic sacrifices for the idea of joining the militia, *La defensa económica* (Mar. 1981) conforms to the pattern of *La defensa militar*. A worker acknowledges not understanding the meaning of economic defense. A song celebrating the struggle for "patria libre o morir" accompanies the titles. Other workers in the film link economic production to the defense of the revolution. Daniel Ortega reports the suspension of U.S. economic aid to Nicaragua and Bayardo Arce stresses the need for greater labor discipline and vigilance against sabotage. Shots of laborers at work alternate with those of workers training with rifles. The concluding titles affirm, "We will remain unflinching in defending to the ultimate consequences the dignity and sovereignty of the homeland and the revolution."

The film uses a new element: extensive archival footage of U.S. aggression, foreign and domestic. After Ortega refers to the U.S. decision on economic aid, a title asserts, "We do not forget what they have done. In Girón. In the Dominican Republic. In Kampuchea." Bombs float out of aircraft, U.S. troops train, bombs explode on the ground. In an abrupt change of scene, uniformed American soldiers are seen beating black people on the street in civil rights demonstrations. Then U.S. soldiers beat a Vietnamese prisoner, and famous shots capture terrified Vietnamese women and children running down the street carrying babies maimed by napalm. The Cuban filmmaker Santiago Alvarez used this footage in several films in the 1960s, such as *Now* (1965).

Legall reproduces the same discursive strategies in *La defensa económica* to indict U.S. hypocrisy, guilty before the world of unjustified aggression against the Vietnamese, a mirror of the racist oppression imposed on its own African American citizens. As Nicaragua's relations with the United States deteriorated, Legall tries to resurrect the world's moral indignation at U.S. policies, hoping to galvanize Nicaraguan opposition to Washington's attitudes. But this was a two-edged propaganda weapon. One title in the film defines economic defense as "making of our workplace a Sandinista trench." Militarizing the workplace meant literally bearing arms at work, but most actual attacks threatened isolated agricultural workers in the countryside, such as along the border with Honduras. Arce's speech, however, emphasizes "struggling energetically against labor indiscipline, against the waste of resources, disorder." These injunctions corresponded to the government's suspension of some rights for workers, including the right to strike. That is, though drawing its strength from the popular classes, the FSLN chose to tamp the momentum of the popular classes in the interests of national security. Just as the FSLN ended land takeovers by campesinos and small farmers to assuage the fears of the larger, agro-export landowners, the FSLN now adopted limits on the relatively small working class, blocking efforts to prevent erosion of real wages. Legall would continue in this vein in several subsequent efforts, but INCINE was on the whole searching for less didactic forms.

Mariano Marín

La defensa política (May 1981) marked the first credited work of Mariano Marín. Marín had recently returned from studying filmmaking with Jean Rouch at the Musée de l'Homme in Paris. He had received a grant in 1978 but remained in Nicaragua to support the FSLN during the insurrection. After the triumph, he accepted the grant. In France, he was demoralized by the condescending, ethnocentric atmosphere at the school and spent his time with other Latin Americans. Still, he had been exposed to the rudiments of filmmaking and even managed to convince Rouch to finance an experiment in Super 8-mm filmmaking in Nicaragua. France shipped film-developing materials as well as cameras and editing facilities. Marín wanted to use this equipment upon his arrival in Nicaragua, but claimed the directors showed no interest, and the equipment remained in delivery crates.[6] Marín instead set to work directing noticieros.

In his first noticiero, the inventive Marín added new touches. Strangely, given the popular nature of the Sandinista revolution, none of the previous films showed Nicaragua's ubiquitous wall painting and graffiti. Marín corrected that oversight with a series of precredit graffiti. Marín then created an elaborate *plan séquence* for the credits. Continuing the graffiti motif, he splashed credits on several white walls of a building, with the camera gliding in a single take from one wall to another. Like the original graffiti artists, the filmmakers become participants in a form of popular communication.

Most of the graffiti are slogans taken from the standard FSLN repertory—Viva la insurrección popular Sandinista, Para la insurrección popular Sandinista—but one, vowing, "We will bury the heart of the enemy in the mountain" is attributed to the FSLN, GPP. In this film, for the first time in a noticiero, Marín hints at the factional strife that riddled the FSLN during the 1970s. Throughout its history as a small guerrilla organization, the FSLN was buffeted by internal debate. The FSLN's first years were inspired by the Cuban revolution and Che Guevara's *foco* guerrilla strategy. In the late 1960s the FSLN suffered crippling military setbacks and eventually rejected the *foco* strategy. Following that impasse, the FSLN split into competing "tendencies": the GPP, or Guerra Popular Prolonga; the TP, or Tendencia Proletaria; and the tercerista (third) tendency. Each tendency analyzed Nicaraguan society differently and proposed a different strategy for achieving victory against Somoza. The GPP took the Vietnamese struggle as its model and envisioned a long campaign based on building solid support in the countryside. The TP pursued a more orthodox line, arguing for the vanguard role of the urban proletariat, a tiny proportion of the Nicaraguan working population. The terceristas, who mediated the split, proposed a broad-based patriotic front that would eventually be forced to choose popular resistance to the increasingly isolated dictatorship. Dramatic military actions would build popular sympathy for the antidictatorial struggle and ultimately ignite a popular explosion, or insurrection, that would topple

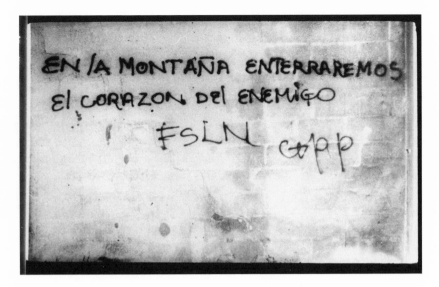

Vestiges of the FSLN tendencies: Guerra Popular Prolongada, or GPP
(La defensa política)

Somoza. The terceristas are often referred to as the insurrectional tendency for this reason.

Marín had belonged to the GPP faction and apparently retained that allegiance after the unification of tendencies in early 1979. Exaggerating the persistence of earlier divisions would be a mistake, but they had not disappeared. Before the triumph, FSLN activists had worked with one of the factions, sharing its ideological analysis and group identity. The FSLN did not openly refer to the tendencies after 1979, but all Sandinistas knew the history. If INCINE depended on tercerista support, and Minister of Culture Ernesto Cardenal was a tercerista, then promoting national unity over any hint of class struggle might reflect this.[7]

Between these graffiti bookends, the film shows the damage the contras have inflicted on the country and depicts Washington's role in training and financing them. U.S. military advisers conduct training exercises with contras in Florida, Kissinger delivers a speech about his doomsday Central American domino theory—claiming the dominoes will terminate in Mexico "which will then be a very grave matter for us"—and a Nicaraguan exile warns that "eventually we are going to have communism right there at the Rio Grande." While the film shows stills of Reagan and his wife eating with their hands, Carlos Nuñez speaks about aggression against Nicaragua, the juxtaposition suggesting the United States wants to gobble up the country. After a man writes "la defensa económica" on a wall, the film then shows

The Second Year

people working. Before the reprise of the opening graffiti, Marín inserts several other graffiti, including one attributed to the FSLN Proletario (Sandino Vive. Muerte al somocismo) and another singling out the "CDS en acción en la vigilancia de nación" ("CDS in action watching over the country").

Though *La defensa política* completed Legall's triptych, Marín tempered Legall's crude style. The contra footage and U.S. archival footage clearly identify the military, as opposed to political, card played by the opposition with U.S. backing. But the film doesn't celebrate military preparedness. The film does not mount montages of Nicaraguan children and soldiers raising weapons in the air. For the first time no leading comandante (Humberto Ortega, Daniel Ortega, Jaime Wheelock, Tomás Borge) appears. Instead, the graffiti anchor the film in the peoples' strength, creativity, and energy. The film shifts the orientation toward FSLN authority. Instead of interrupting the comandantes' speeches at rallies with shots of crowds chanting "poder popular," the film goes to the source of the FSLN's authority, the popular masses that ensured the FSLN victory.

But these independent stirrings were only incipient at INCINE during these months. Legall and Lacayo worked on two perfunctory noticieros about comandantes' trips abroad: *Viaje del Comandante Daniel Ortega a México* (Apr. 1981) and *Viaje del Comandante Humberto Ortega a Indochina* (June/July/Nov. 1981). Sandwiched between these two reportages was the *Segundo aniversario de la revolución popular sandinista* (July 1981). In response to the isolation imposed by the United States, Nicaragua sought aid from other countries. Mexico expressed public solidarity and contributed significant financial aid. Mexico and Venezuela generously shipped petroleum to Nicaragua in the early years of the revolution. The Ortega brothers traveled to Mexico and Indochina partly to solicit foreign support. According to Johnny Henderson, the editor, Ramiro Lacayo had no interest in filming Humberto Ortega in Indochina.[8] However, the famed Cuban documentarist, Santiago Alvarez, who sent a crew with Castro whenever he traveled, secured a plane ticket for Lacayo, so he had no choice. Henderson claimed that Legall was supposed to edit the film of the Mexico trip but refused. A foreign filmmaker who had shot footage of Ortega's stay in Mexico called Ortega to ask if he wanted the footage. Ortega told him that Nicaraguan filmmakers had shot footage and then he called INCINE. Greatly pressed for time, Henderson assembled the film over one weekend.

Criticism

At the end of 1980 as Alberto Legall arrived at INCINE, a new cultural publication, *Ventana*, appeared as a weekly supplement to the

FSLN daily newspaper, *Barricada*. *Ventana* was edited by Rosario Murillo, wife of Daniel Ortega, and provided the ambitious Murillo with a venue to compete with Ernesto Cardenal over the direction of cultural policy, a battle waged publicly over the poetry workshops.[9]

In the following years, poetry and literature remained dominant in *Ventana*, but periodic articles and interviews dealt with painting, sculpture, television—and cinema. In January and February 1981, *Ventana* reviewed two films, signed by INCINE. *Kramer vs. Kramer* was the first. Whatever one's views of the film, it is surprising to encounter such vitriol:

> I think that *Kramer vs. Kramer* has no excuse. A succession of tricks, falsifications and deformations of characters, it is conceived to raise in the least honest way a serious problem of our time: the right of divorced fathers to the custody of their children.
>
> At no point is there any attempt to confront the theme in a deep and profound fashion; instead it is shown as a case so unusual, extreme and macho: the wife is the villain and the husband a hero who succeeds in overcoming his lack of experience through sacrifice and love.[10]

The review, however pointed, essentially attacks the film's melodrama. The next week, in another unsigned INCINE review of the Bruce Lee film *Return of the Dragon*, the critic(s) unfurls a wholly political analysis:

> [*Return of the Dragon*] sets out the individual values: the solutions, rather than resting in the will of the masses, are polarized in the strength of a man who, given his characteristic as superman, does not belong to the human race.
>
> The center of the plot of this type of cinema is the exaggeration of limitless violence and the absurd exaggeration of the martial arts.
>
> In [Lee's] films, there never appears the attitude of work and struggle of the oriental peoples. His setting is the Hong Kong of drugs, of prostitution, protected by the great capitalist powers.
>
> His films will continue to be shown in theaters because this type of spectacular is still useful. Still, until you decide.[11]

In fact, this review is atypical of the filmmakers at INCINE, who appreciated commercial cinema. In any event, no other reviews were printed under the INCINE rubric for the rest of the year.

In the following issue, INCINE head Ramiro Lacayo wrote a thoughtful account of filmmaking in revolutionary Nicaragua, "Memoria histórica del pueblo."[12] Lacayo discusses prerevolutionary filmmaking and INCINE's current plans. INCINE's greatest task is "to preserve in images this history that the people are constructing." From the beginning, Nicaraguan cinema is a "committed, militant cinema, which surges from the heat of combat and documents the revolutionary process."

Lacayo relates that foreigners recommended producing fiction films after the triumph. The "internationalistas wanted to make a big film about Sandino, with Jane Fonda and Robert DeNiro. We would have ended up carrying cables and Pacino's bags." Lacayo implies that Nicaraguans preferred to film ongoing struggles, part of INCINE's "obligation to record all of the effort that our people were going to make to reconstruct the country, to create the truly just society." Perhaps in response to criticism, Lacayo acknowledges that INCINE has been less effective in addressing problems. He calls for learning from the people. Perhaps the filmmakers have had "their own preconceptions, which are at odds with what Nicaraguans really think, what is truly Nica, truly Sandinista." This collapse of identities—Nica, Sandinista—of course highlights a persistent and important tension. If the filmmakers made "truly Nica" films, would they be Sandinista? Or, conversely, would Sandinista films be accepted as truly Nica?

Here Lacayo raises the problem of "panfletario" films. Many filmmakers later viewed the early films as too *panfletario,* and already Lacayo recognizes this danger. He asserts that the *panfleto* is "too obvious, not artistic. That is the criterion. Revolution is art, creation. . . . Noticieros should be a poetic reflection." Lacayo indicates that INCINE has learned from the Cine-Mobil screenings that "audiences do not want long speeches. They want to see themselves on screen, as creators of the revolution. Second, we have to know how to present the spectacular, to amuse audiences. . . . This is difficult to harmonize, for often the political message is given more weight."

For Lacayo, however, the biggest failure has been not "creating a cinematographic culture in our people. . . . We want people to be able to criticize the films themselves, to see how lies operate." This is exactly what regular newspaper film criticism might have accomplished, but the two earlier reviews were little cause for optimism, and INCINE never established a regular column. A short-lived attempt to discuss films critically on television never achieved the success of Cuba's popular weekly show "24 Times a Second."[13]

Television could have offered a natural exhibition space for the new national cinema, but few INCINE films were televised. INCINE personnel claim that tensions between Lacayo and state television head Iván García prevented this obvious symbiosis. García, apparently, wanted to sell airtime, not give it away. INCINE balked, pleading poverty, and in his article, Lacayo bewailed INCINE's inability to use the revenues generated by the film theaters for film production. In a *Ventana* interview, García provided an account of the challenges facing television.[14] He spoke of the financial and ideological difficulties of finding enough programming appropriate for the revolutionary state. In addition to the expense of production, García notes the difficulty of attracting advertisers, for the SSTV monitored advertising. The government had passed a law banning the exploitation of women's images to sell products, but advertising companies made only one commercial for all of Central America. García pointed out, "If Nicaragua objects to a commercial, a company is unlikely to produce a separate commercial for the modest Nicaraguan market."

More important, though, was the different relationship of cinema and television to the FSLN. Historically, the FSLN had not used cinema in the struggle against Somoza, whereas it had operated the clandestine Radio Sandino. After the triumph, the two television stations were grouped together in the new SSTV, an identification with the FSLN that INCINE had deflected when it changed its name from the Sandinista Institute of Cinema to the Nicaraguan Institute of Cinema. Thus, the FSLN viewed radio, television, and the press as key resources in the revolution and placed them in the Department of Propaganda and Political Education (DEPEP). By assigning INCINE, a separate institute, to the Ministry of Culture, the FSLN obviously did not consider Nicaraguan cinema to be a mass medium with the same potential ideological impact as radio, television, and the press, and permitted it to operate under less constant political scrutiny.

In anticipation of the March 1981 meeting in Nicaragua of the fourth Mercado Nuevo Cine Latinoamericano (New Latin American Cinema Market), MECLA, several articles in *Ventana* introduced the relevant topics for discussion. In "A Great Unknown: the Latin American Cinema," the problem of market size is considered.[15] Only Mexico, Brazil, and Argentina had established national film industries with relatively consistent levels of production. The cinemas of other countries produced films occasionally.

> In every one of the Latin American countries, there is
> massive consumption of cinema of the large production
> centers (Hollywood, Paris, Rome, London), but the whole
> cinema which would be the closest culturally is
> unknown: that cinema of the countries with culturally
> similar languages and cultural processes.

The Second Year

At an earlier MECLA meeting in Brazil, an analysis of the situation con-cluded that though various countries had instituted protective measures for national films, in no case were there arrangements to exchange films in Latin America across national borders. The article suggests that "opening a common market would multiply the national markets already existing and trigger a surge of the countries' own cinema in countries where there is no cinematographic creation." Specifically, this arrangement would allow Nica-ragua to go beyond its small domestic market and recover invested capital in the external Latin American market. "All these conclusions and proposi-tions remain, for now, as an instance of this struggle for the surge of a cinema which expresses the necessities, the feelings, the national identity of the Latin American man."

In the next week's issue, *Ventana* carried a history of the New Latin American Cinema, "Apuntes sobre el Cine Latinoamericano," starting in Argentina in the late 1950s.[16] The first task had been to break out of the grip of foreign cultural dependence. The ideological crisis of the bourgeoisie failed to offer intellectuals and artists alternatives to the "nihilist tenden-cies that in very varied forms, particularly existentialism, led to the produc-tion of empty formal games, or in the best circumstances, the symptomatic interior 'breaking free.'" The sharpening class struggle provoked a "rupture with these lame expressions . . . which were wiped out by an event which rocked the life of Latin America: the Cuban revolution."

The heritage of Soviet cinema, Italian neorealism, and the best documen-tary tradition, from Flaherty to Ivens, bore fruit in the work of the young Latin American artists and intellectuals who transformed cinema from "an instrument of domination" into a "tool of liberation":

> [With the] ideological decomposition of the bourgeoisie
> as a dominant class . . . the movement of Latin American
> cinema is now already a visible reality. Its subsequent
> path will be linked to the struggles of the working class
> and its allies to construct a classless society.

Set against Lacayo's more subdued and modest remarks, this militant state-ment appears anachronistic, a vestige of the fiery cultural rhetoric accom-panying political struggles in the late 1960s and early 1970s. In particu-lar, these words echo the most inflammatory manifesto from that period, "Towards a Third Cinema." Despite the relative consistency of FSLN attacks on imperialism, the FSLN never promoted eliminating the bourgeoisie as a class and normally did not proclaim their policies as socialist, whatever sym-pathies the leaders felt for socialism as an ultimate goal. It is not clear who wrote this account, for none of the filmmakers wrote in such militant terms or directed films reflecting these views.

The next week's article, "Nicaragua, Sede IV Reunión del MECLA," concentrates on organizational considerations, primarily distribution of Latin American films in the region.[17] The political aspects are confined to criticizing Western monopolies that traditionally controlled the flow of films throughout Latin America, so that "90% of Latin American film production does not reach the general public," and asserting that the MECLA meeting in Nicaragua

> represents the efforts of our Revolutionary Government to attract a wide participation of the democratic sectors of Latin America in the joint effort to break the barriers imposed by the imperialist economic domination in the terrain of cinema.

A group discussion reproduced in *Ventana* after the MECLA meeting provides a more concrete record of the concerns of the participants.[18] The foreign participants were Pastor Vega (Cuba, director of *Retrato de Teresa* [*Portrait of Teresa*]), Walter Achugar (Uruguay, distributor and ICAIC representative in Europe), Miguel Littín (Chile, exiled director of several influential films, including *Actas de marusia*). Carlos Vicente Ibarra, María José Alvarez, and Alberto Leal (*sic*, presumably Legall) represented INCINE, sponsor of the event. Members of *Ventana*'s staff rounded out the gathering: Rosario Murillo (editor, poet), Gioconda Belli (poet), Guillermo Rothschuh Villanueva (writer on communication), and Francisco de Asís (head of the Institute for the Study of Sandinismo). Most speakers openly discussed INCINE's work. The foreigners praised Nicaraguan film for its maturity and artistry. For Littín, who dominated the conversation,

> film functions here as a tool, as a weapon, and also as an art. This is very important! The compañeros have dedicated themselves not only to express the revolutionary themes, but also to express them as an art form. In this sense the Nicaraguan cinema, in spite of its young age, is one of the most advanced documentary cinemas in Latin America.

Littín suggests that INCINE can convey "the face and identity of the Nicaraguan people, the face and identity completely new and unknown in the cinema." Like the newsreels Littín and others made in Chile under Allende, the Nicaraguan films show exactly what is going on in the country. Legall modestly points out the importance of "our search for a cinematic language ... which shows our identification with the interests of our people. A language which is our own, which allows us to show on the screens the successes, the advances, and the problems of our revolution."

When Littín asks how people respond to the noticieros, Legall describes two categories. Audiences opposed to the revolution try to scream at the screen. When the audience is a more popular one, "we've seen the people clapping, shouting slogans, identifying completely with what they are seeing." Alvarez concurs, and observes, "The people are enchanted with seeing themselves on the screen." But Alvarez alone cites a specific example of Mobile Cinema projections on the Atlantic coast: "When there are speeches, the people don't pay much attention." Belli distinguishes between the news presented on television and radio, and the INCINE noticieros. In the former, the people are depicted as objects, not subjects; in the cinema, "a completely different vision is seen. It is the people who are recounting how the revolution is advancing." While Belli does not elaborate, this distinction corresponded with the bureaucratic separation of the mass media of television and radio under the FSLN propaganda department, and the cinema—with its semiautonomous status in the Ministry of Culture.

Several speakers discuss how INCINE should approach problems confronting the revolution. Ibarra, perhaps the most aesthetically sophisticated of the speakers, gently deflects the praise showered on Nicaraguan film:

> We could fall into the little triumphalism of believing
> that the noticieros which we are showing, that some
> documentaries which we are making, are the maximum
> expression of our possibilities. But while we maintain
> this frequent critical attitude toward what we are doing,
> I believe that we are going forward. For we are trying to
> integrate in the consciousness of the compañeros who
> are making cinema here in Nicaragua, this permanent
> critical spirit, this rigor in study, in political preparation
> and aesthetic-cultural preparation.

Murillo wonders whether INCINE is in fact using its cameras to present problems. Legall refers to his trilogy on military, economic, and political defense, although those films do not explore problems other than the pressures exerted by North American aggression and the need for sacrifices from the people. Ibarra returns to Murillo's point and acknowledges that the noticieros tend to present the "official version," fearing that "the problem that we are considering is going to provoke more problems and . . . we don't want to risk such provocation." He contends that the proper attitude of "revolutionary criticism" should be to raise issues in a critical manner, which INCINE's films had not done to that point.

Belli takes the discussion of addressing problems in an entirely new, and curious, direction. After accepting the idea of dealing with problems critically, she focuses on how INCINE can deal with future problems and suggests that the people need films to offer some hope; they need a *mística*

> which will allow the people to face all these problems
> with a collective sense and with a sense of vision toward
> the future, to take account that they are investing in
> their own history, in their own future. The fundamental
> task of INCINE in this moment would be to help create
> this mística of the people, of the collective and the
> problems of the revolution, to confront them from a
> positive point of view, that is, that we have all these
> problems, but here we are all ready to resolve them.

De Asís cautions Belli that perhaps she is exaggerating, for the *mística* exists and "it began many years earlier, during the war, it is what made July 19 possible." Belli agrees but insists that a new *mística* is needed, one not of war, but of reconstruction.

Belli's call for a *mística* summons up a mythology of the revolution ready to withstand any assault, and she highlights the need for such a mística by describing a factory worker whose wages have not changed since the triumph and who watches the purchasing power of those wages erode. Ibarra and Murillo, argue for a critical, revolutionary attitude to acknowledge these problems, and Ibarra stresses the importance of educating as well as informing the people. They believe that the films should clarify FSLN policies and convince the people of their rightness. Belli fears that people could wilt under pressure unless fortified with a *mística* to endure the "disorienting shock" of future sacrifices. Subsequent events would substantiate these fears, but INCINE did not pursue this *mística*, a concept actually resisted by Lacayo and Ibarra, who saw such triumphalism as a weakness of INCINE's production.

During INCINE's transition, then, after completing the early noticieros and before releasing the first documentaries, some INCINE personnel understood the dangers of becoming an official FSLN organ. Ibarra warns of complacence, and Alvarez cites audience indifference to official speeches. Despite Legall's reference to dealing with problems, Legall's films, including the one he mentions, *La defensa política,* are hardly independent views of the peoples' difficulties. But as Ibarra and de Asís insist, Nicaraguan filmmaking was still in its infancy. In addition, both the filmmakers and the Nicaraguans were inexperienced in seeing films critically. While Littín was impressed with INCINE's first two years, Ibarra called for "rigorous discipline," suggesting the need for constant reevaluation. The release of INCINE's first documentary several months later initiated the next stage of INCINE's continuing maturation.

First Documentaries

The original agreements between the Cubans and INCINE included plans for producing several medium-length 16-mm color documentaries per year. Documentaries allowed a longer production schedule and permitted filmmakers to examine topics in greater depth and to experiment artistically more than was possible with the noticieros. Over time, the noticieros became a training ground for filmmakers, a kind of rite of passage before graduating to documentaries.

In *Ventana* of July 18, 1981, on the second anniversary of the triumph, a short piece entitled "*La otra cara del oro*" [*The Other Side of Gold*], by the Puerto Rican Emilio Rodríguez, appeared. The first paragraph explains the title, a play on words of a common expression equivalent to "the flip side of the coin" in English:

> This marvelous metal that unleashed the bloody avarice
> of the Spanish imperium on indigenous America . . . this
> element which propelled the colonization of the West of
> North America . . . this glittering ingot which determines
> the capital of nations . . . how often have we meditated
> on how it is obtained, on the human cost its extraction
> entails, the ecological devastation which its industrial
> processing causes, the misery of the miner caused by the
> exploitation of the capitalist boss? This is the other side
> of gold.[19]

The article recounts the mining history in the Atlantic coast region since the late nineteenth century. Assuring a percentage to the first (Anastasio) Somoza, the North American companies despoiled the area's natural resources. After Daniel Ortega announced the nationalizations in the first noticiero, the transnational countries demanded millions of dollars in compensation. "INCINE's documentary, *La otra cara del oro*, takes on the theme of the human, mineral, and environmental exploitation in a graphic and metaphorical form." Rodríguez then describes the film's organization, beginning with "the audience penetrating the atmosphere of the mining centers" and concluding with the camera zooming out "to discover a stunning industrial desert." This description corresponds to the film, completed shortly before the *Ventana* article in July, but gives no hint of the difficulties encountered in production.

The final film credits for INCINE's first documentary list two directors, Emilio Rodríguez and Rafael Vargas. Rodríguez started but could not complete the project. Lacayo passed it to Vargas, who claims it is his film. The film's editor, Johnny Henderson, believes that both men deserve credit, and the final version does list both as directors.[20]

Curiously, Rafael Vargas had not worked on any noticieros. However, Vargas had joined INCINE immediately after the triumph. Vargas's work at INCINE makes him a unique figure. Like many educated middle-class Nicaraguans, Vargas had attended university abroad, but he was the only filmmaker who had actually made a film before joining INCINE. After attending the Catholic university in Managua, Vargas studied architecture in Mexico and had a long history of interest in film. With Franklin Caldera, Vargas had organized a cine-club in Managua to show film classics. In 1973 he made *Señorita*, a short film heavily influenced by surrealism.[21]

According to his own words at the time of the triumph, however, he had little political experience. In September 1979, Vargas applied to work at INCINE. His letter, written by someone who had never joined a political party and who describes himself as a Buddhist, presents an interesting self-portrait.[22] The prose is virtually Marxist parody, as he explains that his education took place "within a bourgeois, dictatorial, and capitalist society." On his return to Nicaragua in 1971, he says he attempted "to do something" and puts a militant spin on being president of the architecture students association. After the 1972 earthquake, he worked on the establishment of urban affairs offices until discovering that "within the existing structures there was little that could be done for the masses."

He then landed a job at "these same premises" (i.e., INCINE), run for Somoza by the Mexican Felipe Hernández. But his oppositional stance, such as submitting a script "critical of the bourgeois Nicaraguan system" compromised his position and he was forced to resign. With other cinephiles (Mayra Luz Pérez, Carlos Mohs, and Rodolfo Glenton), he organized the cine-club

ANCINE (*Asociación Nicaragüense de Cine*), but people motivated by financial interests sabotaged that venture. In Vargas's words,

> The existing structures permeated all the social strata, nothing happens without the desire of capital. Yet when the insurrection of September 1978 broke out, I gave all my moral support, but I don't believe that I did much for the insurrection in the practical aspect. I only wrote poems and some other story as a silent protest. Never have I had the courage to grab a rifle, as I did not in July. My wish to collaborate took the form of working as a Red Cross volunteer. Now I wish to contribute my cinematic knowledge to help create the future cinema which will have to recover our national identity and raise the educational level of our people.

Vargas's letter is interesting for its militant leftist tone. This young, urbane, literate, witty, introspective artist sees his dream of filmmaking in the hands of armed Sandinista militants. Adapting to the current situation, Vargas describes his pacifist/passive personal account in political jargon. However, even during the early years at INCINE when "everyone was Sandinista" (according to many of the personnel), Vargas avoided political involvement. He didn't work on the early noticieros, which he characterized as "Marxist-Leninist."[23] The FSLN political representative at INCINE, Vicente Ibarra, attributes the substitution of Nicaraguan for Sandinista Institute of Cinema to Vargas.[24] While many filmmakers deride Vargas as an opportunist, that is probably unfair, even if it is accurate. Vargas always saw himself as an artist and filmmaker. He opposed Somoza but never joined a political group. He was single-minded about making films; the other filmmakers did not separate their aesthetic ambition from their revolutionary engagement so rigidly.

Once at INCINE, Vargas, on at least one occasion, argued in a June 1980 memo that INCINE risked "complete failure" if the filmmakers did not have a "clear comprehension of the Cinematic process (Art and Industry)." Inside the institution, Vargas was calling for greater professionalization. For Vargas, part of the danger was that "we are economically subsidized and we are not working with our own resources." Many at INCINE wanted greater independence. Yet INCINE benefited from its association with the FSLN. With only a modest budget, INCINE depended heavily on services in kind provided by FSLN organizations, access to military training exercises, food and housing from FSLN support groups, transportation funding from the army,

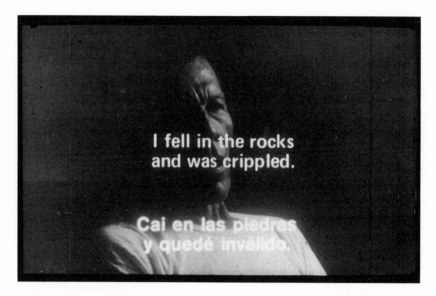

*Miskito miner speaking of dangers in the mines (*La otra cara del oro*)*

trucks from the army or Interior Ministry, and so on. The Cubans' expectations placed additional pressures. Since the Cubans covered many of the actual filmmaking expenses (raw stock, development, postproduction), they could effectively require INCINE to produce noticieros. Furthermore, the newly formed (and forming) bureaucracy was hardly a well-oiled machine. Throughout the government and party apparatus, there were tendencies to build separate, often personal, fiefdoms, leading to bureaucratic disarticulation and loss of efficiency, evident in the conflicts between INCINE and SSTV. However ad hoc, at least INCINE's matrix of connections did support continuous production.

To return to INCINE's first documentary, *La otra cara del oro* does represent a more "professional" work. The 20-minute length permits a more leisurely pace. Freed from constraints of topicality, the film explores its theme in multiple aspects and builds a more complex, less "panfletario" argument. No officials speak in the film. Throughout, the only voices are those of the miners. Perhaps most importantly, the film constructs a rich aesthetic texture, letting black-and-white images and sounds convey a harrowing indictment of the U.S. companies.

Before the credits, a lone miner speaks in Miskito, with Spanish and English subtitles, about the abysmal state of his health caused by mine work. After the credits, long shots of an overcast sky and the mountains give way to shots of adults and children in the dirt streets of the small town. Several other miners describe injuries, from silicosis to physical maiming, as one worker shows missing fingers on his left hand. Shots of rain falling from the wooden housing and dripping into a large barrel establish the recurrent theme of water. Suddenly, a popular song, "Concho Pinto" comes on as the camera peers into the playback mechanism of a jukebox then tracks backward to reveal a popular bar in which workers are now eating and drinking beer. Next, the camera approaches several bottles of Victoria beer (made in Nicaragua), followed by a dissolve to a lone bottle of VSOP brandy framed in the center of the shot, and the sound track changes to 1930s jazz music. The camera now travels through the elegant empty interior of the foreign manager's house and lingers over the elaborate table service in the dining room. After the long takes of the camera movements, there is a series of quick cuts, accompanied by the U.S. Marine anthem "From the Halls of Montezuma," of houses, including a swimming pool and tennis court, formerly occupied by the foreign mining managers. As the song ends, several shots show a bowling ball rolling toward the camera before toppling the pins, a metaphoric coda summing up the preceding images and sounds. Without a word uttered, the sequence dramatizes the former contrast between the hard lives of the workers and the opulent lifestyle of the owners.

Next, miners descend into the mines, water dripping everywhere. As the miners plunge lower and lower and begin working, other destitute former miners testify to the mining companies' callous indifference. When workers succumb to loss of limb or silicosis, the company stops their wages and provides no medical care, simply discarding them as no longer useful. In the only reference to the United States, one miner accuses the "gringo" of leaving behind nothing but destroyed machinery, seen piled in heaps, the "cemeteries" described in the *Ventana* article by Rodríguez.

The next sequence examines the miners' living conditions. The camera glides past women preparing food on antiquated stoves, children crammed into overcrowded rooms, wooden latrines with no plumbing facilities. A miner with a missing arm walks slowly toward the camera down a dirt road, the shot intercut with a chest X-ray, as a voice describes the injuries suffered in the mines and the sound track plays the oppressive sounds of mine machinery. Suddenly, the film cuts to a rapid montage of 76 miner identity photographs, each with a number at the bottom, as the famous musical crescendo from the Beatles' "Sergeant Pepper" album plays.

Darkness and silence fill the screen before the haunting final sequence. The only voice-over in the film catalogues the ecological devastation inflicted on the region by the mining companies. In images reminiscent of the Farm Security Administration's *Power and the Land*, the film shows the environmental cost to Nicaragua:

*A miner who has lost his arm to the mines (*La otra cara del oro*)*

To extract this gold, the companies devastated 1,650 square kilometers of forests. They dumped 34 million tons of crushed stone on fertile land, converting it into deserts. They poisoned eight rivers with 76 pounds of cyanide, one of the most toxic substances for human and animal life, hundreds of children dying of cyanide poisoning in the populations living by these rivers. The contamination has caused the disappearance of thirteen aquatic species, staples of the families of the region. And they have left thousands of Nicaraguan workers dead, mutilated, tubercular or silicosis victims, mainly Miskitos and Sumos.

The Junta of National Reconstruction nationalized the mines, the North American companies withdrew, demanding indemnifications of millions of dollars. But, is it just that, after enriching themselves with our gold, silver and copper, after so much death and ecological damage they have left behind, we still have to pay?

Without naming imperialism or referring to the FSLN, without Daniel Ortega announcing the nationalization of the mines, *La otra cara del oro* makes a devastating indictment of imperialist barbarity. The enclave econ-

*The dessicated legacy of U.S. exploitation (*La otra cara del oro)

omy creates a world apart from that of the indigenous workers, an owner's world reproducing the material luxury and cultural artifacts of a foreign land. The film exposes as false claims about the benefits provided by foreign-controlled capital to poor countries. The simple testimonies of the stricken miners and the quiet inventory of lives mired in poverty are incontrovertible evidence of imperialism and expose the presumptuousness of foreign demands for compensation.

Notwithstanding the remarkable effect of the film, the mines were not a political challenge for the filmmakers. As the base of an enclave economy, the mines were isolated structurally and geographically from the revolution. The FSLN promoted the mining area as the birthplace of Sandino's struggle against imperialism, but the coastal population had little contact with contemporary Sandinismo. Hence, the mines were a noncontroversial canvas for the projection of a depoliticized, unproblematic political vision, the expulsion of the foreign occupiers. Consequently, the film depicts an uninterrupted history of suffering, devoid of Sandinista heroes and martyrs. The foreign companies "withdrew"; they were not thrown out or forced to accept the conditions of sovereignty demanded by the revolution. No one in Nicaragua, or elsewhere, could deny the injustice presented in the film, but the film never tries to mobilize audiences to act. In a sense, the criticisms directed at the drought imagery of Pare Lorentz's Depression films could be applied to *La otra cara del oro.* In the Lorentz films, nature has exacted its toll on the land, through no apparent human agency. The photography transforms desiccated landscapes into sculptures of barren natural beauty. The photography conveys a feeling of inevitability. Many progressives hailed the federal government's intervention to reverse remorseless nature, a statism that does not arise from the peoples' organization, or any particular politics. *La otra cara del oro* leaves a similar feeling of powerlessness, so overwhelming and successful is the evocation of the scourge that the companies inflicted on all life forms.

The experience of completing an earlier compilation film on the revolution may have affected subsequent filmmaking at INCINE, including this first documentary. The FSLN wanted to use the footage shot during the insurrection for the first anniversary of the revolution. Vicente Ibarra and Johnny Henderson worked feverishly to edit the film in Cuba. The footage came from several sources and reflected the divisions among the factions. Henderson recalls that Ibarra devised a careful plan for the film. At a screening in Cuba, attended by FSLN leaders, Carlos Nuñez objected vehemently to the film's bias in favor of the insurrectional tendency and demanded that it be recut to restore balance.[25] That is, the first effort to make an official film on the insurrection and triumph triggered internal conflict, reflecting the still-tender tendency schism. The INCINE heads may have decided, consciously or not, to avoid controversy by choosing "safer" topics. This early skittishness may have inhibited INCINE's agenda for years into the future. Therefore, based on reaction to the first noticiero (*Nationalization of the Mines*), whose agenda showed that the nationalization of the mines was both popular and uncontroversial, INCINE perhaps viewed the topic as a perfect first documentary.

Several months after *La otra cara del oro*, INCINE completed its second documentary, *Del águila al dragón* [*From the Eagle to the Dragon*] (late 1981). During his trip to Indochina with Humberto Ortega, captured in the tedious noticiero *El viaje del Comandante Humberto Ortega a Indochina*, Lacayo shot footage of contemporary Vietnam. On his return, Lacayo made an ambitious, short documentary using that material. In an article printed in both *Ventana* and the independent but pro-FSLN *El Nuevo Diario*, Lacayo prefaces the text by citing Ho Chi Minh: "Once the Yankee aggressor is defeated, we will construct a country ten times more beautiful and wonderful." The article describes the aims of the film:

> With this documentary we wanted to begin a reflection
> on the North American aggression against Vietnam. . . .
> It's not a "rational reflection" on the war, imperialism, its
> causes, interests, etc., but rather an "emotional reflec-

tion," an attempt to construct a metaphor of indignation against one of the most brutal crimes which we have witnessed. . . .

We couldn't make a simple news report on the Vietnam war, given the time lag, but we would have to give the film a creative shake-up which would revitalize the image, which would give it a certain vitality which we wanted to convey. It was about creating a manifesto rather than a chronological description of the events of this war. The documentary would be composed fundamentally of the compilation of historical images of great force and brutality mixed with contemporary images of Vietnam which had a lyric fluidity. We related the latter with images taken by us of the Vietnamese people, its reconstruction effort, its cities, its parks, its daily life, music. . . .

We decided not to use interviews or narration but only to rub images against each other by the rhythm of the editing, white/black against color, music against music. We wanted the spectator to be moved not rationally, but that he should feel it. We wanted to suggest, cry out, confuse, and ultimately, to frighten.[26]

By virtually eliminating spoken words, the 15-minute *Del águila* formally departs from the noticieros and also from Vargas's film. The filmmakers clearly saw the documentaries as an opportunity to exercise their creative energies. As Lacayo indicates, the film is structured around a straightforward contrast between the peaceful, lyrical lives of the Vietnamese, shot in color, and the unbridled aggression launched against them by the United States, shown in black and white. The film essentially combines the pacific footage taken in Indochina by Lacayo's crew with archival footage cannibalized from other documentaries and newsreels, such as the U.S. *Hearts and Minds* (1974), by Peter Davis. The contrast is played out in multiple formal registers. The film's formal complexity works on an emotional level, and the argument unfolds with a lucid logic.

The opening images introduce the serene daily life of the Vietnamese people: junks on the water, statues of Asian deities, temples, street shots. After a title announces "chronicles of an invasion," U.S. air force jets take off from an aircraft carrier. Archival footage and stills show police, including a policeman in riot gear holding a man down with his foot, beating civil rights protesters. In an elaborately edited sequence, a high school football coach speaking to his players violently in the locker room is intercut with stills of Nixon, hecklers at an antiwar march, players rushing out of the locker room, and U.S. soldiers wading ashore. Big-band music from the 1940s ("the glorious and triumphalist music of the forties by Glenn Miller and Art Shaw"— Lacayo) plays over these black-and-white images. The next sequence shows a Vietnamese marketplace and plays Asian music. The big-band music returns as bombs float from planes and fall in slow motion, then there are more shots of the Vietnamese, walking and bicycling in the city, ending with girls jumping rope. Bombs fall as the screen goes black. A longer sequence follows, deploying famous images of Vietnamese suffering: the summary execution of a Vietnamese prisoner by a South Vietnamese officer, a U.S. soldier viciously beating a prisoner, a napalmed little girl running down a dirt road. These images are intercut with more shots of high school football, the players crashing into each other, the choreography of the half-time band, cheerleaders. The intercutting associates the U.S. army aggression with a martial rite of passage, exemplified by the rituals of a high school football game.

The next sequence celebrates the Vietnamese defense against the air war. A lone peasant with two water buffalo walks with his rifle slung over his shoulder. Air defense batteries fire missiles at the U.S. planes, which drop to earth. GIs retreat from battle, dragging the dead and wounded. Gerald Ford stumbles as he walks out of a plane with his wife Betty. Janis Joplin wails, "Tell me whaaa, whaa, whaa, why . . ." over stills of a morose Lyndon Johnson at his desk, followed by an atomic-mushroom explosion. Nazi soldiers march by, then U.S. Marines; there's a shot of the Statue of Liberty, footage of a U.S. soldier sucking the breast of a Vietnamese prostitute (from *Hearts and Minds*), and three shots of Hitler, Nixon, and Reagan. After this barrage, the sedate, rural images of young Vietnamese women tending crops close the film, restoring the traditional rhythm of Vietnamese agriculture.

Despite the pace of the archival editing, the rhetorical messages are clear. The air war interrupts the daily life of the Vietnamese people, a people with an old and rich culture (the images of the deities and temples). U.S. culture inculcates aggressive values in its youth (football games); aggression is then turned loose at home in civil repression (racist denial of civil rights), and abroad in racist imperialist aggression, shamelessly directed against civilians. This rush of images is cut to "a rhythm much more accelerated and violent, alienating in its neuroses and the sickness of decadent western society."[27] The Vietnamese fight back, fell U.S. aircraft, repel ground troops, and bring down the aggressor (Ford stumbling). Like the Nazis, U.S. Marines march to orders of Hitler/Nixon/Reagan; the soldiers mock the meaning of the Statue of Liberty by subsidizing the Vietnamese sex industry.

In addition to condemning U.S. aggression, *Del águila al dragón* also demonstrates the superpower's vulnerability. In this sense, the film both warns and rallies the Nicaraguan people, as the Reagan administration stepped up its threats; as Lacayo noted: "The film is also—and this is important—a demonstration, a repudiation and an opportunity to reflect on imperialist war, faced with the aggression that other peoples have had to suffer and that today our Revolution is threatened with confronting."[28] In a review in *Ventana*, Carlos Mohs echoed this concern:

> At the end [of the film], the triumph of calm, but the reference of a past to the real present of the world remains. The popular memory of Vietnam is rescued for the present moment and the effect, for the action of the Nicaraguan spectator. Conflicting positions of feeling and seeing this culture dominated by blood, so distant from the Vietnamese as from us, this Yankee imperialist power continues its threatening behavior and we breathe within it.[29]

Given claims by Nicaraguans that Nicaraguan audiences had no film culture, the film risked baffling local audiences. The Mohs review implies this, despite Mohs's own ease in deciphering the film. He observes, "The first impression of the spectator has to be surprise and perplexity before the accumulation of dense and complex sensations." So he unpacks the film in detail, sketching a history of this form of documentary, highly edited and often using found footage, assembled for political purposes. He lists filmmakers from the 1920s: Jean Vigo, "poet of the rigorous social documentary," Luis Buñuel, who "scandalized humanity with an identical social perspective, but with violent and explosive images," Dziga Vertov and his "documentary of 'cine-eye' or cine-truth," and the "disconcerting and superstylized explosion of the historic documents of 'cine-montage'" of Eisenstein. Mohs turns then to what makes the film disconcerting, what may perplex spectators: "distasia." For Mohs, the distasia, or "disorder," of the film is the contrast between the assertive, rapid editing and the serenity of traditional Vietnamese life with the violence of the "imperium which dominates by violence in its history of repression and rapine."

But Mohs does not want to say that this technique simply shocks (there is nothing "sensationalist or melodramatic"). The film works by engaging the intellect, eliciting mental effort, "awakening the mind." As the filmmaker, Lacayo defends the film as a new form that can directly impact the spectators more than the noticieros that had by then become somewhat stale and repetitive. Lacayo wanted

> to give [the film] a little poetry, a little protest, and a great deal of solidarity. This entailed a risk, but we were not trying to make something pretty (the war was not pretty) but to create a direct impact on the audience, to communicate with them. Finally, more than a successful solution, the documentary is an open path, a step in the other direction, an attempt to try out the genre of a form less flat, creating new relations, seeking out stronger responses.

As Mohs implied, *Del águila al dragón* is based on assertive montage. In this film, the technique achieves an effect similar to that of *La otra cara del oro*. The images come at the viewer as a kind of assault. Undoubtedly, Nicaraguan audiences unaccustomed to aggressive, didactic editing might have difficulty following the argument, but the rhetorical logic is clear. Still, the overwhelming effect remains the might of the U.S. military machine, somehow heroically defeated by the Vietnamese. Aside from anti-aircraft missile defenses, however, the film does not indicate how. The editor Henderson has said that they intentionally avoided images of Ho Chi Minh, not wanting to attribute victory to an individual.[30] But there is no hint of the political organization of the Vietnamese resistance, no footage of the vast tunnels built for years of underground living, a reality far more significant militarily than the years in the mountains mythologized by the FSLN. That is, the victory in *Del águila* seems magical, and the film's technical virtuosity reinforces that problem, hiding the true strength of the people. Nonetheless, the documentary form did provide Lacayo—and Henderson—the chance to experiment, to step past the noticiero's boundaries, and *Del águila* was part of INCINE's advance.

Rafael Vargas finished *La otra cara del oro*, but he had inherited that project in midstream. He claims credit for the film, but he did not initiate it, and its political thrust, though somewhat muted, nonetheless contrasts with Vargas's preferred political stance and cultural interests. His next documentary, *La brigada cultural Iván Dixon en Cuba* [*The Ivan Dixon Cultural Brigade in Cuba*] (late 1981), was a better fit with his aesthetic interests.

Iván Dixon covers a purely cultural exchange between Nicaragua and Cuba. Political connotations are entirely eliminated. The Nicaraguans do not mention the Sandinistas or the revolution; the film makes no reference to the Cuban revolution or Fidel Castro. Aside from a sequence of Cuban nightlife, a montage of neon bar signs ending with the floor show at the Tropicana in Havana, the film follows black Nicaraguan costeños dancing or speaking in short interviews. Implicitly, the presence of Nicaraguans in Cuba conveys a sea change in the political climate of Nicaragua. The Nicaraguan bourgeoisie had demonized the Cubans as hard-line Marxists eager to convert Nicaragua into another socialist prison in the Caribbean. Unfortunately, this type of discourse found sympathetic audiences on Nicaragua's Atlantic coast, for the FSLN had already committed serious errors there, though most pertained to the Miskitos rather than to the black population to the south.

To judge by the film, the costeños from Nicaragua have developed an extremely sexy dance known as Palo de Mayo. One woman speaks of the pleasure she enjoyed in Santiago de Cuba, the center of black life in Cuba. As in Nicaragua, revolution or no, blacks warm to each other through ethnic/racial affinities, not national or class identities. The revolutionary government in Nicaragua arranged the cultural exchange, suggesting the revolution's inclusiveness, but nothing the black Nicaraguans say, always in Spanish, hints that they live in a revolutionary culture now. Even more than the noticiero *La costa Atlántica, Iván Dixon* concentrates on the costeños' erotic exoticism. Without the polemical thrust of *La otra cara del oro, Iván Dixon* has no real shape. The scenes unroll as a series of dance performances in Cuba, combined with comments by participants and picturesque shots of costeño life.

A film like *Iván Dixon* inevitably raises questions about identity, in this case, identity of the revolution, of Nicaraguan culture, of Sandinismo, of the costeños. The Sandinista revolution consciously tried to forge a national identity. But centuries of neglect of the Atlantic coast could not be eviscerated in one stroke. Large parts of the Nicaraguan territory had few cultural connections to the dominant *mestizaje* culture. When a nationalist president tried to claim Nicaraguan authority over the Atlantic coast in the 1890s, the British navy repudiated the claim, and the United States overthrew the president and found a more compliant replacement in 1909. In short, many factors besides physical isolation separated the Pacific and Atlantic halves of the country: language, history, economic organization, political/cultural allegiance. The Miskitos were committed to their own leaders, and the black population was linked culturally to the Caribbean and economically to the United States. In any event, heterogeneity always interacts dialectically with national identity.

Iván Dixon tries to have it both ways. On the one hand, Vargas emphasizes the pronounced eroticism of the costeños by featuring the Palo de

Mayo, probably the most prominent cultural marker of costeño identity in the Pacific region of Nicaragua, and certainly one that associates blacks and eroticism, a connection widely made in "European" cultures. On the other hand, the film wants to embrace Palo de Mayo, and, metonymically, the black costeños, as part of Nicaraguan culture, a rhetorical catachresis that merits treatment in a film because of the very cultural distance being bridged. Following this logic, the larger the distance and the more stereotypical the markers, the greater the paternalism. In *Iván Dixon*, all the costeños speak Spanish. Yet even in the early noticiero *La costa Atlántica*, Jaime Wheelock's informal chat with costeños must be translated into English for listeners. *Iván Dixon* ignores the language question in what is actually the attempt to construct national identity, inasmuch as such a homogeneous identity certainly did not exist within Nicaragua's territorial borders.

Nor did reservations about the film go unexpressed. Ibarra received a letter from the Foreign Ministry with comments on *Iván Dixon*. The Ministry requested material from INCINE to be sent to Ecuador, and the letter quotes the following observations from the Nicaraguan ambassador in Ecuador:

> To be brief, I refer specifically to the short *La Brigada Iván Dixon*. In the film there is a lamentable poverty in the dialogues and interviews, giving the image of our people as a people of subnormals, falling into a simplistic folklorism and frankly humiliating comparisons, such as when the film shows the worst backwardness and the worst blemishes of our Atlantic Coast.[31]

María José Alvarez, after working on many of the early noticieros, directed the last of this first set of documentaries. Throughout the 1980s the FSLN created yearly slogans. For 1981 the FSLN chose "Year of Production and Defense," and María José Alvarez constructed her first documentary around the theme of production. *País pobre, ciudadano pobre [Poor Country, Poor Citizen]* (late 1981) confronts the problem of imports. Unlike the previous documentaries, however, the 16-mm, black-and-white *País pobre* does not strike out into new formal territory. The film relies on interviews with workers to describe the economic parameters of export dependency and to demonstrate their own political understanding of Nicaragua's relationship to the world economy.

A long precredit sequence, like the opening sequence in Alvarez's *La costa Atlántica* (Noticiero 11), mobilizes sketches, stills, and a dissonant music-over to chronicle the early history of dependency. The Spanish enslaved and murdered the indigenous population, but after independence, the country suffered from economic dependence. The United States controlled the national banking system at the turn of the century, and Somoza installed dependence as a national policy. After shots of printing presses and *Barricada* headlines warning about aggression, a young woman explains that the people have to fight to "defend our political system." This elaborate opening announces the two poles of the film, political independence and economic independence.

After the credits, the camera tracks past houses that are in disrepair and factory machinery that is idle, recapitulating the state of the country after the triumph, a victory whose costs were estimated to be the value of one year's gross national product.[32] A woman emphasizes the urgency of reactivating production, and a male worker explains that workers must act as an "advance guard" to overcome economic problems. Amidst shots of cotton processing, another man speaks about raising productivity to obtain money, and the first man returns to describe the importance of saving to buy dollars to purchase fuel. Nicaraguans must produce their own machinery, for they cannot import from abroad, a fact illustrated by stills of advertisements for cars and whiskey featuring beautiful women, an advertising technique banned in Sandinista Nicaragua.[33] At a port at which containers with foreign lettering are unloaded, a voice-over observes that Nicaragua cannot control the international prices of imported goods, which are always changing. The camera then passes through the Oriental Market, where patrons and merchants complain about rising costs. A highly edited sequence is built around the rising cost of gas. With classical music driving the sequence, the film intercuts shots of cars, buses, and poor Nicaraguans and logos of Texaco and Esso, as a recurring graphic traces the rise in the price of a barrel of oil from $21.96 in 1979 to $43.37 in 1981, a one hundred percent increase in two years. The screen goes black as a voice says, "Despite political independence, we still depend on the rich countries to live." To close, the film intercuts shots of agriculture and industry. Shots of farms being irrigated and fields being sown alternate with shots of harvesting (coffee and cotton), and shots of white-hot steel rolling past the camera. The montage terminates with shots of goods being packaged and loaded onto docks for export.

Overall the documentary paints a bleak picture. Nicaraguans can expect higher prices and greater sacrifices. The individuals in the film are not discouraged, but the film offers no hope for audiences, such as by showing the organization of production in cooperatives, worker control of the workplace, profit sharing, or subsidy of basic consumer goods by the government, all of which were being implemented with extremely varied success. As always, Alvarez lets ordinary people express hopes and fears, instead of letting FSLN militants predict the promised land, or comandantes deliver speeches already memorized by their audiences. But the voice-overs perform a similar function to that of those speeches: logical, but too abstract and chimerical for a population struggling with daily necessities.

These three documentaries, then, represented a step forward for Nicaraguan cinema. The first two consciously broke with the conventions of the noticieros. They were not dictated by conjunctural factors, as were the Literacy Campaign and the departure of Robelo and Chamorro from the Junta. No comandantes spoke, and they did not document particular political events such as the nationalization of the mines. *La otra cara del oro* and *Del águila al dragón* sought new aesthetic strategies, from highly stylized photography and new musical motifs to wordless, aggressive emotional montage designed for maximum audience impact. These strategies may have more successfully conveyed the economic and military power of the United States than the creative responses and collective strength of "popular power," but the films were first efforts in search of a more supple aesthetic, and they succeed admirably in their bitter denunciation of the economic and military rapacity of the U.S. "águila."

Four THE NEW
GENERATION

The breakthrough to documentaries opened space for new directors. Lacayo and Alvarez had worked at INCINE from the beginning, directing most of the first year's noticieros, and their documentary work left a directorial void in noticiero production. Like their predecessors, the new aspirants used the noticieros for their apprenticeship before the next major transformation at INCINE, the great leap forward into fiction. However, the new filmmakers surely benefited from the experience acquired during the first two years. After organizing the noticieros around the comandantes and then, under Legall's stewardship, around national defense, INCINE backed off from this instrumental approach to cinema. There was probably no institutional decision, and the 1982 noticieros still included some highly topical themes, but the new filmmakers displayed more creativity. Politics remained dominant, but more experimental cinematic ideas emerged, as if INCINE's institutional experience of two years of intensive production reduced deadline pressures. No doubt an established routine freed time for more creative reflection and preproduction planning. By the second half of 1982, Noticiero 31, a four-part history of the Sandinista Army, would reach almost 17 minutes, twice the average noticiero's length.

Worker Cinema

Class stratification at INCINE separated the creative personnel (directors) from the technical workers. Lacayo, Alvarez, and Vargas were either upper-class (Lacayo, Alvarez) or solidly middle-class (Vargas). Most of the technicians had not attended university anywhere. No former INCINE participants dwell on class divisions, so tensions may not have broken down along class lines. The most bitter conflicts were among the directors. The class differentiations surely raise questions about the class character of the revolution, but the answers do not contradict the FSLN's goal of basing policies on the interests of the popular classes. No revolution can eradicate years of class formation overnight. Class struggle continues long after a group seizes state power. Left- and right-wing critics of the FSLN use the class contradictions to show either that the FSLN failed to work against the bourgeoisie and consolidate the revolutionary victory or, alternatively, that they restricted the bourgeoisie's economic and political rights.

INCINE represented an atypical case for assessing the integration of the popular classes. First, Nicaragua lacked a filmmaking apparatus before 1979, so there was nothing to reorganize and redirect, and no former state functionaries with questionable political commitments. Everyone at INCINE supported the revolution, whether actual FSLN members or not. Second, the cultural sphere normally contains a disproportionately high representation of the bourgeoisie, particularly in a poor, rural country with high illiteracy and a small middle class.

In fact, there was an ephemeral attempt to produce a workers' cinema in Nicaragua, but not at INCINE. A Bolivian, Alfonso Gumucio Dagrón, obtained United Nations funding to establish a Super 8-mm filmmaking workshop in 1981. He set up shop at the CST, the Sandinista Workers Federation. Gumucio Dagrón had considerable experience, both as theorist of political filmmaking and as an organizer of a Super 8 experiment in revolutionary Mozambique. However, he did not work with INCINE, and took a dim view of INCINE's lack of solidarity with his project.

> The compañeros . . . of INCINE attended in the first days, and then abandoned the workshop because they were not really motivated; they had been assigned by their organization to comply with this task without really believing in it.[1]

Gumucio Dagrón was committed to low-tech, politically engaged cinema produced by workers. Gumucio Dagrón saw his work in the context of "third cinema," a clandestine, revolutionary cinema that he energetically defended in his written account. Apparently this three-month experiment in workers cinema in Nicaragua did not continue with Super 8-mm filmmaking, but with video after the end of the workshop as various participants moved on to the mass organizations.

The Super 8 workers' project highlights two aspects of INCINE's work. First, INCINE had no ties with workers' organizations. INCINE looked up in the bureaucracy, not down, for support. INCINE did not recruit workers, the predominant group in the CST. In fact, INCINE did not connect to the mass organizations. It sought material support at the various ministries. This strategy, conscious or not, effectively isolated INCINE institutionally and politically, and weakened it. Second, unlike Gumucio Dagrón who promoted the Super 8 technology for its low cost and ease of operation, INCINE began working exclusively in 35 mm, a highly capital-intensive and costly medium, just when the cost of raw stock doubled overnight because of an escalation in the cost of silver. The extreme concentration of raw-stock production internationally imposed dependence on most countries, with no recourse to import-substitution alternatives. INCINE's place in the chain of dependence was as recipient of Cuban largesse, primarily, and Mexican largesse to a lesser extent. It couldn't purchase raw stock with its own hard currency. In retrospect, it is clear that shooting film, whether 35-mm, 16-mm, or 8-mm, has become increasingly expensive relative to video, and Gumucio Dagrón has admitted that he would have used video if he had foreseen the cost benefits of video.[2]

Transition

In 1981, however, INCINE was still producing noticieros. While conjunctural factors continued to guide them, this condition was interpreted more loosely, as the prominence of the comandantes receded and the noticieros no longer followed political events or speeches as consistently. Over the course of the next 12 noticieros, the original directors withdrew and new directors completed the rest of the cycle, which essentially ended in 1984. The quality varied, but overall the new directors exercised more creative initiative in choosing topics and cinematic strategies, including some first tentative steps toward fiction.

The choice of topics for the noticieros, as already noted, depended on several factors. The heads of INCINE, Lacayo and Legall, offered a list of possibilities from time to time. The filmmakers themselves suggested topics, following their particular interests. National priorities also affected the choices, especially in response to the intensity of the contra war, which heated up between 1982 and 1984. As INCINE as an institution developed, its personnel acquired more experience, and the films became more ambitious, the filmmakers eventually sought less topical themes. Therefore, the distribution of films according to the following rubrics in this chapter (and chapter 6) eventually shifted away from the war.

Military

With Alberto Legall at the helm, the war figured prominently in these next noticieros.[3] Legall directed four more noticieros, three of them dealing directly with the military. *La contrarevolución* (Feb. 1982) shows contra training in the United States and Honduras. With lampblacked faces and camouflage uniforms, the North American advisers and recruits present a grotesque image, and the film indicts the United States and former Guardia Nacional officers in the formation and indoctrination of the contras, who were drilled with slogans to kill communists. This film was never shown publicly, though the Cinemateca retains a copy. Given Legall's fascination with the military, he probably took advantage of a tie to the army to gather material, but the army may have had reservations about releasing a film outside of its control, for it had its own audiovisual unit making videos for internal use.[4] Similarly, in his last film for INCINE, Legall directed a film about a military training maneuver by the army, *Unidad frente a la agresión* (late 1982), and the noticiero presents footage of the artillery and armor, and the air force's participation. With the exception of a speech by the head of the army, Humberto Ortega, to the troops (and one short report by the director of the military maneuver), the only sounds are those of the weapons reports, explosions, and the motors of the tanks and airplanes.

Legall also contributed one more film that was indirectly about the war in El Salvador, *La decisión* (Nov. 1982). The Salvadoran military had captured a young Nicaraguan working with the FMLN guerrillas and apparently convinced him to testify publicly against the FMLN. However, when sent to the United States for a press conference, the Nicaraguan dramatically and heroically changed the script by describing how the military had tortured him to compel his cooperation.[5] Displaying a lurid flair, Legall begins and ends the film with dark shots reconstructing subterranean torture sessions conducted by the Salvadoran military. Between these two fictional reconstructions, and intercut with them, the Nicaraguan testifies in various venues (including the United States' *MacNeil/Lehrer Report*) about the torture methods.[6]

While Legall tended to take a literal approach to the contra war and the threat of U.S. invasion, Mariano Marín sought more creative possibilities within the confines of the noticiero structure. Like many of the earlier noticieros, *Jornada anti-intervencionista* (Sept. 1981) is constructed around a single event, a day devoted to nonintervention, but Marín mixes graphic archival material with fictional vignettes to place the current North American threat in historical perspective. The final shots come from archival footage of the United States' air war in Indochina (seen in *Del águila al dragón*). The concluding title contains a quotation from a famous Nicaraguan poet, Fernando Gordillo (who was one of the founders of the first *Ventana* and died in 1967): "A century later, the enemy is the same."[7]

While this film doesn't completely fulfill the injunction to "recover our national identity," it represents a step in that direction. Marín has identified a Marxist anthropologist uncle as a powerful influence on him. Anthropology was viewed with derision by his conservative Granada family, but it gave Marín hope about escaping from bourgeois conventions. Granada, long a conservative bastion, was the first large city in Nicaragua and the citadel of Spanish culture. Both influences can be seen in Marín's film. The film posits a link between the Spanish and their successors, the North Americans, and also a continuity between the adventurer William Walker and his reincarnation, the cowboy Ronald Reagan.

With extremely limited means, Marín audaciously weaves in three abstract sequences of live action to evoke these historical continuities. Marín had worked with the experimental Nicaraguan dramatist Alan Bolt before the triumph, and he may have learned from him to devise simple, abstract representations reverberating with historical significance. The horse-drawn carriage and the sound of hoof beats conjure the early nineteenth century. Crowd noises contribute to the film's historical resonance and dramatize historical events represented in intercut still images and the stylized gestures of grenade throwers.

Clearly, Marín wanted to shake off the earlier noticieros' stodginess while retaining a strong polemical thrust. Composed almost entirely from archival material, primarily graphics, the film encompasses the sweep of Nicaraguan history. In the few images filmed specifically for the film, Marín chose simple, powerful fictional reconstructions of iconic staples of the insurrection, the muchachos' urban guerrilla activity. The range of cinematic materials deployed, and the juxtaposition of documentary and fictional registers on multiple levels, of image and sound, were refreshing departures from the mechanical formula practiced under Legall.

Marín was not only trying to rally audiences to defend the country against northern invaders, but also to establish the FSLN's continuity with patriotic nineteenth-century predecessors. Although critics accused the FSLN of being a Soviet pawn and of transforming Nicaragua into a socialist outpost in Latin America, and despite Marín's former closeness to the GPP tendency, the film has no Marxist or foreign references. National sovereignty was key. Adopting the FSLN's nationalist reading of Nicaraguan history, Marín included a progression of official FSLN martyrs of the twentieth century: Benjamin Zeledón, Sandino, Fonseca.

Only three subsequent noticieros covered public acts or proclamations.

Reenactment of "los muchachos" as guerrillas (Jornada anti-intervencionista)

Dispuestos a todo por la paz (Mar. 1982), directed by another new director, Fernando Somarriba, deals with the announcement of a State of Emergency on March 14, 1982. Throughout the war, the government made increasing demands on the population to participate in the country's defense. Over time, these demands took a toll on popular support, as the economy's deterioration wore down the population. *Dispuestos* offers an early view of how INCINE conceived of marshaling support for this first major military measure directed at the civilian population.

Before the credits, grainy documentary footage of contra training identifies the threat, replete with death's head insignia and banners exhorting combatants to "Kill a Sandinista." An unidentified young civilian calmly recounts the government's efforts to use negotiation, "serious efforts of the Sandinista Revolution to find peaceful means to solve the crisis in Central America." The military-clad Daniel Ortega reads the official proclamation of the State of Emergency,

> so that the counterrevolutionaries, the criminals who are
> conspiring against our people, have no possibilities to
> take advantage of the liberties that have been in effect up
> to the proclamation of this decree.

Rather than detail aspects of the proclamation, the film samples activities under way to shore up the national defense. Men and women train with

guns, excavate trenches, build bunkers, and practice firefighting to combat industrial sabotage. Soldiers stand solitary guard on bridges throughout
Nicaragua, an important image after the destruction of two large bridges
on the same day as the State of Emergency declaration. The entire country
was forming brigades—in the factories, on the cooperatives, in the neighborhoods, in health centers—and training for the militias. One person after
another explains, "I believe it is the duty of Nicaraguans to be integrated into
the Popular Sandinista Militias to defend the country, the sovereignty," "It
is our duty as Nicaraguans," "It is the duty of every conscious Nicaraguan,"
"I feel it is a patriotic duty."

The unfortunate irony of this film "for peace" [por la paz] is the evident
militarization of Nicaraguan society. In emphasizing civilian defense, the
film implies that victory against the contras is in the people's hands, and the
government needs popular support to arm the people. While a comandante
has the last word in the film, the people speak throughout, affirming that
they must defend their country. Contrary to the norm elsewhere in Latin
America, in Nicaragua the war will not pit a professional army against civilians. Ordinary citizens, men and women, are not forced into military service; they accept these duties as their responsibility to the revolution.

INCINE's archives indicate that the subject of Mariano Marín's next film
was the third anniversary of the triumph of the revolution. Yet *Homage to
the Heroes and Martyrs of Monimbó* (Aug. 1982) includes no footage of the
official celebration in Masaya, a small city some 40 miles south of Managua.
Instead, Mariano Marín fashioned a tribute to the costly rising of an Indian
barrio of Masaya against the Guardia Nacional in 1978. Though brutally sup-
pressed by Somoza, the barrio's heroic resistance was an important detonator in the final stage of overthrowing Somoza. That the participants were
Indians independent of the FSLN conferred a special aura on the rebellion, for
it illustrated the breadth and determination of popular discontent. Though
surrounded by tanks and bombed by Somoza's air force, the Indians held
out for seven days, sustaining over two hundred deaths. In addition, though
the FSLN had not participated in the uprising, a prominent FSLN combatant,
Camilo Ortega, brother of Humberto and Daniel, joined the fight. His death
put a Sandinista stamp on the Monimbó struggle. Joining indigenous resistance with a Sandinista martyrdom became part of the FSLN mythology of
the insurrection.

The spontaneity and bravery of the Monimbó population probably ap-
pealed to Marín, who bristled at authority. As in his previous noticiero
(*Jornada anti-intervencionista*), Marín designed several fictional sequences
of an agitprop variety to alternate with accounts by several women about
their collaboration with their sons in preparing bombs for use against the

Guardia. After an introductory section establishing the barrio environment, one mother explains how her son passed on the instructions for the preparation of chloride, sulfur, and aluminum. As she wraps a small bomb with her hands, several muchachos are seen running through the forest, their faces disguised by the famous Masaya masks. Having reached their destination in the woods, they hurl the bombs into the clearing in the background.

Marín devotes the film's second half to Camilo Ortega's death. Camilo's memory hovers over the film, because a song dedicated to Monimbó and Camilo, written by Carlos Mejía Godoy, opens the film and returns throughout. An elderly woman who witnessed Camilo's death describes it, and the words of the song play over shots of tombstones:

> Your pure blood, Camilo,
> continues to grow in the pitihayas [an edible cactus],
> in the smile of the children
> of my beloved Nicaragua.
> Your pure blood, Camilo,
> blazing in the mountain,
> Spilled on my country
> Its violent blossoming.[8]

Picking up the motif of death and interment as renewal, the film concludes by intercutting a woman carrying a basket on her head with shots of the cemetery she is about to visit. When she arrives, she takes down the basket and places fruit on an anonymous martyr's grave.

The film exhibits little of Marín's inventiveness, but it contains evidence of the continuing thrust toward fiction. Marín uses fiction to dynamize an uninspired project, otherwise composed of brief, static interviews with Monimbó mothers, and shots of gravestones. In addition, Marín makes another rare foray into prerevolutionary history to examine the source of raw material for the construction of Sandinismo. Normally the noticieros relied on stills or archival footage for such representations, so Marín's use of fiction implies dipping into the unchronicled history of the people.

Lurching back again to more official discourse, *Del ejército defensor de la soberania nacional al ejército popular Sandinista* (Sept. 1982) presents an extended history of the Sandinista army, from Sandino's army, Defender of National Sovereignty, to the Popular Sandinista Army. Again mixing archival images (both still and moving) with interviews with comandantes, the film reveals the FSLN's efforts to transform the erratic flux of events into a burnished teleology. At the same time, the film implicitly incorporates the contra war into the Nicaraguan people's struggle against Somoza and imperialism.

Structurally, the film carves up a half century of Nicaraguan history into four parts, each identified by titles. The first title, "Planting the seed," presents the history as a natural, biological process; nourished properly, history will follow inevitably. After a veteran of Sandino's army cites Sandino's instructions to his troops, as the camera pans across the mountains seen in the first noticiero (on Sandino), Humberto Ortega, in military garb, a cigarette in hand, picks up the thread:

> Sandino brought together our revolutionary, political and military movement, and the Sandinista Front, with the formation of the distinguished vanguard in the 1960s, giving continuity to this historic integration that was, admittedly, set back by the death of Sandino in 1934, and begins to recover its roots with Rigoberto [López Pérez, assassin of the first Somoza in 1956] and all the armed actions of the 1960s.

In "Part II, Foundation of the FSLN, Planting the seed," the narration quickly distinguishes the FSLN from traditional parties:

> The popular masses of Nicaragua have their own political-guerrilla instruments. The Sandinista Front is the response to the imposition of the Liberal and Conservative parties, instruments of the *vendepatria* oligarchy of Nicaragua.

The FSLN's only surviving founder, Tomás Borge, recalls the historic moment:

> One July day in 1961, we were seated around a simple table in the country, drinking coffee and talking in the dawn light, and Carlos Fonseca was speaking to us of the struggle, of the difficulties facing us and of the need to create instruments of combat. He mentioned not only armed force, not only the need to have a powerful fist to fight back and a band to defend ourselves, but also the need to build an adequate political instrument for the new history which we were undertaking to build, and this instrument was the Sandinista Front.

The narration, and Borge's memoir, show the FSLN as a political-military organization, breaking from liberal/conservative collusion under Somoza. Suddenly, images from old Somoza newsreels show the Guardia Nacional rounding up prisoners. Borge acknowledges the bleakness of the time, when "Somocismo reached its highest levels of repression and savagery against the people." Another Somoza newsreel document, with original voice-over, shows the Guardia in action, illustrating Borge's reference to the anticommunist fury of Somocismo with the newsreel's commentary: "the Fidelista movement, misnamed the Sandinista Front of National Liberation, a subversive organization, with the support of the evil sons of the country."

The newsreel footage shows a bullet-riddled house, and crowds peering offscreen at the aftermath of another seminal FSLN event. The narration provides a condensed FSLN interpretation:

> In 1969, the house of Julio Buitrago, national leader of the Sandinista Front, is attacked by more than four hundred soldiers of the Guardia Nacional. Buitrago, symbol of a whole generation of Sandinista fighters, resists until death. It was the battle of one man against an army. A regime that, with incredible cynicism, gives its own version of the facts.

Though the Front, or at least the filmmakers, wanted these images and words to indict the savage repression, the Somoza newsreel contains one accurate, and thorny, charge against the FSLN. Calling the FSLN "Fidelista" indicates the Cuban influence on the FSLN's formation, and more specifically, on the "foco" strategy pursued during the 1960s. This strategy, championed by Che Guevara, called for forming small military cells throughout Latin America.[9] Working in geographical isolation, these *focos* would simultaneously perform political work and stage well-planned attacks against repressive military regimes, converting the local population to the popular movement. Che died pursuing this strategy in Bolivia. The strategy also failed in Nicaragua, for Guardia repression nearly wiped out the FSLN in the 1960s. In this sense, Buitrago's death represented both a "symbol of a whole generation of Sandinista fighters" and the end of the Nicaraguan *foco* strategy, ushering in the FSLN's darkest years.[10]

Humberto Ortega, however, does not mention any of this. Instead, he begins in the early 1970s, a phase "known as the accumulation of forces in silence." The Front's remaining members, perhaps fewer than one hundred in the whole country, had to rethink its strategy. During those years, the Front ceased military actions and rebuilt its membership. The silence was shattered spectacularly with the daring raid on José María ("Chema") Castillo's house during Christmas 1974. Having planned the takeover as a dramatic propaganda coup, the Sandinistas demanded that a Front communiqué be read over the nation's media, that payment of $1 million ransom be made, and that political prisoners be released and promised safe conduct (to Mexico). In a stroke, the FSLN had returned, starkly contradicting Somoza's claims to have eliminated it. While the Guardia surrounded the house, and their commander—and Somoza's son—El Chigüin, strutted about helplessly, Somoza agreed to the demands; cheering crowds lined the road as the busses carried the commandos to the airport. However weak the FSLN's actual political/military strength, the attack's audacity captured the popular imagination. It also unleashed a wave of Guardia repression, including a declaration of a state of siege that lasted almost three years.[11]

By 1982 the names of Rigoberto López Pérez, Julio Buitrago, and "Chema" Castillo were famous in the FSLN's popular history, but the "crucible" of the most committed Sandinistas was "la montaña." The title of Part III names the next period: "The mountain. Where the dream matured." The comandante most closely associated with this period, Henry Ruíz, evokes the difficulty of guerrilla life in the mountains, a life described colorfully by Omar Cabezas in his memoir, *La montaña es algo más que una imensa estepe verde* [*Fire from the Mountain*].[12] Cabezas suggests the nature of the mythic status achieved in the mountains by Ruíz, more frequently called "Modesto" [the modest one]:

> There's one image I'll never forget. At the end of the day, after not having fought the Guardia, waiting for God knows what, without much knowledge of the tactics or strategy of war, freezing cold, in the shittiest kind of shape and all of that—there was Modesto reading Ernest Mandel's *Political Economy*. If somebody had a book floating around up there it would never occur to us to get it out and read. We didn't feel up to dealing with that foolishness. Maybe it wasn't foolishness, but we weren't capable of reading a book on the theory of revolution. So that was the sort of stuff Modesto was made of: he passed the time reading, studying.[13]

Ruíz describes life in the mountains as a rite of passage. From among the aspirants, the Front chose the most qualified members of the "vanguard." As Ruíz cites the campesino's importance to the struggle, the film cuts to a Somoza newsreel applauding the Guardia's successes in the mountains.

Images of urban guerrilla combat terminate this official paean and indicate a fissure in Somoza's calm façade.

The urban conflict foreshadows Part IV: "The Final Offensive. The Dream Blossoms." Headlines from the (prerevolutionary) opposition *La Prensa* announce the outbreak of insurrection, as city after city falls to the Sandinistas. Jaime Wheelock, of the Proletarian Tendency, explains the cities' importance in the final victory, for "the work in the cities was fundamental for the victory of the revolution." At this point, the insurrection's momentum is conveyed through footage of street fighting and shots of mortar and artillery, culminating in the comandantes' historic arrival in Managua, where they were greeted by tumultuous crowds. A short epilogue shows more footage of soldiers exercising before the final title: "This is an homage to our armed forces."

Aside from promoting the Popular Sandinista Army's prestige during a period of rising contra aggression, this 17-minute noticiero provides the only INCINE panorama of FSLN history. The agrarian metaphor—planting the seed, maturation, flowering—sees the FSLN project as an inevitable, natural outgrowth of Somoza's repressive rule. The FSLN forged a political-military organization armed with an accurate analysis of historical forces, the accuracy validated by the victory. By implication, the FSLN still retains a correct analysis, now seeing the need for a powerful military to defend against a foreign threat.

Nonetheless, the film's design betrays contradictions. As in earlier noticieros, only the comandantes speak. The popular classes they represent— campesinos, workers—are silent. Official discourse controls the images, imposing an official interpretation on events, arguably contradicting the film's metaphoric stress on the organic growth of popular opposition to Somoza (and FSLN leaders did pay tribute to the spontaneous aspects of the insurrection, in which the FSLN trailed behind the masses).

Furthermore, the film never distinguishes between urban and rural participants. As the FSLN knew, the final insurrection depended mainly on spontaneous and creative organization in the urban barrios. Competing analyses of the city/country axis had fractured FSLN unity in the battle of the three tendencies. The film overlooks these fissures but proffers a tercerista analysis. It is understandable that the film never identifies the tendencies by name, but neither Borge nor fellow GPP member Henry Ruíz even allude to their earlier belief in "prolonged war" in the countryside. Jaime Wheelock, a leader of the Proletarian Tendency, refers to the urban work as "fundamental" but doesn't mention the working class, the key social group in the proletarian analysis. What remains, then, is the broad rubric of the popular masses, undifferentiated by political or class analysis. The film embraces the tercerista strategy of a broad, multi-class, patriotic alliance to overthrow Somoza, never indicating the class divisions that persisted intensely after the triumph. Thus, in the film, the historic signposts of the FSLN struggle are not building support in the long years in the mountains or forming the mass organizations during the insurrection, but the isolated exploits—those of Rigoberto López Pérez, Julio Buitrago, and the "Chema" Castillo raid—that electrified the country and successfully challenged Somoza's invincibility. In short, the film endorses the ultimately victorious terceristas.

Economy

While the preceding noticieros reflected the omnipresence of the contra war throughout Nicaraguan society, the Sandinistas were also attempting major economic transformations. In an earlier noticiero, *Wiwilí, sendero a una victoria* [*Wiwilí, road to victory*] (Oct. 1981), Legall, assisted by newcomer Fernando Somarriba, constructed the film around a public act devoted to the Agrarian Reform. In a peculiarly anachronistic opening, a Toyota jeep passes over country roads and through a stream before stopping on the crest of a hill. In a bravura stroke, the Toyota's door opens and legs with knee-high boots emerge and walk to a ridge as the camera slowly pans the mountains and fields in a scene similar to those used in the first noticiero about Sandino. The figure seen only from the waist down is immediately recognizable, for the simple iconography of Sandino consisted of the large wide-brimmed white hat and the knee-high boots. As a voice-over of Sandino's comrade explains the general's plans for agrarian reform, there is no question that the figure represents Sandino.

As part of the Agrarian Reform, land titles were awarded to campesinos. Wiwilí was chosen because Sandino founded an agricultural cooperative there shortly before his death. While Wiwilí uses a minimum of comandante footage, the image nonetheless conveys dependence, with the government distributing titles to passive campesinos. The film, however, never clarifies that land titles were awarded to cooperatives rather than to individuals. This decision reflected the Agrarian Reform's concern to retain control over the campesinos' productive activities, including crop choice, credit, prices, etc. Furthermore, the film overlooks the importance that the government placed on state farms, where the land belonged to the state and the workers were wage laborers, members of an agricultural proletariat, not peasants with their own land. Of course, INCINE could not clarify a complicated agricultural situation in ten minutes. (A fuller treatment can be found below in the discussion of the 1983 *Nuestra Reforma Agraria*.)

After completing her first documentary, María José Alvarez directed her last noticiero, *Los trabajadores* (July 1982), commemorating May Day, or International Workers Day. Alvarez again eschews voice-over and lets the workers speak. An opening sequence of graphics, with photographs and drawings, depicts workers at the workplace or in demonstrations. A title defines the worker as "the force in the production of material goods for the existence of society." With the intrusive sound of factory machinery heard in the background, workers pound metal into shape. Another title continues: "Work is the organized creative activity to produce a good." Work in the factory continues. At an outdoor meeting, workers explain the meaning of their work for Nicaragua, each limited to a fragment and edited in a rhythm joining each worker's words to the next worker's, for the next worker's intervention begins while the previous speaker remains on screen. The comments stress the worker's contribution to national well-being:

> . . . the work we are doing is for social benefit, to apply it in education, health, . . . housing of the working Nicaraguan people . . .

> . . . the delivery of raw materials, the costs, all these things we are dealing with, because also we are responsible for . . .

> . . . in more work during the eight working hours, that is, to use the eight working hours to the maximum . . .

> . . . we can open, we the workers ourselves, we are the ones who are going to begin . . . we are going to lead this revolution toward socialism . . .

> . . . we have made the machines, we have done it with the sweat of each of the workers, so that the country can save hard currency . . .

In the May Day march shown toward the end, workers carry portraits of Lenin and Marx with the "International" on the sound track. In the industrial coda, the film presents assembly-line work, the camera angled down banks of mass-production machines. To close, the camera zooms out slowly in low angle from a close shot of a worker with a pneumatic hammer to end on a long shot of the worker in a virile pose, legs apart, bent to the task, a virtual icon from socialist realism: the socialist worker as hero.

Unlike other INCINE films, *Los trabajadores* articulates a clear Marxist interpretation. The film focuses on workers, even citing the "working class." Exegetes of Sandinismo, of course, can find adequate FSLN quotations to

Campesinos reading land titles—awarded to cooperatives
(Wiwilí, sendero a una victoria)

label the movement Marxist, but neither Sandino's eclectic legacy nor the crisscrossing ideologies of FSLN leaders inscribe any consistent Marxist trajectory. Many left-wing commentators upbraided the FSLN precisely for this failure, and no earlier film identifies so unmistakably with Marxism in its visual and aural iconography. Right-wing critics of the FSLN claim to see through the tactical disguise of the FSLN to the dread reality of Marxism-Leninism, but in fact the preponderance of FSLN statements and speeches place Sandinismo firmly on the three foundational pillars of national sovereignty, anti-imperialism, and non-alignment. Some currents within the FSLN (and to its left) were openly Marxist, but Nicaragua under the FSLN was not a Marxist state, or even a socialist one. The government controlled several industries formerly operated by foreign companies, banking, and foreign trade, but the vast majority of property and business remained in private hands. Expropriation of property affected only 20 percent of the land, and with the exception of Somoza interests, the bourgeoisie owned the means of production. To be sure, governmental restrictions significantly reduced the bourgeoisie's economic power, but such controls do not constitute socialism.[14]

INCINE unquestionably did not advance a Marxist agenda. What is interesting in this film is its conception of the working class. For one thing, the workers are politicized, class-conscious. Most workers discuss their contributions as workers to the society, to Nicaragua, to the revolution, to social-

*Rare appearance in INCINE production of Marx and Lenin (*Los trabajadores*)*

*Worker as socialist icon (*Los trabajadores*)*

ism. But they articulate no trade-union demands about wages or working conditions. At the same time, aside from the march banners, the workers do not refer to workers' organizations and are not identified as union members, despite the phenomenal rise in union membership after 1979 and the public exposure given to the CST, the FSLN workers' mass organization. Following the decree of the State of Emergency, strikes and other forms of popular militancy were illegal at the time (though sanctions were rarely applied), and real wages had not yet plummeted precipitously, so such trade-union demands might not surface, but the lack of emphasis on workers as a militant class exerting pressure on private factory owners and directors is surprising.

Culture

While many of these noticieros documented and even promoted the militarization of the country for national defense, other films examined aspects of civil society. Cultural activity burgeoned with the creation of the Ministry of Culture and the appointment of Ernesto Cardenal, virtual poet laureate of the FSLN, as its head. Aesthetic and bureaucratic battles raged inside the Ministry, but Cardenal remained above the fray, and Fernando Somarriba composed his first directorial effort around an interview with Cardenal.

La cultura (Dec. 1981) consists of shots and voice-overs of the Cardenal interview, intercut with images of a variety of cultural activities, presumably all sponsored by the Ministry of Culture. Thus, before the credits, Cardenal speaks about pre-Sandinista Nicaraguan culture but categorizes it as extremely elite, "a tiny group of us . . . belonged to this culture and the people were totally marginalized from the culture." As a member of that elite, Cardenal's remarks carry unquestioned authority. The high illiteracy rate in Nicaragua helped produce this problem of elitism, and after the credits the film shows the Literacy Campaign with many familiar images.

Cardenal then notes that there has been "a resurgence, a cultural rebirth in Nicaragua since the triumph of the revolution, in poetry, in music, in theater, in song, dance, artisanship, reading." Young children play musical instruments while he speaks. Then, as Cardenal speaks about "autochthonous . . . national" culture, Somarriba illustrates his words with shots of a ballet practice and a classical violin recital. Cardenal also mentions the Casas Populares de Cultura, a network of urban cultural centers, the site of community cultural activities, such as the poetry workshops. Cardenal neglects the cinema in his list of cultural activities. Somarriba corrects this with a sequence on a film being shot in Nicaragua by the Chilean-exile filmmaker, Miguel Littín, in which Littín explains on a film set how valuable

*Director Fernando Somarriba (left) with Minister of Culture Ernesto Cardenal
(*La Cultura*)*

raw stock is and that it must be purchased with hard currency. However stirring, Littín's film, *Alsino y el cóndor* set off heated controversy (discussed in chapter 5).

The first part of Cardenal's discussion concentrated on traditional high culture, but the last part settles on artisanal production, including the first Festival of Maize, held in response to the "imperialist aggression cutting off wheat for us." Somarriba inserts shots of pottery workshops and various craftspeople, part of the "indigenous root of our nationality," specifically part of "our cultural tradition of corn," which referred to the Indian goddess of corn whose blood produced a great harvest of corn the year after her martyrdom. "For us, this was also a symbol of all the martyrs of the Revolution who sacrificed themselves for the happiness of their people."[15] The film closes with images of the festival. Somarriba tacks on a title at the end saluting the "Anti-Cultural Ideological-Penetration Day Rubén Darío on the 115th Anniversary of His Birth."

As a film about Nicaraguan cultural accomplishments, *La cultura* has little to recommend it. Cardenal speaks genuinely, but without specifics. Through Cardenal's words, the film does break down traditional elitism and it includes previously disdained forms of expression: maize rituals and Nicaraguan cooking. At the same time, this film about indigenous culture overlooks the irony of having a foreign filmmaker, albeit a Chilean exile, serve as the representative of filmmaking in Sandinista Nicaragua.

For his second film, Somarriba directed *Los mimados* (Feb. 1982), which is about homeless and neglected children. In one sense, the film is entirely naïve and artless. With the exception of a brief voice-over, there is no dialogue, nor any images of adults. Instead, the film shows children selling newspapers or food on the streets, running around garbage dumps, or engaged in activities such as school, swimming, receiving medical care, or simply playing and dancing together.

Though extremely simple, the film was a daring step for INCINE. Commentaries dominated early noticieros, denying the images' autonomy. The early films always supplied interpretations, and too often the comandantes controlled the discourse. Over time, other voices replaced those of the comandantes, and directors like Alvarez interviewed ordinary people. But images were normally subservient to sound. In *Los mimados*, a simple song frees the images to speak. In itself, banishing the word may be unremarkable, but the images in this film indicate the persistent social problem of drifting youth failed by the revolution's social programs. Though the film does show measures being taken to resolve them, in an understated way, barefoot children peddling at Managua intersections were daily reminders of an unmet challenge. Certainly, the Literacy Campaign and health clinics helped children, and the country reduced illiteracy and wiped out childhood diseases, but filmmakers previously ignored recalcitrant issues. In this sense, the seven-minute film opens a small window on an important unsolved social problem.

Ramiro Lacayo, assisted by Somarriba, returned to noticiero production with *Viva León Jodido*, a film about the city considered to be the birthplace of Sandinismo. The images present some of the architectural characteristics of the city, as a voice-over offers a historical account of the foreign influences, including the founding by Spain of the University of León, where "the first steps of the revolutionary movement would take place." While the film does not say so, the FSLN was founded in León by students Carlos Fonseca, Julio Buitrago, and Tomás Borge (the only surviving member of this group). During the survey of the university, the film lingers on a courtyard as several pistol shots ring out, evoking the assassination of Somoza García in 1956, another inventive fictional reconstruction: "On this spot the patriot Rigoberto López Pérez brought justice to the tyrant Somoza the First. Twenty-three years later León would be the first liberated city in Nicaragua."

While this sequence joins León and Sandinismo, the rest of the film steps back from overt FSLN partisanship, as the offscreen Lacayo asks residents on the street why they like León, and the film cuts from one respondent to the next. In stark contrast to Legall's earlier martial films, *Viva León* neither responds to conjunctural factors nor presents a didactic message from the

FSLN. *Viva León* is a more properly cultural film. The architectural profile shows "indigenous" cultural roots, and the music and speech embody popular Nicaraguan culture with few links to the litany of Sandinista successes.

In retrospect, this period from mid-1981 to late 1982 appears transitional. The filmmakers, having thrown themselves behind the revolution in the first years, recognized the limited public interest in the parade of comandantes exhorting solidarity and sacrifice. To reanimate INCINE's work and explore more varied cinematic means, some filmmakers may have wanted more distance from the FSLN, but most wanted to build on their experiences with the noticieros and take a more independent course. The first directors—Lacayo, Alvarez—had graduated to documentaries, which were freer in formal strategies and had fewer time constraints and more generous economic resources.[16] Agreements with Cuba stipulated producing 12 noticieros per year and only several documentaries, so newer directors did not generally make documentaries. Instead, they turned the noticieros into mini-documentaries, still retaining enough of the rubric of noticieros to qualify for Cuban technical support.

At the same time, INCINE was evolving. Franklin Caldera had departed early, leaving Ramiro Lacayo to head production and Quincho Ibarra to head exhibition and distribution. In mid-1982, however, when Minister of Culture Ernesto Cardenal was traveling abroad, a power struggle broke out in the Ministry of Culture.[17] Some department heads expressed differences with Vice-Minister Daisy Zomora and attempted to unseat her. There are different views of the coup's ultimate target. Some interpreted it as an attack on Cardenal. Zamora ultimately dismissed the leaders, including Ibarra. He was reassigned to the Institute of Plastic Arts (still within the Ministry of Culture). Some INCINE members view Ibarra's departure as part of Lacayo's plan to consolidate his own power over INCINE. Subsequent to Ibarra's move, all communications up the Ministry's hierarchy passed through Lacayo alone. Lacayo claims to have supported Ibarra. Still, Lacayo survived as INCINE's sole director. Neither the FSLN nor the Ministry of Culture named a replacement for Ibarra.

Five   I N   S E A R C H
          O F   P O L I C Y

INCINE's film production accounted for one—seminal—aspect of INCINE's activities. Though coming under the umbrella of INCINE, distribution and exhibition had their own bureaucratic structure with little interaction with the filmmakers. INCINE could not control exhibition and distribution as it could production because those functions were potential revenue sources, and the FSLN controlled those revenue streams. Still, as INCINE's founding document announced a commitment to "recovering national identity," that task entailed not only producing *Nicaraguan* films, but also nurturing, even creating, a Nicaraguan cinematic culture. That culture had previously been formed by Hollywood and Mexican films being shown on Nicaraguan screens. After the triumph, INCINE would have to devise strategies for resisting and combating foreign cultural domination of cinema. In some ways, this challenge mirrored the FSLN's assertion of national sovereignty as a way out of the long history of dependency on the United States.

Small, poor countries, and most large, wealthy ones, for that matter, face daunting problems in combating the penetration of films from the United States. In principle, large countries have domestic audiences capable of supporting a film industry, but Hollywood has virtually always aggressively and successfully exported its films to even large foreign markets. While it is impracticable for countries to ban Hollywood films, larger countries can set minimum quotas for screening domestic productions. The national audience size largely determines the limit of the quota percentage. Domestic product competition was impossible in Nicaragua, but the government did resort to censorship through the Commission of Classification. The commission's activities actually stressed moral over ideological criteria, though their occasional application of ideological criteria offers insight into Sandinista attitudes about U.S. cultural imperialism.

The Commission of Classification concerned itself with urban theatrical exhibition. Despite the rapid urbanization of Nicaragua, the rural population was still roughly half the total, and INCINE built up a Mobile Cinema structure for those isolated audiences, offering screenings to millions of rural spectators every year. With that audience, INCINE exercised considerable control over what to show, though not necessarily over the context of the screenings. Because there was a captive audience, the screenings could be and were used by the FSLN for ideological purposes, but there is little evidence of their efficacy. INCINE devoted one film to the Mobile Cinema project, but the didacticism of that film only reinforces such questions.

Another way to combat foreign ideology was to rally audiences to exemplary films made by established filmmakers about the Nicaraguan struggle. INCINE participated in several coproductions shot in Nicaragua during the 1980s, including *Alsino and the Condor*, directed by the exiled Chilean director Miguel Littín in 1981. While some Nicaraguan audiences responded positively to the film, a roundtable discussion published in *Ventana* revealed a barrage of criticism. Nevertheless, Littín returned to Nicaragua to direct a film on Sandino in 1989, but that troubled film was never released in the country.

If the original triumvirate heading INCINE was chosen to represent three complementary prongs of a unified cinema policy—production (Lacayo), distribution and exhibition (Ibarra and Caldera)—only Ramiro Lacayo remained at INCINE by the end of 1982. Caldera had resigned long before, and Ibarra was removed in mid-1982, undermining coordination of distribution and exhibition.

Lacking either control of distribution and exhibition or an organized strategy for resisting U.S. cultural penetration, INCINE contributed to addressing the problem through the Commission of Classification, the Mobile Cinema, and the debate over *Alsino and the Condor*.

Commission of Classification

Operating within the Ministry of Culture, INCINE sought to change peoples' cinematic tastes. National film production documented changes introduced in Nicaraguan life since 1979 and contributed to consolidating popular support for those changes, but the modest annual output of short noticieros and documentaries could not fill the demand for popular film entertainment. Hence INCINE's other departments had to devise an exhibition and distribution strategy that would inhibit the noxious influence of foreign values and inoculate spectators against these ideological toxins. As Ibarra observed in 1979, "the substandard product of cinema and the great 'successes' of Hollywood have constituted for a long time forms of domination and drugging of consciousness."[1]

These concerns led to forming the Commission of Classification of film by the Ministry of Culture on September 22, 1979. Originally part of the Ministry of Culture, the commission bounced around from the Front's Department of Propaganda and Political Education to the Ministry of the Interior, which was also responsible for the Law of Communications and the Media. As the Ministry of the Interior (MINT) controlled the national police and internal security apparatus, moving the commission to the MINT indicated that there was, in principle, a serious concern with film classification. The commission's location, however, may not have affected its operation, for the law of the media stipulated the membership. The law of September 22, 1979, designated the following participants:

> INCINE (three members)
>
> AMPRONAC (Asociación de Mujeres ante la Problemática Nacional/Association of Women Confronting the National Problematic, precursor to AMNLAE) (one)
>
> Ministry of Education (one)
>
> Ministry of Health (one)
>
> Youth Organizations (one)
>
> Nicaraguan Journalists Union (one)

The rating system called for determining appropriate age categories. But the key question revolved around prohibiting films. Because the law did not specify evaluative criteria, sampling commission reports will show how the commission operated, although various retrospective accounts by former participants suggest that the discussions were chaotic; one INCINE cinephile, a provocateur by nature, found the discussions highly diverting but chortled at the ignorance of some members.[2]

As the state nationalized only some 20 percent of the country's 125 theaters and could not control the programming of the private theaters, it fell to the Commission of Classification to weed out the most damaging films. The commission screened films five days a week at Managua theaters. According to internal reports, attendance by members was erratic and probably depended on a combination of interest and daily schedules.[3]

As in many countries, including the United States, violence and pornography were the paramount considerations. In the United States, Hollywood undertook to censor itself (the Hayes Code) heading off government censorship, and the ratings code performs the same function today. The U.S.

government gets into the act occasionally through the little-known Foreign Agent Registration Act, which got some Canadian documentaries labeled "political propaganda."[4] But these methods of censorship serve to inhibit *production* of films. The U.S. ratings system regulates producing films, then, because a warning about violence or sex puts any investment at risk.

The desire of Nicaraguans to protect a nascent revolutionary culture is understandable. With such a tiny market, Nicaragua had little leverage over distributors, often subsidiaries of U.S. companies. In small countries like Nicaragua, such a rating system (for imported films) would have no effect on production. And, as Ibarra noted, because Hollywood entertainment was viewed as an ideological danger for everyone, age restrictions excluding impressionable young audiences alone would not suffice, for adults were also at risk. Though the Commission of Classification guidelines did not explain criteria, they did specify that films be shown uncut, making prohibition the only alternative.[5]

In quantitative terms, the commission primarily banned films considered too violent or pornographic. To judge by many of the films' obscure titles and countries of origin—Mexico, Spain, Italy—they were made for the exploitation market and had no artistic or popular entertainment pretensions. On occasion, applying these criteria resulted in banning films like Australia's *Mad Max* or the United States' *Rocky Horror Picture Show*. The commission report on *Mad Max* cited the "glorification of violence," an "individualist hero . . . outside the law," and a "false moralism." The "mise-en-scène" is described as a "glorification of a 'punk' style or leather jackets (like the savage and marvelous world of the hippies)."[6] These characterizations resemble assessments from U.S. conservatives. On the other hand, some U.S. critics, unconcerned about being moral arbiters, champion films like *Mad Max* for their formal inventiveness.[7]

In developed countries, the criticism market is larger, and consumers read reviews to make viewing decisions. Without a Nicaraguan tradition of film criticism, the commission made viewing decisions for audiences. Some commission members recognized this as paternalism and displayed ambivalence in their evaluations. Faced with Pasolini's *Salo* (1975), the commission's report (July 24, 1980) prohibited the film, without calling it pornography. "It is," the report said,

> extremely complex in the interaction of eroticism and politics, [and] would not be easily understood by our public, still lacking the maturity needed to confront some cinematic works. Nevertheless, this Commission recognizes the interest and quality of said film.

In this case, the commission acknowledged the film's artistic merit. The audience may not have the "maturity" to appreciate the artistic merit, but that could change as audiences gained sophistication.

If standard concerns with sex and violence dominated the prohibition lists, narrow political considerations blocked some films, including *The Alamo, Exodus, The Deerhunter,* and *First Blood* (the title of the second Rambo film). Though there were no official guidelines, one commission document from 1984 refers to the defense of imperialism and attacks on revolutionaries and national liberation movements as grounds for prohibition.[8] The commission interpreted this charge with great flexibility at times. The report on the 1960 John Wayne film *The Alamo* called the film

> a historical manipulation of the events that occurred between the United States and Mexico. . . . The North American intervention in Texas and the theft of large parts of the north of Mexico are brushed aside, leaving the North Americans justified in the end.[9]

More commonly, the commission dealt with contemporary films relevant to the Nicaraguan revolution. The commission banned *Wild Geese,* a film about white mercenaries in Africa, because it is "an apology for the same type of pro-imperialist mercenaries who collaborate with the Somocista dictatorship in the repression and genocide of our people."[10]

The long and elaborate justification written by Ibarra, Vargas, and Mayra Luz Pérez for prohibiting *The Deerhunter* provides insight into the most responsible and sophisticated commission members' thinking.[11] The report gives a fair, if polemical, reading of the film. Robert de Niro kills the Vietnamese "to defend liberty and truth." This is presented in the film as a praiseworthy task, and he is captured together with his friend. In their account, the commission members support the North Vietnamese and object to their being stereotyped. The film presents them as "crazy, bloodthirsty and obsessed with violence," a staple of war films and typical of the depiction of the Japanese in Hollywood World War II films, though interestingly, less typical of the depiction of Germans. Similarly, Nicaraguan solidarity with the Vietnamese struggle for independence is understandable, given the Somoza family's reliance on the United States.

But the commission did not ban the film for these reasons. After all, in an article on cinematic criticism (discussed below), Ibarra argued that the critic should explain distortions of reality as a pedagogical function. Instead, the commission based its decision on the *effect* of the film's structure on the spectator, a psychological argument: "The spectator ends up hating those who have made possible the death of an innocent, stupid gambler and 'loving' the repentance of the war crimes of a man who rediscovers the meaning of animal (not human) life." Concomitantly, the spectator identifies with the evasions offered by the film as substitutes. Unable to resist, the spectator excuses the protagonists' crimes while identifying with the "superficial emotion[s]" proposed by the film. Once that mechanism kicks in, the spectators relinquish their critical faculties and cannot keep the larger perspective of U.S. aggression in view. Maudlin feelings of family and friendship hide individual and group responsibility for war crimes. Consequently,

> The Nicaraguan Institute of Cinema, through its
> Commission of Classification, cannot approve the
> exhibition of such a barbarity. Because the film *is*
> barbarous. . . .
> Our decision is irrevocable. It is a matter of
> revolutionary principles.

Of course this analysis reflects the paternalism built into any system of censorship. Those with critical knowledge can act as sentinels for others more susceptible. This attitude was consistent with Ibarra's views, expressed in an early plan for exhibition:

> Maintain a strict control over the quality and ideological
> content of the films, banning the presentation of those
> that are harmful to the social development of our
> people.[12]

Once instructed by the censors' criticism, the people will develop critical tools. Needless to say, this argument's logic is problematic. Who are the censors? Who chooses them? What are the criteria? Who establishes the criteria? The FSLN enjoined its members to learn from the masses, but the censorship argument reverses this process, effectively demobilizing the people's critical energy.[13]

Despite the commission's vigilance, traditional fare poured into the country. With hundreds of films screened every year, the commission's policy blocked from 10–20 percent of them, mostly cheap Mexican and Italian sex comedies. As indicated, the commission did ban some highly publicized films, but the rationale for classification itself was never publicly discussed or debated. *Ventana,* the Sandinista cultural weekly, never ran an article on these issues. In Ibarra's article on cinematic criticism, he never mentioned censorship. Cinephiles who objected to being deprived of selected cultural products could attend special screenings of banned films at the Cinemateca, for the commission's administrative guidelines provided for such exemptions.[14]

If the commission could not stem the cultural flood at the border, the state distribution arm, ENIDIEC, tried to reorient viewing habits by seeking new distribution sources. The private distribution companies, free to pursue pre-revolutionary policies, had no reason to change their programming. Profits drove their businesses, and Hollywood and Mexican films returned healthy profits. Consequently, INCINE opened the cinema market to the socialist countries.

In this enterprise, INCINE's strategy failed. With such a small market share, ENIDIEC made little headway with the films from socialist countries. In its best year, 1982, the state-owned theaters attracted only 36 percent of the spectators, and that figure fell to 25 percent and 28 percent in 1983 and 1984, respectively.[15] If INCINE hoped to wean Nicaraguan audiences from Hollywood and Mexican fare by transforming their taste for cinema, it would require a period of transition. Furthermore, there was never a popular groundswell demanding films from the socialist countries. Like the attachment to traditional property relations that resisted state intervention, the cinematic appeal of the "American way of life" could not be eliminated overnight.

In the initial exhibition plan, INCINE articulated the need to change popular tastes. One early draft for exhibition noted that

> the task of this department is to see to it that the cultural policy defined for our country by the Dirección Nacional of the FSLN and our revolutionary government not be derailed by a medium of diffusion so effective as the cinema. . . . We have to develop a path that contributes in an integral manner to the formation of the man of social consciousness that our Popular Sandinista Revolution is pursuing.[16]

Clearly, this rhetoric expresses great hopes for making fundamental changes. Everything was possible. INCINE tried to follow these inchoate plans, taking advantage of the films offered at favorable rates, or for free, by socialist countries. But like the television system, INCINE discovered it could not satisfy viewers' demands by replacing all traditional programming. The head of SSTV, Iván García, acknowledged this constraint in the 1981 *Ventana* interview cited in chapter 3.

Would an interest in films from the socialist countries have developed over time? This is unclear, as market logic precluded widespread distribution. Like García, Ibarra knew that the "new" programming was less popular, so he tried to balance the traditional with the new, estimating the latter at roughly 30 percent of programming in the state-owned theaters, or 6 percent of national programming.[17]

INCINE had little impact on popular tastes, but other countries with similar strategies also failed. Ever since Fernando Birri in Argentina started to make films to reflect the national reality in Argentina, many progressive filmmakers have sought to "decolonize" spectators' minds. Cuba has been the only Latin American country able to mount a sustained strategy, which has included efforts to educate the populace in film criticism with such programs as "Twenty-four Frames Per Second," but Cuban writers and filmmakers have consistently remarked on the difficulty of this project. Prominent Cuban film historian and critic Ambrosio Fornet recently wrote, "The production of fiction feature films, limited to a very modest average of three per year, is barely noticed in the five hundred theaters in the country."[18] Julio García Espinosa, author of "For an Imperfect Cinema" and director of Cuba's most popular film (*Adventures of Juan Quinquin*, 1967), discussed this problem during the 1970s:

> We control all the means of production, and all the
> theaters, and after fifteen years, we see sadly that still we
> do not run the theaters, simply because we cannot
> project exclusively the revolutionary cinema, the
> militant cinema.[19]
> It's a shame that good intentions are not enough.[20]

Of course few countries and certainly no Latin American countries can satisfy domestic demand with only national productions. Even theaters in Brazil and Mexico are filled with Hollywood films. More troubling, however, is the historical failure of Latin American cinemas to develop successful distribution within Latin America. Repeatedly, Latin American filmmakers have testified to an unfamiliarity with Latin American films outside sporadic film festivals.[21]

A complementary approach to protecting spectators would be to develop a politically informed criticism to educate spectators, to promote a more discerning taste. Lacayo and Ibarra took on this challenge. On the second anniversary of the triumph, Lacayo described Nicaragua's current cultural backwardness and future challenges in a *Ventana* article, "Annotations on the Culture of Resistance."[22] Lacayo identified elements in Nicaraguan and Latin American history as possible models of "our true face." Four hundred years of colonial domination covered Nicaraguan culture with a maquillage encrusting "our cultural identity." Foreigners "impregnated us with a mentality of being dominated and we were euphoric to take them in as signs of progress." But "communities, peoples, nature, preserve in heroic resistance our American essence," in dances, songs, languages, food. A colonialist bourgeois society does not generate culture, but seeks culture abroad. It seeks only to exploit Nicaragua. The middle class, the petite bourgeoisie, unable to travel abroad, reproduces the foreigner inside Nicaragua and imports culture. Artists suffer from these pressures, forced to adopt and follow foreign trends. Pejorative terms used for Indians reflect condescension toward "all that was really Nicaraguan . . . all that reminds us of our American origins."

But anticolonial and anti-imperialist struggles, against Walker, with Sandino, and for liberation, are all part of recovering Nicaraguan identity:

> Sandino is at once the synthesis of military and cultural
> resistance. As with Sandino, three values have been
> recaptured and integrated in our revolutionary culture:
> anti-imperialism, the popular character, and the
> nationalist reaffirmation.

Lacayo illustrates this synthesis of military and cultural by calling a campesino's access to an M-16 "an important cultural phenomenon"; similarly, street theater, underground poetry, and literature are also part of the synthesis, even artisanal production, which "invests all its inventiveness in the construction of contact bombs, improvised mortars, makeshift weapons." For Lacayo, this culture of resistance has a decidedly militaristic cast.

Still, foreign domination has forced a militarism on Nicaraguan culture. With the revolution, which is "before everything else, and above all, an ideological fact, a cultural transformation. . . . We must begin to study, to analyze, catalogue, understand the cultural phenomena released by the struggle of the FSLN and its historic victory." Lacayo's remarks called for excavating Nicaraguan history and uncovering, preserving, and promoting forgotten and denigrated practices: folklore, artisanship, and indigenous rituals. At the same time, Lacayo recognizes and accepts that some foreign influences "today form part of our legitimate cultural patrimony."

A month later, Ibarra raised these issues in *Ventana*. He analyzed recent Hollywood trends to plan summer blockbusters and reverse setbacks caused by competition from video and cable television. According to Ibarra, the studies have done careful audience "research" to determine how to produce the current wave of hits like *Raiders of the Lost Ark, Superman II,* and *For Your Eyes Only.* But this "gringo production" is a cinema of so-called

> entertainment in which we can speak of 'hidden meanings.' This is an apparently inoffensive cinema, with large audiences but with effects that are generally worse than those of films in which things are said clearly. . . . This type of film takes advantage consciously of the deformations of our cultural development inherited from the past.[23]

Though he does note that the Commission of Classification will have its work cut out for it, Ibarra does not explain how to expose and resist these "hidden meanings."

Nor did he do this in an article several months later entitled "Cinematic Criticism and Revolutionary Society."[24] After an introduction about the "vacuous" criticism under Somoza, Ibarra writes that film criticism concerns

> discovering the means and mechanisms that the cinema uses to have the population internalize ideas which are racist, chauvinist, violent, sexually degenerate, etc. This function means demystifying the cinema, shaking the barriers imposed by unscientific knowledge and having the audience itself appropriate the intellectual means necessary to organize in the best way the world and the society that we are constructing.

Presumably, this task requires teaching spectators how the cinema conveys ideas so that they can protect themselves against hidden meanings. The critic, in approaching films such as *Gone with the Wind* and *Apocalypse Now,* must have knowledge of the historical contexts, and "this knowledge will have to be responsible, mature, to make known the real history and its consequences." However, he does not assess the relation between the film and "real history," nor does he clarify the meaning of that phrase. In fact he concludes by claiming, "Denouncing imperialism and the military dictatorships of the continent . . . is cinematic criticism."

In short, while these statements lay out some general principles, they do not demonstrate what criticism should be. The Hollywood films, cited above (chapter 3), were subjected to a crude sociological analysis indicting individualism and celebrating the "will of the masses." And those reviews were short-lived.

After Ibarra's article in February 1982, two reviews appeared, dealing with two classics of the New Cinema of Latin America, but the reviews displayed a sophistication presumably far beyond a newly literate population. In the first review, of Chilean exile Miguel Littín's *Acts of Marusia* (1975), a big-budget historical film based on the massacre of Chilean workers in 1907 and made in Mexico, Carlos Mohs introduces a Brechtian critique to decode the film, stressing terms such as "distancing structure" and "reflexive."

Adapting Brecht's theory of the theater to cinema was a hallmark of 1960s Marxist film criticism.[25] Using "reflexive" implies an attention to the film's formal organization, at the technical level of shots and camera movement, a sensitivity to detail normally unheard of in popular film criticism in developed countries, let alone in a small Central American country with no tradition of film criticism. Thus, Mohs supports his argument with detailed evidence from the film describing how cinematic techniques are used to present the proletarian masses as individuals with dignity and courage, and the bourgeoisie and its army as outsiders and servile to their foreign masters.

Mohs has not simply written an éloge to working-class fortitude and resolution. He is not trying to convince viewers and readers of the ultimate victory of the workers' struggle. Instead, he plunges into the aesthetic/political structure and texture of the film, showing how Littín embeds his political beliefs and commitments in the arrangement of cinematic elements. This is a far cry from Ibarra's injunction that denouncing imperialism is film criticism.

If Mohs's review reflects familiarity with contemporary film theory, Victor Martín Borrego is more conventional in discussing Pastor Vega's *Retrato de Teresa*.[26] Made in Cuba in 1979, *Portrait of Teresa* relates a woman's difficulties balancing work and union responsibilities with the domestic demands of being a wife and mother. The film provoked fierce polemics in Cuba, for the film, made by a man, broached the problem of machismo and questioned the husband's double standard.[27] Unlike the previous review, the sounds and images of the film are not analyzed. Borrego looks straightforwardly at the plot and concludes that the film's implied criticism of the husband is unfair, and he dismisses the film for "degenerating bit by bit into a 'modern' sentimental drama."

While this dismissal is not unreasonable, Borrego grants no potential educational possibility to the film, unlike a female writer in Cuba who thought the polemics stirred by the film "embraced the broadest sectors of society. The equalities of the Cuban woman became a theme of public discussion, outside the home. Teresa, as a worker, found a very important interlocutor, a fundamental element of our society, the working class woman."[28] Regardless of one's own interpretation, both Mohs and Borrego wrote thoughtful commentaries on the films, but INCINE did not pursue this criticism on a regular basis.

But both films represent artistic interventions fully compatible with Sandinista aspirations. One film comes from a veteran of Allende's Popular Unity struggle (1970–1973) and the other from the socialist Cuban revolution. They are not part of the imperialist wave of "entertainment" films inundating Nicaraguan theaters. According to Ibarra, criticism should be applied to Hollywood films in order to dissect the patina of entertainment secreting hidden meanings. Though INCINE signed several reviews in early issues of *Ventana*, they then disappeared and never returned. Nor did Mohs or Borrega write again for *Ventana*. Thus, during the revolution's early years, Ibarra and others pointed out the need for a pedagogical criticism to guide audiences toward cinematic literacy, but neither INCINE nor others came forward to fulfill this mission.

Mobile Cinema

INCINE had another option. Drawing on the experience of countries with large rural populations such as Mexico, Cuba, and the Soviet Union, INCINE operated an extensive Mobile Cinema system. Mobile Cinema brought cinema to areas without permanent theaters, mainly in the countryside and in poor urban neighborhoods. According to official figures, through 1986, Mobile Cinema conducted 5,000 separate screenings for over one million spectators each year, mainly agricultural workers.[29]

With Mobile Cinema, INCINE never faced the same obstacles as ENIDIEC. The specific raison d'être of Mobile Cinema was to screen films for audiences without theaters, electricity, or any experience of film. Mobile Cinema enjoyed a monopoly, with "unspoiled" spectators, and might thereby have inscribed on this tabula rasa the proper ideological imprinting so elusive for the Commission of Classification and ENIDIEC.

In principle, Mobile Cinema was starting from scratch. Once launched, however, its trajectory was buffeted by multiple pressures. In an early proposal, Ibarra saw Mobile Cinema as having a highly politicized function. He analyzed distribution and exhibition in Nicaragua before the triumph:

> They served as instruments to *direct*, consciously or
> unconsciously, forms of social behavior, habits, custom,
> conceptions about life and proper reactions to specific

problems that have made possible, among other things, the 45 opprobrious years of the Somocista dictatorship. Today, in Sandinista Nicaragua, in the Patria Libre, the Nicaraguan Institute of Cinema, ideological instrument of the Revolution, proposes to transform the current relations between the cinema and the population.[30]

INCINE must help people see the mercantile foundation of commercial cinema, but, according to Ibarra,

we cannot speak of having our people see cinema in the abstract, at the margin of the revolutionary process and outside of its principles and objectives. When we speak of our people seeing cinema, we are referring to the cinema that permits them to transform our reality in a revolutionary way, that permits them to learn to use the necessary revolutionary instruments for the building of a free and Sandinista consciousness. We are referring to a liberation cinema, weapons for the definitive liberation of Nicaragua.

Others at INCINE probably wanted Mobile Cinema to entertain the poor and isolated rural population. Mobile Cinema did target harvest workers doing the most demanding physical work under the most primitive working conditions.[31] Though Mobile Cinema normally included INCINE noticieros in the programming, classic feature films were the main attraction. For the most part, Mobile Cinema worked with the 16-mm format.[32] Often referred to as a nontheatrical format, 16-mm films were lighter, less expensive to print, and the projection equipment was more economical and portable. Mobile Cinema units traveled in jeeps in areas without paved roads; on donkeys, when there were no roads; and on small boats, when rivers were the principal means of transportation, for the commercial format of 35-mm film was too unwieldy for most Mobile Cinema applications. Mobile Cinema depended heavily on foreign contributions for equipment and films, primarily from Cuba (21 films) and the Soviet Union (15). Consequently, Cuban and Russian films formed a majority of the foreign films in the Mobile Cinema collection, along with Chaplin's films, plus a sprinkling of films from Mexico, Bolivia, Chile, and the United States (*Salt of the Earth*).

The films included fiction and nonfiction. The Soviet Union sent Eisenstein films and short documentaries, such as the 20-minute *The Soviet Trade Unions and the Housing of the Workers* (though a Mobile Cinema inventory lists *Potemkin* and *October* as Soviet documentaries). Cuba supplied primarily short nonfiction subjects, including some classic Santiago Alvarez films as well as educational shorts such as *The Forest, A Marvel of Equilibrium*. The great Cuban feature films (*Memories of Underdevelopment, Lucia*) don't appear on the list, though Bolivia was represented by several radical films of the Jorge Sanjinés/Ukamau group, in fact the only films of the New Cinema of Latin America. Thus, Mobile Cinema had many films at its disposal—political, scientific, and educational films, and fictional comedies or animated fairy tales.[33]

INCINE's archives do not indicate a programming policy. In all likelihood, programming depended on the screening organizers, for Mobile Cinema necessarily worked with the local authorities and groups to arrange the challenging logistics. Mobile Cinema supplied films and equipment but had no regional or local headquarters. Projectionists had neither the time nor the local contacts both to publicize screenings and to prepare for transportation, gasoline, and screening space; local groups performed these duties. Mobile Cinema, then, operated with support from the local FSLN unit, Sandinista Youth, CDSs, the Sandinista Army, UNAG (Unión Nacional de Agricultores y Ganaderos/National Union of Farmers and Cattlemen), and so forth.

The political orientation of these groups influenced Mobile Cinema's screenings. Such Sandinista organizations were committed to consolidating the revolution by doing political work and by establishing and promoting services, especially for the campesinos. Mobile Cinema's emphasis on political work apparently overshadowed the goals of cultural development championed by Ibarra in *Ventana*. As late as July 1983, after four years of work, one INCINE evaluation report (written by the former head of Mobile Cinema, Julio Torres) complained that

> the FSLN informed INCINE that the Mobile Cinemas
> in all the Regions should organize exclusively those
> projections that would support its propaganda activities,
> which to some degree slows down the normal develop-
> ment of the activities [of Mobile Cinema].[34]

While this directive may not reflect the norm, other evidence suggests that the projectionists shared this general propaganda orientation. In the same report cited above, Torres recommends improving their "cultural-political and cinematic training," which implies the projectionists have failed to convey the films' messages and intentions. But the very class stratification among INCINE personnel contributed to this problem. As indicated, the class cleavage at INCINE placed privileged class representatives in creative positions as directors and upper-level administrators; the less privileged were concentrated in technical areas, including Mobile Cinema. The salary schedules, all absurdly low, assigned remuneration accordingly, with directors receiving 33 percent more than technicians, including the Mobile Cinema projectionists, as a rule.[35]

The correlation of class and education had a pronounced effect in the field. Lacking political and cultural sophistication, the Mobile Cinema projectionists apparently took inappropriately extreme positions. In a sympathetic homage to the projectionists, the pro-FSLN Nicaraguan writer Michele Najlis described the atmosphere of Mobile Cinema. According to Najlis, the custom in the reserve battalions was to refer to compañeros according to their tasks. Thus, the Mobile Cinema projectionist was known as "Incine." Writing about her experiences in September 1982 in the area newly called Zalaya North, the northern part of the Atlantic coast, where Miskitos were a large majority, Najlis recounts the following episode:

> Incine had one passion: to hurl out a reverent "chagüite"
> [roughly, a spirited "rap"] before every screening. They
> say that Upper River [Río Arriba, presumably the
> projectionist who worked in that area] was speaking of
> things like "proletariat," "class consciousness," "need for
> the worker and campesino masses to overcome" . . . and
> the Miskito compañeros barely speak Spanish![36]

Though sympathetic, Najlis portrays "Incine" as a comic figure, weighed down by films and projector. During one projection, when "he lost the only clothing he was wearing, he had to hide between his backpack and the projector." Another time, when the sound equipment failed, "the film was going to be silent . . . but no, because Incine, who knew by heart the entire sound track, continued reciting the speech, adding the applause and even the music!" In fact, she contrasts the projectionist's diverting comportment with the beginning of the assembly, which was "very solemn, with the political officer of the army and the local magistrate presiding." Evidently, the local authorities viewed the event as a tool for political work. In this mise-en-scène, the projectionist says nothing about the cinematic qualities of the films. Instead, he addresses the bewildered audience with a harder Marxist line than the one in the films, Nicaraguan or foreign.

One fascinating document, however, sheds light on the "cinematic training," in Torres's phrase, of the projectionists. INCINE made one film on its own history, *Historia de un cine comprometido* [*History of a Committed Cinema*] (Feb. 1983). Officially listed as Noticiero 36, the film is one of the later noticieros, and it stands apart in many ways. *Historia de un cine comprometido* was the only noticiero that the Puerto Rican Emilio Rodríguez directed and received credit for, although he had worked with the Leonel Rugama Brigade before the triumph. An early *Cine Cubano* had identified Rodríguez as an INCINE founder. The INCINE archives contain an August 1979 proposal signed by Rodríguez, "director of the Instituto Sandinista del Cine Nicaragüense," for the formation of a Sandinista Filmmaking Institute. In his "Exposición" Rodríguez emphasizes the tight coordination that should exist between the institute and the FSLN.[37]

Though writing when the Junta of National Reconstruction was the governing body, Rodríguez repeatedly refers to the FSLN as the institution with power. In many ways the FSLN was indistinguishable from the government, but Rodríguez's ideological aspirations are expressed as Sandinista, not Nicaraguan. Thus, for the "objectives and functions" of the new institute, Rodríguez maintained that

> the fundamental objective . . . is the creation and development of a national cinematography that responds to the ideological line of the revolution and promotes the new national values to support the development of a culture based on the Sandinista principles.
>
> Finally, given the current lack of Nicaraguan technical cadres to bring this project to fruition, we propose as a first task the technical and ideological preparation of compañeros from the ranks of the FSLN and who have a cinematic bent.[38]

But when the FSLN designated three heads of INCINE, three Nicaraguans were chosen. However loyal Rodríguez was to the FSLN and the revolution, he was Puerto Rican (the son of a U.S. army soldier.)[39] Consistent FSLN policy made Nicaraguans leaders of new institutions. Many foreigners with political expertise and experience rushed to Nicaragua after the triumph, but they normally served as advisers. Furthermore, despite the dearth of INCINE filmmakers, Rodríguez did not direct noticieros (though he sometimes served as cameraperson). In addition, Rodríguez began as director of *La otra cara del oro*, but did not complete the film. Rafael Vargas, who finished the film, thinks that Rodríguez doesn't deserve directorial credit. In fact, as a rule, except for certain "prestigious" projects, only Nicaraguans directed INCINE's films.

Historia de un cine comprometido, then, is the only noticiero directed by a foreigner who worked at INCINE. The noticiero is unusual. As the name

Rafael Ruíz discovering film jammed in the camera
(Historia de un cine comprometido)

announces, *Historia* makes INCINE its subject. INCINE technicians appear on screen for the only time, though the directors occupy more screen time. Alejandro Soza, a head of Mobile Cinema, produced the film. Above all, *Historia* provides a perspective on INCINE by a foreigner, a filmmaker who had worked at INCINE from before the beginning but who had no decision-making power. In addition, to judge by his early "Exposición," Rodríguez took a more politicized stance on cinema culture than INCINE's heads.

The film opens with the 1983 filming in Nicaragua of a coproduction with France and Cuba. The voice-over relates the story of *El Señor Presidente*, "a Latin American dictator who governs under terror and repression, as in so many countries of our America, which still suffer from imperialist dictatorships."[40] The "quality and political commitment" of such a film would have been "an idle dream" before the triumph. This filming, then, "represents an enormous qualitative leap in the national artistic production." At the same time, the beginning emphasizes the heavy equipment needed in such large-scale productions, which require considerable hard currency and so account for the appeal of coproductions. Though the Nicaraguan filmmakers were ambivalent about coproductions, Rodríguez may have seen coproductions as an avenue for his own participation. INCINE represented the mechanism for realizing the cinema they had fantasized about on the battlefield, ultimately, "a cinema of cultural recovery."

Tracing INCINE's history, the commentary cites the training acquired by the Nicaraguans. "Brother filmmakers" visited Nicaragua and taught aspects of production; the images show Nicaraguans first in classrooms, then applying their learning on editing tables. The principal school has been the noticieros, whose time pressures and production regularity produced errors but also led to solutions, recognized at festivals with prizes. Equally important has been Mobile Cinema, seen journeying into remote areas in jeeps, or with mules, or in small rowboats. Once at the destination, the projectionist prepares the equipment and the screening begins. The audience, filled with rapt children, watches. They laugh freely, watching young children cringe at injections (footage taken taken from the earlier noticiero on the Literacy Crusade). After another shot of the Mobile Cinema projector reestablishing the site, new images fill the screen. The sequence proceeds with shots from cheap action and pornographic films: fights, weapons, and naked women. All of this passes on the screen as if being seen by the happy children shown earlier.

The commentary provides a remarkable critique of this medley, which is

Editor Johnny Henderson at INCINE *workshop (*Historia de un cine comprometido*)*

*Ramiro Lacayo, head of INCINE (*Historia de un cine comprometido*)*

repeated while the voice-over continues: "The principal production of the imperialist cinema is of this nature. Its messages, repeated thousands of times, exercise a direct influence on our values and aspirations in life."

Let's look at these images anew.

> The super hero, white, tough, Aryan. Fighting the evil that threatens the consumer society. His principal quality: extreme individualism. With this he always triumphs over the impossible.
> The woman: sexual object, submissive and humiliated, has value while young; if not young, she only provokes laughter.

The film criticizes "imperialist cinema" in the context of Mobile Cinema, implying that rural, campesino, often indigenous audiences, many seeing their first film, wanting respite from hard daily lives, should have to listen to didactic attacks on imperialist cinema. Instead of just enjoying the cinema, audiences had to be warned against insidious messages from this "ideological instrument." Imperialist cinema uses sex and violence to promote capitalist values. Underdeveloped countries cannot resist imperialism's superior technological might, which literally uses the hero's ray gun to melt the face of a technologically under-equipped third-world villain. But the cinema's ideological power cuts both ways. Nicaraguan cinema, "a revolutionary cinema," can promote collective work, the integrity of women, and the pacific resolution of problems.

The Cuban Octavio Cortázar made a film on Cuba's Mobile Cinema in 1967 that served as a model for Rodríguez's. In his study of Cuban cinema, Michael Chanan discusses that film. For Chanan, *Por primera vez* [*For the First Time*], with its "simple and least portentous of images . . . has produced for its audience its own self-discovery *as* an audience." Chanan indicates that in the Cuban film "the audience has become, together with the film-makers, participant observers and observant participators in the same process."[41] Whether the film achieves these results is debatable, but Chanan has identified the filmmaker's attempt to make these new Cuban film spectators see and feel themselves as protagonists of their own history. This attitude contrasts with *Historia de un cine comprometido*, which shows the audience's delight but imposes a rigid ideological and instrumental interpretation of cinema, paternalistically stressing the cinema's dangers rather than allowing untutored viewers their autonomy.

Changing terms, one can find similar discussions in U.S. newspapers. The power of film and television to corrupt naïve people has incited polemics and argument for a century. What is interesting about *Historia* is its source. No other INCINE film or published article advanced such a crude analysis. The Commission of Classification used such criteria, but private distributors imported less objectionable samples of the traditional standard fare. In the case of *Historia*, Rodríguez, a foreigner, is more militant than the Nicaraguans. His representation of Mobile Cinema, a project already shown assuming a militancy dramatically inappropriate to Miskitos, who speak their own language, subjected audiences to Marxist sloganeering, a strategy unlikely to transform them into Sandinista spectators.[42]

The Debate over *Alsino y el cóndor*

One film in Nicaragua received extended critical discussion in *Ventana*. In July 1982, a contingent of the Sandinista cultural elite discussed the first fictional film produced in Nicaragua: Chilean film director Miguel Littín's 1981 *Alsino y el cóndor*, made with a part-Nicaraguan cast and a foreign (primarily Mexican) crew. Notwithstanding the Nicaraguans' sensitivity to a film made by a foreigner (in obvious support of their revolution), the discourse presumably allows Sandinista intellectuals to exercise their critical skills.[43]

In organizing the forum, *Ventana*'s editor, Rosario Murillo, chose participants close to the FSLN: two people from the FSLN's Department of Propaganda and Political Education (Leonel Espinosa and Gioconda Belli), two from the Ministry of Culture (Ramiro Lacayo and José Daniel Prego), and one from the Institute for the Study of Sandinismo (Francisco de Asís Fernández). The director of the National Library (Lizandro Chávez) and a government representative from the Information Office completed the group.

A stunned Miguel Littín also sat in.

Murillo's introduction prepares readers for the acerbic discussion. She indicts the films shown in Nicaragua before the revolution, films that "corrupted the eye and consciousness of the Nicaraguan spectator," only to be expected in a country that only three years before "began to open the doors to cultural expression and creation, with the freedom that only a revolutionary process could guarantee." Murillo, a poet, opines, "Regarding the cinema, we have to say the same thing that we say of poetry: a poem of love is worth as much as a poem about guns and machine guns. A good love poem is worth as much as a good film about love."[44]

With this preface, Murillo summarized prerevolutionary filmmaking in Nicaragua, with two failed feature coproductions (with Mexico) and Somoza's execrable PRODUCINE, turning out films on the "works of progress" of the various ministries (as seen in Lacayo's *Bananeras*, discussed in chapter 7) and "the surrealism of their bacchanals." Against this background, and citing INCINE's noticieros and documentaries, Murillo warns readers about the criticisms of Littín's film in the discussion, acknowledging that the accents, clothes, and settings, as directed by a foreigner, may be jarring to Nicaraguans. She also identifies two reactions to the film, an enthusiastic one from popular audiences, and a more critical one "in more sophisticated circles, that is, those whose thinking is more developed (contaminated?)." Above all, she defends artistic freedom, implicitly criticizing "panfletario," "manichaean," and "triumphalist" tendencies. For her, INCINE quite properly defends the film, arguing that reality is more complex:

> INCINE claims that the creative and learning capacity
> of the people should not be underestimated, that
> propaganda should be done by breaking with the
> manichaean tendencies, entering the field that until
> now only the enemy has controlled, that is, the field
> of subtlety, of imagination, of metaphor.

Essentially, Murillo is preparing readers for critical attacks on the film. According to Murillo, INCINE alone, despite, or because of, its own experience with nonfiction, defends an artist's freedom to transform raw material—a strange accent, a character's hat, etc.—in ways that could violate a literal conception of reality but reach a more profound truth.

Murillo actually performs her own Manichaean reduction opposing "panfletario" and artistic. In her view, "panfletario" always cripples artistic ambition and creativity. But what bothered the critics was not the film's politics but its not adhering to reality. De Asís cites the bizarre use of language, such as the simultaneous and incongruous use of the Nicarguan *vos* and the Spanish *tú* for the second person singular. Some were bothered by the appearance of Sandinista East German trucks (IFAs) being driven by the Guardia Nacional.[45] These glitches might sound trivial, but the dissonances told Nicaraguans that the story wasn't Nicaraguan, and both the associations and expectations provoked by the film led to the rejection of the film by many of these critics.

This is the real crux of the criticism of *Alsino*. Except for Ramiro Lacayo, the critics had difficulty accepting a mix of Nicaraguan and foreign cultural markers and even more trouble accepting elements that contradicted the Nicaraguan reality. The film wanted to draw on the Nicaraguan struggle and make a more general, even allegorical statement about popular struggle in Latin America. For the Nicaraguans, their struggle's particulars anchored the story in a specific time and place; diegetic anomalies interfered with the interpretive leap into metaphor. As Chavez articulated the problem, "the source of all this dissatisfaction . . . is the metaphoric treatment of a reality to which it is difficult to apply this metaphoric language." Nicaraguans applied a criterion of fidelity to reality not necessarily as an inviolate critical principle or protocol, but because the film placed enough Nicaraguan elements in the story to invite this interpretation. They didn't quarrel with artistic license or complain about censorship. They were raising legitimate critical questions about this specific film. Their comments reflect neither the political narrowness nor the underdeveloped critical skills to which Murillo referred.

After hearing the complaints, Littín confessed: "I would have liked to participate in the critical discussion with you and to have agreed with you. But I completely disagree. Frankly, I am disoriented." Early in the session Littín had answered questions in a way that foreshadowed the imminent discord. De Asís and others objected that characterizing the gringos as complex, guilt-ridden villains was *inaccurate, untrue,* for "the gringo who came to Nicaragua was not this type of gringo." In response, Littín cited evidence of psychological problems in U.S. veterans of the Vietnam War! Littín wasn't claiming artistic license as a defense, but documentary truth, found in documentaries and interviews, to the point where the soldiers cry after discovering what they have done. Littín endorses using these ideas in *Alsino* because "human contradiction exists at all levels, in all human beings." The Nicaraguan critics didn't dispute that human contradiction afflicts everyone, even the enemy, but no one believed the Guardia or the gringo soldiers in Nicaragua wrestled with their consciences. For de Asís, they were "pure human beasts"; for Belli, "a guardia was not a tormented person but someone who did things with no remorse or nightmares." The Nicarguans felt that Littín's argument based on veterans of the Vietnam War was irrelevant to their situation.

Littín plowed ahead. He maintained that independently of the gringos' and Guardias' psychology, their bouts with guilt did not palliate a murderous policy. Later, after confessing disorientation, Littín responded to specific criticisms, while insisting he hadn't made a film on Nicaragua's recent history, for only Nicaraguans could do that. He wanted to "make an open film on the movements of struggle in Latin America and all the movements of struggle in Central America, because it seems to me that the participation of the North American advisers is much clearer, more obvious now in El Salvador than in the Nicaraguan struggle." In the end, however, he falls back on the defense provided by Murillo and Lacayo:

> Frankly I regret not agreeing with you but I think that the film is fulfilling its task. I have attended various screenings in different theaters in Nicaragua and I see that the understanding of the public goes far beyond what we could have imagined. Because the public has a cinematic culture and this country has a broad cultural and ideological level much more profound and contradictory than one could imagine. In fact, the film could have been even more complete in this sense.[46]

This defense, of course, contradicts critics' claims that Nicaraguans had no cinematic culture. The public's warm reception of the film might also belie the paternalistic rationale advanced by Ibarra and the Commission of Classification. This argument turns paternalism upside down, transforming the masses into a rich reservoir of creativity and critical perspicacity. Those who join with the enlightened masses renounce artistic restrictions and political pamphleteering.

Ramiro Lacayo belonged to this camp, in contradistinction not only to the critics at the round table, but also to the less-privileged compañeros of Mobile Cinema, with their spirited "chagüites" and critiques of imperialism. Lacayo's position probably corresponded to his own personal and professional commitments. As head of INCINE, which coproduced the film, he could hardly join the attacks. He would not jeopardize his foothold at INCINE when heads were rolling in the Ministry of Culture. Like the other critics, he did not insist on a harder political line, for that stand would impose restrictions on INCINE. Lacayo probably shared the other filmmakers' restiveness not only to push the boundaries of the noticiero, but also to make the crucial step toward fiction. Murillo even notes in her introduction that INCINE's work to that point did not include fiction, implying that Littín's fiction film represented an artistic advance over the more "committed" noticieros and documentaries, as if the Nicaraguan productions lacked cinematic artistry.

Alsino could be seen as INCINE's Trojan horse. Let a prestigious foreign director, whose previous film (*Acts of Marusia*) was a masterful fictional recreation of a popular Chilean struggle brutally snuffed out by a repressive military, demonstrate the value of fiction. INCINE could then use *Alsino*'s success to justify its own fictional productions. Ibarra had already expressed his sense that fiction was premature. INCINE should concentrate on distribution and exhibition. For Ibarra, INCINE's limited resources could not support fictional filmmaking. Lacayo, then, was walking a tightrope, careful to defend fiction's political effectiveness, but not giving ground on artistic freedom.[47]

Throughout the discussion, the participants speak at cross-purposes. While Murillo warns against too "Manichaean" and "panfletario" a criticism, the other critics dwell on the film's jarring inaccuracies. No one calls for more orthodox political analysis. In fact, gleaning any clear sense of Sandinismo from the discussion would be difficult. Certainly no one uses Marxist terms like working class, proletariat, capitalism, or socialism. Nor does anyone object to using metaphor. But metaphor depends on similarity, and the critics thought the disanalogies overwhelmed the similarities and aborted the metaphor. On the other hand, Murillo, Lacayo, and Littín defend the film's artistic freedom and positive audience responses. But the critics questioned the film's artistic success. No one wanted to limit artistic freedom, but artistic independence did not guarantee artistic success. Nor did the populist defense sway them. The critics, as Nicaraguans who had fought a costly struggle against a brutal dictatorship, balked at the film.

Murillo's aggressive defense of the film, coupled with her introductory claim that Nicaraguans still lacked deep cinematic judgment and authority, suggests an additional motivation. Rosario Murillo had founded the ASTC the previous year. From that power base, she waged a ceaseless campaign against Ernesto Cardenal and the Ministry of Culture. The ASTC, with *Ventana* (edited by Murillo) as its organ, functioned as an alternative Ministry of Culture. Murillo wanted to organize professional artists committed to the revolution, not promote *amateur* artists, the goal of the Ministry of Culture in general, and the poetry workshops in particular.[48] The ASTC did not include cinema artists, but her remarks in the debate emphasize the importance of quality, a clear backhanded swipe at Cardenal's policy of democratizing art. Murillo, then, used the artistic defense of *Alsino* as an opportunity to advance her own more "artistic" program of the ASTC.

It is unfortunate that Murillo never saw fit to hold similar discussions about INCINE's own fiction films several years later. In fact, of the assembled critics, only Vicente Ibarra wrote about INCINE's films. Yet Ibarra was removed from INCINE at this very moment (summer 1982) in the Ministry of Culture power struggle, so when he wrote those reviews, he was no longer a member of INCINE. Although INCINE continued producing noticieros, documentaries, and eventually fiction films, the institution ultimately did little to promote its films domestically, or to create "the new spectator."

Six   BREAKING THE MOLD:
NEW NOTICIEROS

In 1982 film production at INCINE reached a new phase. Institutional organization did not change, and the production schedule still adhered to the
early agreements with ICAIC (35-mm black-and-white noticieros and 16-mm
color documentaries). But the boundary between categories was crumbling
and the noticieros began to resemble documentaries in design, length, and
topicality. In addition, the pioneer directors stopped working on noticieros,
and the second- and third- generation filmmakers replaced them. As the
war against the contras intensified and pressures on nonessential material
resources increased, INCINE's bond with the FSLN loosened. While the
INCINE administration probably did not know its future direction, the withdrawal of the first generation from noticiero production reflected an aspiration toward artistic excellence, already foreshadowed in the *Alsino* debate,
and the ultimate cessation of noticiero production by the end of 1984.

Lacayo, now sole head of INCINE, had always sought greater autonomy
from the FSLN for INCINE, and he got funding from other government agencies. This allowed filmmakers to tailor plans to the coproduction requirements rather than adhering to one noticiero per month. As will be seen from
the thematic distribution of this last set of noticieros, only two of these films
concern the military, and then not the regular army. Instead, the filmmakers
granted increasing space to cultural issues, taken broadly, and to grassroots
voices and images. The FSLN as the vanguard of the people and the comandantes recede, as the filmmakers sought to represent the revolution in deeds,
not as illustrations of official words.

Culture

When asked to identify a truly Nicaraguan film, Mariano
Marín referred to his next noticiero, *El maestro popular* (Oct. 1982).[1] Marín

organized this simple film around a young teacher in a village near Managua. The young woman sits in her spare living room and describes her work in adult education. The film follows her to school in the mornings, returning home for a meal, then back to school to meet with other young teachers. Several teachers see that the absence of electricity prevents night classes and impedes completion of homework. Once the adult students express their concern, the instructors seek solutions and "el maestro popular" recounts the story. Marín closes the film with the adult students in class, as the camera zooms out slowly from the window of the schoolhouse to reveal new electric lights.

Presumably Marín chose this woman as an example of the continuing commitment to popular education after the celebrated Literacy Campaign of 1980. As the teacher herself says,

> At the end of the literacy campaign, I returned to my house. Here I discovered another task of education, the stage of sustaining, how the compañeros would be able to continue going forward, to not forget what they had studied.

As she speaks, Marín films her seated in her living room, the kitchen visible and audible in the background. Marín explains:

> There is a mise-en-scène in *El maestro popular* that has very Nicaraguan characteristics. My relation to the dialogue with the camera I believe is one of the successes that you come to feel, that the Nicaraguan way of speaking has something distinctive about it. That is, there is a form of expression of the young woman that reveals the real indigenous characteristics. It's not the child trying to get this effect; it's not the handsome, well-dressed actor, nor the white people of neo-realism, but a new realism that was showing this reality, this was the importance of the search. I filmed it because it was not the first time I made this frame, which seems more like an impressionist frame. It is an open shot, very much of the country. Furthermore there's a refreshing element from the beginning. It has no other purpose than to show her comportment; I try to center the film on what she does. The only thing I do is to change the location.
> The film consists of a clearly defined landscape, a

Nicaraguan one, which I think is very rich, though it is not there for good taste. We are speaking of a film about teaching the public to read. . . . One of the scenes in the film where the woman is making a tortilla, heating the stove, a dog walks by, a chicken, in short a very typical frame of Nicaraguan life, all done in a very natural manner. It is very typical of the region. Of course we had done this many other times, but without filming it and it occurred to me that it is much better than putting myself in a chair and only pointing the microphone. This way is less distancing, an attempt to give this Nicaraguan image of our search.[2]

This nine-minute film conveys a sense of the people solving problems, building on the work of the national Literacy Campaign. The literacy veterans returned to families and villages and applied their experience and commitment to solving problems like the need for electricity. The young teachers solicit the adult students' opinions and constantly emphasize working collectively. Marín notes that the people had been requesting electricity for months and that they helped them have electricity installed. There are several polemical moments in the film—the multiplication lesson includes this problem: Five compañeros came from Masaya to Managua to a meeting. The Sandinista Central paid each one five córdobas for the trip. Five times five, twenty-five—but no other overt references to the FSLN. That is, the film shows daily Nicaraguan life, in the interior shots with random animals coming and going, in the exterior shots of the "maestro popular" walking to school, in the Nicaraguan Spanish spoken extemporaneously and unaffectedly by teachers and students alike.

María José Alvarez's departure for the Atlantic coast created a vacancy filled by newcomer Iván Argüello. Argüello had applied to work at INCINE earlier but received no response. He had produced various publicity videos but, like others, had no previous film experience. He had, however, worked in the theater and he had wanted to work in films for some time.

His first film, La gran equivocación [The Big Lie] (Jan. 1983), shows the effects of North American popular culture/music on Nicaraguan youth. Throughout the Somoza years, North American popular culture, disseminated through radio, television, and cinema, had permeated Nicaraguan life. The revolution did little to restrict Hollywood films, and television continued to rely on imported products. The FSLN recognized, and the Commission of Classification identified, problematic areas: individualism, violence, pornography. Yet apart from La gran equivocación and Historia de un cine

*Adult education schoolteacher at home (*El maestro popular*)*

comprometido (see chapter 5), INCINE's films did not fight this ideological battle.

The structure of *La gran equivocación* suggests INCINE's ambivalence about North American culture. The opening sequence begins by showing rock stars like Jim Morrison and Jimmy Hendrix and playing heavy rock on the sound track. Evoking the psychedelic ambience of the late 1960s, the camera swirls about, spotlights transformed into flashing comets. These lights suddenly go out of focus, ceding the screen to the title and credits. An offscreen commentator indicts the influence, especially on youth, of North American culture. More pointedly, North American culture distracts youth from participation in the revolution, dramatized after the credits as the camera tilts down over a raised rifle.

While this opening suggests a tired left critique of popular culture, the rest of the film straddles the question. After a sequence on some Nicaraguan Olympic games, Carlos Nuñez, head of Sandinista Youth, praises youths for embracing the Sandinista spirit. Invoking the Literacy Campaign, Nuñez speaks of exchanging the book for the gun, the gun for the machete. The film then illustrates various "revolutionary" activities for young people, providing emergency relief following heavy storms and working as soldiers in coffee-harvesting brigades. All document a youth responding to the revolution's challenges, leaving childish pastimes behind. However, the film ends with a long sequence of youth leisure activities edited to rock music by

Santana, though a final voice-over commentary enfolds the recreation in a nationalist and revolutionary discourse by referring to the "blue and white flag of the country and the red and black of the Sandinista Front."

The film's ending, then, is surprisingly similar to its opening sequence. Perhaps the references to the youth culture are meant to criticize the packaging of this youth culture—television screens, magazine advertising, radio broadcasts—in addition to its being a foreign culture imported from abroad. None of the final sounds or images are mediated in any way, hence they can be understood as Nicaraguan youth activities uncontaminated by the imperialist media. Nonetheless, Carlos Santana was still a North American import, so the film remains ambiguous.[3]

The year 1984 was the fiftieth anniversary of Sandino's assassination, and Iván Argüello constructed a noticiero around Sandino. *Esta tierra es ese hombre* (June/July 1984) mobilizes a variety of cinematic materials, from stills of Sandino and the first Somoza to archival footage in video and even a short animated insert at the end. He also introduces some fictional representation, using a series of doors closing to symbolize the setback to the revolutionary cause at Sandino's death; the doors later open with the overthrow of Somoza and the continuing struggle against imperialism.

Argüello's key rhetorical effort involves the campesinos. Jaime Wheelock appears at a meeting, followed by a graphic announcing the Agrarian Reform. The government officials embrace campesinos who have come forward to receive land titles. As in the earlier *Wiwilí*, the film leaves out who is actually receiving the land, probably the single most important fact for the campesino audience. A final quote from a poem by Ernesto Cardenal illuminates the birth and death metaphors earlier in the film: "But the hero is born when he dies, and the green grass is born again from the ashes." *Esta tierra* is transitional, retaining some past excesses, yet anticipating the fiction of the future (and specifically Argüello's future as director of INCINE's first fiction feature film). Argüello himself was not completely satisfied with the film:

> If I did it again, I think it should cover more popular
> legends about Sandino; for me it's not very successful.
> There is a surrealist tendency in it that I was able to
> express well. It's not a problem of [a film] being *panfle-
> tario* if I want it, but if it's *panfletario* when I don't want
> it, that's a problem.[4]

Though Humberto Ortega is not seen in the film, his speech from the July 19 (1984) celebration of the triumph is heard, invoking Nicaragua's heroes and martyrs. And again repeating early mistakes, Comandante Ortega's words accompany shots of soldiers on military maneuvers, instrumentalizing the Dirección Nacional discourse for political purposes, in this case recruiting campesinos for defense of the patria of Sandino.

At the same time, the film has fictional aspects. The first sequence reconstructs Sandino's murder. Sounds of horses provide sound-over to a series of stills of horses. A gravedigger asks the men standing over him who has died, but they tell him to mind his own business and finish his work, a reference to the mystery surrounding Sandino's grave, which has never been found. Hence the symbolic importance of the veterans of Sandino's army, as the opening scene motivates two veterans and Sandino's "novia" (girlfriend) to describe how they have guarded and passed on the legacy of Sandino's struggle. As one veteran puts it, Sandino's blood was fecund, for it sustains the country's new defenders. At that moment, the doors seen closing earlier are thrown open in a repetition of the same tracking shot. The "narrative" thread picks up the idea of fecundity with a fictional village official registering Sandino's birth in 1894, carefully inscribing the information in the town registry. Sandino was a "natural son," son of a bourgeois landowner and a servant, i.e., a humble man.

These fictional thrusts contribute to making Sandino father of the revolution, and Carlos Fonseca his son. Images of both, and slogans from their writings, dominated the FSLN's iconography. In an interesting way, this public campaign to construct a new national iconography contrasts with Somoza's self-promotion during his dictatorship. During a sequence of insurrection stills, *Esta tierra* includes a famous newsreel of a crowd tearing down a statue of Somoza. Later, after the campesinos receive land titles, a life-size statue of Sandino is unveiled, in his casual pose, with iconic uniform, hat, and boots. Unlike Somoza, who was raised above the earth, Sandino stands on the ground, beside the people, human-sized.

But the FSLN did not simply celebrate installing a powerful leader, a staple of fascism and socialist realism. While the FSLN treated the *dead* Sandino in heroic terms and added Fonseca to the pantheon after his death in 1976, the FSLN avoided elevating living individuals as icons.[5] The FSLN's highest governing body, the Dirección Nacional, *always,* on principle, made decisions by consensus. Before the electoral defeat in 1990, no DN member broke ranks with this policy. In addition, gigantic representations of FSLN leaders never appeared at rallies, official functions, fêtes, etc. No doubt the experience of the tendencies in the late 1970s influenced this practice. Thus, the campaign to create a Sandinista iconography applied mainly to Sandino himself and was consciously restricted to dead figures. In this sense Nicaragua broke with a Latin American tradition of *caudillismo,* the installation of a cult around one leader, a practice grotesquely pursued by some socialist countries as well.[6]

Argüello devoted his last noticiero, *Bienaventurados los que luchan por la paz* (*Blessed are those who fight for peace,* Oct.–Nov. 1984), to another individual, the national poet Rubén Darío. Once again Argüello uses the narrative conceit of bookends to frame the film, in this case showing the pages of a book by Darío tracing Nicaragua's long quest for national sovereignty. In between, images of death and destruction wreaked by the U.S.-funded contra dramatize Nicaragua's current difficulties. There are images of fresh graves and still-smoldering wreckage, as mothers mourn lost sons. Footage of the immediate aftermath of a contra attack flickers identifiably as video footage, taken from television coverage.

At this time, the television footage underlines the semantic stretching of the term noticiero. When the Cubans began making weekly newsreels in 1959, they covered current events. Like most countries at that time, Cuba had limited television development. Newsreels presented the only moving images of breaking events, even if the news—already reported on radio and in newspapers—was several days old. Twenty-five years later, in much of Latin America, television covered current events. Nicaragua was no exception, though Mobile Cinema continued to bring moving images of news to remote areas.

The film, then, has a clear rhetorical structure. Loved ones go through the rituals designed to express grief, rife with Christian iconography. Once rituals end, people steel themselves to defend the country, construct fortifications in the countryside, and form self-defense militias in the cities. Lest the efforts be seen as a partisan defense of the FSLN, the words of Darío, *the* national poet, place the current struggle for sovereignty in the context of a century of repeated U.S. aggression.

The use of Darío is interesting, since his credentials as a revolutionary are debatable. He was opposed to imperialism, and no one contests his importance as a literary figure, but he lived most of his life outside of Nicaragua and was never involved in Nicaragua's political life. He returned to Nicaragua before dying in 1916 at 49. Since he opposed imperialism, the FSLN claimed him as a pre-Sandinista patriot. But Darío had said little on these matters. In fact, Darío's political sympathies were so ambiguous that many political formations, including Somoza, have tried to claim him.[7]

Economy

After *El maestro popular*, Marín took on another local initiative, again using several interesting cinematic ideas in *Los innovadores* (Dec. 1982). The destruction during the war of liberation affected much of Nicaragua's capital stock, the machinery needed to process and produce goods like milk and boots. Third-world revolutions inevitably face this problem. They are dependent on capital goods exclusively available in developed countries in exchange for hard currency. Small countries like Nicaragua may not have the raw materials to produce capital goods, so they continue to rely on historical links with a developed supplier. Commentators recognized this problem early, but the premium on hard currency discouraged large-scale purchases of goods abroad. In the film, the opening images survey factory destruction: twisted and idle machine parts, mangled metal graveyards that were once factory shop floors. Suddenly stop-motion filming resurrects a gear rolling forward into the foreground accompanied by the upbeat commentary: "We were starting to pay the price of our liberty, but quickly, everything sprang into movement again: the innovators leapt to their feet." In the film's first part, Marín uses footage shot for earlier noticieros. In this case, however, the workers describe the challenges they face and their concrete solutions to fashion spare parts. Unlike the *Plan económico*, in which the milk pouring into bags illustrates the precision of the annual plan—a macro view that scants the workers' contributions—here the workers subordinate the machines to their own creativity.

In one sense, the film's discourse has been depoliticized, for the workers do not refer to political organizations nor do they cite the much-promoted "social wage" as compensation for falling real wages. They dwell instead on their expertise in their respective jobs, proudly detailing the minutiae of the tasks:

> At the company we have saved the country a lot of money. The trick I would say is in the mold; the mold was made of iron, we made it with iron and before pouring the aluminum in the mold the mold was preheated, because the sudden change of temperature, you know, the aluminum is hot and if you put it in the chilled part, that begins the heating, then the mold was preheated and that resolved [the problem] for us.

The molds stamp the boot soles marching through the machinery. Suddenly Marín cuts to a low-angle shot with the camera placed beneath train tracks as a slowly advancing locomotive blackens the sky, gliding forward to a Beatles song, a staple of Marín's sound tracks. Marín later introduces an unusual sound element. When a reconditioned bus emerges from an assembly line, a simple guitar version of the International celebrates the event. After several workers discuss ways to construct formerly imported parts, the International resumes, as the film shows farmers tilling a field. Not only do the innovators work in factories; they also learn from the campesinos:

*"International" yoking peasant and worker (*Los innovadores*)*

> We start off with the basic goal of increasing production,
> trying to improve their agricultural tools and in this way
> we begin to develop, to work with some information
> provided from the campesinos themselves, some work
> done empirically, to come up with an improved
> traditional plow, based on the knowledge of the small
> farmer.

The film ends with two campesinos with a yoke of oxen directing a new and improved plow while the guitar slowly picks out the International.

Los innovadores dispenses with the top-heavy discourse of the earlier noticieros about production. While the FSLN initially placed great store in mechanized production, in industry and agriculture, this film favors the workers' creativity. Raised solidly middle-class in Granada, Marín claims to have campesino roots. Without renouncing mechanization, Marín locates increased productivity in working people's intelligence and commitment. There are no paeans to the miracles of cooperatives, nor visual odes of tractors covering the landscape as in Eisenstein's *Old and New*. Here the International forms a conceptual bridge between country and city, the worker-peasant alliance, summed up by the narrator's final words: "We are making an effort, said one mechanic. Imagination is free."[8]

One of the last noticieros, *El abastecimiento* (June–Oct. 1984), takes on an

*Merchant explaining situation of food supply (*El abastecimiento*)*

increasingly important daily problem, food supply and distribution. Many
key decisions swirled around the food question. The importance of feeding
the population had to be balanced against the need to produce export crops
to earn hard currency. Export crops required large numbers of agricultural
(wage) laborers. Part of the Agrarian Reform debate concerned the consequences to the rural wage-labor supply of distributing land to campesinos.
With increased access to land, campesinos could subsist by working their
own plots and might withdraw their labor from the market. With a reduced
labor force, export production would decline. To induce campesinos to produce for the internal market, the FSLN had to offer relatively high producer
prices, but they also wanted to keep prices low for urban consumers (the
key supporters of the FSLN), requiring food subsidies. When the war became
an additional factor, the army was another preferred competitor for food,
pressuring producer prices down and (urban) consumer prices up (to shift
some of the food subsidy to the army). This undertaking required a system
to control many tasks, one being food distribution, always privately handled
in the past. In Nicaragua, keeping control over distribution was virtually
impossible.

Despite the freshness and importance of food as the subject, *El abastecimiento* is an awkward film. New director Ronald Porras, with the support
of the ministry (MICOIN) responsible for the official food subsidy program,
Empresa Nicaragüense de Alimentos Básicos (ENABAS), went to the Orien-

tal Market with a camera and asked merchants about distribution problems. The technical quality of sounds and images is poor, and the film does not shape the responses conceptually. The film lurches from one sequence to the next with little shape or organization. A government representative says he will refer to four problems in the distribution system, but the film apparently eliminated the last two, suggesting rushed editing. Some sequences in the script do not appear in the final cut, such as a "popular inspector" visiting an official neighborhood distribution outlet (*pulpería*) to check prices. Many first directorial projects suffered from similar problems; in this case, the noticiero cycle was about to end, and the inadequacies may reflect this shift in institutional priorities.

Government Programs

INCINE's efforts to seek greater financial independence led to a number of coproductions with various government agencies. Mariano Marín directed his next noticiero about a revolutionary program administered by the MINT. *Generosos en la victoria* (Mar. 1983), to be blunt, is a Potemkin village account of the new Nicaraguan prison system. The film's narration and the testimony of former and present prisoners construct a prisoner's dream world. The prisoner passes through several stages of incarceration, culminating in the "régimen abierto" (open regime), in which forms of confinement have disappeared: no walls, no barriers, no guards, no weapons; instead there is self-government. Prisoners undergo reeducation and work, but they are paid wages and enjoy periodic conjugal visits and even unsupervised leaves. Many serious inmates express appreciation of the system. The final speaker, a former prisoner, says, "I felt happy and it seemed to me that even if I had had a sentence one or two years longer, I would have spent it calmly, because . . . there it's not a penal center; it's a, for me, it's a work center."

Prison officials also praise the system. The officials stress reintegration of prisoners, which entails analyzing their conduct according to criteria like class background. Crime is "seen as a vestige of Somocismo, as a vestige of the enemy which we want to wipe out completely." Various mass organizations—ATC, CST, AMNLAE—support prisoner reintegration, so freed prisoners are not cast adrift. But the prisoners themselves supply astonishing encomia:

> Without question the "régimen abierto" as an institution has a root deeply planted in the revolutionary principles and which is found clearly announced in a principle of

the Commander in Chief of the Popular Sandinista
Revolution Carlos Fonseca Amador, when he spoke of
the warmth toward one's enemies, of being generous
with enemies.

Admittedly, one does not expect indictments of the prison system from
prisoners in a film financed by the prison system. Nor do citations from
the Commander in Chief of the Popular Sandinista Revolution bespeak an
absence of partisanship in the reeducation process. Nonetheless, Marín insists on the film's truth and says he was amazed himself. It would be difficult to find a less credulous observer than Marín, whose indifference and
even hostility to authority were indelible aspects of his personality (though
his sympathy with the GPP tendency, dominant in the MINT, should not be
discounted).

For his last noticiero, Mariano Marín collaborated again with the MINT
to make *Los centinelas de la alegría del pueblo* [*Guardians of the Happiness of the People*] (Aug.–Nov. 1983). Or at least so the credits read. Marín
renounced credit for the film, claiming that its final form traduced his conception. Once Marín was called for military service, INCINE began to find
many problems with the film and finally turned it over to Rafael Vargas.
Marín felt that Vargas destroyed it "because he likes to destroy things."[9]
Nonetheless, the film does retain many elements from Marín's plans, and
the footage was shot under his watch. But regardless of "authorship," *Los
centinelas* edges closer to full-fledged fiction, a docudrama seeming to represent real events, though the final product resembles delirious drama more
than scrupulous documentary.[10] Marín certainly saw it as an opportunity to
work with fiction:

> *Los centinelas* . . . in reality is a crazy short fiction that
> was . . . like *Miami Vice,* something in that style that I
> like. I wanted to do these things that were a chance to do
> this *chi chi chi* . . . capturing what I've seen for I don't
> know how many years of American cinema . . . the angle
> of the camera, the lighting, these hard contrasts, all
> of this.[11]

Though ostensibly about the efficiency of the modern Sandinista Police,
the film takes off into pure stylization in a nighttime chase and shootout in
"downtown" Managua that is so realistic that the cameraman, Frank Pineda,
was actually wounded when someone forgot to put blanks in the guns.[12] After
the triumph, the FSLN separated police and army functions, placing them in

separate Ministries, that of the Interior and the Defense, respectively. The FSLN prided itself on revolutionizing the police department, now dedicated to criminal, not political, matters (though special units of the Ministry of the Interior were established for internal security). The film's title conveys the new police's official role, to safeguard the people.[13]

First, the film portrays the new police's rigorous training. A credit sequence is constructed around police directing traffic, and modern police equipment, including a communications center and forensic laboratory. A training sequence covers physical instruction, such as guiding police dogs over barriers, and carefully explains responsibilities to attentive young students. Emphasizing these changes makes sense in the context of Somoza's brutal Guardia. Somoza kept the Guardia isolated, systematically severing their human ties to ensure absolute loyalty, inhibit sympathy for victims, and reinforce their terrifying mystique.

Marín may have realized that an account of antiseptic police training had dramatic limitations, for in the opening he inserts moving-camera night shots of cruising police cars. These shots parallel the daytime tracking shots gliding past rows of students in the classroom, but they also introduce a potential narrative—patrol cars searching for criminal activity on Managua's dark streets. Once three students receive diplomas at an official ceremony, the story can leave the school and concentrate on the evening's events.

Their car radio directs three young officers to a specific street and a probable armed assault. A man greets them at the gate to the house, identifying himself as a member of the CDS. Fortunately, a female Volunteer Police member (in uniform) has noticed three men driving a car and told the police. The first officer enters the house, gun drawn, and he discovers a corpse. Almost immediately, the house is swarming with forensic experts, painstakingly collecting blood samples and fingerprints and even tracing a chalk outline of the body.

Meanwhile, control central calls all patrols to look for the men and car described by the witness. One patrol locates the car and reports its location, "in the rubble, from the Margot Cinema, two blocks toward the lake, one up." Soon after, they locate the criminals, "donde fue el palacio de Justicia" (where the Ministry of Justice used to be). These directions confer an unmistakable authenticity, for they are immediately identifiable by Nicaraguans as uniquely from Managua. With few street names, Managua addresses are given in relation to (more or less) familiar local landmarks, which can be as modest as "the little tree." While this system is not unique to Managua (or Nicaragua), what is unique is the phrase "donde fue," for that designation refers to landmarks that existed only before the big Managua earthquake— in 1972! Hence, the policeman informs control central that the three crimi-

*Steel-trap efficiency of Sandinista Police (*Los centinelas de la alegría del pueblo*)*

nals have holed up where the Palace of Justice used to be, now just another gutted building littering the desolate landscape of downtown Managua.

Marín chose this site for its irony, but also as a perfect set for a spectacular gunfight. With spotlights, the police request reinforcements and deploy them outside the building. Several high-angle shots spot the thieves counting their booty as the police tighten the cordon to flush them out. With police affecting stances indistinguishable from those seen on *Miami Vice,* a Sandinista shooter hits the gun of a thief. But the final coup de theatre takes place on what looks like a proscenium, with a door in the center and two decaying stone staircases flanking it. In long shot, the last criminal rushes out with a gun, and the police converge on him from two sides and disarm him; everyone freezes; cut. The implacable Sandinista Police have served justice and honored their commitment to protecting "the tranquility of the city" (according to the script).

By the climax, the sober schoolroom has become a mere pretext for a dramatic chase. Marín clearly indulges his excitement about fiction with shots of flashing police lights and sirens. At one point he devotes an entire sequence to a parade of eight police cars speeding to the crime scene, the camera filters turning the flashing lights into electric sparklers. Once deployed around the building, seen in several high-angle shots, the police advance methodically, the inexorable movement of Sandinista justice. Exploiting the location and the lights, Marín throws large shadows of the "actors" sliding mysteriously across the crumbling walls, the shadows sometimes preceding their owners in the shot. Probably, these sequences lacked the ideological depth of the Ministry of the Interior's own video work, but the cinematic sophistication and bravura of Marín's film highlighted the amateurishness of the MINT's fictional productions.

In effect, Marín took on the noticiero assignment and made it a fiction workshop. He had been moving in this direction (as with the staged reconstructions of *A los héroes y mártires de Monimbó*, the 1821 declaration of independence in *Jornada anti-intervencionista*). Working with the Ministry of the Interior again may have given him confidence to experiment, assuming the MINT was pleased with his recent noticiero on the prison system (*Generosos en la victoria*). Marín's GPP background (and continuing respect for the GPP, as evidenced in the graffito from *La defensa política*) corresponded to the orientation of the people around Tomás Borge at the MINT. And fiction was in the air, with Rafael Vargas beginning the long process of transforming his noticiero into fiction (*Manuel*/Noticiero 40), and other directors eager to take the plunge.

Iván Argüello's next film filled the noticiero mold to perfection, representing perhaps the acme of noticiero production, and received a number

Melodramatic atmosphere of Sandinista Police closing in on criminals (*Los centinelas de la alegría del pueblo*)

Breaking the Mold: New Noticieros

A Miskito boy singing in Miskito to open and close Rompiendo el silencio

of international awards. Following the recent pattern, *Rompiendo el silencio* (June 1984) was a coproduction with the national telephone company, TELCOR. A brigade of TELCOR workers volunteered to extend telephone service to remote parts of the Atlantic coast. In addition to the difficulties of cutting through the jungle, the brigade also faced contra attacks, for the contra concentrated its assaults on precisely such social services. *Rompiendo* documents the final push to reach a Miskito village.

The film accomplishes what many others fell short of aesthetically. Eager to promote government policies, the noticieros often forced some official line on the films. Argüello eschewed voice-over commentary, for he wanted the images to carry the film. There is relatively little speech in *Rompiendo*, though the film's theme is the transportation of speech. Aside from a few words spoken over the telephone or sung, only brigade members speak in the film, without government representatives or spokespeople.

Speech, however, does open the film. A young boy sings in Miskito, which conveys the film's setting in Miskito territory somewhere on the Atlantic coast and puts Miskito onto a noticiero sound track for the first time. The film also has a Miskito title, printed below the Spanish title in the opening credits.[14] A zoom-out reveals the open space of the community. Argüello cuts abruptly to workers, Kalyshnakovs slung over shoulders, slashing away at the dense growth of a forest with machetes, clearing the space. Only the percussive rhythm of machetes can be heard. After several shots, one worker describes the project in physical terms, with no obvious political subtext. They are extending communication on the Atlantic coast, one line from Rosita to Siuna (two mining towns), one from Rosita to Bonanza (towns 32 kilometers apart), and so on. Several other workers add more background information. They never claim the project for FSLN glory. The last worker explains why he worked in the brigade: "Right now to me it's important that all of Nicaragua—including the most distant corners, the furthest mountain—be in constant communication, in the Pacific region and the Atlantic."

After a fade-out, night falls and the workers return to a barracks. The camera tracks past the workers singing folk songs and eating dinner, bunched together on their bunks, with no dining table. No one arrives with orders for the next day's work, nor is there the forced camaraderie of a summer-camp songfest. Various small groups talk among themselves, with one worker saying,

> All of us who take part in this project see ourselves as brothers, you see, we see each other in our difficult times, in happy times, and we live everything together. So, under the same roof, like this, our barracks, and we work together in the field, we see each other all the time. The relations among the compañeros are very fraternal. Apart from various jokes that are a part of our humor.

For the following day's work, Argüello found a way to represent—cinematically—this fraternalism. At dawn, several armed brigadistas leave for defense duty. Then, with no speaking, Argüello mounts a five-minute sequence of coordinated collective work, whether lifting and carrying heavy trees in unison, movements cut to the rhythm of the physical exertions, cutting back and forth between distant spots connected by shouts of the team, or pulling a zoom back from a boat carrying a telephone line across a river as the line rises triumphantly from the water. The workers discuss their tasks. The crisp editing matches, or creates, a powerful sense of teamwork, efficiency, organization, and morale. Though they are working hard with machetes, the cutting transforms the work into a well-oiled machine, the human parts harmonizing physically and psychologically, the successful work taking shape on the screen, as the telephone poles rise majestically against the sky and the wires stretch across cleared space and descend to a village in the distance below.

This passage of the film incarnates the noblest hopes, aspirations, and successes of the revolution. The workers, in their own words, identifiably Nicaraguan in rhythm and aural punctuation (pues ... pues ... pues ...), describe their experience as volunteers. No official voice sanctions their words or robs their speech of its poetic autonomy. Rather than describing the fraternal bonds of the workers, the editing shows the bonds formally. The sounds of the work cut together with the images highlight the quiet but firm revolutionary commitment of the brigadistas, not as an abstraction, but as the successful construction of something lasting and beneficial for the workers and for the recipients, the Miskito villagers.

Once the telephone line reaches the village, the film comes full circle. From a small telephone office, an operator tries to get a connection for a Miskito man waiting with the phone. When the line comes through, the man begins chattering in Miskito, and Argüello returns to the opening scene, the rousing song heard earlier carrying forward the excitement of the accomplishment. But this time he reverses the zoom's direction. Just as the telephone line has brought the Miskito village, the Atlantic coast closer—to the Pacific, to the present, to the revolution—so the zoom-in brings the audience closer to the Miskito village, a powerful coda ending with the young boy again bursting into song, in Miskito, as the credits roll, and finally the FSLN slogan of 1984: After 50 years . . . Sandino lives.

Though only Argüello's second noticiero, *Rompiendo el silencio* succeeds in accomplishing what INCINE noticieros had been seeking since the beginning. Without mentioning the FSLN, without FSLN representatives speaking, *Rompiendo shows* what the revolution means, and *represents* an accomplishment of the revolution. The film shows an effort to reach a marginal group, already alienated by the invasive treatment of the FSLN on the Atlantic coast, an attitude that drove many into armed opposition to the FSLN. The telephone can bring the Miskitos into the national "territory" without displacing them or disturbing their traditional ways of life. Furthermore, the film opens and closes in the Miskito language, an early source of tension between the FSLN and the Miskito population, for the Literacy Campaign initially failed to use Miskito in its plans, which the Miskitos saw as another paternalistic and insensitive Spanish, colonial effort to "improve" them. The film assumes that the Miskitos would welcome breaking this historical silence. However, the director Argüello said that the Miskitos were hostile during production, although the Sumos and Ramas offered help.[15]

The film's title plays on this tension but also has more specific connotations. In one sense, the silence never existed, for the Miskitos were constantly speaking. The FSLN did not hear, or did not understand. The telephone line breaks the communications isolation of the coast and facilitates the passage of Miskito language to the Pacific. But the phrase also evokes the victorious FSLN assault on the home of "Chema" Castillo in 1974, emblematically ending the period known in FSLN mythology as the "years of

*Bringing the telephone to the Miskitos (*Rompiendo el silencio*)*

silence."[16] Almost ten years later, the FSLN has finally awakened to the needs of the Miskitos, and INCINE has returned to the terrain after more than three years of silence.

Earlier noticieros had eliminated the comandantes' speeches but hadn't discovered new ways to communicate FSLN goals. INCINE was torn between its status as a government entity (within the Ministry of Culture) and a group of young middle-class bohemian artists trying to support the revolution with personal expression. In *Rompiendo el silencio*, Iván Argüello found a new way to express support for the revolution. *Rompiendo* foregrounds Miskito as the central language by placing it at the beginning and the end, as well as including the film's title in Miskito at the beginning. But there is no patronizing celebration of unsullied exotic "native" culture. The brigadistas want to extend a service to the Miskitos on the Atlantic coast in order to break down the physical—and cultural—barriers that divide the country.

Most important, however, is the way the film's editing captures the brigadistas' teamwork. The FSLN direction of the revolution evoked fears about collectivizations and coercion. The Agrarian Reform pressured agricultural labor into unfamiliar forms of collective work, whether turning agricultural laborers into state workers on state farms, pegging terms of credit to the degree of cooperativization, or restricting land titling to the cooperative movement. Worker testimony about the benefits of cooperatives could suggest state pressure (though the pressure was economic, not physical). In *Rom-*

*Teamwork of volunteer telephone brigade (*Rompiendo el silencio*)*

piendo, volunteers who work for TELCOR make a commitment out of revolutionary belief, without material incentives.[17] They choose to work and live in the middle of the jungle for months. Argüello breaks their work into parts; sometimes many lift a tree, sometimes brigadistas work in tandem, aligning telephone poles. In both cases, the editing captures the collective spirit, yielding aesthetic pleasure in its own right, linked to the brigade's coordination.

Of course one might edit sequences on a cooperative in a similar manner, but in that case a state/party interest would lie behind the editing, making it a sterile exercise. Technique alone cannot ensure political persuasiveness, nor can simplicity guarantee authenticity. *Rompiendo el silencio* succeeds by finding an adequate and supple form for a convincing political project, which resonates at the local level and more broadly at the level of government relations with the Miskitos. On the ideological battleground, Miskito militants fighting the government could not indict the TELCOR project as another wound imposed by the FSLN. The TELCOR project's neutrality made it an effective ideological and artistic means of repairing the early government errors.

For *La ceiba, autodefensa* (August 1983), directed by Marín, INCINE worked with UNAG to tackle pressing issues in the countryside. The earlier noticieros reflected the revolution's oft-noted urban bias; few films presented the campesinos' problems in detail. References to the Agrarian Reform mentioned the campesinos, and they were seen illustrating Sandinista speeches, but no film placed the camera inside campesino life from beginning to end. Jaime Wheelock had visited state farms (Noticiero 7); Ernesto Cardenal, sitting on his comfortable veranda, extolled the richness of campesino culture (Noticiero 22); and Marín traced the contributions of "los innovadores" to the campesinos' simple technology (Noticiero 33); but campesino life played mainly an illustrative role. Campesinos, of course, always figured in the FSLN's plans. As far back as 1969, the Historic Program of the FSLN included Agrarian Reform and a worker-peasant alliance.[18] Immediately after the triumph in 1979, the Junta nationalized Somocista land with the idea of transforming it into the "motor of the revolution" with the establishment of large state farms, and the state provided many services to campesinos—particularly those in cooperatives—virtually throwing credit at them, and later forgiving the debt.

But with the welcome changes came problems. Intervening in the agricultural sector shattered traditional customs. Suddenly an inefficient state bureaucracy replaced the usurious but knowledgeable *compadrazgo*, a middleman "godfather" who could loan money on the spot or find transportation for crops before they rotted in the fields.[19] The peasantry had learned to distrust the government over many years. When the government changed, the peasantry did not shed its distrust. While the government trumpeted agrarian reform, it barred land seizures.

The contra war aggravated and exploited these tensions. Contras concentrated attacks on health clinics, schools, cooperatives—all new improvements in rural life. The contras could also rely on the Somoza legacy of deep anticommunism among the peasantry, many of whom fled the expansion of agri-business during the preceding decades in order to preserve some independence while scraping together hard lives on less fertile land.

The contras' success in disrupting the campesinos' already difficult lives provoked government responses that sometimes made things worse. Military defense became paramount, and defense against the contras required large manpower resources, in regular army and militias, in addition to training. When the military deemed defense unfeasible, it recommended relocating communities to safer terrain. Thus, the war imposed hardships on a population not necessarily predisposed to making sacrifices for the Sandinistas. Hence the Sandinistas emphasized nationalism and defending national sovereignty against foreign aggression, although the contra foot soldiers came from the same Nicaraguan rural population. In the opening shot of *La ceiba*, a man with a rifle bangs on a piece of hanging metal to summon villagers: "Militias forming. Four columns. Close ranks. Line up for the front [line]." As the credits roll, the scene shifts to a small boat gliding along the

Rio Coco along the Honduran border. Marín then drops the militia and fills in the village's background, finally restoring the frame at the end of the film as the four columns receive their orders for the day. Once the camera leaves the boat, moves through the forest, and arrives at a village, the first shots show young children reciting with a teacher; one shot pans from a soldier to the students. As the introduction unrolls, a voice-over describes contra attacks that forced the community to move in 1982:

> Afterward they took us to a Miskito village, where we stayed three months, after which we left for here, La Ceiba. The last day of November 1982 the Front gave us this land and with the help of the district [government], we built a house, a cooperative and we began to work. In December of this year, we have fifty families living here in this settlement.

The commentaries and interviews—all by and with men—lay out the government's position. Contra attacks threaten lives and crops, so villages must be moved to consolidate defense and protect the food supply. Once relocated, the population is organized into cooperatives, explained by a villager:

> In this cooperative, the work is done collectively, what one does, all do. We plant what we harvest; it is for everyone. For example, if one person has to stand guard, the others work in the field and then the other does guard duty and we work in the field by turns. Then what we harvest in the work we eat ourselves, and the rest we sell and what we get from the receipts is distributed in equal parts to every member of the cooperative. But in order to be able to bring in the harvest we have to work armed to prevent attacks by the Chilotes [contras].

Nonetheless, La Ceiba is no utopia. Neither images nor sounds hide the hardships. The man who gives the background also expresses hopes for another permanent home, under "more comfortable and better conditions." After the vice-president of the cooperative notes the lack of medicine, another voice-over elaborates:

> This community, the problem of health is key. Above all with the children who are the ones who suffer most from

the climate and because the makeshift housing doesn't protect them adequately . . . from the rain and this makes the children sick in the throat and chest, see? To cure them sometimes we have to take them away from here, as far as Wily . . . and sometimes it's difficult, for we have petitioned the Ministry of Health, but until now we have nothing concrete.

These complaints reflect poorly on the government, so publicly committed to child welfare. Similarly, *La ceiba* does not celebrate any official organizations, whether the comandantes and the FSLN or the peasant mass organization UNAG, which sponsored the film. After the initial credits, UNAG appears only once in the sound track of the film.

To judge by this film, the contra bases are located on the other side of the Río Coco, in Honduras. The last shot of the film shows a militia soldier seated on a hill above the Río Coco looking toward Honduras. This coincides with the government's characterization of contra aggression as a foreign-directed and -supported military interference in Nicaragua. That characterization was largely accurate. But it was simultaneously true that contra groups recruited members within Nicaragua and found local support.

La ceiba, then, while supportive of government-mandated population transfers, relies on local participants to tell the story, as in Marín's earlier *El maestro popular* and *Los innovadores*. In *La ceiba*, Marín sets his camera up for interviews, with daily activities, like washing clothes in a stream, seen clearly in mid-background. The women performing manual chores do not speak, but Marín nonetheless includes them in the visual representation of the community. Later, cooperative members hack away at crops with machetes as they construct underground shelters for protection against contra artillery. Marín may have wanted to capture the physical aspects of his subjects' lives. That commitment may have fostered a more open, less confined aural style at the same time. Consequently, as the filmmakers pushed against the confines of the noticiero, some films represented qualitative leaps forward beyond the rough, early noticieros.

Fernando Somarriba's *Río San Juan—a este lado de la puerta* represents the first fully realized break with the standard pattern of noticiero production. Its production extended from July to September 1983, longer than the normal one month for preproduction, filming, and postproduction. The film also includes a flashback to two months earlier. A flashback filmed within a noticiero virtually explodes the premise that a noticiero covers current events. The film lasts over 20 minutes, three times the length of some early noticieros and more than twice the length of most others.

Though it has a muted feel, *Río San Juan*, like *La ceiba*, addresses the problem of relocating whole communities in response to contra aggression. Beginning with the cowbell call to militia duty, *La ceiba* sounds a military note, stressing self-defense. *Río San Juan* provides a more supple structure, filling in the region's history since the sixteenth century and identifying the dominant foreign threat since the nineteenth century as North American imperialism.

Instead of presenting the population transfer as beyond discussion, *Río San Juan* includes a general meeting at which residents pose practical questions about relocation and express fears about debts and crops. Recording these anxieties acknowledges that government policies impose hardships on the campesinos. *Río San Juan* tries to justify the fiat. The transfer will proceed whether the campesinos agree or not, but the film does not imply that everyone accepts this. Many campesinos objected to disrupting their own lives for reasons that were not their fault.

Somewhat awkwardly, *Río San Juan* describes gains delivered to the campesinos by the revolution. Prompted by an offscreen request to "speak a little about what the education is like," one campesino praises the literacy teachers and health care. For each response to his questions, Somarriba inserts shots of the school and health center. FSLN strategy was built around this exchange. If campesinos formed cooperatives, the FSLN would improve their education and health services. The campesinos would lose the freedom to sell their produce to any buyer, though that had often meant accepting terms dictated by a single monopsonistic buyer. The FSLN offered what it felt was a fair trade-off: Campesinos might receive less cash for their products, but new services would more than compensate. The FSLN gambled that campesinos would see this themselves. Ultimately, for complicated reasons, the FSLN lost this gamble. But they did not understand this failure for some time. Hence, the government and the filmmakers advanced what they hoped were persuasive arguments, not realizing that many campesinos were not converted.

On some level the film perceives the need for rhetorical argument. The revolution hadn't solved the country's problems overnight, or over the decade. In many ways, material conditions deteriorated. Real wages fell, prices paid to campesinos were kept low, manufactured goods were scarce in the countryside, etc. Yet the government heavily subsidized social services proudly displayed in *Río San Juan*. Cinematically, these inserts recall the officialist illustrations from the early noticieros, rigidly touting FSLN policies.

But unlike the rhetorical fait accompli of an already constructed community shown in *La ceiba*, *Río San Juan* approaches policy as an ongoing process. Formally, the flashback marks time passing, with clear transitions as the image goes in and out of focus. The title "Two months earlier" quantifies the amount of time. Secondly, the film allots many shots to clearing the ground, splitting fronds with machetes and weaving them into roofs, securing with rope the joints of the buildings, preparing food for the community. Relocation requires hard work; the film doesn't disguise this. If audiences had to be convinced to move, they would immediately think of the physical ardors involved. They would also think of crops and working conditions in the new location. The general meeting provides a forum for voicing those concerns. While the filmmakers of earlier noticieros learned to replace the upbeat discourses of military-clad comandantes with the campesinos' more authentic and halting cadences, those campesinos had been chosen to testify to the benefits of FSLN agrarian policy. In the general meeting of *Río San Juan*, campesinos express real fears. Admittedly, the film muffles those fears with the uniformed government representative's speech. He allays their concerns satisfactorily, so the film does not question the policy's wisdom. But the film is transitional and a dry run for Somarriba's highly controversial later film on the problematic of the Miskitos (*Los hijos del río*; see chapter 9) and their forced move to Tasba Pri.

For its final noticiero, INCINE essentially hired itself out to the newly formed Supreme Electoral Council to produce a film on the first election in Sandinista Nicaragua. Two of the first noticieros had broached the topic of elections when the FSLN spoke of participatory democracy. When the FSLN avoided holding elections for several years, the United States called this a betrayal of the people and a violation of the government's promise in 1979.[20] Eventually, the FSLN decided to hold elections, hoping to alleviate the pressures of the war, the embargo, and the scarcity of international loans. The FSLN understood that tainted elections would tarnish them, and they invited a wide spectrum of international observers to legitimize one of the most-observed elections in history.

Once the Nicaraguan government agreed to elections, the United States' true concerns became clearer. In February 1984, the government announced that elections for president and the legislature would be held on November 4, 1984. The Council of State passed election rules, including registration periods, access to media, etc. U.S.-backed candidates immediately raised objections. After indicating that he would run, Arturo Cruz, the primary candidate supported by the United States, withdrew at the last minute, apparently with the approval of, if not under the order of, the United States (later revealed to have been paying Cruz $10,000 per month during this period). Another conservative, Virgilio Godoy, also backed out, causing a split in his party.

The title of the noticiero on the elections indicates the position of the film: *Nicaragua ganó* (*Nicaragua Won,* Oct. 1984–Jan. 1985). By holding elections, the *nation* has won, having proven its democratic credentials. Furthermore, the introductory FSLN hymn is never heard, but the Nicaraguan national anthem is heard for the first time in the entire noticiero cycle. Daniel Ortega's inauguration ceremony on January 10 opens and closes the film. In between, participating parties, left and right of the victorious FSLN, get screen time. For the most part, the presidential candidates, including Arturo Cruz, speak. At the huge FSLN rally concluding the campaign, Daniel Ortega accurately, if polemically, attributes the withdrawal of some (Cruz and Godoy) to a decision by the United States. Ortega asks the massive outdoor audience if elections should be postponed to accommodate the demands of nonparticipants. The crowd repeatedly chants "poder popular" ("popular power") as the camera pans past hundreds of thousands of celebrants.

Once the parties have spoken, the film moves on. Several voters outside polling places endorse the elections. Afterwards, foreign electoral observers (from Mexico and England) compare their experiences observing elections in many countries and affirm the success of the Nicaraguan elections. Despite the opposition's carping, virtually all of the observers ratified the orderliness and fairness of the elections (balloting was disrupted by contra attacks in seven locations in the north of the country).[21]

With 67 percent of the votes, the FSLN won both executive posts and as well as control over the new legislature. That legislature, however, no longer included seats for the mass organizations, the rhetorical and institutional bedrock of the claims about participatory democracy. Inclusion of seats for the mass organizations in the Council of State in 1980 had provoked Robelo's resignation from the Junta of National Reconstruction. Given the association between representing the mass organizations and promoting participatory democracy (along with thinly veiled hostility to elections per se), the FSLN's eliminating representation of the mass organizations could appear to replace popular power with bourgeois democracy. Despite the FSLN's progressive spin on elections, resorting to elections to "demonstrate" democracy contrasted sharply with their previous position.

Similarly, *Nicaragua ganó* is a sort of reductio ad absurdum of the newsreel form. At 26 minutes, it is the longest noticiero. *Nicaragua ganó* wasn't timely news. Voices of ordinary people are drowned out by party officials. This time political parties get a chance to bore audiences. Once again, the film ignores difficult election issues, specifically the charges of weighting the electoral process in favor of the FSLN *prior to* the elections. Certainly Nicaraguans could see various biases at work—government trucks brought

FSLN supporters to rallies, and FSLN candidates were allotted disproportionate time on the government television. The report of the U.S. academic
group, Latin American Scholars Association (LASA), acknowledged that the
government in power enjoyed privileges but viewed these advantages as normal perquisites of incumbency, whether in Latin America or the United
States.[22] Rather than responding to the charges, the film elides them, cham-
pioning only the feat of holding successful elections.

Then again, the Supreme Electoral Council picked up the bills. With the
scarcity of internal INCINE funds for production (salaries were still being
paid by the Ministry of Culture), filmmakers sought funds where they could,
such as from the government ministries. The recently formed Supreme Electoral Council contracted with INCINE for the film, and according to director
Fernando Somarriba, the council wanted the film completed and released
quickly.[23]

In some ways, then, *Nicaragua ganó* is a lame-duck noticiero. The noticieros no longer had a future. Somarriba probably finished it as quickly as
possible. Touching noncontroversial bases, the film passes by topics that
might have encouraged viewers to think more deeply about the implications
of suffrage or glimpse the rifts splitting the country, and in particular the
countryside.

By late 1984, *Nicaragua ganó* was not relevant to the questions people
confronted in their daily lives. The vote ratified popular confidence in the
FSLN, but *Nicaragua ganó* did not respect its audience or argue for the value
of elections, which, according to the FSLN, were imposed from without.
While this objection is applicable to many noticieros, they had been improving over time, and films such as Somarriba's own *Río San Juan,* Marín's
Centinelas, or Argüello's *Rompiendo el silencio* demonstrated both political
and aesthetic strides. The filmmakers hoped to make more ambitious and experimental films, though still within the FSLN political orbit. The first directors' "graduation" to documentaries suggested a possible trajectory. But the
second (Somarriba and Marín) and third (Argüello) generations transformed
the noticieros into short documentaries with fictional elements. *Nicaragua ganó,* then, ended the noticiero cycle appropriately enough, as an arid
project without the energy provided by anticipation of future creative work
on noticieros.

Seven   DOCUMENTARIES

As the noticieros changed—in shape, length, ambition, and sponsorship—
bending their initial restrictions, the "veteran" filmmakers, those with two
years' experience, were starting documentaries. While the noticiero cycle
unfolded under the tutelage of Cuban advisers and followed the model of the
Cuban newsreels, the documentaries offer an opportunity to examine the
directions the filmmakers pursued with more creative latitude and the degree to which they manifest more personal styles that collective work on the
noticieros may have obscured.

As discussed in chapter 3, the first INCINE directors, Ramiro Lacayo,
María José Alvarez, and Rafael Vargas, completed documentaries in 1981.
The agreement with ICAIC projected an annual production of three to four
short documentary films each year, shot in 16-mm color. Longer production
schedules for documentaries enabled the filmmakers to consider subjects
at greater length with less topical pressure. The same three directors dominated the next group of documentaries as well, as second- and third- generation filmmakers assumed greater responsibility for the noticieros during
1982 and 1983.

Bananeras

After completing *Del águila al dragón* late in 1981, Ramiro
Lacayo decided to make *Bananeras* in 1982, a film about the banana plantations in the Pacific region, near the port of Corinto. Though the Standard
Fruit Company owned and operated banana interests in the country, Nicaragua was not precisely a banana republic. Foreign capital figured prominently in the banana industry, but bananas occupied a relatively minor part
of Nicaraguan exports.[1] After the 1979 victory, the new government signed

a five-year agreement with Standard Fruit. The government assumed control over banana production and Standard Fruit took over responsibility for transportation, export, and marketing of the bananas; Standard Fruit broke this agreement in October 1982 after the film was completed.

Bananeras contrasts the reality of the workers' plight with excerpts from Somoza newsreels. The bright, cheery Somoza footage describes how technology will improve efficiency. Somoza visits a new packing plant with mechanized processing, cleaning, and packaging of bananas, before showing the port where cranes hoist boxes of bananas to waiting ships. The film intercuts this black-and-white archival material with color shots of a man hauling a cable attached to his waist leading to a large mass of bananas suspended from an overhead wire in the trees. This repetitive and backbreaking task recurs throughout the film, clearly contradicting the claims of modernization made by the Somoza newsreels. The workers recount details of the work; offscreen, Lacayo sounds astonished by the revelations, as he asks why the hauling can't be done by mule or machine.

The workers never refer to union organizing or the role of the pro-FSLN Central Sandinista de Trabajadores (CST). Nor does the film cite new laws about minimum wages or worker management of state-run farms and businesses. The Sandinistas worked with two labor organizations before the triumph. These were officially recognized by the new government in 1980 when the Council of State included seats for the industrial workers and agricultural workers, represented by the CST and the Asociación de Trabajadores del Campo (ATC). In the early years after the triumph, the CST organized the banana workers and apparently obtained gains for them.[2] But the CST represented urban industrial workers, factory workers. The workers in *Bananeras*, cutting and hauling the bananas in the fields, perform manual work and the film emphasizes the *lack* of mechanization as an implicit criticism of the company. Even more significantly, the workers often supplemented their wages with individual farming plots, and most were from peasant backgrounds. The ambiguity of class identity was recognized officially in 1986 when the ATC replaced the CST as the labor representative for the workers "since banana workers had more in common with seasonal agricultural workers than with urban factory laborers."[3] Thus, Sandinista developmental strategy prioritized the importance of industrialization and sometimes imposed an industrialization perspective where it did not apply.

Similarly, the film ignores the plantations' gender dichotomy. Men work in the fields, ostensibly the heavier work requiring more skill and returning higher wages; women wash and load bananas in the packing plant. The Sandinista revolution wanted to reduce gender differentials, but a 1983 study found that gender segregation remained the norm and was a source of re-

*Back-breaking manual work of banana workers (*Bananeras*)*

sentment by women.[4] This evidence on the screen elicits no comment from the filmmaker(s).

Politically, then, *Bananeras* exposes the superexploitation of the banana workers under Somoza but fails to provide any worker or government response to this inequity. Speaking about the film years later, Lacayo said he was aware of the ambivalence in the film regarding the hesitation to criticize the FSLN, on the one hand, and the implicit criticism on the other.[5]

The 16-minute *Bananeras* resembles *La otra cara del oro* in its exposure of the legacy of the Somoza period, but it has a confused political analysis and a less assured aesthetic strategy. *La otra cara del oro* dealt with an isolated, remote area in the Atlantic region in which several foreign countries operated an enclave economy.[6] That is, Vargas's film functioned as an accusatory obituary, for the companies have left, and the workers ravaged by injury and disease remain to testify to the human devastation, while the haunting coda dramatizes the ecological ruin left behind. The absent companies emerge as obvious villains. *Bananeras* confronted a different situation, for the banana plantations were still operating and were government-run. Thus, the appalling conditions documented by the film can be attributed to practices introduced during the Somoza period in the 1970s, but the persistence of those conditions two years after the revolution creates a strange dissonance. While the new government could not solve such problems overnight, the specific problems cited and illustrated are precisely what government economic planning aspired to address.

The construction of *Bananeras* implies both that the filmmakers did not understand Sandinista development strategy and that they seemed barely conscious of the negative associations that the film could authorize. The film's indifference to labor organizing and union affiliation marks the filmmakers as outsiders without sensitivity to the policy issues involved. Do men and women in the film see themselves as campesinos [peasants] or obreros [literally, workers]? Do they belong to a union, do they know if they belong to a union, do they know which union? Can they live on their wages, or must they supplement wages with subsistence farming? Is the union adequately representing them?

La otra cara del oro could ignore these questions, for the companies left the country in a scorched earth policy. The abandoned workers belong to an alien world, vacant eyes staring into emptiness as their voices wheeze from ruined lungs. The film constructs these men as witnesses, in a litany of faces flashing on the screen, in the X-rays of lungs shimmering as inorganic shadows, in the pointless march of a one-armed miner toward the camera. Resonant with horror, these images sculpt historical memory, reminding audiences of Somoza's dictatorship.

Bananeras used techniques similar to the ones in *La otra cara del oro*, such as the sequence of the living quarters, rag-clad urchins running about, and an emaciated dog nosing in a pail swarming with flies, but these are images of the present, the Sandinista era, surely an unintended result. With more research, with deeper analysis, the filmmakers could have critically and sympathetically examined labor questions, worker participation in management councils, and the role of wage incentives in getting higher productivity from the workforce. As late as 1994, Lacayo, himself scion of a large sugar-growing family, claimed total ignorance of the debates roiling the agrarian sector and the agrarian reform bureaucracy.[7] Like Vargas, Lacayo wanted to develop his art; unlike Vargas, Lacayo was constrained by political concerns, both as head of INCINE and as an FSLN militant. Vargas fashioned his aesthetic efforts according to his humanistic vision without partisan commitments. *Bananeras,* set in the Pacific region, habitat of the Sandinistas, cannot present a horrific past sealed off from the present by the triumph of the revolution.

In fact, the issues in *Bananeras* represented challenges for INCINE. How could the filmmakers consolidate support for the revolution while acknowledging persistent problems? Could they develop an independent critical voice without endangering their financial and institutional support or their potential to reach and affect audiences? Finding a balance when the country was under a State of Emergency (decreed March 14, 1982) and in constant fear of military attacks, or even a U.S. invasion, was obviously not an easy matter.

While the filmmakers say they had freedom from political interference, a document in INCINE's archives suggests that Ramiro Lacayo may sometimes have had to look over his shoulder. In a letter dated November 24, 1982, on official FSLN Dirección Nacional stationery, Comandante of the Revolution Carlos Nuñez wrote to Vice-Minister of Culture Francisco Lacayo about (Ramiro) Lacayo's recently completed *Bananeras:*

> In this documentary, part of the history of the FSLN is shown, in addition to the situation of the Bananeras and some passages where Somoza appears returning to the country and being received by the Somocista Guardia [Nacional]. The point is that these two parts have led the audience to respond with applause.
>
> I believe that INCINE should review the content of the documentary in question, and also verify once more the information that was conveyed to me. (See Appendix for copy of original letter.)

Such a communication could only have a chilling effect on INCINE's artistic freedom, though Lacayo may have kept these pressures to himself. In fact, he maintained that in the ten years he was with INCINE, he "was totally free and independent."[8]

Various filmmakers complained about cuts imposed on their films. The evidence, however, does not point to political considerations but rather to conflicting interests of the filmmakers themselves. In one example, Fernando Somarriba bitterly objected to the removal of archival footage of Somoza from his *La cultura,* asserting that Lacayo seized the material for his own film, *Bananeras,* which likely was true. In the full version of the original print found in the INCINE archives, *La cultura* indeed does begin with newsreel footage of Somoza and the bourgeois elite attending cultural events and parties, providing effective documentation of Cardenal's opening comments about Nicaraguan culture previously confined to a tiny elite. Lacayo uses footage of Somoza touring the banana-processing plants. Somarriba's accusation corresponds to charges voiced by many about Lacayo's peremptory manner and arbitary decision making.

Pan y dignidad

As the war intensified during 1982, repercussions reverberated throughout the society, including INCINE. War preparation was a central theme in María José Alvarez's second documentary, *Pan y dignidad:*

Carta abierta de Nicaragua [*Bread and Dignity: Open Letter from Nicaragua*] (1982). Alvarez says that finding successful structures for her films is always a problem. Though the 30-minute *Pan y dignidad* is no exception, sometimes this difficulty had virtues. While the Nicaraguan filmmakers adopted the Cuban model, Alvarez was the first to break with this pattern. She understood the pitfalls of letting the commandants' rhetoric dominate and displace other discourses. Probably, Alvarez simply felt diffident about imposing structures. Her insistence that Johnny Henderson's editing helped shape the material confirms her unease with structure.[9] Given her accounts of the sexism operating at INCINE (particularly in the early years), Alvarez may have rejected a strong structure as political and/or artistic male posturing. She may have recoiled at the discourses of the male commandants, instead of being awed. She did not have administrative or bureaucratic ambitions that make respect for authorities a protocol.[10]

It is interesting to consider *Pan y dignidad* in this context. The subtitle itself, *Open Letter from Nicaragua*, announces a more personal discursive voice. Alvarez doesn't appear in the film, but her voice reads the "letter" on the sound track. The film mobilizes three separate discourses. As Alvarez explains, she is continuing an open letter by Sandino in 1929 to President Hoover in which he wrote: "Nicaragua does not owe a single penny to the United States, but you owe us the peace lost in our country since 1909, when the Wall Street bankers introduced the corrupting vice of the dollar in Nicaragua."[11]

The letter anchors Nicaraguan history in the struggle against the U.S. The struggle did not conclude with the 1979 triumph. Now the United States has again robbed the country of peace. The third discourse weaves through the other two: the role of women in the overthrow of Somoza, the problematic of women in military defense.

Alvarez begins with a lyrical opening sequence. A woman in close shot, wearing a scarf, picks cotton off the twigs between her face and the camera. Alvarez reads: "I want to tell a story. It's the story of my country. It's my people." Over shots of the countryside, Alvarez quotes poet Joaquín Pasos demanding that the Yankees get out of Nicaragua, a refrain picked up throughout the film: "Get out of here. Get out of here."[12] Nicaragua's land, fruit, and beauty are "only for us." As this introduction fades, the history unfolds, first with footage of U.S. troops landing in Nicaragua in 1909, followed by stills of Sandino and his army while Alvarez continues her commentary: "they are my heroes." After the titles, the Somoza era has begun, with footage of Guardia Nacional searching a bus and Somoza delivering a speech. Alvarez says that Nicaraguans never felt Somoza was Nicaraguan, "for us he was a foreigner . . . appearing on television speaking English." Then anti-

Somoza rallies are shown, footage of the insurrection, and a demonstration by AMPRONAC, the women's organization that preceded AMNLAE before the triumph. Here Alvarez wants to demonstrate women's participation in the revolutionary struggle. A musician plays a guitar intercut with shots of mourners. A cut from scenes of the guitar to those of loading a gun effects a transition to the formation and history of the FSLN. "The best men and women formed it."

These best men and women forced Somoza to flee Nicaragua, leading to the July 19 celebration as the combatants streamed into Managua. "It was the first time we were all together." Once victorious, the country turned to reconstruction, as people in the countryside work with machetes and city dwellers return paving stones ripped from the streets to build barricades. "No one told us to do it, but we felt ourselves owners of our own country. We felt Nicaragua as one big family."

This project continues with the 1980 Literacy Campaign, still in 1982 a symbol of the human potential of the Nicaraguan people. Alvarez had already made two previous noticieros about the Literacy Campaign (see chapter 2), which displayed the disproportionately high participation of women. Alvarez notes that the activity was not hierarchical, "not just teaching, but a meeting of the big family." Reinforcing women's role in the crusade, a woman teacher instructs an adult female student.

Having demonstrated women's importance in the revolution and in reconstruction, the film turns more didactic. Women in the market, women in the factories, and women in the squares express the desire to join the militia, for they have won the right to participate. They complain that men have prevented them from joining the militia; one man says single women should be welcome, but not married women. One woman holds her uniformed daughter's rifle. Alvarez states that Nicaraguan women want peace but points to increasingly belligerent U.S. actions through 1981 and 1982. Women are seen receiving mortar training, cleaning rifles, and preparing to defend the country, for "there were many women in the insurrection, many who fell." At this point Alvarez returns to the poem telling the Yankees to get out, but with a feminist twist. Sandino's widow appears, quoting her husband's defiant warning: "We'll die first, we'll die first. . . . We will not surrender."

Using an open letter as a formal device, and the first person both singular *and* plural, distinguishes *Pan y dignidad* from all other Nicaraguan films.[13] The woman's face in the first image of the film, and the concentration on women combine with the first-person voice-over to emphasize the filmmaker's identification with women's struggles. Alvarez presents women, including the women *organized* in AMPRONAC, as central participants in the revolution. Alvarez also supports women's participation in the country's defense. That debate is often cited to demonstrate the effectiveness of the mass organizations, or, more specifically, AMNLAE, the successor to AMPRONAC. The mass organizations were supposed to guarantee FSLN responsiveness to popular will. The FSLN could tap the peoples' creativity through the mass organizations. In practice, questions quickly arose about the mass organizations' autonomy and actual significance as brokers of "poder popular." There is little question that the mass organizations, except UNAG, saw their influence dissipate over time. Assessments of AMNLAE and other mass organizations are always relative. Typically, defenders acknowledge modest gains and find encouragement in women's participation in various debates. The FSLN made the final decision, but at least they listened to the organizations. Critics demand a concrete look at gains, find them perfunctory, and assail the subordination of the organizations to the FSLN's will. According to several commentators, military service for women is the test case for AMNLAE. AMNLAE fought for women's equal access to military service, but in 1983 the FSLN decided against the AMNLAE position.

Curiously, while lauding AMPRONAC's work before the triumph, the film does not refer to the recent formation of AMNLAE in late 1981. In other words, Alvarez unequivocally supports women but doesn't mention the only mass women's organization formed after the triumph. Here again, the evidence suggests a more voluntarist vision of political action, not through the party channels of a mass organization, but independent of them. This vision probably reflects INCINE's isolation, as discussed in earlier chapters. Also INCINE had its own separate premises, shielded from daily administrative oversight.[14] Finally, many observers, Nicaraguans and foreigners alike, have commented on INCINE's permanent disorder, an enclave of young bohemian Sandinistas on a long, frayed leash.[15]

In fact, *Pan y dignidad* comes closer to the mass organizations than most INCINE productions, for the problematic of women in the revolution was the raison d'être of AMNLAE. Though the film preceded the formal debate over the military draft, AMNLAE did successfully campaign for equal female participation in the militias, precisely the film's position. It may be that the film reproduces a common tendency to denigrate AMNLAE as an elite group of educated women with an agenda different from that of the FSLN. Alvarez may have shared this view or she may have preferred to sidestep the issue.

Nuestra Reforma Agraria

After the CDSs, the largest and most significant mass organizations represented the campesinos. However central the issues of national sovereignty, political pluralism and a mixed economy, economic reform and modernization, the revolution's success would depend on the success of the Agrarian Reform, "the most important chapter in the revolutionary agenda."[16] Hence, it is worth considering carefully the *only* major film devoted to the Agrarian Reform: *Nuestra Reforma Agraria*.

Though an unlikely choice for such a politically charged topic, Rafael Vargas directed the 33-minute film in 1982.[17] Never an FSLN member, Vargas avoided partisan matters, and agrarian reform was a topic for highly partisan policy discussion from the beginning. In poor agricultural countries, revolutionary change places a high priority on agricultural policy, and agrarian reforms are a staple of Latin American revolutionary movements. Since the countries' agricultural profiles differ considerably, agrarian reform comes in many varieties. The title, *Nuestra reforma agraria*, already suggests an emphasis on *Nicaragua's* Agrarian Reform, not a generic brand, nor a copy of another country's.[18]

Arguably, the Agrarian Reform offers a clear insight into Sandinismo's core tenets. Commentators could easily find citations to support many interpretations of the FSLN's "true" beliefs, for there were no fundamental FSLN texts.[19] Certainly Marxism's classic works never had the status they achieved in the Soviet Union and China. Sandino's written record could not provide solid theoretical guidance, nor could Carlos Fonseca's work. In a country dependent on agriculture, especially for the hard currency essential for development, how the FSLN approached questions of land ownership, planning, technology, and so on might clearly reveal the FSLN's "real" designs for Nicaragua's future.

Agrarian reform entails transforming agriculture from the exploitative conditions of the past. As Nicaragua did not have a tiny elite of large landowners operating enormous plots of land, but a large number of small peasant landholders, the agrarian reform could not simply reduce or eliminate large landholdings. The key decisions would revolve around how much land to take over and whether to use it for private or state farming. In Nicaragua, the government nationalized the land of Somoza and his closest business associates, most of whom had fled the country, but that early decree affected only 20 percent of the land under cultivation.[20]

Disposing of that land posed a key dilemma for Nicaragua's agricultural planners. Nicaragua earned most of its hard currency from agricultural exports and the related agro-processing industry. Those exports were mainly produced on relatively efficient large farms. The 20 percent of the land taken over by the state was primarily composed of such large estates (though their actual weight in export production was small.[21] Distributing the land to individual campesinos would result in lower export production, for campesinos would not choose to be salaried laborers if they had their own plots to raise food for consumption, marketing any surplus. Such withdrawal from export production would reduce export earnings and the investment potential for technological innovation. Hence, the FSLN decided to keep the nationalized land intact in large units of state farms producing for export.

The bias in favor of exports resulted from political as well as economic considerations. The FSLN included the patriotic bourgeoisie in the new revolutionary Nicaragua, even if the reasons behind this decision remain unclear. The FSLN probably had no consensual opinion on the ultimate role or fate of the bourgeoisie. What is clear is that the FSLN made no definitive move to eliminate the bourgeoisie as a group or class. Ultimately, the FSLN believed that the viability of revolutionary Nicaragua, at least in the medium term, depended on the participation of the patriotic bourgeoisie in the economic sphere, as the bourgeoisie held a virtual monopoly on technical knowledge and experience at all levels of the economy and government. The FSLN soon discovered the difficulty of managing the former Somocista enterprises; taking over additional technologically advanced agricultural properties would have overwhelmed their managerial and technical resources, and exacerbated the political tensions caused by the alienation and flight of qualified personnel.

In addition, export production required a salaried labor force to work on harvests. State farms shared this interest with the bourgeoisie; both the FSLN and the bourgeoisie needed an available, salaried labor force. Freeing land for individual farming might attract that labor force. If significant numbers of the salaried labor force, whether labeled semi-proletarian, proletarian, or sub-proletarian, *considered themselves or aspired to be (once again) campesinos*, then the land question could interfere with generating needed hard currency for industrial development through export production.[22]

An additional factor was the essentially urban profile of the FSLN. For the most part, the insurrection and war were urban phenomena.[23] In its overall orientation, the FSLN looked first to the urban centers for support. Among the mass organizations, the most powerful and most mass-based were probably the CDSs. The campesinos were numerically the largest category of the economically active population but had no mass organization representing their needs in the original FSLN structure. Initially, the rural workers association, the ATC, included wage laborers as well as campesinos, but the organization fought for the salaried workers, not the campesinos, who eventually formed UNAG in 1981 (though still in a subordinate position vis à vis the wealthier elements among rural producers).[24]

Agrarian reform went through three stages. On the day following the triumph, July 20, 1979, the government issued Decree No. 3 nationalizing

holdings of the Somoza family and their closest associates. This nationalization was largely completed by November. The Institute of Agrarian Reform
(INRA, later MIDINRA, Ministerio de Desarrollo Agropecuario y Reforma
Agraria), headed by Dirección Nacional member Jaime Wheelock, of the Proletarian Tendency, assumed responsibility for this land. MIDINRA either
managed the land as state farms or distributed land to farm cooperatives.[25]

In 1981 on the triumph's second anniversary, the government released the
Law of Agrarian Reform. The law did not extend expropriation of land per se,
but stipulated various conditions under which the state could take control
of land: abandonment, underutilization, and exorbitant rentals. Only farms
above specified sizes (for different regions and crops) were subject to these
conditions.[26] Large landowners could farm properties, following guidelines
on land rents to campesinos, drastically reducing this form of rural exploitation of labor. So long as these landowners kept land in production, they
were free of direct state interference. The third stage came in 1986, well after
the production of this film, and made changes in the law to try to give more
latitude to the government in the application of agrarian policy.

The formal decrees show the FSLN's agricultural policy goals but don't
convey the complexity and ferment of the situation on the ground.[27]
Decision-making circles debated the direction and meaning of the Agrarian
Reform, struggling with insufficient data, inexperienced and untrained personnel, and considerable variations in agricultural reality across regions,
class identification, quality of land, level of technology, etc. Despite a clear
bias in favor of collective work, it would be difficult to characterize the
Agrarian Reform as socialist. In fact, most refer to the revolutionary years
as "transitional." Carlos Vilas uses a less ideologically charged formulation:
"the transition to development."[28]

Sorting through the complexities of land reform was difficult, and
INCINE's only major film about the Agrarian Reform could not present a
complete picture. According to Rafael Vargas, Jaime Wheelock insisted on
changes in the film's first version, so the final version presumably conforms,
grosso modo, to MIDINRA's image of the Agrarian Reform in mid-1982.[29] As
for artistic elaboration and organization, Vargas's hand is clearly evident.

Like the very first noticiero, and like some of La otra cara del oro, also
(co)directed by Vargas, Nuestra Reforma Agraria opens with a form of testimony. Before the credits, an offscreen male voice describes the heroic death
of a compañero, Germán Pomares. When mortally wounded, Pomares concealed the gravity of his wound and ordered the others to continue fighting.
The camera zooms out to reveal a lone candle on a table at which a man is
seated at night. An interviewer asks the man what Pomares thought about
the campesino, about the land:

Polo adrift in darkness speaking of realizing Sandino's dream of Agrarian Reform
(Nuestra reforma agraria)

> Bueno, what he thought was that the land should belong
> to the campesino who worked it, to the campesino
> because we still had a long way to go, and what he
> wanted was that we all work the lands that still had
> landlords.

As he finishes speaking, the candlelit man is in a dark space, which fades
to black as the titles appear. As in the earlier films, the introduction refers
to a historical event—the death of Germán Pomares, an early campesino
guerrilla killed in June 1979. The film ends with the same candlelit campesino seen in the opening, Polo, whose final words trace the connection
with Pomares further back to Sandino:

> Yes, the agrarian reform is fulfilling its task, because the
> ideals that Pomares had were the same that Sandino had.
> Because the struggle that Sandino waged was open to the
> campesino who was exploited by the owners. In this
> sense, we will never go back. We have to end with all of
> the people, because all those people united are like
> stones that nobody can move.

Modern agroindustrial processing, hands never touching the product
(Nuestra reforma agraria)

This frame wraps the film in the rhetorical folds of the campesino, but the film's substance is far more ecumenical. Traveling down the technological scale of Nicaraguan agriculture, roughly from the most advanced to the least, the film proceeds through five geographical regions of the country. A title identifies regions, and Vargas constructs a short cultural and topographical précis to introduce each.

In "The Pacific," a series of long-lens close shots of leaves set the scene. Two hands pull a phalanx of knob-tipped bars, triggering a symphony of technological wonders, gears turning and machinery churning, implacably transforming raw cane into sugar. Technicians seated at sparkling control panels monitor the processing. Human hands touch the metal controls, not the sugar itself. Here is high technology, the San Antonio complex, still in private hands. A manager explains that they are expecting the largest harvest in their history and adds that the Junta de Gobierno is subsidizing the price of sugar, paying a high price to the company but not passing the real cost to the consumer.

Abruptly, the film cuts to an enormous vacuum tube sucking cotton up; the next mechanical process packs cotton into bales, which are lifted by cranes onto waiting ships. Here cotton, the crop that radically transformed Nicaraguan agriculture after World War II (doubling its production every few years during the 1950s), is efficiently processed and sent directly to ships for export. In this *state-owned* plant, human hands never touch cotton, not even for ginning—the film shows pits bouncing like hail pellets on a conveyer belt below. Again, workers comment on the enterprise's success. It has doubled output in each of the three years of operation.

The second section, "The North," deals with more labor-intensive crops: coffee and tobacco. After the deft if arty montage about León (where Vargas was born), full of religious associations in the architecture and iconography, hands sort through beans already spread out in the factory. Without elaborate mechanical steps, the coffee ends up in bags ready for transport. A man perched atop coffee bags lauds the "Construction Junta" in improving the workers' housing and roads. A campesino enumerates advantages of belonging to a Credit and Service Cooperative (CCS): easier access to credit and higher prices for coffee. The following sequence on tobacco begins with harvesting individual leaves but quickly displays the skill involved in cutting the leaves to proper specifications, rolling them into cigars and packing them neatly in boxes. The speakers give an organizational breakdown of this company, with 36 sites, and emphasize the creation of jobs, some 6,000 in that year. One worker claims that the company directly or indirectly supports 40,000 people in the region.

After leading with coffee and tobacco, the section concludes with a sequence of clearing land and irrigating it for planting (irrigated) rice. A worker supplies an overview of the crops: corn, beans, rice, and others. He adds that by increasing land devoted to rice, they can "solve partially the food problems which exist at the national level."

The third, middle section takes place in Managua, seat of the Agrarian Reform administration. After another stylized prologue, with visual references to the FSLN—Sandino's portrait, the Rojo y Negro flag, the eternal flame at Carlos Fonseca's tomb—the title identifies "The Center." Seated around a table with colleagues, Jaime Wheelock offers a revealing account:

> We are going to continue transferring the land to the
> campesinos, because each time it will be done more
> frequently. But really, the land is only one element,
> not everything, because on the other hand we have
> also the question of technology, investments, fertilizers,
> improved seeds. Regarding the infrastructure of
> production, we must work on improving the roads in the
> countryside, the transportation and also the systems of
> supply. And lastly, the supply of credit, which is a tool,
> a source.

Agrarian Reform head Jaime Wheelock surrounded by Managua bureaucrats
(Nuestra reforma agraria)

Repressed dream of the campesino—working his own land
(Nuestra reforma agraria)

During the overview, Vargas intercuts a simple peasant story. In the first shots, a young boy guides an oxen team through a field as his father wields the plow behind. As the campesino finishes work and returns home, various officials address specific questions. A UNAG representative expresses the interest in pursuing the "struggle for the land" and sees the value of the Agrarian Reform as a basis for "resolving the problems of the campesino." According to the next speaker, the ATC, originally constituted as the mass organization representing all agricultural labor, now works with workers involved with export-crop production.

Though unidentified, the next man is a prominent young FSLN political theorist, Orlando Nuñez, who worked on agrarian reform for many years and headed the Institute of the Agrarian Reform. Not representing any particular group interest, he speaks as resident, home-grown intellectual with post-graduate education at the Sorbonne. Nuñez had written an article in 1981 for a prominent academic journal in the United States, boldly claiming that the Nicaraguan revolution was a new form of revolution, one distinguished by what he called the "third social force."[30] Nuñez insisted on the particularity of Nicaragua's revolution, that it was forging a new path, still under construction, hence unlike preexisting models. In the film he asserts that "we do not have to change substantially the forms of property [ownership]." Placed at the film's center, and called "The Center," this section is the film's policy pivot, though its formal organization offers another perspective on policy, probably unintended. The Agrarian Reform bureaucracy is located in Managua, and the minister of the Agrarian Reform, Jaime Wheelock, also member of the Dirección Nacional of the FSLN, is the first to speak. By virtue of occupying both posts, Wheelock sets policy. He may vary emphases depending on the time, place, and audience, but his comments reflect the orientation of the Agrarian Reform at that point. He observes that land will continue to be distributed to the campesinos, then adds that the land question is only one issue, and expatiates on the great promise of high-tech production. That is, after a nod to the question of land and the campesinos, Wheelock forthrightly sets out a modernization agenda, which translated into capital intensive, high-tech projects clustered in the agro-processing sector. Wheelock favors projects requiring proletarian wage labor over traditional campesino small-holder farming methods and work rhythms. Following Wheelock's logic, the land question would not receive a high priority at the level of the individual campesino.

The other four speakers, all presumably government functionaries, discuss the agrarian problematic, though without mentioning the deep tensions of agricultural policy. The UNAG representative describes UNAG as the organization for small and medium producers who have a "trajectory of struggle for the land." No one mentions the pressures that led to UNAG's formation. UNAG did represent individual producers, but it also potentially threatened FSLN hegemony in agriculture. Though formed as a Sandinista mass organization, some claim that the FSLN accepted the creation of UNAG in order to corral significant dissident campesinos and prevent the establishment of a truly independent farmers' organization.[31]

As befit the interests of the organization's membership, the ATC spokesperson does not broach the question of land. With a clear *class* identity as proletarian, the ATC worked in the agro-export sector, and its interests coincided with those set out by Wheelock when he deemphasized the importance of land and concentrated on "development, . . . getting out from underdevelopment . . . from backwardness."

After Nuñez intervenes with a reassurance about the mixed economy, the final speaker in the section addresses the land question for poor campesinos. In one sentence he invokes the magic incantation of *cooperatives* that will "resolve the historical situation of exploitation in the country." Cooperatives were to answer the campesino demand for land, and, at first, the FSLN awarded land almost exclusively to cooperatives. Furthermore, despite pressure from campesinos, the FSLN was reluctant to frighten large landowners. Three months after the July 20 decree on the expropriation of the Somocista properties, the FSLN ended the expropriation of property and prohibited peasant land takeovers. The FSLN then either kept land for state farms or made it available to cooperatives.

The cooperative movement exploded in the early years in response to the offer of land. As with the state farms, the government virtually threw money at the cooperatives to induce campesinos to join. With lucrative incentives like credit, machinery, price supports, etc., many campesinos did sign up. However, though the figures indicate massive participation, campesinos generally chose the least collective forms of cooperative organization, despite more benefits being offered to more collective forms.[32] Thus, interest rates on loans were lower on cooperatives with the most collective forms of farming, on which all land was farmed collectively. Conversely, where all land was held collectively but worked individually, credit terms were less favorable. In short, the FSLN pursued policies to transform campesino attitudes, to dislodge them from traditional individualistic views of the land and convert them to collective farming.

While the bureaucracy speaks, the intercutting evokes an idealized campesino life precisely opposite to the new model described by each of the officials. Beginning during Wheelock's commentary, images of a male campesino plowing the field with two oxen, led by his son, alternate with images of the bureaucrats. As the Managua personnel describe a technological transformation of agriculture, a lone campesino methodically guides his plow through furrows, trudging past the camera and framed against the sky, the bright red sun setting magnificently and dramatically in the background. After the day's hard work, the campesino meticulously unyokes the oxen and returns home. Slowly sitting down at a small table with a single candle, the campesino watches patiently and impassively as his wife places food before him and then leaves him alone in silence. Here Vargas depicts a timeless campesino idyll, cut off from any social existence beyond the entirely self-sufficient family. As the script describes it, "While they [the Managua bureaucrats] speak, we see the campesino working all day; in the late afternoon, he returns to his house, where his family awaits him, and night falls."

The juxtaposition of macro planning discourses and this campesino idyll suggests a specific and polemical logic. The other four geographical regions all have a particular imagery associated with them, and the film dips into that reservoir of popular images to situate the action. Managua, the capital city, has above all an urban identity. Vargas constructs the picturesque opening around this urban identity, with the only tall buildings in Managua towering over the landscape. The city has drawn many former campesinos, and Vargas fashions a fantasy out of the accumulated nostalgia for that life left behind, cleansing it of the grinding poverty, soil erosion, depletion of fertility, dispossession of land, and so on. Policy makers and experts behind desks spew out words about the transformation of Nicaraguan agriculture, a torrent of words about hard manual labor. The campesino is silent, his only voice the iconic eloquence of his solitary labor.

The remaining two regions follow "The Center" as concluding vestigial pendants, for the economic weight of the Pacific and the North far outweighs the economic significance of the interior and the Atlantic coast. The prologue to "The Atlantic" revolves around cutting trees and gliding over an inland waterway as birds fill the sound track. Unlike the dissonance between the verbal and audiovisual discourses in the previous section, this introduction provides an efficient and accurate image of the Atlantic region, labeled "The Atlantic." In form, these sections follow the pattern of the first two parts of the film. One speaker comments on a particular aspect of the agricultural activity of the region, and assorted images illustrate that activity. The content differs significantly but still falls within the administrative concern of agricultural policy, if not of the Agrarian Reform directly.

The sounds of saws clearing trees and birds singing place the action in the reality of the Atlantic region. In previous decades, with the rapid growth of agro-export farming in the Pacific and the North, peasants were forced off the land and went east into the virgin jungles of the coast, the agrarian frontier.

Once there, the peasants raised staples of the Nicaraguan diet: corn, beans, plátanos [plantains]. Understandably, there is less emphasis here on production, for the peasants presumably apply traditional methods, unlike the highly mechanized production of agro-export and the state sector. Actually, that traditional method filled the visual vacuum in "The Center," where it functioned as an idealized fantasy. Instead, Vargas films vignettes of village life, segueing from cooking and sewing to assembling a rifle: Defense against the contra has become part of daily life. Most appear to be mestizo men with some official responsibility. They speak about production in larger terms than their personal plots. One black Costeño explains in English a successful new method for using the machinery, translated in Spanish subtitles. The section concludes with a discussion of cocoa oil, as seated black women hack coconuts with machetes, followed by the machinery processing the oil. The script of the film describes this scene in a startling paternal rhetoric, even if the paternalism is not particularly marked in the scene: "The women of the Atlantic Coast of Nicaragua, with this special beauty of our black race, which we share with the whole Caribbean, cut, open and drain the water from the coconuts."

The final title identifies the last region: Río San Juan. Nestled in Nicaragua's southeast, the Río San Juan area is one of eight administrative subdivisions in the country. According to this sequence, the revolution is changing a way of life, not just agricultural life. Director Vargas asks about their baseball league, apparently as the pretext first to show a baseball game, but more importantly to show them later working the fields in baseball uniforms, suggesting a new interpenetration of work and leisure in their lives. According to Martha Clarissa Hernández, the assistant director, Vargas was responsible for the uniforms and for instructions on how to act, bringing up the question of exactly what is a documentary.[33] Later, a worker at a state cattle-raising enterprise proudly explains the work of the state organization, and a coworker notes that the workers decided to organize collectives.

In the introductory images of this section, Vargas included drawings produced in an archipelago of islands dotting the eastern corner of Lake Nicaragua, near the Costa Rican border. During the 1970s, the poet and priest Ernesto Cardenal, later Minister of Culture, established a religious-artistic community in these small isles of Solentiname. Before the insurrection, Somoza's Guardia Nacional destroyed the community, forcing its members to flee. The artworks, then, carry both artistic and political connotations, and the Río San Juan area occupies a special cultural status within Sandinista lore. Vargas closes this section with a theater group, with the actors introducing themselves popping into frame one by one, each adding one word of the sentence "We are doing theater for the people." At an old Spanish fort, the group mounts a piece of agitprop theater that condenses central themes in *Nuestra Reforma Agraria:*

> And now, the land will be ours?
>
> No, compa[ñero], not only the land. We need the sticks, the axes, the seeds, the fertilizers. We need to learn to write; to read. We need to learn to work together. We need to be different people all over Nicaragua.

With this gentle deflection from the hunger for land and the insertion of a new agenda, an expanded field of campesino uplift, the geographical itinerary is complete, and the candlelit campesino returns to tie agrarian reform to Sandino.

In a country dependent on agriculture, any agrarian reform process would stimulate debate. A reform aiming at a radical transformation of the countryside would unleash powerful forces and vigorous discussion. As the central axis of social and economic transformation, Nicaragua's Agrarian Reform had profound consequences throughout the 1980s. However, establishing the relationship between the Agrarian Reform and its consequences poses problems for discussion and analysis, problems that must be considered when viewing *Nuestro Reforma Agraria.* Without getting lost in details, the question of the peasantry illustrates the complexity. One might begin with a straightforward question: Did the peasants benefit from the Agrarian Reform? But first, one would have to know what the category "peasant" means. Then, how many Nicaraguan peasants were there in 1979? Experts disagree on even such ostensibly neutral data, and not only because little data was kept during the Somoza years. The definition of a peasant affects the number. Furthermore, what was the Agrarian Reform trying to do? The question assumes that the Agrarian Reform was a coherent, noncontradictory policy. In fact, the reform was a process, lurching in contradictory directions simultaneously, affected by factional infighting, ignorance, incompetence, indecision, pressures from the war, incorrect assumptions, and so on. The process of the agrarian reform also responded to the effects of its policy, adapting to ever-changing conjunctures.

When Vargas made *Nuestra Reforma Agraria* in 1982, experts may have glimpsed some contours of the problem, but the issues weren't clear to most outsiders, and certainly not to the INCINE filmmakers. For that reason, *Nuestra Reforma Agraria* is a valuable document on the Agrarian Reform, toeing the official line, but also secreting a kind of unconscious doppelganger. The bookends of the candlelit peasant speaking of Germán Pomares bridge the historical gap between Sandino's dream of agrarian reform and its realization in the FSLN Agrarian Reform. The four agricultural regions accurately reflect the emphases of the Agrarian Reform to that point. The MIDINRA has opted for modern technology in a mixed economy, with large state farms and a substantial private sector, both concentrating on export production. The ATC, mass organization of salaried workers, represents the interests of those members. Other farmers, producers of basic grains to feed the population, will form cooperatives and receive preferential treatment to promote more collective forms of work. The images essentially illustrate the themes of mechanized work processes and the stages of production from the field to the port for export or to packaging for the consumer.

But conveying the diversity of the agrarian reform process obscures a fundamental aspiration of the historical subject of Nicaraguan agriculture: the campesino's dream of owning land. In the most elaborate sections, the two devoted to the Pacific and the North, high-tech production predominates while managers applaud the strides of the Agrarian Reform. When campesinos speak in the less developed eastern regions, they proudly describe forming cooperatives and raising production levels. Only amidst the bureaucratic discourses of Managua does the repressed world of the individual campesino surge to the surface, but still without its own voice. While the policy makers *speak* of agrarian transformation, the *image* of a campesino working alone on the land presses through into their discourses. This powerful, irrepressible fantasy of the past, idyllic, nostalgic, elegiac even, haunts the reformers' vision, as if the film somehow has exposed the reformers' unspoken fear that the campesino will reject the inducements of a collective, technologized future. As at the center, so at the two ends, the other campesino, Polo, does speak, but only as a purely ideological construction, adrift in the frame's darkness, soldering the campesino connection with Sandino. Certainly unconsciously, director Vargas has fashioned a brilliant picture of the Agrarian Reform, an uncannily prescient analysis, for the unanswered desire for land ultimately turned a significant part of the peasantry against the FSLN.

Teotecacinte

If *Pan y dignidad* showed the self-defense preparations and training, and *Nuestra Reforma Agraria* touched on the military function of cooperatives, the first documentary of Iván Argüello went to the war's front lines. Argüello used footage shot in contra camps in Honduras by a Dutch filmmaker (Peter Tolbertson) to expose not only the damage the contras inflicted, but also the barbarity of their tactics and ideology. Argüello patched the contra material together with Reagan's 1983 speech to Congress and material he gathered in the Jalapa area in the north of Nicaragua, on the border with Honduras, called Teotecacinte, source of the film's title, *Teotecacinte, el fuego viene del norte* [*Teotecacinte, the fire comes from the north*] (1983).

Flickering video images of Reagan addressing Congress open the film, identifying the war's sponsor. Reagan is asking for funds to support the contra war. The 35-minute film cuts the speech, periodically inserting segments of it. With ample justification, Nicaragua characterized the contra armies as mercenaries paid by the United States to bring down the Sandinista government. Reagan's image alone establishes that association. However, this speech also illustrates the fantastic arguments dreamed up by the Reagan camarilla (Kirkpatrick, Elliot Abrams, etc.) to justify the carnage. In this first excerpt, Reagan, the most spectacular budget buster in U.S. history, minimizes the $600 million requested for Central America in 1984 as "less than a tenth of what Americans will spend this year on coin-operated video games." Typically, Reagan finds a folksy concrete image—American kids popping coins into amusement games—to cut through the fog of numbers and statistics for the audience, the American public, more than for Congress, which knew its way around numbers well enough. This first Reagan segment ends with the ominous claim that "this evening there can be no doubt that the national security of all the Americas is in play in Central America."

However receptive the American public was to this warning, Nicaraguans could find it only a macabre joke. According to Reagan, Marxist Nicaragua's existence threatened the region's stability. As the president of the United States, Reagan made this claim without proof and without fear of a pliant Congress demanding facts. With the Nicaraguan army so occupied with the contra war, Nicaraguans, whatever their political opinions, could never have directed any significant efforts to the struggles in neighboring countries.

The contra interviews expose Reagan's escalating fantasies. One contra complains of Sandinista pressure on his father, a captain in Somoza's army; another about being in exile himself, for he too served under Somoza. A fourth contra speaks about training with foreign advisers in Honduras. Essentially, then, the contra's own testimonies confirm Nicaraguan charges that the contra are former Somoza Guardia Nacional and receive training from foreign advisers in Honduras.

A government representative explains the situation in Jalapa, where the contra have caused damage worth 129 million cordobas, concentrated in Teotecacinte. The contra aggression requires measures to protect the harvest and transfer hundreds of families from the border. Reagan reappears describing the geographical proximity of Central America to the United States, with "El Salvador closer to Texas than Texas is to Massachusetts, Nicaragua is as close to Miami, San Antonio, San Diego, and Tucson as these cities are to Washington, where we are meeting tonight."

Perhaps the most incredible charge raised against the Sandinistas concerns religion. A contra leader gives the following account of why the contra will win:

> We can't lose this war. It is a holy war in which we are
> shoulder to shoulder with Jesus Christ. We could call it a
> holy war because we are confident that our actions are
> guided by God and when we go into combat we ask God
> that He guide us with the gun and make us do what
> is right.

A priest from Jalapa conveys his astonishment at such beliefs:

> Christ is the defender of life. He says that he wishes that
> everyone live, so these people cannot be Christians,
> because they have killed campesinos here, defenseless.
> They went where campesinos were working on their land
> early in the morning, they have killed women like
> Victoria Rayo, in the line, here in Jalapa. They have killed
> children, ambushed civilians, even ambulances. So if
> they were Christian they would not attack the defense-
> less, so it's impossible that God is with them in this
> struggle.

After these two positions, Reagan continues his harangue:

> The government of Nicaragua has imposed a new
> dictatorship, has failed to hold elections it had promised,
> it has taken over the majority of the media of communi-
> cation and submitted all the media to heavy censorship.
> It has deprived bishops and priests of the Catholic
> Church of the right to say mass during Holy Week on the
> radio, they have insulted and mocked the Pope.

Finally, a contra soldier claims the Sandinista policy is "that God does not exist, that God never has existed, that the Catholic religion has never existed." The stunned offscreen Dutch interviewer asks how priests could say this; the soldier can't answer.

The Sandinistas encountered many problems with the Catholic Church, especially with its traditional hierarchy. Archbishop Obando y Bravo, its Nicaraguan head, opposed the FSLN and supported the contras. The Sandinistas proposed a different vision of religious practice based on liberation theology and placed two priests in charge of Ministries (the brothers Fernando and Ernesto Cardenal, Ministers of Education and Culture, respectively). The Pope's short visit to Nicaragua was embarrassing, but mainly because he failed to call for peace as hundreds of thousands of listeners had expected. So many people waiting hours at the airport for the Pope were expressing their faith, not a wish to mock His Eminence.

Another contra adds the final plank to the Reagan/contra argument: anticommunism. Somoza had played the anticommunist card successfully, and the contra forces, dominated by Somocistas, carried on the crusade. Once again a contra soldier reveals the "politics" driving the aggression:

> Soldier: I haven't killed Nicaraguans. I've eliminated, removed Sandinista-communists found in our country. I'm a soldier not to kill but to get rid of communism.
>
> Interviewer: But what does that mean, to kill?
>
> Soldier: Well, the word kill is fairly controversial.

Argüello then places various witnesses after this contra to recount incidents of cold-blooded murder of unarmed innocents, including children and campesinos going to the fields.

The first part of the film lays out ostensible justifications for the contra war. Reagan's television speech clarifies the U.S. role as the war's initiator, both ideologically and economically. The fantastic assertions of the contra soldiers and their admissions of Somocista backgrounds expose the hypocrisy of claims that the contras are freedom fighters. The contras indict themselves; repeatedly the interviews short circuit into incoherence, such as calling "killing" a controversial word.

The United States accused Nicaragua of imposing a repressive Marxist state on the Nicaraguan people. *Teotecacinte* juxtaposes two discourses, that of the U.S. president and the contra army he finances and trains on the one hand, and Nicaraguan campesinos, civilians on the other. The contra soldiers mouth words they do not understand, placed there by Somoza in the past, now by U.S. military and their own former Guardia Nacional "officers." They speak in abstractions, of the existence of God, of communism, of semantics, all received secondhand as purely ideological discourse. The campesinos speak concretely, of facts they have witnessed and experienced, such as seeing a child shot in the head, attacks on campesinos in the fields, burning crops, etc. The campesinos never mention the FSLN, Sandino, collectiviza-tion, socialism, or religion. Their unforced testimony is eloquent, colloquial, entirely devoid of political partisanship. The campesinos without question mount a more persuasive argument than the contra soldiers.

To that point in the film, blame falls palpably on the contra, who ap-pear as mannequins manipulated by foreigners. Nicaraguans can have no choice. They must side with other Nicaraguans to defend their children, land, and crops. They must defend Nicaragua, its very sovereignty, against foreign interference. The film evokes a nationalist response rather than a de-fense of the FSLN.

The first part of the film alternates between the contra and the local com-munity; the rest deals with the military question. The campesinos must move to safer environs where they construct makeshift housing. The regu-lar army, with artillery, advances toward the vacated areas, while the camera surveys sites of attacks, bodies strewn about a still-smoldering terrain, the wounded loaded onto trucks. Refugees offer details of the attacks, and several Ejército Popular Sandinista (EPS, or Sandinista Army) soldiers speak some-what mechanically about holding positions, following orders, "fighting on to the final consequences in the battle, there where they assigned us." Some footage was taken during combat, with weapons reports ringing on the sound track and the camera careening wildly at times, familiar markers of combat, where abrupt movements signify danger, as the images are unreadable on their own.

Argüello reported that the army had discouraged filming at the front, but cameraman Frank Pineda and Argüello managed to reach the battle zone on their own.[34] But this kind of traditional war reportage was uncharacteristic of INCINE's work and was the last of this genre, though the experience did lead Argüello to return to the same area to film INCINE's first fictional feature several years later.

Despite planning to produce several documentaries per year, none of the directors of these films—Lacayo, Alvarez, Vargas, Argüello—worked on documentaries in the following years, with the exception of Argüello's 1988 *Días de crisis.* Several other directors made documentaries later, but regu-lar output ended after 1983. Furthermore, most of the later documentaries dealt with literary themes, not the political issues at the heart of the ones discussed above: foreign exploitation, the domestic pressures of U.S. aggres-sion, the Agrarian Reform, and the contra war.[35]

By the end of 1983, fiction began absorbing INCINE's resources and imagi-nation. The troubled history of Noticiero 40, converted into a fiction project by Rafael Vargas, opened the door and the other directors rushed in, with first-, second-, and even third-generation filmmakers signing on. The rhythm of documentaries ended in 1984, as did the noticieros, with fiction usurping INCINE's time and shrinking resources. The scope of fiction expanded progressively through shorts (1984–1985) to one short color feature (*Mujeres de la frontera*, 1985–1986) to a final full-length color feature (*El espectro de la guerra*, 1988).

Eight   THE REALITY
            OF FICTION

By 1984 INCINE's filmmaking had reached a turning point. As the state de-voted more resources to the war, support for cultural production shriveled. Most INCINE filmmakers had already made noticieros and the most experi-enced began experimenting with fiction. INCINE quickly discovered that fic-tion monopolized the institution's resources, abruptly ending the noticiero cycle and curtailing the flow of documentaries. Big-budget coproductions also took a toll, accelerating the momentum toward fiction and feeding un-realistic fantasies of developing a viable industrial base for cinema. In the rush to fiction, the filmmakers probably did not understand the risks. The de-cision proved costly. Just when INCINE needed new means to sustain itself, the novelty and difficulty of fictional production impeded reliable planning. The effective end of INCINE came with the completion of two feature films in 1987–1988, one fiction and one documentary.

The leap into fiction did not happen overnight. Some INCINE filmmakers maintain that fiction appeared during the second year of noticiero produc-tion. Mariano Marín viewed all his films as fiction, because they all included material "puesto-en-escena"; that is, for Marín, setting up shots in advance, with proper lighting and careful placement of individuals.[1] There was in-creasing evidence of directorial intervention throughout the noticiero cycle. Even though all the noticieros presented themselves as nonfiction, many filmmakers engaged in recreating historical events within them—Sandino's announcement of an agrarian reform in Legall's *Wiwilí, sendero a una vic-toria,* registering Sandino's birth and digging his grave in Argüello's *Esta tierra es ese hombre,* the declaration of independence of Central America in Marín's *Jornada anti-intervencionista,* the assassination of Somoza García in Lacayo's *Viva León.* The increasing frequency of sequences "puestos-en-escena" shows an expanding interest in fiction, but none of these examples, based on real events, violated the noticieros' nonfiction premise. Generally, the sequences were historical references, and obvious as such, not *documentary* reconstructions of the historical events. When the high laced boots of "Sandino" stride to the hilltop (in *Wiwilí, sendero a una victoria*), the film neither suggests it is using newsreel footage nor even that Sandino really stood on this spot.

Later in the noticiero cycle, some sequences are ambiguous but still embedded in the rubric of nonfiction. For example, the elaborate ending of Marín's *Los centinelas* was entirely invented and staged. The thieves divvy up the loot in the old Palace of Justice, and the backlit police stalk their quarry with guns drawn, ultimately converging on the trapped perpetrators frozen on a virtual stage. The film doesn't pretend to be reality. The scene resembles, as Marín readily acknowledged, the stylized television fare of *Miami Vice* more than documentary. But the noticiero does claim that the Sandinista Police have an inexorable reach, the nonfiction premise.

Various factors pushed INCINE toward fiction. Effectively, the changing format of the noticieros eliminated the distinction between the noticieros and the documentaries, though the agreement with the Cubans still included the slots for noticieros. Two of the most veteran filmmakers, Lacayo and Vargas, wanted to experiment with fiction, thinking that fiction would allow INCINE to temper the *panfletario* thrust of the earlier films. The cameraperson, Frank Pineda, claimed that Lacayo fought with the Vice-Minister of Culture, Francisco Lacayo, but that Daniel Ortega had intervened on Ramiro's behalf.[2] Once the FSLN reduced INCINE's funding in May 1984, INCINE had less reason to worry about FSLN monitoring. No doubt several of the other filmmakers shared the fascination for fiction of Lacayo and Vargas. In the words of Rafael Ruíz, the first fiction film, *Manuel*, set off the "epoch of fever, the joy of beginning to make fiction films."[3]

However, not everyone caught the fever. María José Alvarez objected to the cessation of noticieros, but "they thought I was crazy, for they considered it a lesser genre."[4] Alberto Legall opposed the move to fiction because of its expense, for "it shouldn't be allowed to dominate documentary production; the political situation needed counter-information against the gringo propaganda, and fiction was the germ that ended up killing the whole project."[5] One of the original founders of INCINE, Vicente Ibarra, looked back on the decision as a fateful one: "INCINE became dedicated to fiction, of grand fiction, but with increasingly fewer resources. . . . For me, this could have been avoided. . . . I'm not saying that they couldn't have made fiction films, but they should not have been the nucleus, the principal activity of INCINE, which is what occurred."[6] But Ibarra had been removed from INCINE in

1982, so in this sense Lacayo had no significant internal opposition from someone of the stature of Ibarra.

The move into fiction was abetted by the momentum that had been building for some time to redesign INCINE as an "empresa," or business. Lacayo had been seeking for years to gain control over state film distribution (ENIDIEC) and exhibition (Cine RAP), which would provide INCINE with direct access to those revenues, and INCINE's archives contain various documents that speak of these plans, including one that proposes producing films fundamentally for the exterior, and that states "in the medium and long run, fiction should be our fundamental activity."[7] Apparently, Lacayo thought that fiction would be the strategic linchpin of INCINE's future as they contemplated selling the films abroad.

Manuel

In fact, the first planned fiction film undertaken began life as a noticiero. Marín proposed a film about the military draft. He had opposed the draft in Nicaragua, but during his stay in France, he learned that military service could train people. On his return, he wanted to make a film to elicit public discussion about the possible purposes and uses of military service, such as education, for "service here [in Nicaragua] had no other meaning than being cannon fodder."[8]

As the contra attacks increased, the government initiated discussions about compulsory military service. The Junta sent a proposal to the Council of State in early August 1983. Despite vigorous opposition, the law of Compulsory Military Service passed in September, taking effect in October. During this period, Rafael Vargas took over the project. Many subsequent details remain cloudy.[9] Some maintain that Noticiero 40 coincided with the so-called *talleres*, or workshops. Fernando Birri, founder of the Documentary School of Cinema (El Instituto de Cinematografía de la Universidad del Litoral) in Santa Fe (Argentina) in 1957 and a progenitor of the New Cinema of Latin America, suggested that INCINE organize the directors and technical personnel into two filmmaking *talleres*.[10] Working collectively, the filmmakers would increase efficiency and creativity. Some directors recall this plan with derision, because they say one *taller* grouped together the "good" filmmakers, and the other the "bad." In any event, the results of the short-lived talleres contradicted such evaluations, as the second or "bad" taller produced the excellent *Rompiendo el silencio*.

Rafael Vargas maintains that he completed a nonfiction film, a noticiero, about a young soldier, who died before the film was finished.[11] According to Vargas, the film carried a note on screen at the end rhetorically asking the United States why it supported military aggression against Nicaragua. Alberto Legall recalls the film as a documentary.[12] Lacayo remembers it as combining documentary and fiction, "fiction illustrating interviews. Like a docudrama. But it was weird."[13] Martha Clarissa Hernández claims to have been present when Vargas convinced Lacayo to allow him to transform the project into fiction, saying he had an actor all picked out and talking about a script, wanting "something well made and subtle."[14] Unfortunately, as memories have faded, most people recall the more dramatic events that happened later. Vargas did not understand why, but he claims there were political objections to the noticiero. Yet the soldier had died, so it was impossible to change it. Hence Vargas proposed remaking the film as fiction—and Ramiro Lacayo accepted.

By all accounts, Vargas was difficult to work with. The filmmakers and cameramen (all male) caustically lampoon Vargas's habit of suddenly announcing in the middle of work that he had to stop to meditate. On two occasions, frustrated crew members struck, walked off the set, and left production in limbo.[15] Vargas may have had professional peculiarities, but co-workers also may have questioned his political commitment—a suspicion Vargas claims had prevented his work on earlier noticieros. With a definite sense of artistic vocation, Vargas was perhaps less open to compromise than his colleagues. Though the two heads of INCINE, Lacayo and Ibarra, had great respect for Vargas's artistic sensibility, many of the others interpreted Vargas's stance as pretentious affectation.

By mid-1983, the rhythm of noticiero production was changing, distending, but Noticiero 40 was probably scheduled for completion during the middle of that year. However, a July 1 memo, referring to the film as Corto (Short) No. 40, contains many complaints about the project's progress.[16] The producer, Brenda Martínez, alerted Alberto Legall (head of noticiero production at the time) that Vargas had used too much film, exhausted the crew, and yet had completed only half of the shooting. Exactly three weeks later, Vargas wrote to Legall protesting the two-week limit for editing, and demanded four weeks, which Legall refused, warning Vargas that INCINE would take "necessary measures" in the event of further delays. Apparently Vargas ended up resigning in August or September, for Lacayo wrote to Vargas on September 20 specifying conditions for Vargas's return. He reminded Vargas to adhere to production schedules, noted that absences from work or delays in production would be deducted from his salary, and imposed a probation period of three months.

Three months later, Legall had to sanction and fine Vargas for further transgressions.[17] Apparently, Vargas resigned again, for he wrote a remarkable mea culpa the following March asking to be reinstated and attributing the problems to a "nervous crisis":

> It's because of all of this that I wish to withdraw my resignation and excuse myself for the comments therein, as well as try to express through your good office to the crew and the *taller* the fact that this same nervous tension led me at times to take arrogant attitudes and to put pressure on the work beyond the real limits of the crew.[18]

Meanwhile, successive INCINE work plans kept pushing back the dates for the film. In July 1983 the production department estimated that final copies of *Manuel* would be available at the end of August. *Ten months later,* another report includes the astonishing note that Vargas would present to the Executive Committee a new script.[19] Another full year later, Julio Torres suggested to Vargas that the film be released in Nicaragua in August 1985, over two years after shooting began![20]

Though INCINE personnel ridicule Vargas's working methods, the interminable production history of *Manuel* reveals its centrality in the transition to fiction. Despite these delays, INCINE did not shelve the project. By 1983, with three years of (roughly) monthly noticieros and short documentaries behind them, the veterans were poised to move to a new level. For the old guard, torpor had set in with noticiero production, which, as has previously been mentioned, was also changing in length, depth, sponsorship, and so on. Lacayo no longer worked on noticieros, Alvarez had left INCINE, and Legall had withdrawn from production. Lacayo had indicated an interest in graduating to fiction and even published a short story in *Barricada* in 1983, which would be the story for Lacayo's first *projected* fiction film. Lacayo, then, sought a way to break into fiction, knowing his superiors in the Ministry of Culture and the Dirección Nacional might question this move.

At that moment, *Manuel* fell into his lap. Several filmmakers said that Lacayo revered Vargas. The severe memo from Lacayo to Vargas setting out conditions for accepting Vargas's return to INCINE does not indicate awe, but Lacayo did defer to Vargas's artistry. Appointed by the Dirección Nacional, Lacayo was a Sandinista charged with a heavy political responsibility. Vargas, then, could be his guinea pig. Timid by nature, Lacayo would greenlight *Manuel* as the first fiction film and let Vargas test the waters. This decision unleashed a rush to fiction, Lacayo himself leading the pack. Whether by design or not, Vargas drew all the flak for the problems associated with the first fiction film, while none of the fiction films that followed encountered the opprobrium heaped upon Vargas for *Manuel.*

In the final 28-minute version, Vargas acquitted himself quite adequately. Manuel, a young reservist, relates to his fellow soldiers various incidents from his past. The plot proceeds through flashbacks intercut with Manuel's banter with his comrades in a truck headed for a war zone. The script's structure simply strings together scenes that develop the central character. The scenes unroll chronologically, most built around a dramatic conflict, some devoted to Manuel's purely subjective experiences. For the most part the conflicts revolve around political questions, while the subjective sequences have no explicit political content.

In a typical Vargas touch, the film begins with a prologue preceding the credits. A well-known Nicaraguan theater actress, Pilar Aguirre, speaks about her grandson, Manuelito, abandoned by his worthless father and raised by her:

> As a child he was very quiet, but very studious. He spoke
> to me of great things, of the great men and of that
> struggle for liberation of the oppressed peoples, of things,
> frankly, which had very little interest for me.

This introduction immediately puts Manuel in the new revolutionary generation, while an older generation remained relatively indifferent, uninvolved as it had also been during the Somoza years. This generational tension will tighten in a later scene, but this shot with the grandmother already describes a conflict between the two characters. Equally important, the prologue announces a new cinematic path into fiction and a homage to a grande dame of Nicaraguan theater. Her appearance alone establishes the screen world as fictional.

After the credits, the men in the truck trade stories and then ask Manuel why he has never been in the reserves before. He explains that he served one tour and was injured. The first flashback interrupts the scene in the truck with an ambulance racing down a street carrying Manuel to the hospital. Once at the hospital, he is wheeled down a corridor, his carriage gliding smoothly past the camera, while his heartbeat is amplified on the sound track. These shots, already within a flashback, reinforce the sequence's subjectivity, which then extends to Manuel's delirious fantasy. Suddenly, he is in a large, dark, cavernous new space. Bewildered, he walks forward to see revelers at a long table, one woman raucously laughing; another woman mocks him, saying it is "your fault, your fault." He sees a woman lying on a hospital stretcher. Apparently recognizing her, Manuel falls upon her and begins to

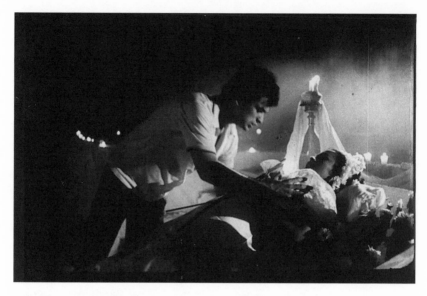

Manuel encountering his girlfriend in dream: "The Andalusian Dog howling in a corner of the cathedral" (Manuel)

embrace her violently. The young woman abruptly sits up, which ends the fantasy and returns the scene to the hospital, before it rejoins the soldiers in the truck. According to Vargas's later account, this is Manuel's dead girlfriend, clad in a wedding dress. She says his actions have killed her, but he does not regret them. Instead, he grabs her "in a fit of voluptuousness . . . The Andalusian Dog howling in a corner of the cathedral."[21]

Vargas acknowledges the influence of Buñuel and surrealism, but it is more evident in this fictional film than in the earlier documentaries.[22] This influence manifests itself as a strong subjective thrust, usually associated with camera movement, sometimes with slow motion and distortion of conventional sound and dialogue, and often with a disjunction between dreamlike images and disembodied sound. Normally, a shot of a face signals a transition to or from subjectivity, such as Manuel's opening his eyes on the hospital stretcher. Vargas likes the camera to personify a character, moving silently forward through a mysterious space, where objects and other characters assault and slip by the invisible visitor. Vargas used this technique in *La otra cara del oro* when a dissolve from a jukebox leads to a forward tracking shot through the luxuriously appointed, now-empty North American manager's house, and noises of drunken revelry fill the otherwise silent sound track. So powerful is the pull toward subjectivity that Vargas places a fantasy within a flashback in the first sequence of INCINE's first fiction film.

The other flashbacks are tendentious. Manuel's narcissistic girlfriend Xiomara argues with him about joining the reserves; she wants him for herself. Rather than treating Xiomara sympathetically as someone legitimately fearful of losing a loved one, the film repeatedly indicts her character. She offers to sleep with Manuel if he does not go off to war. She accuses him of wanting to leave her for another woman. In a later scene, Xiomara tells a friend that another man has invited her out and that she is tired of hearing Manuel babble about revolution. Later she joins a birthday celebration where everyone sings "Happy Birthday" *in English*. In short, Xiomara represents the self-centered, selfish, unproductive Nicaraguan bourgeoisie deformed by U.S. culture.

The grandmother performs a similar function, though she brings an auto-referential note to the role. Having raised Manuel, she worries about his welfare and opposes his military service. With Christmas approaching, she complains about shortages of consumer goods. Having just returned from a Sandinista Youth meeting, Manuel responds: "But Grandmother, that's not the most important, it goes way beyond a glass of whiskey or an apple. It's the dignity of a people." When Manuel asks about her life under a "regime imposed by the gringos," she enters a reverie, stepping outside the space of their conversation into her own frame, an adjacent sitting room festooned with bric-a-brac accumulated during the Somoza regime. This shot evokes the superficial seduction practiced by the Somoza regimes, a shallow façade of material well-being hiding an actual material and spiritual void. Apparently, Grandmother had not heeded the message of the great Nicaraguan clarion of spiritual identity and independence, Rubén Darío, whose portrait hangs prominently in the dining room where Manuel speaks with her.

When the soldiers arrive at their destination, the flashbacks end, and Vargas concludes the film with an ambiguous coda. In a brief night battle, Manuel is shot, fatally. The light theme music bridges the transition to the finale and continues, as Manuel runs joyously through what was downtown Managua before the earthquake, and into Luis Alfonso Velásquez Park, named after a young Sandinista martyr, a boy of ten killed by "the genocidal dictatorship."[23] Manuel is jumping on benches and swinging on a lamppost. He spots a young boy deftly fashioning a paper boat. After they exchange glances, freezing the action, the boy places the boat in the water next to him. The music builds as the camera leaves the characters and follows the boat bobbing on the water, slowly dissolving to the waves of a large lake, with one of Nicaragua's many volcanic peaks towering on the horizon. If Manuel has died, his spirit gambols freely in the park, the locked glances passing his spirit to the next generation. That new generation, however, is yet unformed, oblivious to Manuel's struggles and the victory of the revolution. At

*Grandmother surrounded by memories of a past under Somoza (*Manuel*)*

*Grandmother with Manuel, with portrait of Rubén Darío in background (*Manuel*)*

the same time, the boat set adrift, rudderless, on choppy water, implies uncertainty about the future. Manuel has died for a cause he believed in, but what is his legacy? Will the revolution succeed? Will new blood replenish the Sandinistas' ranks? To judge by the film, Vargas is not sure.

Qué se rinda tu madre

No such ambiguity pertains to the next fiction films, though the chronology gets jumbled here. *Manuel* was the breakthrough film to fiction, but production problems delayed its completion. Sometime in mid-1983, soon after it was decided to transform *Manuel* from noticiero to fiction, *Manuel* became the first part of a planned 90-minute trilogy on the war.[24] With Vargas running interference for Lacayo, Lacayo planned to direct the second part, *Daniel*, based on his short story in *Ventana* two years earlier. Fernando Somarriba would direct the third part, *Noel*, from his own script. The production difficulties with *Manuel* quickly scuttled the trilogy plan. Then Lacayo contracted hepatitis, so he turned *Daniel* over to Mariano Marín.

Into this breach stepped Fernando Somarriba with *Noel*. As the names suggest, the trilogy dealt with three stories about young men, all "designed around the theme of the aggression we are suffering on the part of Imperialism."[25] *Manuel* concerned the problematic of military service, though it avoided the sensitive issue of the draft, for Manuel served in the reserves *voluntarily*. Daniel, a young Sandinista schoolteacher, travels to an isolated village to establish its first school but becomes a target of contra violence. Noel is a Sandinista soldier imprisoned by the contras in Honduras. In the end, the films were shot and released in reversed order from the original plan. Somarriba finished the 45-minute *Noel* at the end of 1984, Marín completed the 40-minute *Daniel* early in 1985, and *Manuel* came out later that same year. Once the trilogy idea unraveled, Somarriba proposed changing the title of *Noel* to *Qué se rinda tu madre* [*Let Your Mother Surrender*], but Lacayo overruled him, objecting to the vulgar connotations of *Qué se rinda tu madre*, and imposed the title of *Nunca nos rendiremos* [*We'll Never Surrender*].[26]

If *Manuel* constructed its design around schematic conflicts and concluded with an ambiguous coda, *Noel* eliminates gray areas entirely. The contra leaders are monsters, bloodthirsty and sadistic. The Sandinista soldiers are innocents, literally stripped naked and chained like animals to their cages. Character development, such as it is, dominates any narrative drive. Hidden in the mountainous Honduran border area, the prison camp provides the background for a series of set pieces, and the characters act out their respective functions.

The opening sequence takes an inventory of the contra camp. The camera moves first to Noel, shackled naked in a bamboo cage outdoors in a small clearing. Uniformed contra soldiers are exercising nearby, completing the anticommunist couplets begun by their instructor:

> What do you want to do?
> Kill, kill, kill.
> Unity and Patriotism,
> We will overthrow communism.

A contra radio station describes the influence of the Soviet Union and socialist bloc countries on "Marxist Nicaragua," while the camera pans past a virtual supermarket of U.S. products, including whiskey, cigarettes, and weapons. Finally, a contra soldier shoves food at the prisoners, who eat with their hands manacled.

Anyone familiar with the Sandinista representation of the contra aggression will recognize this picture. The United States finances mercenaries based in Honduras and provides incentives of liquor and cigarettes as well as unlimited weapons of death and destruction. Radio broadcasts and training methods supply the ideological underpinning to the material lure; wild reports about the communist yoke falling on Nicaragua fan xenophobic resentments of impressionable young Nicaraguans.

A jeep pulls into camp with a Honduran officer, an obvious proxy for the gringos. Young, confident, somewhat imperious, striding dynamically in his spotless uniform, the officer inspects the troops. He congratulates the burly, paunchy, older, raddle-faced contra leaders and quickly disappears with them into a tent.

Noel contemplates his fate and remembers his capture. On a quiet evening, while a man on his porch plays a guitar, the contra rush in, beating the defenseless and terrified family. One contra holds a gun to the young boy's head as the leader presses the mother for information. At that moment, a contra interrupts Noel's flashback to summon him for interrogation, perhaps the central scene in the film.

Interrogation scenes have a long cinema pedigree, often indicating the moral compass of the captors. Mistreating prisoners of war violates the rules of war. Normally, in films, the enemy ignores standards of decency strictly observed by one's own side, and the contra follow this tradition. Somarriba deploys a panoply of strategies to demonize the contra, from the acting and the dialogue to the aggressive, associative editing and tendentious ideologi-

*Contra torturer with the blessing of the Pope (*Qué se rinda tu madre*)*

cal argument. Close-ups of contra officers emphasize their distorted facial features as they scream threats and obscenities at Noel. Their shouts eventually become part of an abstract sound montage, liberated from their sources in a cacophony of aural aggression. As the rhythm of the editing accelerates, Somarriba inserts shots of printed propaganda material introducing the religious dimension, with posters proclaiming that "Christ is the Liberator" and "The Pope is with us." Furthermore, in the film, candles scattered about the tent during the interrogation transform the session into a virtual religious service, collapsing the contra brutality with religious fanaticism.

The film constructs a grotesque image of the contra leadership and also tries to separate those brutes from the young recruits. Whiskey and tobacco from the United States, too expensive and unavailable to most Nicaraguans, indict the manipulation of the U.S. handlers and the depravity of the contra leaders, for peasant recruits cannot be blamed for susceptibility to such blandishments. One young contra complains of not seeing the dollars promised to them. Here, the film offers an explanation for the successful recruiting of the contra: While preaching anticommunism, the contra have built a mercenary army, held together by promises of money.

The interrogation of Noel includes another recruiting "tactic." The contra officers importune Noel to join them, arguing that his former comrades think he has already joined the contra and will never trust him again.

While documenting such charges is difficult, there are many accounts of the contras' kidnapping peasants and forcing them into counterrevolutionary forces. Resistant "recruits" would be threatened with reprisals against surviving family members in Nicaragua.[27]

Lest any contra consider escape, the film conveniently ends the interrogation session by announcing that a prisoner has escaped. The soldiers recapture the prisoner, and the officers strut and shout about what they do to anyone trying to escape, directing their words more to the young contra "recruits" than to the prisoner. Dramatically drawing his knife, one of the officers cuts deeply into the man's throat, prolonging the execution, while Somarriba cuts to several close-ups of terrified young contra soldiers watching the body crumple to the ground in extended death throes, the sound of the gushing blood recorded on the otherwise silent sound track.

The positive and negative poles of contra service having been clarified, the wages of sin versus the risks of apostasy, the film concludes. That night, peering through his cage's bamboo bars, Noel sees a vision, a single athletic figure's slow-motion acrobatic dance. Noel has already feigned agreement to participate in a terrorist mission into Nicaragua (using explosives), so he leaves the camp the next morning with several young contras. With a voice-over revealing his thoughts, Noel wonders what to do. While the others sleep, he slips into the forest. A contra discovers his escape and they chase him. Thinking only of his country, Noel soon recognizes the impossibility of escape, and maneuvers to die and take the others with him. Worried about triggering the explosives if they shoot at Noel, the contra corner him in a narrow ravine. Having successfully set his trap, Noel pulls the pin on a grenade. The film ends with the detonation, sealing Noel's martyrdom.

The finished film more or less conformed to the original plan, despite production problems.[28] In a sense, everything suffered in the graduation to fiction. The acting is either wooden (Noel) or hyperactive (contra officers). The editing is awkward, lacking the proper shots to cut together. No rhythm develops; shots often appear too long or too short. Perhaps most harmful, the narrative has no forward thrust. The attempted escape occurs without warning. The execution scene follows, but without narrative resonance or expectation. Normally, narratives rest on expectations communicated to the audience by dialogue or situation; the script of *Qué se rinda tu madre* limps from incident to incident without proleptic direction.

In his own commentary on the film, Carlos Vicente Ibarra concentrated on the interrogation scene:

> What is particularly arresting is the sequence which
> creates an hallucinogenic climate to highlight the

fetishism of an evangelical discourse full of fanaticism
which, it is true, breaks the unity of the cinematic
rhythm, but at the same time makes possible the
establishment of the links among the very ideological
elements of the followers of our enemies.[29]

Perhaps to burnish the film's political and aesthetic luster, Vicente Ibarra
opines that Noel's self-sacrifice "recalls two moments of our historical con-
vergence": when Darío warns that "a great flight of crows blackens the blue
sky," and Sandino writes that he will kill himself in a great explosion, refusing "to allow profane hands of traitors and invaders to profane his remains."
It is unlikely that any other spectator would "recall" these two moments,
surely not Somarriba, who wasn't given to poring over Sandino's collected
letters. The defensive references to Darío and Sandino may not only be an
unconscious acknowledgment of the film's weaknesses but also a barome-
ter of the pressures placed on fiction to spring full grown as art, without the
long training period granted the noticieros.

Esbozo de Daniel

While the film passed on to Mariano Marín from Ramiro
Lacayo suffers from similar problems, the 40-minute *Esbozo de Daniel* is less
heavy-handed. The action unfolds in an isolated fishing village, untouched
by Sandinista reform efforts or contra violence. Furthermore, the anecdote
hinges on a young boy's consciousness as first the Sandinistas and then the
contra arrive. The film sides with the Sandinistas, but the action takes place
in a more fluid space, as opposed to the highly symbolic spaces of *Manuel*
and the overtly Manichaean mise-en-scène of *Qué se rinda tu madre.*

Perhaps *Esbozo de Daniel*'s less strident tone derives from the original
story. Lacayo published it in *Ventana* in September 1982.[30] In the story, a
narrator recounts the life of Daniel, an 11-year-old loner in a remote fishing village. Daniel is an expert at fishing, but the narrator describes him
as if he were part of the natural habitat, blending into lush descriptions of
secluded areas where Daniel passes his time, with tattered clothing and no
shoes. At one point the narrator compares Daniel's fishing technique to a
pre-Columbian dance:

He would explain it to me patiently, he would untangle
the hook for me. At other times he was far away, still,
holding the fishing pole or throwing it into the water, or
he would be inside the water up to his waist, holding the

net, one end in his mouth, the other in his hand, he
would make a movement toward his back, circular, like
the lost step of some pre-Columbian dance and the net
would go flying in its arc, held down by the lead weights,
covering the whole sky, and it would fall in the water
making the sound of waves crashing.

A visitor from the city, the narrator brings with him a television and a
typewriter:

Sometimes when I sat down to write at the typewriter
he stopped watching television and moved next to me,
enraptured to see what I was doing and stayed there
watching, intrigued, curious: he has never seen a
typewriter.

The story ends when the narrator returns the following year and looks for
Daniel to give him a new fishing pole, only to find out that Daniel and his
family have moved on, and no one knows to where.

Presumably, Lacayo wrote this story long before the trilogy idea arose.
Certainly, its Rousseau-like evocation of l'enfant sauvage takes place in an
imaginary state of nature outside historical time. Daniel does not understand television conventions—he asks if the program has ended when a commercial interrupts it—and makes no comment on the stories the narrator
reads from the typewriter, stories the narrator feels "too inhibited to ask
him about."

In any event, by the following June, Lacayo had written a treatment based
on his story. The outline remains, but now Daniel's identity with nature has
become a pivot in the struggle between the revolutionary government and
the contra. A schoolteacher arrives to establish a village school, and Daniel,
the children's leader, fears that the newcomer will usurp his position. A competition ensues, Daniel boycotting school and claiming that a teacher, from
the city, cannot teach the practical skills they need. The schoolteacher sees
Daniel as a troublemaker who must be punished.

Eventually, the teacher realizes that he must win Daniel over as an ally.
Slowly, a new relation forms, with Daniel and the teacher "going off fishing
together, shrimping, and riding horseback together on the beach." For his
part, Daniel can now release his suspicion and enter the teacher's world. He
becomes an excellent student and once again leads the others.

But into this Sandinista idyll of city/campo bonding intrude the contras.
In front of the whole defenseless village, the heavily armed contras execute

the teacher as a communist. They burn the schoolhouse and destroy the village's food reserves. They threaten that if another teacher shows up everyone will pay. The next day the adults discuss what to do, and as the discussion gets increasingly heated, Daniel and his friends are already arranging stones for the new school's foundation.

Lacayo subsequently wrote a full script, but after contracting hepatitis, passed the project to Mariano Marín. In the case of *Esbozo de Daniel*, the transfer caused problems, for the volatile Marín complained that he was chained to a project he had not chosen; as Marín expressed it years later à propos *Daniel*, "in the end, I think the script was weak. A bad film can be saved with a good script, but a bad script cannot be saved in any way."[31] Nonetheless, Marín's name appeared in the credits as cowriter, which apparently elicited an angry memo from Lacayo, for Marín wrote Lacayo a spirited riposte offering to withdraw his name (an offer evidently not accepted by Lacayo, for Marín's name remains as co-screenwriter on the final print).[32]

This narrative follows a standard conversion formula, the youngster falling from the grace of ignorance into the world of knowledge and consequent political commitment. Such trajectories are standard in political filmmaking, from Pudovkin's *Mother* (1926) to Costa-Gavras's *Missing* (1982). The formula inevitably entails accession to political consciousness through personal tragedy, putatively warning the audience of the risk of ignorance. The dependence on the personal—the conversion mechanism—always poses problems, for moving to the abstraction of knowledge requires a considerable leap. The contras kill Daniel's new friend, but for unexplained reasons. According to the film, Daniel doesn't understand what Sandinista or communist means. Obviously the audience recognizes that the schoolteacher promises entrée to a new world, breaking the village's isolation. Yet the film doesn't actually argue for the benefits of modern social exchange. The village has not suffered from isolation: There is no poverty, disease, or material want. Daniel demonstrates the abundance of nature's bounty. The schoolteacher may bring knowledge, and culture—for Daniel is surprised at the idea of an imaginative literature—but aside from this, the film shows little to be garnered from education.

Once again, a film betrays unconscious biases of the revolution. The urban revolutionaries—and at INCINE, the urbane revolutionaries—having honed their aesthetic sensibilities abroad in foreign universities, tend to overvalue culture's importance. The new government's first great victory was the Literacy Campaign, heralded as a long-deserved gift to the people, especially the rural population. Yet these beneficiaries could not live by literacy alone. As the agricultural planners waited for the long-term investment projects to kick in, the government imposed collectivist rules and conditions on agricultural production. Campesinos were not forced to join cooperatives, but if they signed on, they could gain access to preferential benefits. Many did, only to drop out soon afterward. During the early years, the rural population sank deeper into poverty, their customs trampled in clumsy attempts to reduce exploitation in traditional commercial practices.

By the time Lacayo wrote the story, and later when the film was made, many knew of the problems, but *Esbozo de Daniel* ignored them. Campesinos undoubtedly welcomed schools, but as their economic situation deteriorated, they also wanted better prices and reliable transportation for their crops, as well as availability of manufactured goods.

Esbozo de Daniel elides these issues by setting the action in a fishing village, picturesque, but apparently entirely and happily self-sufficient before the arrival of the Sandinista and his cultural beneficence. Only after the teacher arrives do the contras appear. The contras did terrorize rural communities and target government personnel for death and mutilation. An unacknowledged reality was that the contras were supported by significant numbers of campesinos with legitimate complaints about the revolutionary government.[33] According to the film, only Daniel, his friends, and Daniel's aunt, mourning her lover, decisively recognize the Sandinista commitment to their well-being. The adults worry that the community will be caught in a political crossfire. But the adults don't complain about government policies. That is, the community is isolated not only geographically but also politically from any material or economic ties to the revolution; from their point of view, they have nothing to lose but their illiteracy and their lives.

Perhaps Marín's criticisms were justified. The introduction of the contras places too weighty a significance on Daniel's relationship with the teacher. In the original story, Lacayo imagined crossing the gulf separating the city and the country, a crossing in both directions, a fleeting social epiphany not repeated the following year. Adding the contras transforms it into a parable of winning indifferent youth to the revolution. The cautious, mutual discovery of each other sinks like a rock in the sand where they frolic. Marín admits that he overdid these scenes, and sees an unintended suggestion of homosexuality in the beach scene.[34] The film may include the teacher's romantic attachment to Daniel's aunt to dispel this idea.

Nonetheless, Daniel's relationship to the teacher remains the film's narrative fulcrum. As with subsequent fictional films by other directors, Marín introduces subjectivity. When the teacher arrives on the bus, Daniel stands watching, and Daniel's voice-over provides a commentary: "As soon as he got off, it was clear he was from the city." Later, after the teacher's death, Daniel sits on a large rock jutting into the sea. When his friends report that the teacher is dead, Daniel does not move, and they run off. Marín then

Teacher's "vision" of Daniel's aunt bringing fruit drink to teacher
(Esbozo de Daniel)

inserts shots from the seashore bonding sequence, in flashback, to convey
Daniel's interior state. Less overtly, Marín includes point-of-view shots of
the teacher. In one, after a close shot of the teacher looking off into the distance, at the end of a school lesson, the beautiful Aunt Lucia walks toward
the camera, clearly understood as the teacher's erotic attraction to Lucia as
she delivers a fruit drink from the grandfather.[35] At the same time, the film
is ambiguous about the teacher. In one lesson, he refers to the multiplication tables, though without polemical examples about FSLN largesse as in
Marín's earlier *El maestro popular*. In a later lesson, however, he asks the students about a sentence written on the board: "We are struggling for peace."
While innocuous, this is the ideological role for which the FSLN's critics
maligned the popular education project. The students don't know what he
means, for the only student response is that this is what's always on the
radio. Furthermore, the teacher puts a poster of Che on his wall. Che was
the original promoter of popular education in Cuba. In addition, the contra
leader specifically asks Daniel if the schoolteacher is Cuban. Certainly the
FSLN had a right to claim that it fought for peace, but the film also implicitly
endorses the ideological inflection of the popular-education campaign.

   Esbozo de Daniel completed the original trilogy of *Manuel*, *Noel*, and
Daniel, but the term trilogy suggests more connected parts than the reality
supported. Vargas was still following the noticiero production schedule,

Rural schoolteacher with his poster of Che mounted in Daniel's room
(Esbozo de Daniel)

shooting in 35-mm black and white according to the ICAIC production agreement. INCINE recognized that fiction projects could not be listed as noticieros, so *Noel* and *Daniel* were shot in 16-mm color, and processed at the Cuban radio and television facility (ICRT—Instituto Cubano de Radio y Televisión). But the momentum building around fiction ended the noticiero cycle forever. However misleading the trilogy rubric, the INCINE personnel viewed them as part of the same fictional thrust. Because of his illness, the head of INCINE, Ramiro Lacayo, had not yet weighed in with a fiction film, with the exception of the experimental, non-acted short *Más claro no canta un gallo* in 1982. When he did, however, he did it in a canny way, which provoked resentment among some other directors.

El centerfielder

From the beginning, INCINE benefited from Lacayo's friendships and connections. Lacayo had been friendly with the martyred Camilo Ortega and also knew Daniel and Humberto Ortega. He had direct contact with Sergio Ramírez, vice-president of Nicaragua after the 1984 elections. Ramirez acted as guardian angel helping INCINE in ways that the Ministry of Culture could not. At this time (mid-1984), furthermore, the government cut off funding for INCINE's production apparatus, so INCINE needed new ways to finance filmmaking.

With INCINE's production future uncertain, Lacayo proposed making a film based on a 1969 short story by Sergio Ramírez. Lacayo interested a Hollywood screenwriter with leftist sympathies, Robert Young, in writing the screenplay. And he found resources to produce the film in 35 mm (black and white), unlike *Qué se rinda tu madre/Noel* and *Esbozo de Daniel/ Daniel*, both shot in 16 mm.

Sergio Ramírez had a distinguished reputation as a writer active in the struggle against Somoza. With others, he had founded the leftist literary group "Front Ventana" in 1960 at the University of León.[36] At the end of the 1970s, Ramírez was a member of the Group of Twelve that offered to negotiate a transition to a non-Somoza government. As a prestigious Nicaraguan writer and intellectual, Ramírez brought considerable nonpartisan legitimacy to this group of 12 oppositional figures who were instrumental in offering an alternative to a capitulation to guerrilla forces. At the time, he had been studying abroad in Germany, and only after the triumph did he emerge publicly as a powerful Sandinista figure. As vice-president, Ramírez led the Sandinista representatives in the National Assembly, but as a cultural figure with a long-standing interest in cinema, he was INCINE's real lifeline to power within the FSLN.

Selecting a Ramírez story, then, provided both artistic heft and insurance to the project, but it also followed a well-trod path of revolutionary filmmaking previously unexplored by INCINE. Revolutions in the Soviet Union and Cuba had quickly filmed stories set in prerevolutionary times, the most famous being Eisenstein's *Potemkin* in 1925. Ambrosio Fornet identifies one of the two specific characteristics of revolutionary Cuban film as "its profound historicity,"[37] seen, for example, in the stunning *Lucía* (1969). In the same year, Miguel Littín made *El chacal de Nahueltoro* and Sanjinés directed *El coraje del pueblo* (1971) in Bolivia, both stories set in the past. Ramírez's story, published in 1969, takes place in the epoch of Somoza, and thus avoids current events, the subject of almost all previous INCINE noticieros, documentaries, and fiction films.

The story of *El centerfielder* follows the interrogation and murder of a Sandinista guerrilla's father. In the cold, damp depths of prison, a sweating prisoner is summoned for questioning. Walking past the field above, he imagines escaping while chasing a fly ball toward the center-field wall. A rifle butt interrupts his reverie and he arrives for questioning. The Guardia Nacional captain refers to the prisoner's dossier, asking him about playing baseball for Nicaragua in Cuba, before asking about his son's involvement with clandestine weapons transportation. The baseball questions trip childhood flashbacks as the prisoner replies monosyllabically. In the flashbacks, his mother complains gently about her son's obsession with baseball as he makes a winning catch in center field and is fêted by his friends. The prisoner protests that he knows nothing. Failing to garner any information, the captain tells the guard to take the prisoner away. The guard asks what he should write on the dossier, and the captain advises him to write that the prisoner was killed trying to escape—following the prisoner's fantasy, though with an altered ending. The film concludes with his murder.

The story's publication in 1969 coincided with a quiescent period for the FSLN, following several devastating military setbacks costing many lives and ultimately ending the FSLN's foco strategy. As discussed, the FSLN saw this period as one for "the accumulation of forces," a time to rebuild the popular movement, especially the mountain support networks among the peasants. This physically difficult time is described graphically and earthily by Omar Cabezas in *Fire from the Mountain*. Ramírez organizes his story around a guerrilla's father, a shoemaker too poor to have a shop, who works at home. The father pleads ignorance of his son's political involvement, but the FSLN depended on precisely this form of passive support, less active than the guerrilla militants who had broken ties with family and friends to disappear into the mountains.[38] The story takes no position on the son's politics, nor does it reveal what the father knows; but it clearly sympathizes with the shoemaker, helplessly cut off from justice, his body carelessly tossed on a garbage heap to rot. The captain does not torture the prisoner. Rather, Ramírez simply denies any legitimacy to authority. Of course the regime's methods are inhuman, but Ramírez boldly challenges its authority instead of concentrating on abuses. The regime is illegitimate and must be uprooted, a fundamental FSLN demand that distinguished it from the reform-minded opposition.

The film follows the story faithfully, finding successful equivalents to the subjective passages of the story, as well as the concrete physical descriptions. Flashbacks pose no problem for the cinema, but the film distends the time within the flashbacks, specifically the time it takes the protagonist in center field to run after the baseball on his way to the wall—a scene shown twice, as in the story, first as the character's fantasy, second as the fabricated police account of his murder.

Apart from the baseball scenes, the action takes place in prison, the drama built around dialogue. Two newspaper articles on the film during its production discussed the adaptation, and Lacayo specifically singled out the acting as key: "The actors here are more essential, the success depends on them."[39] At the same time, Lacayo makes some more general, and peculiar, comments about adaptation. Taking up the position of García Márquez against a cinematic treatment of *One Hundred Years of Solitude,* Lacayo explains that "the work of Gabo contains metaphors that cannot be translated cinematically"; the work of Ramírez, on the other hand, "lends itself to cinema, for it is very realistic."[40] Yet the flashbacks, the main character's dreamlike state, his just having awakened from sleep, the several levels of subjective imagining, all in the space of a five-page story, certainly constitute elements that depart from any conventional realism. They constitute the obvious *unrealistic* fabric of a literary work that does not simply record an interrogation session, but rather tries to convey the agitated mental state of victims of such interrogation.

In fact, all four fictional shorts reflect the tension between the realistic and unrealistic. At the same time, the trilogy's three films take on the reality of the war, whose intensity reached its height between 1984 and 1985, when the films were produced. Clearly, the filmmakers wanted to confront the enormous psychological stress and human and material suffering of the war. Those pressures pushed the filmmakers, consciously or not, to seek ways to convey psychological trauma, hence the subjective cinematic strategies.

Similarly, the trilogy provides case histories of three "muchachos," the popular term for Sandinista youth. These muchachos are not simply caricatures, but individuals, struggling to defend the revolution. They honor a public, civic commitment to their people but also struggle to build private lives under extreme circumstances. The filmmakers used subjectivity to express these private battles to defend personal space. At the same time, as the filmmakers sought to fashion their own creative contributions, the subjective offered an escape from the party dogmatism found in many early noticieros. In addition to capturing the dislocation and disorientation of a war-torn society, the filmmakers associated artistry with interiority, with flashbacks, reveries, and altered psychological states, a creative tension that Vicente Ibarra praised (in *Esbozo de Daniel*) as "the trench of war that joins art and gun."[41]

Nine　　　DASHED AMBITIONS:
THE REACH FOR FEATURES

After completing the first fiction films in early 1985, INCINE ended noticiero production. Instead of continuing to produce both noticieros and short fiction, INCINE proceeded into the uncharted realm of feature films. There is no doubt that various foreign filmmakers' feature productions in Nicaragua fanned the ambitions of INCINE's filmmakers. Large crews from Cuba, France, and the United States were working on a scale far beyond INCINE's experience. But the filmmakers believed that feature production was the next step toward consolidating a real national-production entity. Given the qualitative leap in the resources and time demanded by feature films, the consequences were serious. By the time Lacayo finished his first feature, *El espectro de la guerra*, in 1988, INCINE effectively imploded.

Los hijos del río

The first planned feature, however, was a documentary, not a fiction film. After working on his own *Río San Juan, a este lado de la puerta,* and after seeing Iván Argüello's *Rompiendo el silencio,* both set on the Atlantic Coast, Fernando Somarriba proposed a project on the Miskito Indians.[1] While FSLN problems with the Miskitos broke out early after the triumph in 1979 and rapidly deteriorated, INCINE had not reported on the situation. María José Alvarez and Ramiro Lacayo had produced *La costa Atlántica* in 1980, but that was before violence had erupted; and that short film tried to offer an overview of the coast for the Pacific mestizo population that knew little of the Atlantic Coast. Once war broke out, security considerations restricted intercourse with the Atlantic Coast. More significantly, the war caused serious problems for the government, and the Sandinistas were reeling from the negative international publicity about the problems. The Atlantic Coast was an extremely sensitive issue, and INCINE may have wanted to avoid confrontation with their sponsors, the government. At the same time, the obstacles to operating in a war zone were not insuperable, for Frank Pineda and Iván Argüello succeeded in filming *Teotecacinte* in 1983 in a war zone near Honduras in the Pacific region.

But the Miskito controversy presented a far more delicate political problem. In the Pacific half of the country, the contra were led initially by former Guardia Nacional officers and supported financially, logistically, and politically by the United States. The contra forces recruited some campesinos, but the government never recognized the contra's legitimacy and refused to negotiate with them. Apart from the United States and client states such as Honduras, international opinion did not sympathize with the contra. The Miskitos, on the other hand, represented an entirely different problem. Since the revolution was fought mostly in the Pacific half of the country, the Atlantic coastal populations did not participate, so before 1979 the revolution hardly affected people living on the Atlantic Coast. After the triumph, the Sandinistas' attempts to extend revolutionary policies to the Atlantic Coast met considerable resistance.

The Sandinistas wanted to include the Atlantic Coast as part of Nicaragua in a real way, not simply formally. However, developmentalist blinders prevented them from seeing the centrality of the ethnic question, quite aside from some mestizo cadres' traditional prejudices, born of total ignorance of coastal realities. Correlatively, the coastal peoples traditionally saw the Pacific region mestizos as "the Spanish," interlopers with less understanding of them than the foreign companies that had employed—and exploited— them over so many years.

Many factors contributed to these problems. As revolutionaries, the Sandinistas wanted to transform the country according to the "will of the majority." But clearly any Nicaraguan majority would be the majority mestizo population living in the Pacific, most of whom had supported the revolution at appalling human cost. When the Sandinistas arrived, knowing that the coastal population was inactive in the revolution, they didn't appoint local inhabitants to significant administrative posts.[2] The Literacy Campaign, so popular elsewhere, initially did not include the coastal languages (though that mistake was rectified). Probably the single worst error was failing to establish ties with the Moravian Church on the coast.

The first Moravian missionaries arrived from Germany in 1848 and the Moravians integrated themselves immediately, learning Miskito and translating the Bible into Miskito. Moravian pastors became leaders of the Indian communities. They were the essential interlocutors in any dialogue with the new government. While the FSLN emphasized social, economic, and political changes, they seriously miscalculated the spiritual/ethnic axis and the Moravian leaders' standing. When the Sandinistas arrested and mistreated these leaders in a sweep of arrests in February 1981, the results were catastrophic.

This is not to say that the Moravians were innocent victims. Moravian doctrine had contained a fervent vilification of godless communism. Furthermore, the coastal population depended on the foreign, often U.S.-based companies for a century, so they were more familiar with U.S. values than those of the Nicaraguan mestizo population.[3] Consequently, the Moravian leaders and the Miskito population already harbored suspicions about the "foreigners" from the Pacific promising to "awaken the giant," the unfortunate slogan used by the FSLN to characterize the putative somnolence of the Atlantic Coast.

The war on the coast offered volatile propaganda material. Mistreatment of ethnic minorities, and in this case indigenous peoples, aroused the concern of many human rights groups. Indigenous rights activists protested the treatment of the Miskitos from a different perspective. For the most extreme activists, those advocates of so-called Fourth World Theory, indigenous groups hold inalienable rights to traditional lands.[4] States, with centralized authority and fixed territorial borders, are a Western invention and have no rights over the "nations" of indigenous peoples. Thus, the "border" of the Miskito nation does not end at the Río Coco in northern Nicaragua, the international border adjudicated in 1960 between Honduras and Nicaragua. The Miskito nation exists independently of territorial claims, with its own system of laws, cultural practices, and traditions. Paradoxically, the Somoza regime did not intrude on these rights, as it more or less ignored the Atlantic Coast. Instead, the Miskitos suffered barbaric depredations working for foreign companies granted concessions on the coast, some of which were documented powerfully in La otra cara del oro.

Somarriba cited the "manipulation" of the indigenous rights question as a central reason for making the film.[5] Ramiro Lacayo sounded the same note when he wrote to Bayardo Arce, member of the Dirección Nacional of the FSLN (and, as head of the party apparatus, responsible for propaganda), complaining about the lack of cooperation from "ranks of the FSLN."[6]

While the Miskitos form a minority of the coastal population, for the FSLN, the problem revolved around the Miskitos.[7] Even today, many details remain obscure, with little written documentation from the time. In November 1979, at the FSLN's suggestion, MISURASATA was formed.[8] At the new organization's assembly, Steadman Fagoth, a Miskito Indian, was elected to head the group. In the two years after the triumph, the FSLN attempted to apply policies successfully pursued in the Pacific, forming co-

operatives, building health clinics and roads, and establishing a local bureaucracy run by mestizos. The Miskitos resented the sudden changes and felt
that the mestizo Sandinistas were arbitrary and sometimes racist. Fagoth
and others launched increasingly ambitious and intransigent demands, at
one point claiming rights to almost 40 percent of Nicaragua. At the end of
1980, the Sandinistas tried to prevent a mass demonstration against the presence of Cuban personnel (doctors and teachers) in Bluefields, and friction
intensified. In 1981 the situation worsened. Some Miskitos joined U.S. advisers and contra guerrillas encamped across the Río Coco in Honduras. In
February, Sandinista soldiers arrested many Miskito leaders. The following
day, at Prinzapolka, Sandinista soldiers stormed a Moravian church looking
for several Miskitos. The gunfight that ensued left eight dead, four Sandinista
soldiers and four Miskitos.

The Sandinistas soon released the arrested leaders, except for Steadman
Fagoth. When Fagoth was released, in May, instead of going abroad to study
as agreed, he rounded up thousands of Miskitos from the Río Coco area and
crossed into Honduras to join the contra group (Fuerza Democrática Nicaragüense, or FDN). Fagoth then changed the name of MISURASATA to MISURA
(that is, without the Sandinistas). Another leader, Brooklyn Rivera, coordi-
nator of MISURASATA, initially joined Fagoth in Honduras but later took
his group, still named MISURASATA, to Costa Rica, where he joined former
Sandinista Edén Pastora's contra force, Alianza Revolucionaria Democrática
(ARDE).[9]

By late 1981/early 1982, the FSLN saw the situation in strictly military
terms. Hence, they decided to move the Miskito population away from what
had become a war zone along the Río Coco. This may have made military
sense, but the political cost was enormous, as was the material cost of trans-
porting the population and building a new community, Tasba Pri [meaning
"free land" in Miskito], at a place 60 miles inland.[10] Some under pressure,
some of their own volition, fled to Honduras; others traveled to Tasba Pri.
As soon as the villagers left, the Sandinistas burned their homes.

Tasba Pri was a fiasco. Forced to live away from the river, unable to grow
traditional foods on small plots adjacent to their homes, the Miskitos never
accepted the move, despite considerable FSLN investment. Meanwhile, the
United States and human rights organizations, including the United Nations
High Commissioner for Refugees, publicized the Miskitos' situation in Honduras as a refugee problem, a propaganda disaster for the Sandinistas.[11] By the
end of 1983, the FSLN recognized that a military solution, probably impossible, was certainly ill advised and began searching for a political solution,
initiating a long process known as Autonomy.

Early in 1985, INCINE drafted a proposal for a film entitled "MISKITO."

We believe it is important to make a documentary on this theme, given that this problem has been used abroad to discredit the Sandinista Revolution and until now, there is no national film which responds to this, a film which lays out the position of the Revolution and its interest in searching for solutions. Similarly, almost all the films that have been made about the Miskitos approach the problem in a superficial and anecdotal form, without looking in depth at its historical roots. We propose to make a deeper analysis that touches on the historical, social and political aspect of this problematic.[12]

While the proposal suggests that the film will make the Sandinista case, the synopsis clearly acknowledges Sandinista "errors," including

the Sandinista limitations in the treatment of the ethnic question: the non-coast origin of most of the Sandinista cadres in positions of authority . . . [and] the inappropriate form with which the religious question was treated by some sectors of the Government. We will clarify that this effort [the resettlement] was done with the intention of protecting this people from the effects of the war, and that despite some errors already mentioned, there have never been concentration camps, massacres or military repression against these people.

In short, INCINE took a pro-FSLN line, while acknowledging errors and misunderstandings in FSLN policy. Such an attitude may not demonstrate complete independence, but neither did INCINE whitewash Sandinista culpability.

The attached budget projects a production schedule of 11 months at a cost of $108,114.[13] INCINE, financially independent since May 1984, would raise 44 percent and seek outside funding for the remainder. The filming would take three months and allow for 18 hours of footage—a high shooting ratio of 18 to 1—but it is normally difficult to estimate shooting ratios for documentaries covering ongoing events accurately. A later budget ballooned to $150,000, the increase to be assumed by INCINE. At that point INCINE was still looking for outside financing. The earlier budget included a long postproduction stay in the United States. But the later one indicates that postproduction would take place in Mexico, and Ramiro Lacayo signed a coproduction contract in August.[14]

The contract specifies that the film will be a medium-length documentary (approximately 60 minutes) in 16-mm color, filmed on the Atlantic Coast of Nicaragua and "in the Miskitu camps on the Atlantic Coast of the Republic of Honduras." The film will cover

> the theme of the Miskitu ethnic group on the Atlantic
> Coast of Nicaragua, its history, its situation at the time of
> the Sandinista triumph in 1979; its contradictions with
> the new Government, the displacement and return to the
> area of the Río Coco.

The research and filming were to be completed by the end of October; the editing was to take from November to January, with postproduction to end by mid-February 1986.

As with *Manuel*, however, problems beset the project from the beginning. Untangling the reasons behind production problems is generally a hopeless task. Here they were aggravated by the challenge of filming in the inhospitable Atlantic coastal region, with weather, transportation, and communication problems, as well as complications of the national economy, political tensions, military threats, etc. Thus, for example, director Fernando Somarriba wrote to the current head of production at INCINE, Julio Torres, on August 28, 1985, that

> During the last three months (92 days), we have worked
> effectively only 8 days. That is, out of 92 days, our
> effective return has been only 8 days, for the rest of the
> time we spent trying to coordinate our departures.[15]

Five months later, in January 1986, Somarriba wrote to the region's administrator, introducing yet a new problem with production. An earthquake forced Mexico to cancel the contract, and INCINE had to seek new support. As a result, he estimated that *filming* would conclude at the end of February.[16] In a letter to Julio Torres in May, Somarriba expressed concern about the already shot footage, for there were problems with the first seven hours of footage, another nine hours waited to be developed, and two more hours had yet to be shot.[17] While the original contract projected a completion date of February 1986, Somarriba had still not finished filming in August 1986.[18]

The difficulties extended into 1987, but Somarriba did finish the film—or, rather, two films. After completing an hour-and-a-half Spanish-language version in 1987, he returned to the National Film Board in Canada in 1988 where Somarriba, fluent in English, completely recut the film and produced an hour-long version in English. Both films draw on the same material, but neither includes footage from the refugee camps in Honduras. In addition, because of scheduling delays, he couldn't shoot footage of the return to the Río Coco, nor is there much material on the Autonomy process. Hence, the films lack some material he had wanted, though he sought footage from the Sandinista Army and various foreign filmmakers.

Nonetheless, the films are an impressive accomplishment for INCINE. For the first time, INCINE took on a sensitive topic that had drawn justifiable criticism from abroad. From the vantage point of the late 1990s, years after the Sandinista electoral defeat in 1990, the FSLN criticisms may appear muted in the film(s). But many Sandinistas at the time objected vigorously to the film; some saw it as a contra film. Ultimately, INCINE resisted pressure to change the film.

Somarriba views the English version as the superior film, but both versions are stimulating historical documents. It is true that the Spanish version stays too close to the material, containing a bewildering number of interviews and positions. But this overload tries to avoid the oversimplification an overly streamlined treatment might have risked. The production history indicates that Somarriba sorely missed the footage he had planned, and the interviews are an attempt to compensate for gaps. Apparently Somarriba recognized the overload problem. In the second version he eliminated almost half of the interviews.

In addition, the Spanish version, while arguably more sympathetic to the FSLN, is more diffuse. The glut of information blurs the argument, but the rush of material accurately captures and conveys the complexity of the situation. Alternatively, the English version does not necessarily oversimplify, but it is clearer, stating at the outset, "This is a film about the rights of native people." The first film engages the issue as a more multifaceted problematic that includes the question of native rights, but not as the dominant theme.

The Spanish version announces the context with a title "Atlantic Coast, 1985" over the opening high-angle shot of a field. Then a series of shots of shells of buildings and houses underlines the destruction and absence of inhabitants. The voice-over refers to January 1982, the time of the MISURA attacks, when the events, "like a river, overflowed." The film, then, like its English successor, gives the river, a source of material and spiritual sustenance for the Miskito population, its rightful place as the stabilizing axis of Miskito life. Still, the metaphor of a river overflowing elides the question of responsibility by invoking a natural process, lending inevitability to what transpired.

As images of destruction cascade past, the commentary describes the toll of dead, disappeared, kidnapped. Armed men have wrought this tragedy, but "the Sandinistas were confused by the tactics of the U.S. government." A slow tilt down the empty frame of a church with a large cross illuminated against a wall whitened by sunlight concludes the prologue, and the title and credits scroll over shots of a calm, tranquil Río Coco.

The following section traces the coast's history in voice-over. The exploitation by the foreign companies engaged in mining, bananas, and wood emptied the region of its natural resources, after which they withdrew, leaving poverty and disease (silicosis) in their wake. The commentary then goes back to the creation of the Miskito kingdom in the seventeeth century. Despite the constant presence of foreigners, the Miskitos maintained their culture. Images of Miskitos displaying their fishing skills indicate their attachment to the river and their self-reliance. The Río Coco is central to Miskito life, a cultural and economic lifeline that would later be sundered by the forced relocation to Tasba Pri.

A village bell introduces a sequence on the Moravian Church arriving from Germany in 1848. The film describes the church's commitment to preserving the Miskito language, especially by translating the Bible. Preserving the language would be key in protecting against foreign influences. At the same time, the Moravians introduced changes in Miskito customs, such as raising fruit and domesticating animals to supplement hunting and fishing. Though the film does not mention these changes, Vilas associates them with a Moravian religious strategy to inhibit the Miskitos' nomadic tendencies. The nomadic life had included dissolute activities in the mining towns. Domestic crops and husbandry tethered the Miskitos to homes and villages.[19] In an effective coda to a Moravian church service sequence with the singing of Miskito hymns, the camera zooms out slowly on the rural church as the voice-over notes the Miskito community's isolation from the war going on in the rest of the country (before the Sandinista triumph of 1979).

With this background, the film moves to the 1980s, proceeding chronologically. The voice-over describes the formation of MISURASATA, supported by the FSLN, and the election of Steadman Fagoth as president. At this point, the film tries to expose Fagoth as a villain, asserting that he used the Literacy Campaign to advance his own political plans, which were designed by outside sources such as the CIA and the United States. Then several short interviews air different interpretations of what caused the confrontations between the FSLN and MISURASATA and other Miskito organizations. The first speaker, Leonard Hogson, a representative of Centro de Investigaciones y Documentación de la Costa Atlántica (CIDCA), a Sandinista think tank on the Atlantic Coast (headed by a mestizo), accuses Fagoth of making unrealistic promises to the Miskitos and then blaming the Sandinistas when they did not come to pass. Hazel Lau, a Miskito member of the National Commission on Autonomy (and one of the first leaders of MISURASATA), says when she heard of the Literacy Campaign in September 1979, she approached government officials about including the Atlantic Coast languages. "This is when they became antagonists: the Ministry of Education, the National Association of Educators, and the local leaders."

Then, in a television speech, Luis Carrión, Dirección Nacional member and vice-minister of the Interior, expresses outrage at MISURASATA's manipulation. Dressed in a green Sandinista uniform, he accuses MISURASATA of taking credit for the health, education, and other social services brought to the coast by the FSLN. Furthermore, Carrión sees Yankee imperialism as the hidden puppeteer behind this calumny. Hogson continues his indictment of Fagoth, for "Steadman Fagoth pushed things to separatism." Because of the fear of a U.S. invasion, the Sandinistas had to arrest the MISURASATA leadership, who confessed publicly to their manipulation of the indigenous people. Indeed, a videotaped confession of Fagoth, giving a haltingly cadenced "confession," follows. Two additional interviews discredit Fagoth. Brooklyn Rivera, Fagoth's leading rival within MISURASATA, claims that Fagoth accelerated the confrontational tendencies with his "irresponsibility." Tomás Borge, sole living FSLN founder and the minister of the Interior, acknowledges Sandinista failures, but, "Steadman Fagoth became the principal agent of the CIA leading to the first armed confrontation. The other leaders were not the same."

While the film does not push a single interpretation, it does target Fagoth as the principal instigator of the problems. In this sense, it tends to downplay FSLN errors. Thus, while Luis Carrión may have cause to be outraged at the denial of the FSLN's real contributions in improving the welfare of the indigenous population, he appears not to recognize the resentment fomented by FSLN paternalism in bestowing these benefits, the exclusion of Miskitos and others from powerful positions in the coastal bureaucracy, the fight over the Literacy Campaign, the suspicion of indigenous groups. This myopia, which leads him to see the FSLN as the injured party, betrays the Sandinista blind spot. The reflexive attack on Yankee imperialism clouds an understanding of the non-mestizo population. The voice-over following these interviews picks out this theme:

> This sad conflict was provoked. The United States had decided to use all its means and resources to destabilize the Sandinista revolution. . . . The Miskitos were part of the [CIA's] strategy toward Nicaragua. . . . The government of the United States had achieved its goal. It had unleashed war.

Luis Carrión attacking the machinations of Miskito contra leader Steadman Fagoth
(Los hijos del río)

Steadman Fagoth's "confession" (Los hijos del río)

Dashed Ambitions: The Reach for Features

This interpretation absolves the Sandinistas of responsibility, and simplifies the situation. The only two contemporaneous documents from the early days of the conflict, statements by Carrión and Fagoth, appear to support such an interpretation.

But the rest of the film restores a good deal of the complexity. The opening 20 minutes, after all, deal only with the first years of the problem, through early 1982, when Fagoth and the Sandinistas adopted extreme positions, as Borge noted in his first appearance: "Instead of trying to persuade them, which we could have done, we adopted methods which led to taking extreme positions." Less didactically, the rest of the film chronicles the process of seeking dialogue and building trust.

In the next set of interviews, lasting eight minutes, a less Manichaean picture takes shape. The same Hogson who had attacked Fagoth earlier now expresses his own, and the Miskitos', astonishment at the arrest and mistreatment of Moravian pastors. The superintendent of the Moravian Church, Andy Shogreen, insists on the inextricability of the church and the indigenous population. By implication, attacks on the church are attacks on the Miskitos. Hazel Lau explains that a real fear of the Sandinistas spread throughout the Miskito communities after the February 1981 arrests and the ideological campaign waged against the Sandinistas.

The Sandinistas responded to the conflict with a military decision that reflected the extremity of their position. They decided to transfer the Miskitos from their traditional homes along the Río Coco to a newly constructed community named Tasba Pri, arguing that the Miskitos needed protection from attacks by contras based in Honduras. Of course Miskito villagers did not necessarily share this perspective. Some 10,000 Miskitos fled to Honduras, while the Sandinistas transported several thousand to Tasba Pri. Hogson explains that some communities requested to be moved, but that the Sandinista soldiers terrified the Miskitos by burning their houses left behind to prevent the contras from using them. The voice-over elaborates on the Miskitos' disorientation, observing that some believed this was the biblical exodus. And, unequivocally, the narrator states, "Tasba Pri was a mistake. It was another world."

Here the film does not avoid calling the centerpiece of the Sandinista response to the descent into war, the abrupt displacement of the indigenous people, a mistake. Tomás Borge, who assumed responsibility for handling the problem on the Atlantic Coast in 1985, acknowledges this when he describes the mechanical application of ideas from the Pacific to different realities on the coast. They hadn't understood the cultural importance of the Río Coco for the Miskitos; the water, the crops, the environment, were different at Tasba Pri. Miskito life could not be separated from the Río Coco, plucked from its ancestral home and replanted in alien soil. In establishing Tasba Pri, the Sandinistas tried to separate the ethnic from the political. The failure of Tasba Pri after three years dramatized their inextricability.

The film then addresses the intervening three years of war. Since the crew shot no footage during this period, the film relies on shots of Puerto Cabezas and the mining area. Mirna Cunningham, a Miskito doctor in charge of the regional government in 1984, fills in some history of the foreign companies in previous decades, describing the enclave economy. After years of exploiting and exporting natural resources, the companies pulled out, leaving no infrastructure behind. Even industrial fishing was impossible, for the fishing fleet sailed off to neighboring Costa Rica after the Sandinista triumph. Her interview emphasizes the coast's economic devastation, a developmentalist perspective that occludes the native peoples' right to autonomy. But the interview bridges the gap between the relocation to Tasba Pri in 1982 and the shooting of the film in 1985. A title concludes this transition to the village of Yulu in 1985.

By this time, multiple splits had divided the armed Miskito camp. Fagoth, head of MISURA, remained in Honduras allied with the FDN. Rivera went to Costa Rica and allied with former Sandinista comandante Edén Pastora. The United States tried to unite Fagoth's MISURA and Rivera's MISURASATA under the new name of KISAN (Kus Indianka Asla Nicaragua ra, Union of Coast Indians in Nicaragua), but that organization split into KISAN for War, based in Honduras, and KISAN for Peace, comprised of armed Miskitos living on the Nicaraguan coast.[20] After 1983 the Sandinistas recognized the folly of a military solution and sought negotiations with Miskito leaders. They arranged some fragile cease-fires, often disrupted by groups from Honduras and Costa Rica. But the Sandinistas had accepted the need to move forward with plans for Autonomy. By opening dialogue with Miskitos, the FSLN managed to exclude the unstable Fagoth as the power broker representing the Miskitos, as the commentary concludes: "Steadman Fagoth was out of the scene." During this update, soldiers from both sides are shown speaking informally. The film does not list atrocities committed by various Miskito groups. Instead, it accents the mutual search for solutions to end the fighting and fortify the truce.

After additional interviews, the film returns to the unhappy Miskitos marooned at Tasba Pri. In a 15-minute sequence, the Miskitos dismantle their houses, load their belongings and families into trucks, and start back to the Río Coco. The narrator describes the problems with the Tasba Pri design, including houses being placed too close together, the inability to grow traditional crops, the absence of fishing, and the inappropriateness of Sandinista cooperative ideas to the community's traditional forms of organization. Still, Miskitos and Sandinistas got to know each other, creating a climate of confidence. "Tasba Pri was not ideal, but it was an awakening of their becoming conscious of their nationality, what is their Nicaraguan being." To compound the return's arduousness, the rains came. As 120 trucks neared their destination, rain halted them, truck and tractor wheels spinning helplessly in mud. Finally, the Miskitos grabbed their belongings and set off on foot.

The film's final 20 minutes sketch the latest stages of the situation. Tomás Borge speaks at meetings of the Autonomy process, publicly acknowledging Sandinista errors and referring specifically to the burning of houses and repressive measures. Throwing his authority behind the Autonomy process, he avers that the Autonomy process will proceed independently of the ongoing hostilities. Shogreen, Hogson, and Cunningham admit the difficulty of the path ahead, but each endorses the importance of continuing. Only Brooklyn Rivera questions the integrity of the process. For him, "it's just a re-organization of central power, not a real autonomy for the native population. What we think is that there must be a limit and control over the central government, not vice versa." His obstructionism sets up a dramatic sequence of Sandinista soldiers rushing into helicopters and flying off to confront Rivera's forces, as the commentary explains that Rivera returned in January 1986 with a plan for insurrection, aimed at sabotaging the talks and recuperating his ebbing prestige. Somarriba then cuts to a quiet village where several Miskitos respond to Rivera's plan. The villagers fled when Rivera arrived with gringos; they had never heard gunfire before. The narrator comments, "Many felt they had returned to paradise and that the war had ended. But these illusions were shattered when soldiers from Honduras came, setting mines, launching ambushes, and kidnapping and attacking Sandinista camps."

After recounting efforts to disrupt peace, the film shows a tranquil Miskito village. Men work on their new houses; babies huddle with their mothers who are cooking food. One young child looks shyly at the camera, the image freezes, and the credits roll. Over these serene scenes the final voice-over summarizes the current state of affairs:

> The situation remains subject to external forces, which
> make good propaganda with it against the Sandinista
> Revolution. While aggression by forces supported by the
> United States does not stop, the Miskitos continue to
> suffer, wandering in their own territory. The autonomy
> project, the dialogue for peace, the return to the river,
> goes on, marking the path where hope is nourished.

The film does not explain the Sandinista mistakes or the gravity of their consequences. Neither does it demonize the Miskitos who fought the Sandinistas. Luis Carrión, in his early Sandinista statement, blames Yankee imperialism without admitting government errors, but Tomás Borge, his superior at the Ministry of the Interior, later takes responsibility for Sandinista errors. Borge sees the hand of the CIA but also recognizes the centrality of the native rights issue. The government cannot apply the same policies to the coast. As the filmmakers learned with the noticieros, Somarriba did not rely solely on comandantes' and cadres' repeating an official line. He understood the film's credibility depended on a wide range of interviews, including the head of the Moravian Church, Miskitos working with the Sandinistas, Steadman Fagoth, Brooklyn Rivera, and several Miskito guerrillas who had joined the contras.

Too often in earlier INCINE films, real *political* problems were avoided. A triumphalist rhetoric prevailed, even after the filmmakers stopped relying on comandante speeches. In one of the best noticieros, *Rompiendo el silencio*, the film about hacking through the jungle to bring telephone lines to Miskito villages on the Atlantic Coast, the issue of Miskito autonomy is never broached. The film effaces this political problem in favor of the military problem, the contra threat. The film assumes that the villagers would welcome a commitment to infrastructural improvement. Though the film opens and closes with the young boy singing in Miskito, the Miskitos never speak, and according to the filmmaker, the Miskitos did not help on the film; the crew had better relations with the Sumos. Thus, even in 1984, after the Sandinistas had witnessed Miskito resistance to their paternalistic attitudes, this excellent film adopts similar attitudes, extolling the collective self-sacrifice of the mestizo telephone brigadistas. Just as the FSLN insensitively coined the slogan of "Awakening the giant" in its early work on the coast, so *Breaking the Silence* projects silence onto a group that had been speaking in its own voice and language, for years, even to the point of speaking with guns. *Breaking the Silence* is deaf to that speech.

Similarly, the sole film on the Agrarian Reform, *Nuestra Reforma Agraria*, elides the tensions in the process, suppressing *political* issues raging inside the agricultural ministry. Like *Breaking the Silence* vis à vis the Miskitos, the film shows, but does not hear, the campesinos who are supposed to benefit from the government's policies. Instead, the film constructs an ur-campesino, a symbolic precipitate of campesino magma, the diversity and variousness of campesino interests distilled out and stripped of speech.

In *Los hijos del río*, there is a cacophony of voices, mostly Miskitos, including two vociferous and important Miskito leaders who led the military opposition, Steadman Fagoth and Brooklyn Rivera. The Moravian pastor, Sandinista Miskitos, other Miskito military commanders, and even simple villagers speak, each bringing a differing perspective to the discussion. With the sole exception of Carrión, none of them absolves the FSLN of responsibility for the conflict. Only two high Sandinista comandantes speak.

This first, Spanish version of *Los hijos del río* marks a real advance for INCINE. For the most part, the film withholds judgment on the speakers. This reticence provoked anger among Borge's colleagues at the Ministry of the Interior. But Somarriba maintains that Borge overrode their objections and approved the film (with only minor changes).[21] And despite the resentment that Somarriba felt toward Ramiro Lacayo's direction of INCINE over the years, he affirms that Lacayo supported him during discussions with the Ministry of the Interior. According to Somarriba, the film played for three days at the Cinemateca to packed houses; 1,200 people attended.[22]

The English version reflects a greater historical distance from the events. That film, designed more specifically for foreign consumption with an English voice-over, takes the metaphor of the relationship of the Miskitos to the river more literally and radically reduces the number of interviews. The English version is more polished and succinct, but loses some of the complexity found in the first film. Thus, while the Spanish version began by questioning what could have caused the destruction seen in the succession of shells of houses, churches, and machine detritus lodged in the earth, the second film opens with shots of the river, home to the Miskitos, and announces that this is a film about native rights.

Somarriba eliminated about half the interviews. Luis Carrión does not appear, nor do many of the less familiar Miskito military figures.[23] The English version retains the basic chronology, but condenses the story, reducing the cast of characters. The commentary also adopts a less polemical, less defensive tone. The film specifically contrasts the larger (contra) war over larger issues with the more circumscribed, if still daunting, problem of native rights that motivates the Miskitos: "The rhetoric of communism and counterrevolution hardly applies to this region."

Somarriba also introduced an idea absent from the first version. Repeating the claim that "what the Miskitos really care about is native rights," the commentary offers an analogy to the Iroquois, who had tried to play off the French against the English in the United States two hundred years earlier:

> The Miskitos are acting in much the same way. But it
> didn't work then and it won't work now. There is no
> chance of an independent Miskito state now either.

After discussion by Tomás Borge at an Assembly of Atlantic Coast people of the Autonomy process, the film closes with a sequence seen in the Spanish version, but the commentary corresponds to the second version's new global perspective about native rights and the general question of indigenous peoples:

> No other country in the Western hemisphere has solved the problem, and neither has Nicaragua. After some very bad early mistakes, the Sandinistas recognize the difficulties, that they don't have all the answers, but it's a start.

This perspective distinguishes *Los hijos del río* from INCINE's previous work. The two versions do not eliminate political questions that are endemic to social transformation. In the early years after the triumph, the FSLN often tarred political opposition as counterrevolutionary. For both historical and economic reasons, though, the campesinos and workers, independently of ideology, did not always embrace the measures designed to improve their lives. The mass organizations became increasingly bureaucratized, were led by unelected FSLN militants, and eventually lost representation in the National Assembly. What Tomás Borge says in the film about failing to use persuasion on the coast applies to other political issues as well. *Los hijos del río,* while sympathetic to the Sandinistas, makes Miskito opposition to their policies understandable. As the films and the Sandinistas admitted, the FSLN had transformed a political problem into a military one. War may not have been inevitable without U.S. meddling, but the FSLN did not, or did not know how to, defuse the potential for war.

Mujeres de la frontera

While Somarriba was starting *Los hijos del río* at the end of 1985, INCINE committed resources to its first fictional feature. During a visit by Lacayo to the Soviet Union, the Russians expressed interest in coproducing a film with INCINE. Iván Argüello submitted a proposal, and Lacayo accepted it. Other directors resented the choice of Argüello, who arrived at INCINE later than the others, but Lacayo claimed that there were no other script candidates. Furthermore, Argüello had distinguished himself with the quality of his work. He had traveled to a war zone (in Jalapa) to film *Teotecacinte,* which was very popular among the local population. *Rompiendo el silencio* was acknowledged by everyone at INCINE as a success and won a prize at Leipzig, garnering international prestige. His script for *Mujeres de la frontera* proposed returning to the area where he had shot *Teotecacinte,* so it could be construed as another INCINE contribution to the war effort. Some INCINE personnel suspected that ancillary factors played a role in the choice of Argüello, such as Argüello's status as a committed Sandinista militant with political connections, but Argüello's personality probably did not endear him to the more bohemian elements at INCINE, for he was reserved, serious, "timid" by his own description, and did not mix easily with others.[24]

The Russians promised to send a screenwriter to work with Argüello, but that person never arrived, so INCINE ended up coproducing the film with ICAIC. As with Los hijos del río, the coproducer would supply postproduction and some production support personnel, but INCINE would do the filming. The budget indicates that INCINE would assume 45 percent of the cost, UNAG 20 percent, and AMNLAE 35 percent.[25] This distribution suggests that INCINE successfully found internal funding, though Lacayo claims that Bayardo Arce refused to allow AMNLAE to make good on its commitment.[26]

Argüello wanted to use footage not included in the final cut of Teotecacinte to fashion a film with three 30-minute episodes, a mixture of documentary and fiction, but that conception was eventually scrapped. Argüello encountered many difficulties during the shooting. He couldn't see the rushes regularly, for they were being developed in Cuba; some footage did not come out, and some of the negative was damaged; once in Cuba he found himself editing with incomplete material. According to both Argüello and Lacayo, the first cut was incoherent, delaying the planned release for the December Havana festival. The final cut includes a voice-over by the main character, not in the script, to cover gaps in the story.[27]

The final 55-minute cut follows the growth of a revolutionary feminist consciousness over four years. A young woman, Josefina, receives a letter summoning her to a meeting in Managua to discuss the new Nicaraguan constitution. She marvels at how much has happened in a few years, and the rest of the film unfolds in flashback. Her father leaves the house for guard duty one night and is killed by the contras. The army arrives to enlist men for the militia, and they all go off, including Josefina's husband. The women and children move to town, living in overcrowded and unhealthy conditions in the town hall, entirely dependent on the government for food. The government official argues with the military official over distribution of scarce resources, but the captain brushes him off, saying he needs the men and supplies for the war; the official must make do with what he has for the civilian population. The women approach the captain, but he rebuffs them, though he offers to deliver mail to the men.

When a child dies, Josefina sets out for Jalapa, where the army is constructing new homes. Josefina reasons that the women must organize, return to their land, and take responsibility for feeding themselves. The army tries to dissuade them, but Josefina and the others set off anyway. They travel by

*Josefina leading women against Sandinista Army (*Mujeres de la frontera*)*

foot as Josefina defies the captain's order to return, occupy the unfinished buildings, and begin to clear and sow the fields. A local official informs Josefina that they have been assigned three tractors for their work. But no one knows how to drive them. The official says there is a course teaching how to use the tractors, and three women volunteer.

Josefina wages her own struggle when her husband writes that he will remain in the militia after the other men have returned. She reads the letter in voice-over during the celebration for the other men's return. Even as Josefina endures these pressures, her mother carps at her daughter's budding assertiveness, wondering where it will lead, apprehensive of her absent son-in-law's reaction, saddened that her daughter has not given her a grandchild. Obviously the mother articulates the attitudes of the older, prerevolutionary women, subservient to and dependent on their men, passively accepting their traditional domestic roles. Meanwhile, the men have joined the women in the fields. As they walk through the furrows tossing seed, one man teases another about the latter's wife driving the tractor. In a silent fury, the man forces his wife to stop the tractor and demands the keys, as the other women crowd around to watch the confrontation. The woman refuses to hand over the keys. The man grabs the woman to wrest the keys from her, but the other women restrain him, and he sullenly relents.

In the next scene, Josefina's mother again expresses fears about the changes she sees. Josefina asks why they should return to old patterns, for the men could leave again. In their absence the women have taken responsibility for food and housing and shouldn't relinquish these responsibilities just because the men have returned. The next day, the radio announces that the women from Jalapa have been granted land titles as a cooperative. By the end, despite her discomfort, the mother cannot contain her pride in Josefina: "Before she knows it, Josefina will be a Minister."

While the film is awkward in parts, it tells a didactic story in a modest and credible fashion. Many actors had no experience, and during two weeks of rehearsals prior to filming, the director found that the nonprofessionals outperformed the actors, who invariably overacted. What is most impressive is the unforced development of consciousness among the women, in particular Josefina's emergence as a leader. She responds to concrete situations—the lack of food, the housing problem, concern for the children—with her own solutions. She speaks with common sense, never slipping into jargon. Never once does she invoke the FSLN or UNAG, and she actively struggles against the insensitivity of the Sandinista army, exclusively preoccupied with the military situation. In the confrontation over the tractor, the film does not exploit the scene to launch an attack on machismo. The criticism remains subdued and implicit.

For the first time, in collaboration with two Sandinista mass organizations, INCINE effectively illustrated grassroots struggle and organizing, without mentioning either UNAG or AMNLAE. Simple campesinos, women no less, are forced by circumstance to organize. Though reluctant, the state accedes to their demands. They have not been indoctrinated to form or join a cooperative, no FSLN cadres descend to guide their path. The women do not discuss their oppression as women and suddenly convert to feminism, clamoring to join the middle-class AMNLAE. They do not seethe against the Yankee-sponsored contras who assassinate their parents and force the departure of their husbands and compañeros. Their political consciousness takes shape incrementally, following small successes in obtaining relief through their own courage and creativity.

El espectro de la guerra

INCINE's next project entailed a qualitative leap beyond the modest *Mujeres de la frontera. Mujeres* was budgeted at $26,000 for one month of shooting. *El espectro de la guerra* carried a budget of some $750,000 and projected three months of shooting and two months of editing, with postproduction to be completed in Cuba. The director, Ramiro Lacayo, emphasized this during the shooting:

I am trying to make a film professionally well made, so
I am taking advantage of all the resources. I have used
all my influence to avoid having an excuse for failure.
Qualitatively, it's the first time that we are mounting a
production of these proportions, a Nicaraguan director is
the director. I believe that a film that lacks the necessary
means for its realization implicitly bears the stigma of
failure. But this is not a failure.[28]

Unlike in the previous Nicaraguan fiction films, Lacayo was working with
talented and experienced foreigners, an advantage noted by other Nicaraguan directors.[29] Serge Reggiani, who had worked with Gillo Pontecorvo, collaborated on the screenplay; the Cuban Livio Delgado, veteran of the films
of Humberto Solás, was the cinematographer, and the American Michael
Bloecher edited the film, replacing the original editor, Johnny Henderson.
Articles that appeared during the shooting emphasized the scale of the
production.

Despite this wealth of resources, the finished film contained one debilitating technical flaw. As a coproducer (along with Mexico and Cuba), Spain
provided the dubbing, but they dubbed it poorly. Not only does the dialogue not match the lip movements, but also they used Spanish spoken in
Spain, not Nicaraguan Spanish. No Nicaraguan could watch the film without wincing.

Like *Mujeres de la frontera*, the story traces the coming to consciousness
of a politically inexperienced character. A young black man from the coast,
Reynaldo, travels to Managua to become a professional dancer. He promptly
falls in love with an attractive woman at a party. At the national dance
school, he watches a film of a professional dance, and when the school's director tells him he would need years of study abroad to acquire those skills,
he decides to study dance in France. His draft notice interrupts this plan:
Despite his vain catalogue of excuses, military service is obligatory. Once in
the army, he begs his girlfriend to get him out. When she arranges his escape,
he is confused, for life protecting a mountain community in a war zone has
begun to change him. The camaraderie of his mates and his relationships
with the campesino effect his conversion. He cannot put personal ambitions
above the villagers' safety. A contra attack leaves him wounded in the knee.
Rushed by helicopter to the hospital, the doctor operates, but Reynaldo will
never be able to dance professionally. While recuperating, the hero imagines
a dance with Death, the "Espectro de la guerra," and the film ends.

This synopsis omits the frequency of extended dance sequences. The film

Dance with Death (El espectro de la guerra)

opens on an elaborate production number shot during the Palo de Mayo festival on the Atlantic Coast. The first night after Reynaldo reaches Managua and meets María, there is a long break-dancing scene. At the school,
Reynaldo watches a dance film and then dances with the teacher. Later, he
visualizes an elaborate dance in the ruins of Managua's Grand Hotel (destroyed by the 1972 earthquake). That is, the film constantly breaks into
dance, though unlike classic American musicals, there is no courting ritual
with his girlfriend, except the initial break-dancing encounter. Obviously,
Lacayo wanted the dance episodes to give the project artistic ballast.

For years, Lacayo had been trying to deflect charges that INCINE's
films were too *panfletario*, too propagandistic. Again, in an interview about
Espectro, he repeated the idea, referring to films about Nicaraguan youth:

> I have seen films and documentaries that try to treat the
> situation of youth faced with the question of war, and
> they do it from a triumphalist perspective. At no point is
> there human conflict, and if it appears, it's very super-
> ficial and with a *panfletario* solution. I'm sure that our
> youth is all for the Revolution, but there's a process of
> consciousness that cannot be forgotten. For this reason I

think that to present a stereotypical and perfect vision of our youth in a revolutionary process is to devalue it totally.[30]

One critic complained that the film's war images were too aesthetic, that the "very particular vision of this war is presented as a succession of flashy and exotic post cards."[31] The choice of Delgado as cinematographer may have contributed to this result. Delgado had worked with the celebrated Cuban director Humberto Solás, whose films treat grand themes in a highly stylized manner, particularly the nature of the cinematography, whether in the first part of *Lucía*, an early film for him, or the recently completed *Un hombre de éxito* (1987), another period piece. And Solás was also responsible for the superproduction disaster *Cecilia* that forced a complete reassessment of ICAIC's structure because the project had run out of control and then failed at the box office.[32] Solás's reputation rests on his successful epic films, yet Lacayo said about *Espectro* that "for me, . . . I'm not interested particularly in the epic hero, but in the anonymous hero, the unknown man who daily reflects and confronts the contradictions of his time."[33]

The problem of realism often arises when a filmmaker tries to show contemporary life. The Chilean Miguel Littín had to take responsibility for the language distortions, costume, and sets in *Alsino y el cóndor*, a debate in which Lacayo defended Littín (see chapter 5). In *Espectro*, one Nicaraguan critic saw the "well-to-do and easy-going" campesino "totally different from our own [campesino]. We could be watching a Spanish or Portuguese peasant." The critic also questioned Reynaldo's credibility when he returned to the army from Managua with gifts of a model Eiffel Tower and an Andalusian fan. "In what market would he buy [the Eiffel Tower]?"[34] Lacayo wanted both art and realism, but the anxiety about the lack of art forces him to have art dominate realism, a shortcoming not found in *Mujeres de la frontera*.

On the other hand, *Espectro* is not didactic. Reynaldo is not converted into a Sandinista militant; as in *Mujeres*, no one mentions the FSLN throughout the film. Reynaldo appreciates the needs of and dangers to the campesinos, but he does not become one. In this sense, the choice of a costeño as the central character reduces the conversion pressure, although it raises other questions. In the beginning, Reynaldo appears never to have thought about the war. He thinks only of dancing and his girlfriend. As a black costeño from Bluefields, he may not have experienced the war directly, and the Creoles mostly did not join the counterrevolution on the coast. Like many from the Atlantic Coast, he felt that he was not, in fact, from Nicaragua. Among the excuses he cites to avoid the military is that he's "not even from here," presumably meaning not from the Pacific half of Nicaragua. But the film cuts to him marching with other army recruits. Accepting military service, then, requires him to accept being Nicaraguan.

Despite Lacayo's intention to avoid stereotypes, Reynaldo unfortunately conforms to a Nicaraguan stereotype of costeños. The only cultural artifacts he brings to Managua are the Palo de Mayo and his lithe body. Aside from his passion for dancing, nothing distinguishes him; the few stereotypical costeño details pour into that character vacuum. Though he crosses the deep cultural divide between Pacific and Atlantic, he says nothing about the food, language, transportation, shortages, the revolution, the war, the beach at Xiloa, and so on. He may have already lived in Managua, but the film suggests the contrary: He has no friends there and stays in a shack belonging to a mechanic he doesn't know (someone gave him the address before he left the coast). One effective scene offers an opening for his thoughts. He delivers a letter to his army friend Miguel's house. There, Miguel's father confesses to having been in Somoza's Guardia Nacional and tries to justify this by the limited opportunities available to people like him. Reynaldo sits mute, and then leaves. When he recounts the visit to Miguel, he asks no questions, perhaps from respect, but Reynaldo's mind remains a cipher.

At the first screening in Nicaragua in April 1989, Lacayo remarked in *Barricada*, "The intention was to make a film which was not heavy or dramatic but light and full of color and happiness in the musical genre." Of course this hardly corresponds to the goal of capturing a *Nicaraguan* reality, for INCINE had never previously experimented with the musical genre.

Yet this question of Nicaragüensidad—Nicaraguan-ness—is exactly what other INCINE filmmakers appreciated in *Mujeres de la frontera*, despite its faults. In trying for international acceptance, *El espectro de la guerra* wrapped itself in foreign garb, producing a hybrid of musical and standard conversion drama.[35] Lacayo may have hoped that "autochthonous" and "folkloric" coastal elements would qualify as Nicaraguan, but that hope would be lost on foreigners and peculiar to Nicaraguan mestizos. To return to the rhetoric of Mariano Marín talking about the "typicality" of the young schoolteacher's house in *El maestro popular*—the details like the mother in the background kitchen, the dog passing by—these random details were recognizably "Nica" to Marín. In *Mujeres de la frontera*, in the world of fiction, a rural mailman negotiates the rutted rural road to deliver a letter to Josefina; in *El espectro de la guerra*, the delivery of the draft notice is not shown. The drama of *Mujeres* is slow, distended; time passes. Undoubtedly, that rhythm conveys the atmosphere of the Nicaraguan countryside. From the opening number in *Espectro*, the drama explodes, the pulsing music and strenuous dancing fill any dramatic pauses. In the scene of Reynaldo and María at Xiloa, a volcanic lagoon just outside Managua, the camera moves up María's long naked leg. Xiloa is a popular bathing spot, with female vendors passing by constantly with food and refrescos (Nicaraguan fruit drinks). The physical and dramatic tension between Reynaldo and María, as he explains his plan to leave for Paris, excludes any "authentic" traces of the setting. In some ways, *El espectro de la guerra* sacrifices Nicaragüensidad on the altar of "art."

In considering INCINE's fiction films, the war's influence is pervasive. All the films, shorts and features alike, construct stories around the military conflict. The protagonists, save Josefina in *Mujeres de la frontera*, are killed (Manuel, the schoolteacher in *Daniel*, Noel, the centerfielder) or wounded (Reynaldo). And Josefina in *Mujeres* steps forward as a leader following her father's murder. The war dominated daily life in Nicaragua. Everyone participated. This fact may explain the constant reversion to subjectivity, as an escape from the war's daily pressures.

At the same time, subjectivity was two-edged. As a respite from a constantly mobilized social existence, subjective excursus and fantasy could construct a new cinematic space, even if it didn't offer a safe haven. But the filmmakers often viewed subjectivity as a sine qua non of artistic expression, perhaps in overreaction to the more prosaic constraints of the noticieros. Only *Mujeres* resisted this temptation (the director resorted to Josefina's voice-over only as a salvage method to compensate for production problems), and Argüello was probably the most militant FSLN member at INCINE. All of the Nicaraguan filmmakers, including Lacayo, prefer *Mujeres* to *Espectro*, despite the earlier film's awkwardness. Thinking back on the decision to embark on fiction, INCINE cameraperson Rafael Ruíz recalled that Rafael Vargas had referred to *Manuel*, the first fiction, as the "point of the lance" of Nicaraguan cinema; Ruíz viewed *Espectro* as the "tail of the lance."[36]

Argüello had both the political acumen and artistic restraint to choose a powerful theme and not clutter the story with subjective embellishment. Like AMNLAE itself, INCINE had largely ignored women's issues; yet women, particularly in the campo, also bore heavy burdens from the war. In *Mujeres,* rather than folding themselves into "the people, united, will never be defeated," the *women* unite to protect their own interests, even to the point of challenging the army's bureaucratic rigidity. They respond to the pressures by organizing, not withdrawing into an interior space.

After the Fall

The completion of *Espectro de la guerra* in 1988 effectively ended INCINE, though the institution remained afloat for several years. With *El espectro de la guerra* as his swan song, Ramiro Lacayo, founder and head of INCINE for ten years, left INCINE, his hope of founding a viable film enterprise in Nicaragua having foundered, now a virtually empty shell.[37] The country had been reeling from the war and economic strain for years, and the government had attempted a series of adjustments during that time. In 1988 the government resorted to radical measures, in a year that saw the staggering inflation rate of 33,000 percent enter the history books as one of the highest ever. Aside from devaluation, the government finally moved to reduce the size and expense of the bloated governmental bureaucracy. The Ministry of Culture was shut down entirely, and INCINE remained in limbo for a number of years, nominally assigned to a new Institute of Culture, run by Rosario Murillo, who finally triumphed in her long battle with Ernesto Cardenal for control over culture. But the victory was a Pyrrhic one. By that point, there was neither energy nor funds to sustain the Sandinista cultural project.

A skeleton crew oversaw INCINE's final eclipse. A series of replacement directors—Ronald Porras, Rodolfo Alegría, Eddy Meléndez—tried to keep the institution functioning by renting out equipment, but the work was intermittent and only minimally remunerative. Some of the former INCINE filmmakers tried to put together independently financed projects with INCINE as a coproducer. Some of the people who left INCINE continued to make films, but these films were no longer part of the national cinema project which INCINE once articulated, produced, and incarnated.

With the opposition Unión Nacional Opositora (UNO) coalition's victory in the 1990 elections, the new government displayed no interest in INCINE or the cinema. Undoubtedly, the new government saw INCINE as a Sandinista operation. Starved for funds, unable to sustain itself on occasional publicity spots and music videos, INCINE slowly expired. In 1993 Felipe Hernández, the former Mexican owner of the PRODUCINE premises that INCINE had expropriated in 1979, returned to Nicaragua and sued successfully for the property. INCINE was transferred to a small building across town next to the former Sandinista television studio, where it died a final death. In January 1996, the government posted a notice (see Appendix) on the door putting remaining personnel on indefinite unpaid leave.

Ten   TOWARD THE END OF
          THIRD CINEMA

Ever since the "heroic" decade of the 1920s in the Soviet Union, countries undergoing rapid, usually Marxist or socialist revolutionary social change, have made a national cinema project a high priority in establishing a new social order, often citing Lenin's remark that "for us, cinema is the most important of the arts." In 1959 the Cuban revolution reaffirmed the cinema's importance in the new state, officially declaring, "The cinema is an art," and founded the Cuban Institute of Cinematographic Art and Industry. ICAIC was designed as a virtual ministry unto itself, reporting directly to Fidel Castro. Just as the Cuban revolution inspired revolutionaries and militants throughout Latin America, ICAIC inspired militant Latin American filmmaking during the 1960s and 1970s.

In this nexus of militancy and creative filmmaking, Latin American filmmakers, like the Soviet filmmakers, attempted to theorize militant cinema. In a number of countries—Brazil, Argentina, Cuba, Bolivia, Chile—filmmakers wrote manifestos articulating a political role for cinema during years of political ferment. In 1979 the future Nicaraguan filmmakers were not familiar with these writings, but the theoretical statements provide an essential background for understanding INCINE's experience during the 1980s. One manifesto in particular, "Towards a Third Cinema," might have helped guide INCINE through its conceptual and institutional problems.

Except for the one in Cuba, INCINE lasted longer than the filmmaking institutions in other Latin American countries. In 1979–1980, INCINE confronted a different historical conjuncture, though the changes were only dimly perceptible as the Nicaraguans embarked on filmmaking. Technological and social changes had demoted the status of cinema in Latin America. No new militant cinema manifestos were written in the 1980s. While these changes began years earlier, INCINE's history dramatizes the transformation. As no new militant filmmaking movements in Latin America have appeared in the 1990s, INCINE may have written the epitaph on national militant filmmaking projects in Latin America.

Manifestos

Most manifestos were composed by filmmakers protesting their countries' economic and political conditions. Fernando Birri founded a filmmaking school in the late 1950s in Santa Fé, Argentina. After completing several films, the school drew the authorities' attention and Birri had to leave Argentina. Birri believed that film should document social reality, and he attacked commercial Argentine cinema in his 1967 article, "Cinema and Underdevelopment." Birri called for producing documentaries to combat false images of "both society and our people":

> So, the first positive step is to provide such an image.
> How can documentary provide this image? By showing
> how reality is, and in no other way. This is the revolu-
> tionary function of social documentary and realist,
> critical and popular cinema in Latin America. By
> testifying, critically, to this reality—to this subreality,
> this misery—cinema refuses it. It rejects it. It denounces,
> judges, criticizes and deconstructs it.[1]

Ultimately, the "revolutionary function" of Birri's cinema is "the awakening of the consciousness of reality. The posing of problems." In short, Birri argued for documenting reality, to show a "national, Latin American identity; which is authentic."[2] As a project, Birri's statement remains politically ambiguous. Apparently, a revolutionary cinema should raise consciousness and be directed to the workers and peasants, but Birri suggests no avenue of political action. Once consciousness is raised, this cinema has fulfilled its function; the transition to the creation of "a new person, a new society, a new history and therefore a new art and a new cinema" is elided. And, in fact, even before Birri's forced exile, his films never played a role in any political movement.[3]

In Brazil, Glauber Rocha was an unofficial spokesperson of the Cinema Novo. Like Birri, Rocha primarily attacked the traditional Brazilian cinema. Any film departing from that tradition should be considered revolutionary:

> If the commercial cinema is the tradition, the auteur
> cinema is the revolution. To say that an auteur is

reactionary in the cinema is the same thing as
characterizing him as a commercial director, as
identifying him as an artisan, which is not an auteur.[4]

To the extent that cinema novo was political, its politics were limited to exposing poverty.[5] Filming actual conditions would raise consciousness, a central theoretical concept popularized by Paulo Freire in Brazil and adopted by
many Latin American political activists. This form of consciousness raising
did not necessarily affiliate with specific political movements or parties.
Grassroots movements, like Freire's literacy movement, avoided political
parties because they previously ignored vast numbers of the poor in their
electoral gamesmanship.

Only a few years later, after the "coup within a coup" that overthrew
Goulart in 1968, Cinema Novo defined itself even more exclusively in cinematic, not political, terms. Despite its heterogeneity, Cinema Novo directors, as filmmakers, saw themselves as cinematic pathbreakers, influenced
by Italian neorealism and the French New Wave. As auteurs, they wanted to
forge a new Brazilian cinema. They applied their ideas to exposing poverty
and intellectual hypocrisy but fought their battles in the morass of the Brazilian film industry, skirmishing constantly with commercial interests to
produce an artistic cinema, one renowned at international film festivals (not
in Brazil). The filmmakers' resilience in surviving the country's deteriorat-
ing political situation testifies, in part, to their political isolation, just as
their formal recourse to allegory reflected an ambivalent adaptation or accommodation to commercial cinema rather than a retreat underground into
guerrilla cinema.[6]

Cuba incarnated the national liberation impulses of the New Cinema,
for the Cuban revolution had seized and successfully consolidated state
power. By virtue of their victory, the Cubans stood on the other side of
national liberation. This fundamental difference distinguished Cuban filmmaking from all other putatively national projects. Nonetheless, the Cuban
cinema's energy and artistic success peaked in the late 1960s, just as the New
Cinema was becoming a self-conscious movement and articulating goals and
methods.

In 1969 Julio García Espinosa published "For An Imperfect Cinema," the
most influential Cuban statement on contemporary Latin American filmmaking. While the concept of "imperfect cinema" charted a possible course
for Latin American cinema, in fact most of the article explores the role of
art and artists in a revolutionary society under construction. García Espinosa proposed rethinking the artistic enterprise, returning to Marx's hopes
on the one hand, and the meaning of "popular art" on the other hand. Marx

had predicted a future when men freed from work could devote themselves to painting. García Espinosa understood this as destroying art as an elite vocation. Rather than a privileged few monopolizing artistic production, the masses would make art, eviscerating the separation between producer and consumer. In this future, people would use many technologies—Super 8-mm, a 35-mm Mitchell, videotape, television—with one goal: "He should place his role as revolutionary or aspiring revolutionary above all else."

> The only thing [imperfect cinema] is interested in is how an artist responds to the following question: What are you doing in order to overcome the barrier of the 'cultured' elite audience which up to now has conditioned the form of your work?[7]

The penultimate paragraph uncovers the final hope for such a cinema:

> Imperfect cinema cannot lose sight of the fact that its essential goal as a new poetics is to disappear.

Such a vision has been problematic for Cuba itself. It hardly provided a program for countries still struggling against the neocolonial yoke.[8]

In Chile, after the 1970 elections brought Popular Unity to power, Chilean filmmakers produced a short "Filmmakers Manifesto" (probably written by Miguel Littín). The film festival held at Viña del Mar the previous year emboldened and politicized Chilean filmmakers, though their own films at the festival lacked the militant resistance coursing through films like *Hour of the Furnaces* (Argentina) and *Blood of the Condor* (Bolivia). Although Raúl Ruiz's film, *Tres tristes tigres,* won a prize, he claimed that it was not political, though he was the only member of a political party within Popular Unity. As with many utopian projects of the first great revolutionary cultural explosion in the Soviet Union, the Chilean program described in the Filmmakers Manifesto expressed unrealized, and unrealizable, hopes.

The manifesto sounds the themes of national liberation and national identity, twin constants of this period of liberation struggles:

> Chilean film makers, it is time for us all to undertake, together with our people, the great task of national liberation and the construction of socialism.
>
> It is time for us to begin to redeem our own values in order to affirm our cultural and political identity. . . .
>
> Against an anaemic and neo-colonized culture, a

pasture for the consumption of an elite, decadent, and
sterile petit[e]-bourgeoisie, let us devote our collective
will, immersed within the people, to the construction of
an authentically NATIONAL and therefore REVOLU-
TIONARY culture.[9]

The "construction of socialism" was a project of the distant future, although
the filmmakers did not appreciate that reality. The manifesto soared above
reality and, if anything, encouraged the ensuing frustration, bureaucratic
disarticulation, and retrospective recriminations. In fact, the filmmakers'
sectarianism contributed to Chile Films' failure to produce a single feature in
two and a half years, though, as the first head of Chile Films, Littín planned
eight features *per year!*[10]

Of all the important theoretical statements from the late 1960s, only
"Towards a Third Cinema" offers cinema both a compelling theoretical
analysis and a militant practical program.[11] While other writings inspired
individual Latin American filmmakers, they didn't translate into an agenda
for a national cinema project dedicated to recuperating and reconstructing
a decolonized national identity. "Towards a Third Cinema" appeared when
anti-imperialist sentiment was gaining momentum in Latin America and
coincided with the creative explosion of New Cinema in Latin America, de-
finitively established at Viña del Mar in 1969.

"Towards a Third Cinema" was unparalleled in fundamental ways. First,
the written manifesto accompanied the diffusion of Fernando Solanas and
Octavio Getino's *La hora de los hornos* [*Hour of the Furnaces*]. The film
itself was also unprecedented in its four-hour-and-twenty-minute length,
and it had a powerful impact on other Latin American filmmakers. Raúl Ruiz
claimed at Viña del Mar that the film "hurled us against the walls and left
us breathless."[12] Though the film did not earn unanimous praise, its undeniable power guaranteed wide exposure, particularly in Europe, where it first
showed at the Pesaro (Italy) film festival in 1968. In subsequent interviews
in Europe and Latin America, the filmmaker/theoreticians discussed their
manifesto, conjoining theory and practice around the dual text of film and
manifesto.

Second, the Cubans published the manifesto in *Tricontinental. Tricontinental* first appeared in 1967, simultaneously published in four languages
(Spanish, French, English, and Italian) by the Organization for the Solidarity of African, Asian and Latin American Peoples (OSPAAL). The journal expressed the aspirations from peoples of three continents struggling
against "the criminal policies of intervention, plunder and aggression employed by the world-wide imperialist system and particularly by U.S. Im-

perialism against the Afro-Asian-Latin American peoples" (inaugural issue, July/August 1967). The first issue included articles by Franz Fanon, Kim Il Sung, and Fidel Castro. It also affirmed that "the guerilla detachments of Latin America demonstrate their solidarity with the combatants waging daily combat for national liberation on a tricontinental scale," and cited a message from Che Guevara:

> And let us develop a true proletarian Internationalism, with International proletarian armies; the flag under which we fight shall be the sacred cause of redeeming humanity. To die under the flag of Viet Nam, of Venezuela, of Guatemala, of Laos, of Guinea, of Colombia, of Bolivia, of Brazil—to name only a few scenes of today's armed struggle—would be equally glorious and desirable for an American, an Asian, an African, even a European.[13]

Launched at this historical and geographical intersection, "Towards a Third Cinema" was translated into 12 languages and had more international exposure than the other manifestos.

Third, Solanas and Getino did not let the manifesto, with its inevitable ambiguities, gaps, slippages, and elisions, rest as a final document. They clarified and elaborated their thinking in multiple articles and interviews in Latin America and Europe, responded to criticisms and questions, and even published retrospective comments on their original formulations.[14] No other filmmakers so systematically articulated a theory of cinema for third-world filmmaking.

However, the filmmakers' assiduity had mixed results. Critical attention lavished on "third cinema" stripped the writings of their specificity. In some cases, commentators omit the historical and theoretical features of "third cinema," subsume Third World Cinema under the rubric of "third cinema," and even remove geographical location as a criterion.[15] Often critics fail to emphasize, or even acknowledge, the fundamental importance of the fact that "Towards a Third Cinema" emerged from a specific and concrete practice: the production, distribution, and exhibition of the epic *Hour of the Furnaces*.[16] That experience ensured both a strong polemical thrust following the film's success and a conceptual flexibility. The manifesto resonates with many influences, from Africa (Fanon) and Asia (Mao Tse-tung) as well as Latin America (Arregui, Che). For the filmmaker/theoreticians, the paramount criterion was the film's effectiveness as a political tool, not an aesthetic product. Above all, the filmmakers do not work in isolation from mass movements. The upsurge of organized popular movements provides the preconditions for their work as artists and intellectuals, theoretically and practically.

The manifesto opens by attacking the cinema of spectacle. This cinema, a cinema of consumption, "a digesting object," creates and depends on a passive spectator. This key idea, one with clear affinities to Brecht's radical ideas, simultaneously being resuscitated by European filmmakers and intellectuals, does not stop at strategies of distantiation intended to promote lucidity, a central category for García Espinosa, Willemen, and other commentators.[17] Solanas and Getino insist on "intervention":

> revolutionary cinema is not fundamentally one which illustrates, documents, or passively establishes a situation: *rather, it attempts to intervene in the situation as an element providing thrust or rectification.* It is not simply testimonial cinema, nor cinema of communication, but above all *Action Cinema.*[18]

While Solanas and Getino supported the importance of raising consciousness, the central aim of Birri's work ten years earlier, they wanted to go beyond this. In the same passage, they cite Marx's well-known 11th Thesis on Feuerbach: "It is not sufficient to interpret the world; it is now a question of transforming it." Many invoke this injunction, but Getino and Solanas draw on their own experience distributing and exhibiting their film to demonstrate concrete ways of applying this principle. As many theorists rediscovered Brecht, they also read his comrade Benjamin, in particular the article on "The Work of Art in the Age of Mechanical Reproduction." Benjamin's article welcomed mechanical reproduction for its role in dissolving the aura traditionally attached to the artwork, effectively democratizing the availability and accessibility of art.[19]

Solanas and Getino extended this process beyond the idea of mechanical reproduction. They rejected the very existence of a final product multiply reproduced. For exhibition, they encouraged organizers to project the film in whatever manner was appropriate for their own purposes. The film itself announces several breaks in the projection, allowing for discussion among the spectators. The "act" of screening presupposed the presence of "relators" prepared to stop the film:

> The act is guided by one or more relators [*relatores*] in the room who can interrupt the projection when the participants find it necessary so that the relation between the film and the protagonists eliminates definitively the spectator.[20]

The film's ending includes commentaries from "protagonists" (spectators) obviously not part of the original film.

That is, the film changed over time with these additions, and these changes implied an even more radical repudiation of the notion of an "original" than Benjamin had envisioned. For Benjamin, reproducibility removed the traditional "aura" of art by demoting the status of the original. With multiple changeable copies, there is no original. For Solanas and Getino, any individual copy should be viewed as malleable. In a later article, they refer to films made by their group, Cine Liberación ("or by analogous groups") as "modular" films, ones which could be rearranged according to the purposes of a given screening, cutting out reels, changing the order, etc., "changes which were never questioned by us, inasmuch as we gave priority to the person and the concrete process itself, more than to the life of the film."[21] This formulation prioritizes the "concrete process" of the screening situation. In fact, Solanas and Getino prefer the term "film act" to "film" per se. The film is "important only as a detonator or pretext." Attendance at screenings of such a cinema already constituted an action. Just as Brecht had called for breaking down the barrier between proscenium and audience, for putting the spectators at ease so that they could enjoy the didactic experience, Solanas and Getino developed similar methods to solicit participation:

> As we gained in experience, we incorporated into the showing various elements (a *mise-en-scène*) to reinforce the themes of the films, the climate of the showing, the 'disinhibiting' of the participants, and the dialogue: recorded music or poems, sculpture and paintings, posters, a programme director who chaired the debate and presented the film and the comrades who were speaking, a glass of wine, a few *mates*, etc.[22]

However, unlike Brecht and other writers on the epistemology of radical artistic practice, which would include the Argentine Birri (whose *Tire dié* is "cited" in *Hour of the Furnaces*), Solanas and Getino insist on the importance of knowledge that leads to action.

Furthermore, this subordination of the film text to the particular exhibition circumstances presupposes that

> the space where it takes place, the materials that go to make it up (actors-participants), and the historic time in which it takes place are never the same. . . . This means that the result of each projection will depend on those

who organize it, on those who participate in it, and on the time and place; the possibility of introducing variations, additions, and changes is unlimited. The screening of a film act will always express in one way or another the historical situation in which it takes place.[23]

Just as the filmmaker/theorists try to deflect significance from themselves or their group as directors of the films, they stress the particular historical conjuncture of their interventions. They do not believe that their ideas will mobilize the masses in some illusory imputation of power to cultural work. They state at the very beginning that questions about a revolutionary cinema before the revolution cannot be answered in some ahistorical debate, but only by the masses in struggle.

Despite this emphasis on the international revolutionary upsurge—the impetus for launching *Tricontinental*—both the film and the manifesto concentrate on Argentina, and their particular insertion in the Argentine reality has drawn criticism.[24] The manifesto does not address the correlation of forces in Argentina at that time, but the authors made no secret of their political affiliation as militant Peronistas. Some leftist critics hesitated to endorse the manifesto for this reason, and the film quite explicitly supports the Peronista trade union movement.[25]

But these criticisms do not apply to the theoretical (and practical) project outlined in the manifesto. In interviews and later articles, Solanas and Getino distinguished between their own personal political commitments and the program of the manifesto, though they did tend to view all anti-imperialist struggle in Argentina as part of a broad "National Liberation Movement (Peronism)."[26] But they understood revolutionary cinema less narrowly as any cinematic practice developed within a militant political organization:

> Its primary responsibility is the complete mastery of the resources that it manages and which defines the group precisely as *militant filmmaking group.* . . .
> *The militant filmmaking group does not aspire to win people for itself, but for the organization and the space in which it works.*[27]

or

> *Militant cinema is that cinema which sees itself integrated as instrument, complement or support of a*

specific politics, and of the organizations that carry out
the plan together with the diversity of objectives which it
pursues.[28]

On many occasions, Solanas and Getino stressed this uncompromising position on the "instrumentalization" of filmmaking. Filmmakers bring their
expertise to the militant organization, but their work acquires value only
as it advances the organization's strategy. The film itself has no intrinsic
value.[29]

The subordination of filmmaking to the work of political organizations
contains a certain conceptual confusion, implicitly recognized by Solanas
and Getino. After the manifesto's publication, the writers tried to clarify
"militant cinema," which they referred to as an "internal category of third
cinema."[30] They acknowledge that the term "third cinema" is "sufficiently
new that it still lacks a rigorous level of analysis and criticism." This admission corresponds to the manifesto's claims that "third cinema" is an
open category, not fixed and rigid, hence the critical importance of specific
and changing historical circumstances. By concentrating so exclusively on
the original manifesto, critics have overlooked the significance of "militant
cinema" for third cinema, a distinction available in articles and interviews
for the most part untranslated (from Spanish and French) into English.

In their first discussion of the distinction, after listing militant films made
by groups in Chile, Colombia, and Argentina, Solanas and Getino hazard a
provisional distinction:

> the instigators of a *cinema of militants* are not trying
> now only a work of cultural decolonization or the
> recuperation of a national culture, but are proposing to
> complement through their militant activity (which they
> place above any political-cinematic work) a *revolutionary*
> *politics,* that which leads to the destruction of neocolo-
> nialism, to the national liberation of our countries and
> to the national construction of socialism. . . . Can we
> establish perchance hermetic definitions or theses? If we
> did that, would we not be violating precisely the greatest
> virtue and quality of this attempt: its character of
> *hypothesis* and *inconclusiveness?*[31]

They imply that the more global term "third cinema" refers to the struggle
of "cultural decolonization" and the "recuperation of a national culture,"
themes discussed by Gabriel and Willemen. But subsequent articles and

interviews of Getino and Solanas dwell almost exclusively on this more nar-row concern of "third cinema," such that militant cinema clearly represents a privileged internal category of third cinema.

Militant cinema, according to later elaborations, is a cinema committed to working within and for militant, political, revolutionary organizations. Solanas and Getino's examples of "third cinema" support an extremely flex-ible understanding of the term, for the key criterion is the relation between the spectator and the work. Therefore, not only does their criterion de-emphasize the text's significance, but they also judge a text according to its effect on spectators, its "use value." For example, in 1971, Solanas and Getino asserted that

> *A cinema is militant and revolutionary to the extent that*
> *the people, through the representative and revolutionary*
> *organizations that propel the process of liberation, shape*
> *implicitly or explicitly its nature. . . .*
>
> *This cinema recognizes in the first instance no other*
> *specificity than politics, no other function or front. . . .*
>
> Filmmakers [cannot] be considered militant if the
> work is not part of the work and practice realized within
> organic militant formations.[32]

Judging film on its efficacy as an organizing tool radically changes the status of the film object and indicates an extremely malleable view of the role of aesthetics. Various critics, though acknowledging the third cinema's goal of making revolution, have sought a revolutionary aesthetic in the mani-festo. Despite occasional remarks by Solanas and Getino about finding new forms for new situations, the theorists of third cinema did not restrict the form that third cinema should take. For example, contrary to the assertion that the revolutionary film must have a revolutionary form, they praised Bolivian filmmaker Jorge Sanjinés's work, even though Sanjinés may use

> conventional and old language, which, perhaps in
> Bolivia, would allow it to play a role superior to what
> that same language would signify today in the
> Argentinean context; that is, it might play a more
> significant role in Bolivia.[33]

Based on the relation between the film and the spectator, one of transform-ing him/her into a protagonist, their criterion for a revolutionary act derives from a similar instrumentalization:

> *What defines the revolutionary act* [in film, for example]
> *in fact is not the form in which it is expressed, but the*
> *transformative role that it reaches in a specific (tactical)*
> *circumstance in a strategy of liberation.*[34]

Furthermore, taking this de-emphasis of a film as a fixed text to its logical conclusion, a single film may qualify as militant or not depending on the context of its use. Thus, "a militant Cuban film, for example, is not necessarily a militant film in Argentina *if it does not serve the political necessities of the local revolutionary organizations.*"[35]

Far from being independent of a geographical and historical context, third cinema must serve a specific political purpose for the particular political organization using it. At the same time, even films from the "metropolis" might qualify as third cinema, or at least as militant cinema. Solanas and Getino acknowledge that one Italian theorist's dismissal of *Battle of Algiers* as reformist "is correct from his perspective," but the same film may become a militant film in Argentina

> if such works in our context play a role of stimulation
> and mobilization, of transformation of consciousness and
> of sharpening of contradictions, which is what valorizes
> such films in Argentina today.[36]
>
> What characterizes First, Second or Third Cinema is
> not the theme, the type of distribution, narration
> structure, direction format or economic size of the
> production, but the ideological sustenance and the
> project toward which it is oriented or of which it
> consciously or unconsciously forms a part.[37]

Solanas and Getino also display a bias toward documentary. In the manifesto, they state: "Documentary [cinema] is perhaps the main basis of revolutionary filmmaking." Here they mean revealing the national reality to the people, anticipating the use of the "testimonial" that achieved critical currency during the 1980s: "Testimony about a national reality is also an inestimable means of dialogue and knowledge on the world plane." But their orientation corresponds to an unproblematized belief in the truth of the image:

> An image is a fact [datum] of reality, a proof which is
> defined by itself. . . .
> The documentary image, which cannot be disputed,

that is the proof, reaches a total importance faced with the "proofs" of the adversary.[38]

For many years, film theorists have debated the "ontology of the photographic image," to quote André Bazin's title of a celebrated 1945 article. In the late 1960s, the moment of *La hora de los hornos* and the manifesto, French critics and filmmakers were attacking this naïve realism as a foundation of bourgeois aesthetics. Godard's adage from *Vent d'Est* (1969) that "Ce n'est pas une image juste, c'est juste une image" is a typically Godardian intervention in this debate. Solanas and Getino accept some ontological character of the photographic image, but as the reference to Sanjinés's fictional work (cited above) indicates, Solanas and Getino had no theoretical objection to fiction filmmaking, and both made fiction films after Perón's triumphant return to Argentina in 1973.

No doubt Argentina's reputation as the most "European" Latin American country partly accounts for the emphasis on concrete historical and political circumstances. Aside from nods to European filmmakers like Chris Marker and Joris Ivens, the manifesto carefully concentrates on Latin American and other third-world theorist/activists, for Solanas and Getino identified Argentina's principal enemies as the local neocolonized bourgeoisie, repeatedly excoriated in *La hora de los hornos* as craven imitators of European culture. Promoting national culture motivates them to repudiate inclusion in European militant filmmaking.

Ironically, *La hora de los hornos* acquired its international celebrity in Europe, at the Pesaro festival in 1968. French critics also received third cinema sympathetically, and the French militant film journal *CinémAction* organized a lengthy dossier in 1979 on "the influence of 'third cinema' in the world." The introduction to the dossier calls the manifesto "the most important" of the Latin American theoretical statements, "the one which has best synthesized this new inspiration [for decolonization] and we repeat that it is the only one to have touched on, thanks to its universalist spirit and programmatic value, the context out of which it came."[39] The Latin American respondents claimed "third cinema" had had little influence in their respective countries for this very reason, its emphasis on context. Gumucio Dagrón, on the other hand, in his 1979 survey of "Militant Filmmaking in Latin America," considered the manifesto more influential than García Espinosa's "Imperfect Cinema":

> The theory of Third Cinema is precise, referring to a concrete process, and was developed parallel to the elaboration of the films of the Cine-Liberation Group,

i.e., from the experience itself. It is, furthermore, a true essay, conceived as such from the beginning, with this thrust for ideological precision, and not as an article destined for a journal, in which it was intended to grab some idea out of midair.[40]

In the same article, Gumucio Dagrón observed that "ten years earlier the so-called New Latin American Cinema began to die," a judgment with grim implications in 1979 for initiating a national film project ab ovo in Nicaragua.

Transformation of the Media Landscape

Like the Sandinista revolution, INCINE faced daunting challenges in consolidating a viable national film institute in 1979. The Sandinistas knew they would confront domestic resistance from the bourgeoisie and hostile measures from the United States, including economic and political isolation and a sophisticated amalgam of military pressures. The United States did pursue destabilizing moves, exerting influence to deny international loans to Nicaragua and eventually imposing a complete trade embargo. It pressured allies to reduce support for Nicaragua and poured money into support for the domestic opposition. Most important, the United States financed the contra war waged primarily in the countryside, the weakest domestic sector of Sandinista support.

However devastating, these tactics could be anticipated by the Sandinistas. Unfortunately, Nicaragua also had to contend with a region-wide economic recession, the implosion of the Soviet Union, the collapse of the eastern European socialist states, and the economic crisis in Cuba. And perhaps inevitably, the Sandinistas made mistakes. Commentators disagree over the relative weight given to each factor, but the Sandinista defeat in the 1990 elections reflected the erosion of popular support for the Front.

INCINE eventually suffered from all of these developments. In the euphoria accompanying the victory, resources were relatively plentiful. The Cubans contributed equipment, advisers, and extensive postproduction technical support. Foreign sympathizers flocked to Nicaragua to work with INCINE and sent donations. Ramiro Lacayo eventually succeeded in gathering distribution (ENIDIEC) and exhibition (Cine RAP) under INCINE's administrative umbrella, but the U.S. distributors refused to supply films, and insufficient funds led to the deterioration of the theaters, theaters that some had coveted as the "goose that laid the golden egg."[41] Even before the 1990 elections, INCINE had virtually ceased to operate, as the Front progressively withdrew support from cultural work, and finally in 1988 dissolved the Ministry of Culture and dismissed most of INCINE's personnel. INCINE's rise and fall, however, reveals something far more profound than one more insignificant victim of U.S. cultural domination. One hundred years after the invention of the cinema, national cinemas themselves may be anachronistic as a project of national identity. Independently of the collapse of the socialist world, constructing national cinemas no longer has either the cachet or the social purpose once attached to it.

A variety of factors have contributed to this transformation. Perhaps most significantly, the cinema no longer occupies the privileged place it once held as a projection of national consolidation. Hollywood has increased its domination of exhibition throughout the world, severely limiting opportunities for self-sustaining national industries. The massive introduction of television has, in 20 to 30 years, displaced the cinema as the mass medium of the popular sectors. From the 1960s to the 1990s, movie theaters across Latin America have closed at an astonishing rate. The mass availability of videotapes and VCRs has accelerated this process. Young people still attend the cinema, but they have been raised on television and videotapes.

In a book Julio García Espinosa referred to in his address at the 1988 Havana festival as "required reading for all of us," Octavio Getino exposes the swath television has cut through cinema culture in Latin America over 20 years.[42] Getino, coauthor of "Towards a Third Cinema," has no illusions about a return of militant cinema. With copious data, he catalogues the astonishing shrinking of cinema audiences during this period. In Brazil, cinema attendance declined by 42 percent; in Chile by 58 percent; in Argentina by 78 percent.[43] Even Cuba, which has continued to maintain 500 theaters, suffered an attendance drop of 75 percent, from over 100 million in 1970 to just over 25 million in 1989.[44] Theaters have been closing at comparable rates: Brazil—66 percent; Chile—55 percent; Argentina—41 percent.[45]

The figures for television penetration tell the other half of the story with the rise of television ownership skyrocketing: Brazil—154 percent; Chile—123 percent; Argentina—69 percent; Cuba—173 percent.[46]

Film production has not fallen off as radically as theater attendance, but probably in most countries, the audience has changed. Theaters in poor neighborhoods have closed at disproportionate rates; popular sectors now make up a smaller percentage of the national cinema audience.[47]

Nor does television provide a new compensatory space for screening national films. Conditions vary from country to country, but the overall trend is unmistakable and consistent. Brazil, for example, still has an annual quota of 140 days per year for screening Brazilian films.[48] But television stations are private, so the projection of Brazilian films on television is minuscule.[49] Getino estimated that for every 17 films shown on television, only one Brazilian film is shown.[50] The quota system and various other governmental measures ensure continuing national production, but almost 70 percent are *pornochanchadas.*[51] Even in Mexico, which has a history of protecting national production, U.S. films will soon occupy over 80 percent of the market.[52]

Such figures illustrate the transformation of the media landscape over the past 30 years. Television has supplanted cinema as the mass popular medium.[53] Production costs have risen, audiences have shrunk, theaters have closed, all part of a downward spiral driving production figures down. Privatization has swept the region, drying up potential state funds to support and subsidize cinema. Those cinemas that continued to function, or rebounded after the dark years of military rule, no longer speak of revolution. Still in 1977, Julio García Espinosa proclaimed that such a cinema was the goal in Cuba: "What defines our cinema concretely is anti-imperialism."[54] Ten years later, almost INCINE's precise lifespan, the German Peter Schumann, a champion of Latin American film, delivered a scathing assessment of Cuba's retreat from that goal at the tenth anniversary of the Havana festival:

> In the 1960s, Cuba was the germ cell of revolutionary thought, not only for America. And its cinema was an example for everyone who understood the cinema as a weapon, and also for those who wanted to study the liberation of the screen and wanted to know, how does a revolution transform the cinema, when it has taken power?
>
> Now it's a cinema for broad taste, for easy understanding. The workshop of experimentation, called ICAIC, has become a factory, and the enormous abyss which separates the cinema from television, which separates the cinematic art from the culture of the masses, has disappeared to the detriment of the cinema.[55]

This nostalgia for militant cinema, however, probably represents a minority position. Other observers view the militant, overheated discourse and aspirations of the 1960s as a purely historical phenomenon. Following their logic, revolutionary struggles ran aground throughout Latin America. As social movements have replaced revolution, so liberation is no longer considered "the highest expression of culture," as Sergio Ramírez called it in 1982. One prominent literary critic from the United States, John Beverley, views the current situation with apparent equanimity:

If the dominant tone of ICAIC's early production reflected the more dramatic, transformational stage of the Revolution in the 1960s and early 1970s, the films made in the 1980s on the model of *Portrait* [*Portrait of Teresa*, 1979] reflect a situation in which the Revolution has become the new form of everyday life, "the daily." They are similar in style and content to the American television genre of the "problem movie," dealing with family life, education, young people, work, careers, racism, sexism and so forth, in terms of the lives of "ordinary" people.

The direction suggested by some of the "second wave" films may be toward a revival of melodrama as a mode of progressive filmmaking. . . . It is clear that the "telenovela" and not the feature film will be the decisive cultural form of Latin America's near future.[56]

Viewed against the figures cited above, Beverley's prediction that telenovelas may become the paradigmatic cultural form in Latin America looks persuasive. Filmmaking will not necessarily disappear, at least not in countries with some production infrastructure, but it will no longer represent the aspirations of the popular sectors. Though television will be increasingly inundated with foreign offerings as cable and satellite spread their reach, the success of Mexican and Brazilian soap operas, complemented by more modest output from Chile, Argentina, and Colombia, will undoubtedly retain some market share throughout the region. They may even surpass the historically meager distribution of Latin American cinema across national borders.[57]

While Nicaraguan cinema was not exempt from these long-term trends, neither did INCINE's situation correspond to the specific conditions applying in these other countries. Brazil's domestic audience was large, and with a long if fluctuating tradition of filmmaking, the government could siphon off some theater revenue to support national production through protectionist measures, but it did not sponsor a particular national film project. Chile Films failed to mount a national film project through internal administrative and political disarray, though the small size of the domestic audience limited its potential in the first place, and it did not nationalize the film apparatus. Cuba did nationalize the industry, thereby controlling the national market, but it also made an early commitment to subsidizing a national film project, a legacy from before the incursion of television.

With minimal control of the national film apparatus, INCINE could not compete with domestic distributors and exhibitors who had a long history

Toward the End of Third Cinema

of commercial ties to U.S. companies and their local Latin American subsidiaries. Hence, INCINE depended on Cuban largesse and FSLN goodwill to survive. INCINE probably would not have lasted as long as it did without the Cubans, for their assistance meant that the FSLN effectively did not have to invest significantly in INCINE. Following perhaps an archaic tradition dating from the establishment of ICAIC in 1959, Cuba counseled the establishment of a film institute and the FSLN went along.

Consequently, INCINE was not operating with real costs, since it received so much of its funding in kind. The Cubans covered production costs of raw stock, development, postproduction, and regular travel back and forth to Cuba. The FSLN funded travel and lodging within the country, modest production resources, and minimal salaries. By the middle of the 1980s, INCINE attempted to secure more financial independence by acquiring financial control over Cine RAP and ENIDIEC, but by that time the economy was in a tailspin.

Conclusion

Could INCINE have survived? Has the media landscape changed so radically that national cinema projects in countries like Nicaragua are no longer viable, politically, culturally, or economically? In different ways, the efforts of those in other countries met similar fates, and the repeated aspirations of a pan-(Latin) American cinema have yet to be realized, though the demise of these national projects may ironically see a continental cinema rise from the ashes.[58] Broad trends in cinematic culture throughout the region have vastly altered the playing field, severely constricting the space for national cinemas.

In this context, INCINE emerges even more as an anachronism. As audiences were staying home to watch television, the number of television sets doubled between 1975 and 1980 in Nicaragua.[59] INCINE embarked on cinema production for the first time in the country's history. The establishment of a national filmmaking institute followed the Cuban model. But in 1959 cinema offered the most promising way of popularizing the revolution and exporting its revolutionary culture abroad, a standard bearer for a liberated culture and the "new man." ICAIC's status as an autonomous entity responsible only to Castro underlined Cuba's high expectations for cinema. The elaborately written law creating ICAIC, opening with the assertion that "The cinema is an art" reflected the ambition of ICAIC's mission.[60] The utterly prosaic official decree announcing INCINE's formation accurately expressed the relatively tepid enthusiasm for the cinema on the part of the Dirección Nacional. Lodging the cinema side by side with poetry, music, and plastic arts within the Ministry of Culture conferred no special role on film in the Sandinista revolution.

Other countries encountered difficulties in establishing stable film industries, but INCINE faced an even more challenging situation. Virtually no one at INCINE had experience with film distribution and exhibition, and film production barely existed. Objectively, television had already cut into cinema's status as the most significant mass medium, and that trend would only accelerate during the 1980s. Subjectively, the FSLN leaders had little interest in cinema production. They had never seen the more militant films from Argentina, Chile, and Bolivia, and Cuban films obviously were not shown in Nicaragua during the Somoza years. The FSLN did establish INCINE within the Ministry of Culture, but almost undoubtedly the Cubans were responsible for that initiative, and ICAIC immediately supplied advisers and matériel to begin production. Hence, INCINE did not need a strong commitment from the FSLN to begin, but the administrative scattering of production, distribution, and exhibition ensured a debilitating irrationality in the revolutionary cinema infrastructure.

Given such odds, INCINE managed valiantly during the first half of the decade. The monthly noticieros came out fairly regularly for four years and improved over time as the nascent filmmakers gained experience. Impressive documentaries soon followed. Finally, fiction absorbed INCINE's resources, aborting the noticiero production just when government funding ended (in 1984). The war, hardly a low-intensity conflict for Nicaraguans, consumed the government's attention and budget and shook the entire country. All the while, the head of INCINE tried to obtain control over the state-owned theaters as a source of revenue, but by the time the reorganization came, Nicaragua's economic deterioration had reduced consumer purchasing power, and inflation depressed the local currency's value. Though the government refused to raise admission prices, potential audiences could not afford the cinema, and exhibitors could not maintain the theaters. Reduced attendance also exacerbated the difficulty of replacing parts from the traditional suppliers in the U.S. following the blockade. With distribution, the blockade short-circuited access to United States distributors, though ideological considerations obviously complicated the purely financial possibilities in both distribution and exhibition.

Here is where "third cinema" might have offered a solution. While many critics have faulted the manifesto for its schematism, Manichaeanism and Peronism, Solanas and Getino were proposing a highly flexible program for filmmaking.[61] They concentrated on the relationship between the film and the audience. So long as the film helped transform the spectator into an active participant in the national liberation struggle, the film qualified as "third cinema." But above all, and herein lay perhaps the decisive possibility for INCINE: Militant cinema, that privileged category of third cinema, was part of a mass movement. The task of militant cinema was not just to mobilize the masses, but also to win them to the filmmaker/militant's particular political analysis developed by the mass movement. That is, the content of the political position did not count as much as the film's insertion in the political struggle, perhaps even a struggle among leftist positions. Had INCINE developed this strategy, committing itself to the interests of the mass organizations and even strengthening them, it might have succeeded where the FSLN ultimately failed. The FSLN's greatest strength was its popular support as the vanguard of the revolutionary struggle. As a vanguard organization, the FSLN's formal members probably did not exceed 1,500 militants at the triumph, and during the 1980s, its profile as a vanguard never changed.[62] Its claim to mass support depended largely on the mass organizations' functioning as popular conduits for the people's will. As the pressures mounted, externally from the United States and internally from the U.S.-financed and -directed war, the relationship between the Front and the mass organizations deteriorated. Ultimately the beleaguered vanguard tried to use the mass organizations as executors of Dirección Nacional decisions.[63]

There has been considerable debate over this issue. The Front claimed to represent the interests of "the people." Some leftist critics viewed this phrase as a retreat from a class analysis.[64] So long as the Front refused to deal with the class contradictions, its project was doomed, for there could be no accommodation with the bourgeoisie; Chile provided the lesson for this view. Yet critics also disagreed about what class or classes the Front should represent. With such a small proletariat, the Front could not rely exclusively on that class. The class panorama in the countryside was very complicated, for the agricultural reality was crisscrossed by contradictions of class, property relations, ownership patterns, etc. The agrarian reform process grappled with these problems but could never clearly identify a class project in the countryside, and that is where the contra took root.

On some level, INCINE recognized this phenomenon. After several years of noticiero production, the directors allotted less screen time to the commandants, for they observed the indifference and even hostility manifest by audiences in the theaters. Over time, INCINE also struck deals with various ministries and other institutions, but often INCINE was competing with in-house production units of those ministries, and reliance on the Front for funding and logistical support probably inhibited autonomy. Furthermore, the ministries did not necessarily battle for the interests of the mass organizations.

But INCINE did not pursue links to the mass organizations. Such ties might have built an audience and provided a forum for debate. In any event, as the experiences of other Latin American countries, including Cuba, have demonstrated, national cinema production cannot compete with U.S. production and distribution, even if Nicaragua had nationalized all the theaters. INCINE could have constructed an alternative audience and drawn from that audience to address and articulate their independent concerns.

At the same time, institutional feudalism throughout the state and party apparatus impeded collaborative work. At the highest levels, ministries fought for turf. Jaime Wheelock, head of the Agrarian Reform, battled and eventually prevailed over Henry Ruíz at the Ministry of Planning. In principle, the Ministry of Planning should have guided intersectorial connections at the macro level, but the technical challenges—as well as the political obstacles—proved insuperable. In particular, the Front resisted using market values to peg pricing, resulting in massive subsidies to many interests, including prolonged negative interest rates for agriculture when rationalization of agriculture was a high priority. In recognition of this problem, the Ministry of Planning itself was eliminated in 1985.[65]

Under such conditions, ministries and organizations sought their own survival by defending their own interests. The three most powerful ministries, each headed by a member of the Dirección Nacional—Defense, Interior, Agriculture—ran media projects. Though designed primarily for internal use, Interior and Agriculture aired productions on television, an arrangement INCINE never held with regularity because of friction between the two heads of the institutions.

INCINE produced films with several ministries, but squirreled away within the impoverished Ministry of Culture, INCINE lacked political clout. As throughout the state bureaucracy, INCINE personnel had little administrative experience and for most of the decade couldn't rationalize the cinema sector under one roof. Like many state enterprises, INCINE concentrated on quantitative output, exercising virtually no control over "inputs," or the revenues from theaters and the purchase of equipment. The state was so possessive of hard currency (i.e., dollars) that INCINE depended on services in kind, from transportation, fuel, food, and lodging from the Front to the provision of equipment, film stock, development, and postproduction from the Cubans and other donors. Consequently, filmmakers and producers were not working with "real" budgets. Paper budgets were devised with córdoba costs and dollar costs, but often the enormous córdoba figures bore no relation to reality, given constantly escalating inflation and the difficulty of estimating services in kind.

In addition, the Ministry of Culture was racked with dissension with the early rise of the ASTC, pitting Rosario Murillo against the popular Ernesto

Cardenal. Accounts of this struggle characterize it as both a personal battle driven by Rosario Murillo's ambition and a principled competition between two conceptions of revolutionary culture. Cardenal and his Costa Rican assistant Mayra Jimenez promoted the poetry workshops to democratize culture, encouraging workers, soldiers, and campesinos to write. Murillo set up a rival organization for "professionals," some of whom saw the poetry workshops as propagating restrictive aesthetic and political rules. Though INCINE was not part of this debate, the filmmakers surely viewed themselves as professionals vis à vis the amateur video producers in the other ministries and mass organizations, and their work justified such a view.[66]

It is tempting, and even plausible, to see INCINE's trajectory as symptomatic of the revolution itself. In the early years, despite its precarious status as a capital-intensive entity within a minor ministry, INCINE benefited from external support both financially and ideologically from the Cubans and other friendly countries. Ramiro Lacayo, the inexperienced and timid head of production, managed to parlay his personal connections with Sergio Ramirez into additional back-channel political and material support. The savvy veteran Front militant Carlos Vicente Ibarra oversaw distribution and exhibition (policy, not finances) until the middle of 1982. During this period, Lacayo sought and eventually achieved greater autonomy for INCINE with control over distribution (ENIDIEC) and exhibition (Cine RAP), each formerly housed in the COCULTURA and MICOIN, respectively. As the contra war placed ever-greater demands on the national budget, the government reduced support for the ministry and left INCINE to fend for itself. But with purchasing power plummeting and the U.S. trade blockade radically changing the terms of trade, theaters fell into disrepair, and the quality of the films exhibited deteriorated.

Though the odds were seriously stacked against it, INCINE failed to devise a successful survival strategy. Coproductions in 1983 (*El Señor Presidente*) and 1985 (*Walker*) probably whetted the filmmakers' ambitions as noticiero production ground to a halt. Instead of establishing itself as the essential center for quality film and video production, and instead of building firm ties with the ministries and the mass organizations, INCINE competed with many small video production groups strewn throughout the state and party apparatus. Faced with this institutional disarticulation among media producers, INCINE's earlier grace period probably caught up with it. Just as state sector Area de Propriedad del Pueblo (APP) agricultural managers could ignore cost efficiency while interest rates were negative and the government remained committed to the state farms, so INCINE had not had to confront real production costs. When the subsidies dried up, INCINE, with a rickety infrastructure and few internal dollars, had little political capital to draw on.

At this point the historical conjuncture probably doomed INCINE. Cuba had committed itself to the cinema as a prestige product in the 1960s. Though cinema as a militant weapon lost its luster after the late 1960s and 1970s throughout Latin America, Cuba maintained a commitment to ICAIC. But that commitment was an anachronism, increasingly so during the 1980s with costs of production escalating and television replacing the cinema as the medium of popular choice. And even in Cuba, which had placed a high priority on cinema, creating ICAIC as an autonomous entity directly under Castro in 1959, ICAIC's status fell when it was assigned to one part of the newly formed Ministry of Culture in 1977. INCINE enjoyed no special status in the eyes of the commandants. According to the popular adage, Nicaragua was a country of poets, not filmmakers (nor painters, musicians, or playwrights, for that matter). In most of the world today, even in countries with long histories of distinguished production, such as the industrialized countries of Western Europe, cinema requires state support.

Like the Sandinista revolution itself, INCINE did not, or could not, survive. For the revolution, the United States successfully applied a wide array of economic and military destabilizing measures. With the inevitable challenges facing a government committed to social transformation, the Sandinistas struggled to find a workable strategy and often relied on an inconsistent series of reactive tactics. To some extent, their conflicting policies reflected divisions within the Sandinista leadership: the role of the campesinos and how to distribute land; the attitude toward the bourgeoisie and the blurred distinction between "patriotic" and "unpatriotic" bourgeoisie; pricing policies in the countryside versus the cities; etc. The simultaneous collapse of the socialist bloc removed any cushion of maneuverability.

INCINE modeled itself on the Cuban example of ICAIC. Frank Pineda even described it as ICAIC's "pampered child."[67] But INCINE, unlike ICAIC, did not control the national cinema apparatus. It did not nationalize the theaters or eliminate private distributors. Essentially, INCINE produced a luxury good, a prestige product, at a time when cinema had been displaced by television as the medium of mass communication.[68] Once cut from state support, INCINE foundered. In addition, INCINE probably made some bad decisions, some of omission, some of commission. Failure to establish links with the mass organizations and the ministries left INCINE isolated. Ending the noticieros weakened ties with ICAIC. The 35-mm noticieros had ensured a strong institutional bond with ICAIC; the 16-mm fictional shorts were produced through Cuban television, which operated independently of ICAIC, and the Nicaraguan filmmakers complained about the poor quality of those services. The production of *El espectro de la guerra*, completed during the year of runaway inflation (33,000 percent!) and massive layoffs of state employees (8,000), including the closing of the Ministry of Culture, provided the coup de grace for INCINE.

Can national cinema projects in small Latin American countries exist? The experiences of the large Latin American film "industries" leave little room for optimism. With neoliberalism and globalization sweeping the region, state support has become increasingly problematic. The plummeting production figures, galloping theater closings, and shrinking audiences testify to the precariousness of those cinemas. In the wonderful formulation of Randal Johnson,

> Two questions might initially be asked. First, can a culturally or aesthetically significant cinema survive in Latin America without state support? Second, can one survive with state support? The answer to the first is almost certainly "no." The answer to the second (which may seem facetious) may well also be negative. In tandem, a response can only come in the form of a familiar paradox expressing the double bind many if not most Latin American filmmakers have confronted over the last thirty years or so: they cannot live with it, and they cannot live without it.[69]

But a national cinema industry differs from a national cinema project.[70] A national cinema industry does not necessarily have any inherent value. That is, with the exception of large countries, with large domestic markets, cinema is not economically valuable. If a government represents a new national project, cinema can disseminate and promote that project. Despite its contradictions, Peronism, with wide popular support, particularly among the working class, was that project in Argentina. Getino and Solanas conceived of "third cinema" riding the wave of that project. Before television, the Soviet Union (in the 1920s) and eastern European countries and Cuba (in the 1960s), projected and exported films as cultural products that demonstrated their artistic vitality. However bleak the economic and political realities, the state produced international artistic triumphs. In a time of ideological struggle, these films conferred value, albeit ambiguously when films criticized the regimes.

With the demise of socialism as an ideological alternative to capitalism, such national industries no longer have ideological content. Individual films may have political meaning—feminism, multiculturalism, democratization —but they do not necessarily reflect a national project committed to shared goals. One might read the transformation of Latin American cinemas since the Cuban revolution and the "third cinema" manifesto as the delayed transition in cinema from modernism to postmodernism. Following the Cuban revolution's success, politicized auteurs emerged with the popular surge of anti-imperialism, committed in different ways to national liberation: Littín, Soto, Guzmán (Chile); Sanjinés (Bolivia); Birri, Solanas, Getino, Kuhn (Argentina); Rocha, Guerra, Diegues (Brazil). That generation came of age cinematically following the Cuban revolution's success. Their politicization varied, but all these filmmakers wanted to carve a space in the national cinema for a new national project. Many sympathetic critics lauded the undeniable formal invention of the films and saw them as part of the modernist renewal in Europe during the 1960s. With the failure of mass movements in Chile, Argentina, and elsewhere in Latin America, new, younger auteurs emerged, but these newcomers no longer believed in the grand narratives of the "older" generation. Even Cuba could not resist this trend.[71]

Given INCINE's mission to "recover national identity" in its 1979 "Statement of Principles," to what extent did INCINE fulfill that task? INCINE never found a reliable popular base. Lacayo increasingly sought greater independence from the FSLN, but as he admitted, INCINE was always seen as an Institute of *Sandinista* Cinema. It didn't establish itself as an Institute of Nicaraguan Cinema. Throughout the decade, the FSLN tried to graft its identity to the national one. It consciously avoided the pitfalls of traditional caudillismo by practicing collective decision making in the Dirección Nacional. But that did not prevent the defection of its base, when the DN did not, perhaps could not, make good on its commitment to participatory democracy. Ultimately, the graft did not take.

INCINE's identification with the FSLN sapped its effectiveness in another way. INCINE did not explore sensitive issues: the Atlantic coast, the lived experience of the campesinos, the role of women, the Catholic Church, the mass organizations. The counterrevolution exploited these problems, distorting them to be sure, but with some success. Like the FSLN, INCINE failed to confront these questions directly. In the few exceptions, as in *Los hijos del río* and *Mujeres de la frontera*, in which the films acknowledged real difficulties, they were read as critical of the FSLN. As a new government institution trying to balance ideological commitments with aesthetic aspirations, INCINE moved closer to balance and began to develop a more supple cinematic language of the people, but campesinos, women, Miskitos were not always identifiable in the Sandinista version of "the people."

INCINE rose with the FSLN and ultimately fell with the FSLN, though INCINE's demise in 1988 more accurately reflected the chronology of the FSLN's project than the FSLN's electoral defeat of 1990. In one sense, consistent with the goals of the militant third cinema, INCINE had represented the interests of a particular popular political organization riding and directing a rise of popular forces. But INCINE never proved its utility to the FSLN, nor did it necessarily subordinate its own interests unequivocally to the FSLN, the fundamental condition of militant cinema for Solanas and Getino. While institutionally tied to the FSLN, INCINE wanted more independence. The U.S.-sponsored war, of course, imposed pressures on every aspect of Nicaraguan society during the 1980s, so the FSLN did not have the luxury of stabilizing what it viewed as only a marginal ideological strut.

INCINE cast its lot with the FSLN enthusiastically in 1979. But the early name change from Sandinista Institute to Nicaraguan Institute of Cinema presaged a potential bifurcation of interests. So long as the FSLN retained its popular base, the attempt to identify Sandinista with Nicaraguan had some chance of realization. INCINE could straddle that identification following the fundamental premise of "Towards a Third Cinema":

> The existence of masses on the worldwide revolutionary plane was the substantial fact without which those questions could not have been posed.

But the masses in Nicaragua, like the masses in other Latin American countries before them, could not withstand the multiple pressures of a violent counterrevolution and the consequent demands of an increasingly embattled FSLN in the midst of world historical changes. Inevitably, INCINE was yoked to the fortunes of the FSLN, and the young revolutionary filmmakers at INCINE produced a body of work that dwarfed, in quantity and longevity, the more ephemeral experiments in militant filmmaking in those other countries. Nonetheless, as the Sandinista revolution became the "revolution that fell from the grace of the people,"[72] its revolutionary cinema became the anachronistic heir of third cinema. In the words of Iván Argüello, "INCINE was a utopia that had to fail."[73]

At the same time, the history of INCINE offers the most sustained practical laboratory of third cinema. Solanas and Getino, after all, did not establish a successful filmmaking apparatus in Argentina after the return of Perón. INCINE may not have produced many feature films, but the variety of themes, formal invention, and implicit political interpretation in its corpus provides a rich reflection of and commentary on an exciting popular revolution. Writers on Cuban film understandably laud ICAIC's feature films, but those films represent only five percent of ICAIC's production from 1959 to 1987.[74] For reasons already noted, the FSLN frustrated INCINE's quest for independence. As artists, as revolutionary artists, the filmmakers at INCINE wanted not only financial independence, but also artistic independence. They were seeking space *within* the FSLN to develop their critical voices.

But the political-military conception of the beleaguered FSLN could not accommodate that degree of internal criticism. The most interesting INCINE films—*Pan y dignidad, Nuestra Reforma Agraria, Rompiendo el silencio, Mujeres de la frontera, Los hijos del río*—to name only a few, took on sensitive topics that merited more public discussion. Unlike the earliest films, these films might indeed have rallied audiences to the FSLN, following the theory of Solanas and Getino. The move to fiction, in itself, need not have dealt a fatal blow to INCINE; after all, Brecht's theory of a didactic theater in fact emphasized the importance of entertainment. The third cinema manifesto, however, was written in opposition to a repressive government. Maintaining popular support after the triumph of the mass popular movement probably entails allowing more space for self-criticism, not less. Even if INCINE's trajectory was unaccompanied by theoretical reflection, its legacy remains as the most sustained test of joining third cinema's theory and practice.

Appendix DIAGRAMS, PLANS, CHARTS,
AND DOCUMENTS

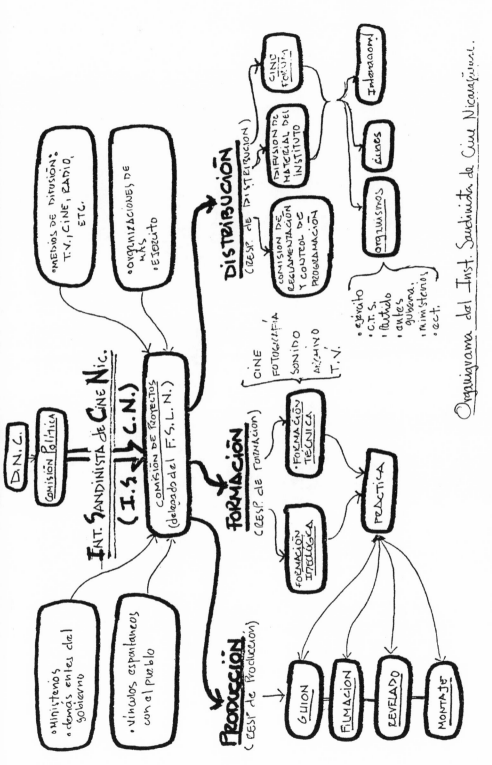

Flow chart for Instituto Sandinista de Cine Nicaragüense. August 3, 1979.

Comisión Coordinadora

| Franklin - Ramiro - Quincho |

Producción
| Ramiro |

Exhibición - Distribución
| Quincho/Angeles |

Comisión Clasificadora
| Franklin | | Franklin | | Quincho |
| | | Hopal |

Rel. Internacionales

Early proposed flow chart for Instituto Sandinista de Cine Nicaragüense.

2.

Cine Movil
|
Org. & Ms.
Eg.
Ruby / Julio

Cine T.V.
Quirche / Frankl

Distribución ┌ Exhibición
Quirche / Angeles

Cinemateca
Frankl / Rafael / Rodolfo

Saus INCINE

Admo.
Vilma / Maruca
Contador
Sr...

Archivo.
Angeles

Early proposed flow chart for Instituto Sandinista de Cine Nicaragüense.

Early proposed flow chart for Instituto Sandinista de Cine Nicaragüense.

INCINE in Ministry of Culture

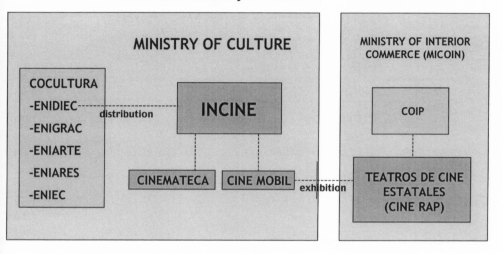

Organization of Production at INCINE

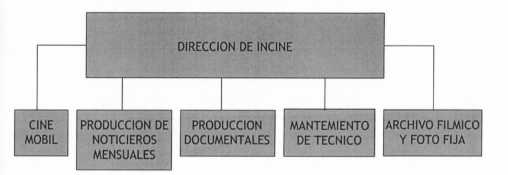

DECLARACION DE PRINCIPIOS Y FINES DEL INSTITUTO

DECLARACION DE PRINCIPIOS Y FINES DEL INSTITUTO NICARAGUENSE DE CINE.

Hasta el día del triunfo de la Revolución Popular Sandinista, Nicaragua fue un país dominado por la más bestial de las dictaduras latinoamericanas: La Dinastía Somocista.

Esta fue nada más que la expresión de una secular dominación ejercida por el imperialismo norteamericano sobre nuestra Patria. Sometida al saqueo, a la explotación, al hambre y a la miseria por esa tenebrosa fuerza reaccionaria y anti-popular, Nicaragua tuvo también que enfrentar una sistemática y profunda agresión destinada a socavar su identidad nacional.

En el fragor de la guerra contra esa fuerza, nació el cine Sandinista, por la necesidad de recoger el testimonio cinematográfico de los más significativos momentos de esa lucha para contrarrestar la desinformación promovida por agencias noticiosas enemigas y mantener viva la solidaridad internacional. Asimismo se proponía conservar para las futuras generaciones el documento del inmenso sacrificio que costó a nuestro pueblo llevar adelante su guerra revolucionaria.

En el cumplimiento de tales tareas germinó lo que hoy -al asumir las responsabilidades del triunfo- se perfila como Instituto Nicaragüense de Cine. Es éste una respuesta al compromiso de rescatar y desarrollar nuestra identidad Nacional. Es igualmente instrumento de defensa de nuestra revolución, en el campo de la lucha ideológica y nuevo medio de expresión de nuestro pueblo en su sagrado derecho a la autodeterminación y a su plena independencia.

A través de todos y cada uno de nuestros trabajos, deberemos satisfacer las necesidades inmediatas de movilización, de educación, de recreación, que nos exige la actual etapa de reconstrucción Nacional, esforzándonos por realizar obras cinematográficas de valor permanente que se inserten en la mejor tradición del cine progresista y revolucionario que se ha producido y se produce en Améri-

INSTITUTO NICARAGUENSE DE CINE

ca Latina, y finalmente en la cultura universal, como parte de una lucha regional, continental y mundial por la liberación definitiva de todos los pueblos oprimidos.

Al iniciar la tarea que como Instituto Nicaragüense de Cine nos hemos propuesto, somos conscientes de que en Nicaragua no existe tradición alguna en lo que a cinematografía se refiere.

Crear el cine nacional desde la herencia de ruinas que la dictadura nos deja es todo un reto. Con la total destrucción económica y material, disponemos de insuficientes recursos para alcanzar los objetivos señalados, pero estamos seguros de poder cumplir porque nos anima el mismo espíritu que nos llevó a la victoria.

Contamos por lo pronto con la singular experiencia cinematográfica obtenida durante la guerra de liberación, y con el aporte valioso y necesario de compañeros internacionalistas latinoamericanos que a nuestro lado enfrentarán el gran desafío que nos espera.

El nuestro será un cine nicaragüense, lanzado a la búsqueda de un lenguaje cinematográfico que ha de surgir de nuestra realidad concreta y de las experiencias particulares de nuestra cultura.

Partirá de un esfuerzo de investigación profunda en las raíces de nuestra cultura, porque sólo así podrá reflejar la esencia de nuestro ser histórico y contribuir al desarrollo del proceso revolucionario y de su protagonista: El pueblo nicaragüense.

Al definir hoy los orígenes y fines del Instituto Nicaragüense de Cine, hacemos un fraternal llamado a las cinematografías y a los cineastas de todo el mundo, para que unidos en el espíritu del General de Hombres Libres, Augusto César Sandino, respalden nuestra iniciativa y así tendamos estrechos vínculos de solidaridad que en este campo de la expresión auspicien el avance y desarrollo de nuestra revolución Popular Sandinista.

¡PATRIA LIBRE O MORIR!

Declaration of Principles and Goals of the Nicaraguan Institute of Cinema

Until the day of the triumph of the Popular Sandinista Revolution, Nicaragua was a country dominated by the most bestial of Latin American dictatorships: the Somocista Dynasty.

This dynasty was nothing more than the expression of a secular domination imposed on our homeland by North American imperialism. Submitted to sacking, exploitation, hunger, and misery by this shady, reactionary, and anti-popular force, Nicaragua also had to confront a systematic and entrenched aggression bent on uprooting its national identity.

In the heat of war against this force, the Sandinista cinema was born, out of the need to gather the cinematic testimony of the most significant moments of this struggle to counter the disinformation promoted by the enemy's news agencies and preserve international solidarity. At the same time it was proposed to conserve for the future generations the document of the immense sacrifice borne by our people to carry forward its revolutionary war.

In the fulfillment of such tasks germinated what today—upon assumption of the responsibilities of the triumph—is known as the Nicaraguan Institute of Cinema. This is a response to the commitment to recover and develop our National identity. It is at the same time an instrument in the defense of our revolution, in the area of the ideological struggle and a new means of expression of our people in their sacred right to self-determination and its full independence.

In each and every one of our works, we will have to satisfy the immediate needs of mobilization, education, recreation, that the current stage of National reconstruction requires of us, strengthening us to produce cinematic works of permanent value which take their place in the best tradition of progressive and revolutionary cinema that has been produced and is being produced in Latin America, and finally, in universal culture, as part of a regional, continental, and world struggle for the definitive liberation of all oppressed peoples.

To begin the task that we, as the Nicaraguan Institute of Cinema, have proposed for ourselves, we are aware that there exists no tradition of cinematography in Nicaragua.

To create the national cinema out of the legacy of ruin that the dictatorship leaves us is a challenge. With the total economic and material destruction, we have insufficient resources to reach our indicated objectives, but we are sure of being able to fulfill them because the same spirit that brought us victory inspires us.

We benefit immediately from the unique cinematic experience obtained during the war of liberation, and with the valuable and necessary contribution of international Latin American companions who at our side will confront the great challenge that awaits us.

Ours will be a Nicaraguan cinema, launched in search of a cinematic language that must arise from our concrete reality and the specific experiences of our culture.

It will begin with an effort of careful investigation into the roots of our culture, for only thus can it reflect the essence of our historical being and contribute to the development of the revolutionary process and its protagonist: The Nicaraguan people.

In defining today the origins and objectives of the Nicaraguan Institute of Cinema, we make a fraternal appeal to the cinemas and the filmmakers of the whole world, so that, united with the spirit of the General of Free Men, Augusto César Sandino, they support our initiative. We will thus have close bonds of solidarity that in this field of expression will favor the advance and development of our Popular Sandinista Revolution.

A Free Homeland or Death!

_____ ~~DE CLASIFICACION~~

1.- FICHA TECNICA.-

Título (en español o idioma original) _Mad Max_

Director _George Miller - Mel Gibson_

Protagonistas _____

País - Compañía _____

Duración _____

A.-SINOPSIS _Entre los policías de tráfico de carreteras hay un héroe que consigue reducir a todas las bandas de delincuentes motorizados. El "trabajo" exige una violencia "legal" tan salvaje como la delictiva. Pero hay una banda especialmente sangrienta, centro de interés del film. El héroe bueno, influido por su dulce esposa, y a causa de tanta violencia e injusticias, se retira del cuerpo, hasta que la banda les cae a ellos, mata a su esposa e hijo, momento en que_

B.- POLITICO IDEOLOGICOS _el héroe decide actuar como "poli" por su cuenta y los extermina en un dos por tres con su camaza de motor impresionante._

Glorificación de la violencia inconsciente, más ??? durísima, ??? individualista, ??? es fuera de al margen de toda ley;
Velocidad en carreteras ??? ??? de la juventud, su ideal (motos); vinculación clara

C.- FOTO~~GRAFIA~~ (COLOR, ILUMINACION) _de las anteriores y de todo el film al negocio_
y a la publicidad comercial más descarada de la venta de motos y automóviles.

- truculencia sanguinaria constante a nivel
Banda ~~Sonora~~ (efectos, música y Diálogos) _formal y de contenidos._

- falso moralismo con que se les condena
por el triunfo del héroe todopoderoso.

REALIZACION _Pésima_

_____

MONTAJE _Igual_

PUESTA EN ESCENA (VESTUARIO, ESCENOGRAFIA, LOCACIONES NATURALES O FABRICADAS. _glorificación de la moda "punk" o chaquetas de cuero (como mundo salvaje y maravilloso del hippismo), y los automóviles y motos como símbolos de "Poder".-_

D.- CALIFICACION

Archivar V

Managua, 24 de noviembre 1982

DIRECCION
NACIONAL

FRENTE
SANDINISTA
DE
LIBERACION FSLN
NACIONAL

Compañero
FRANCISCO LACAYO
Vice-Ministro de Cultura

Estimado Compañero:

Reciba un fraterno saludo revolucionario, impregnado de calor sandinista.

El motivo de esta comunicación es informarle lo que me fue transmitido en relación a un documental que se está pasando actualmente en los cines Cabrera y Dorado.

En dicho documental, se pasa parte de la historia del FSLN, además del caso de las Bananeras y algunos pasajes donde aparece Somoza regresando al país y siendo recibido éste por guardias somocistas. El asunto es que estas últimas dos partes han motivado al público responder con aplausos.

Considero que INCINE debe revisar el contenido del documental en mención, y además, verificar una vez más la información que me fue transmitida.

Sin más a que hacer referencia, me despido fraterno,

PATRIA LIBRE O MORIR
Comandante de la Revolución

Comandante de la Revolución
CARLOS NUÑEZ TELLEZ

¡PATRIA LIBRE O MORIR!

Letter from Comandante de la Revolución Carlos Nuñez suggesting revision of film that had elicited applause for Somoza.

Announcement of suspension of work at INCINE because of lack of funds. January 16, 1996.

INSTITUTO NICARAGUENSE DE CINE
   I N C I N E

Apartado Nº. 4660   Tel. 667977
      Managua, Nicaragua   M E M O R A N D U M .

A   :   TODO EL PERSONAL DE INCINE.

DE   :   LIC. CESAR OBANDO NARVAEZ.
              GERENTE GENERAL.
              INCINE.

REF   :   COMUNICACION RECIBIDA VERBALMENTE DE
              LIC. LUIS A. PALACIOS.
              DIR. ADMITIVO. FINANCIERO CANAL 6 T.V.

FECHA   :   16 DE ENERO DE 1996.

Por este medio se les comunica a todo el personal de Incine
que a partir del día de hoy 16 de los corrientes se saldrá
de vacaciones, presentándose todo el personal hasta el día
1º de febrero del año en curso.
Todo esto según versión verbal y orientación que diera el
Lic. Luis A. Palacios, Director Admitivo. Financiero del –
Canal 6 de T.V.; En visita que hiciera el día de hoy a nues-
tras oficinas a las 9:20 am. de los corrientes.

No omito en manifestarles que esta orientación obedece a no
tener fondos para liquidar salario de la segunda quincena –
del mes de enero/96. Remarcando que todo el personal deberá
hacerse presente el día 1º de febrero del 96. A saber el re-
sultado final del destino de Incine.

                              Atentamente,

----

cc : Lic. Luis A. Palacio.
     Dir. Admitivo. Financiero. Canal 6 de T.V.

     Contabilidad.
     Archivo.
     ▬▬▬▬

     Lic. Amanda I. Carrillo. DICS.
     Marvin A. García.
     Marlene Solano G.
     Juan Ortíz U.
     Francis Obando.
     Osmin Morales.

CON/msg.

                    Dirección: Shell las Palmas, 1½ c. abajo

Filmography

The credits below are taken primarily from the films. For roughly the first half of the noticiero cycle, the films had no credits except for the Director (of Noticieros) and the Realizador. In those cases, I have listed only the name of the Realizador, and the names found on the "fichas técnicas" in INCINE's archives. The credits below do not list all of the names included in the films. In some noticieros, the films include only a group of people not broken down by category, and I relied on the "fichas técnicas" for the distribution. The abbreviations refer to the following categories: d/director; sc/script; prod/producer; ph/photography; s/sound; mus/music; ed/editor; res/research; B/W/black and white. The dates reflect my best estimates of the film's completion.

Noticieros

1. *Nacionalización de las minas.* d: Frank Pineda; ph: Alvaro Jiménez and Frank Pineda; s: Moisés Rodríguez; ed: Alejandra González and Johnny Henderson. Color, 35 mm, 10', December 1979.
2. *1979: Año de la liberación.* d: Frank Pineda; ph: Rafael Ruíz; s: Moisés Rodríguez; ed: Alejandra González. B/W, 35 mm, 19', January 1980.
3. *Plan económico 1980.* d: María José Alvarez; ph: Rafael Ruíz; s: Moisés Rodríguez; ed: Alejandra González. B/W, 35 mm, 9', February 1980.
4. *Jornada patriótica de Sandino.* d: María José Alvarez; ph: Frank Pineda and Rafael Ruíz; s: Moisés Rodríguez; ed: Alejandra González. B/W, 35 mm, 9', March 1980.
5. *Inicio cruzada nacional de alfabetización.* d: María José Alvarez; ph: Frank Pineda; s: Moisés Rodríguez; ed: Alejandra González. B/W, 35 mm, 10', April 1980.
6. *Acto del primero de mayo.* d: Ramiro Lacayo; ph: Rafael Ruíz; s: Moisés Rodríguez; ed: Alejandra Gonzalez. B/W, 35 mm, 12', May 1980.
7. *La Reforma Agraria.* d: María José Alvarez; ph: Frank Pineda; s: Moisés Rodríguez; ed: Alejandra Gonzalez. B/W, 35 mm, 10', June 1980.
8. *Primer aniversario de la revolución popular Sandinista.* d: Ramiro Lacayo; ph: Frank Pineda and Rafael Ruíz; s: Moisés Rodríguez and Eddy Meléndez; ed: Johnny Henderson. B/W, 35 mm, 15', July 1980.
9. *Clausura de la cruzada nacional de alfabetización.* d: María José Alvarez and

Alberto Legall; ph: Frank Pineda; s: Moisés Rodríguez; ed: Johnny Henderson. B/W, 35 mm, 15', August 1980.

10. *La democracia.* d: Alberto Legall; ph: Rafael Ruíz; s: Eddy Meléndez. B/W, 35 mm, 11', September 1980.

11. *La costa Atlántica.* d: María José Alvarez; ph: Rafael Ruíz; s: Eddy Meléndez; ed: Johnny Henderson. B/W, 35 mm, 12', November 1980.

12. *Resumen del año 1980.* d: María José Alvarez; ph: Rafael Ruíz; s: Eddy Meléndez; ed: Johnny Henderson. B/W, 35 mm, 12', December 1980.

13. *El Salvador vencerá.* d: Alberto Legall; prod: Brenda Martínez; ph: Frank Pineda; s: Eddy Meléndez; ed: Johnny Henderson. B/W, 35 mm, 7', January 1981.

14. *La defensa militar.* d: Alberto Legall; ph: Rafael Ruíz; s: Eddy Meléndez; ed: Johnny Henderson. B/W, 35 mm, 9', March 1981.

15. *La defensa económica.* d: Alberto Legall; ph: Frank Pineda; s: Eddy Meléndez; ed: Johnny Henderson. B/W, 35 mm, 9', March 1981.

16. *Viaje del Comandante Daniel Ortega a México.* d: Alberto Legall; prod: Brenda Martínez; ph: Emilio Rodríguez; s: Moisés Rodríguez; ed: Johnny Henderson. Color, 35 mm, 8', April 1981.

17. *La defensa política.* d: Mariano Marín; prod: Brenda Martínez; ph: Frank Pineda and Rafael Ruíz; s: Eddy Meléndez and Moisés Rodríguez; ed: Johnny Henderson. B/W, 35 mm, 10', July 1981.

18. *Segundo aniversario de la revolución popular Sandinista.* d: Alberto Legall; prod: Brenda Martínez; ph: Frank Pineda; s: Eddy Meléndez, ed: Johnny Henderson. Color, 35 mm, 19', November 1981.

19. *Viaje del Comandante Humberto Ortega a Indochina.* d: Ramiro Lacayo; ph: Raul Pérez; ed: Johnny Henderson. Color, 35 mm, 18', August 1981.

20. *Jornada anti-intervencionista.* d: Mariano Marín; ph: Armando Marenco; s: Eddy Meléndez; ed: Johnny Henderson. B/W, 35 mm, 9', January 1982.

21. *Wiwilí, sendero a una victoria.* d: Alberto Legall; ph: Frank Pineda; s: Eddy Meléndez; ed: Johnny Henderson. B/W, 35 mm, 10', November 1982.

22. *La Cultura.* d: Fernando Somarriba; prod: Brenda Martínez and Alejandro Soza; ph: Frank Pineda and Armando Marenco; s: Eddy Meléndez. B/W, 35 mm, 10', February 1982.

23. *La contrarrevolución.* d: Alberto Legall; prod: Brenda Martínez and Alejandro Soza; ph: Armando Marenco; s: Eddy Meléndez; ed: Johnny Henderson; story consultant: Mario Santos. B/W, 35 mm, 10', May 1982.

24. *Los mimados.* d: Fernando Somarriba; prod: Brenda Martínez and Alejandro Soza; sc: Fernando Somarriba; ph: Frank Pineda, Armando Marenco, and Guillermo Granera; s: Eddy Meléndez; ed: Johnny Henderson; res: Mario Santos. B/W, 35 mm, 7', June 1982.

25. *Dispuestos a todo por la paz.* d: Fernando Somarriba; prod: Brenda Martínez and Alejandro Soza; sc: Mario Santos; ph: Armando Marenco and Emilio Rodríguez; s: Eddy Meléndez and Guillermo Granera; ed: Johnny Henderson. B/W, 35 mm, 9', May 1982.

26. *Los trabajadores.* d: María José Alvarez; prod: Brenda Martínez and Alejandro Soza; ph: Armando Marenco; s: Guillermo Granera and Moisés Rodríguez; ed: Johnny Henderson; res: Mario Santos. B/W, 35 mm, 7', June 1982.

27. *La decisión.* d: Alberto Legall; prod: Brenda Martínez; ph: Armando Marenco; s: Moisés Rodríguez; ed: Johnny Henderson; B/W, 35 mm, 8', November 1982.

28. *Unidad frente a la agresión.* d: Alberto Legall; prod: Brenda Martínez; ph: Frank Pineda; s: Moisés Rodríguez; ed: Nelson Avila; Color, 35 mm, 18′, January 1983.
29. *Viva León Jodido.* d: Ramiro Lacayo; sc: Fernando Somarriba; prod: Brenda Martínez; ph: Armando Marenco; s: Moisés Rodríguez; ed: Johnny Henderson; res: Edgardo Buitrago. B/W, 35 mm, 9′, January 1983.
30. *A los héroes y mártires de Monimbó.* d: María José Alvarez and Mariano Marín; ph: Armando Marenco; s: Moisés Rodríguez; ed: Eduardo Guadamuz and Miriam Loasiga. B/W, 35 mm, 6′, August 1982.
31. *Del Ejército defensor de la soberanía nacional al ejército popular Sandinista.* d: Fernando Somarriba and Ramiro Lacayo; ph: Armando Marenco and Rafael Ruíz; s: Guillermo Granera; ed: Eduardo Guadamuz. B/W, 35 mm, 17′, September 1982.
32. *El maestro popular.* d: Mariano Marín; ph: Frank Pineda; s: Guillermo Granera; ed: Jacinto Calero and Eduardo Guadamuz. B/W, 35 mm, 9′, November 1982.
33. *Los innovadores.* d: Mariano Marín; ph: Armando Marenco; s: Guillermo Granera; ed: Jacinto Calero. B/W, 35 mm, 10′, December 1982.
34. *Más es mía el alba de oro!* d: Rafael Vargas; prod: Alejandro Soza, Lilia Alfaro and Rodolfo Alegría; ph: Rafael Ruíz, Frank Pineda and Armando Marenco; s: Eddy Meléndez; ed: Eduardo Guadamuz. B/W, 35 mm, 14′, January 1983.
35. *La gran equivocación.* d: Ivan Argüello; prod: Alejandro Soza, Brenda Martínez and Mayú Cabezas; ph: Frank Pineda; s: Guillermo Granera; ed: Eduardo Guadamuz. B/W, 35 mm, 8′, January 1983.
36. *Historia de un cine comprometido.* d: Emilio Rodríguez; prod: Alejandro Soza and Mayú Cabezas; ph: Emilio Rodríguez and Frank Pineda; s: Luis Fuentes and Guillermo Granera; ed: Eduardo Guadamuz; res: Iván Uriarte and Ronald Porras. B/W, 35 mm, 15′, June 1983.
37. *Generosos en la victoria.* d: Mariano Marín; ph: Rafael Ruíz; s: Luis Fuentes and Eddy Meléndez. 35 mm, 12′, March 1983.
38. *Radiografía de una ciudad.* (never made)
39. *La ceiba, autodefensa.* d: Mariano Marín; prod: Brenda Martínez; ph: Armando Marenco; s: Guillermo Granera; ed: Eduardo Guadamuz; res: Ronald Porras, Ivan Uriarte and Mariano Marín. B/W, 35 mm, 12′, August 1983.
40. *Manuel.* (remade as fiction, see below)
41. *Nicaragua en los no alineados.* d: Alberto Legall and Fernando Somarriba; prod: Rodolfo Alegría; ph: Frank Pineda; s: Eddy Meléndez; ed: Johnny Henderson. Color, 35 mm, 10′, July 1983.
42. *La amistad y la unidad de nuestros pueblos.* d: Alberto Legall and Fernando Somarriba; prod: Rodolfo Alegría; ph: Frank Pineda; s: Eddy Meléndez; ed: Johnny Henderson. Color, 35 mm, 15′, August 1983.
43. *Río San Juan, a este lado de la puerta.* d: Fernando Somarriba; prod: Brenda Martínez and Rodolfo Alegría; ph: Armando Marenco; s: Guillermo Granera and Eddy Meléndez; ed: Eduardo Guadamuz; res: Ronald Porras, Martha Clarissa Hernández. B/W, 35 mm, 21′, October 1983.
44. *Los centinelas de la alegría del pueblo.* d: Mariano Marín; prod: Brenda Martínez and Danny Pérez; ph: Frank Pineda; s: Eddy Meléndez and Guillermo Granera; ed: Eduardo Guadamuz. B/W, 35 mm, 15′, January 1983.
45. *Daniel en Caracas.* d: Pedro Martínez Laya, Ramiro Lacayo y Tamanaco de la Torre. Color, 35 mm, 12′, 1983.

46. *Rompiendo el silencio (Lamnika laka ba krinkl).* d: Iván Argüello; sc: Iván Argüello and Ronald Porras; exec prod: Rodolfo Alegría; prod: Arlez Muñoz and Manuel Beteta; ph: Armando Marenco; s: Moisés Rodríguez and Guillermo Granera; ed: Eduardo Guadamuz; mus: Cedrick de la Torre. B/W, 35 mm, 14', June 1984.

47. *Esta tierra es ese hombre.* d: Iván Argüello; prod: Arles Muñoz and Salvador Martínez; ph: Armando Marenco and Uriel Molina; s: Moisés Rodríguez; ed: Eduardo Guadamuz. B/W, 35 mm, 10', August 1984.

48. *El abastecimiento.* d: Ronald Porras; prod: Fernando Galo; ph: Armando Marenco; s: Moisés Rodríguez; ed: Eduardo Guadamuz. B/W, 35 mm, 9', October 1984.

49. *Bienaventurados los que luchan por la paz.* d: Iván Argüello; exec prod: Alejandro Soza; ph: Frank Pineda and Iván Jarquín; s: Moisés Rodríguez and Carlos Fernández; ed: Caita Villalon and Maricela Soza. B/W, 35 mm, 10', November 1984.

50. *Nicaragua ganó.* d: Fernando Somarriba; asst dir: Martha Clarissa Hernández; ph: Armando Marenco, Rafael Ruíz and Frank Pineda; s: Moisés Rodríguez and Eddy Meléndez; prod: Alejandro Soza and Fercila Rojas; ed: Jacinto Calero; mus: Groups "Praxis" and "Mancotal." B/W, 35 mm, 26', January 1985.

Documentaries

1. *País pobre, ciudadano pobre.* d: María José Alvarez; prod: Lilia Alfaro; ph: Emilio Rodríguez; s: Moisés Rodríguez; ed: Johnny Henderson. Color, 16 mm, 16', 1981.

2. *La otra cara del oro.* d: Rafael Vargas and Emilio Rodríguez; exec prod: Rafael Vargas; asst. prod: Lilia Alfaro; ph: Emilio Rodríguez; ed: Johnny Henderson. B/W, 35 mm, 20', 1981.

3. *Del águila al dragón.* d: Ramiro Lacayo; ph: Raúl Pérez Ureta; s: Héctor Cabrera and Jerónimo Labrada; ed: Johnny Henderson. Color, 35 mm, 15', 1981.

4. *La brigada cultural "Iván Dixon" en Cuba.* d and sc: Rafael Vargas; prod: Lilia Alfaro; ph: Frank Pineda; s: Eddy Meléndez; mus: José Antonio Bornot; ed: Gloria Arguelles. B/W, 35 mm, 12', June 1981.

5. *Pan y dignidad: Carta abierta de Nicaragua.* d: María José Alvarez; prod: Pierre Hoffmann; ph: Rafael Ruíz, John Chapman and Andreas Schultze-Kraft; s: Moisés Rodríguez; ed: Johnny Henderson and Miriam Loasiga. Color, 16 mm, 32', 1982.

6. *Nuestra Reforma Agraria.* d and prod: Rafael Vargas; exec prod: Lilia Alfaro, Oscar Sanchez and Martha Clarissa Hernández; ph: Rafael Ruíz; s: Eddy Meléndez; ed: Johnny Henderson; mus: Manuel Tercero. Color, 35 mm, 32', 1982.

7. *Nicaragua, un país para descubrir.* d: Emilio Rodríguez; prod: Lilia Alfaro, Mayú Cabezas and Zaida Mendieta; ph: Emilio Rodríguez; s: Moisés Rodríguez; ed: Alfonso Borrell; mus: "Mancotal." Color, 16 mm, 18', 1982.

8. *Más claro no canta un gallo.* d: Ramiro Lacayo; ph: Frank Pineda; s: Moisés Rodríguez; ed: Johnny Henderson. B/W, 35 mm, 5', 1982.

9. *Bananeras.* d and sc: Ramiro Lacayo; prod: Lilia Alfaro and Martha Clarissa Hernández; ph: Frank Pineda and Roberto Fernández; s: Eddy Meléndez; speaker: William Argüello; ed: Johnny Henderson; text: *La hora cero* by Ernesto Cardenal. Color, 35 mm, 16', 1982.

10. *Managua de sol a sol.* d and sc: Fernando Somarriba; ph: Frank Pineda and Rafael Ruiz; s: Moisés Rodríguez; ed: Johnny Henderson; Color, 16 mm, 24', 1982.

11. *Teotecacinte, el fuego viene del norte.* d and sc: Iván Argüello; ph: Frank Pineda; s: Moisés Rodríguez; ed: Johnny Henderson. Color, 35 mm, 35', 1983.

12. *Estos sí pasarán.* d and sc: Rossana Lacayo; prod: Danny Pérez; ph: Rafael Ruiz; s: Moisés Rodríguez; ed: Stacey Ross. Color, 16 mm, 20', 1985.

13. *Una canción de amor para el otoño.* d and sc: Ronald Porras; exec prod: Moisés Rodríguez; ph: Frank Pineda; s: Moisés Rodríguez; ed: Jacinto Morales. Color, 35 mm, 27', 1986.

14. *Un secreto para mí sola.* d and sc: Rossana Lacayo; prod: Julián Gonzales, Rossana Lacayo; ph: Rafael Ruiz; s: Guillermo Granera; ed: Edith Baker and Katia Sevilla. Color, 16 mm, 29', 1987.

15. *Los hijos del río (Wanki Lupia Nani).* Spanish version: d and sc: Fernando Somarriba; prod exec: Carlos Alvarez; ph: Armando Marenco; s: Eddy Meléndez; ed: Johnny Henderson. Color, 16 mm, 90', 1987. English version: sc: Gwynne Dyer, Tina Viljoen and Fernando Somarriba; ed: Johnny Henderson and Tina Viljoen. 58', 1988.

16. *Escuchemos a las mujeres.* d and sc: Rossana Lacayo; prod: Martha Clarissa Hernández; ph: Rafael Ruíz; s: Guillermo Granera; ed: Sarah Minter. Color. 16 mm, 26', 1989. ENCI (Empresa Nicaragüense de Cine).

Fiction Films

1. *Manuel.* d and sc: Rafael Vargas; prod: Alejandro Soza, Mayú Cabezas, Danny Pérez and Salvador Martínez; ph: Rafael Ruíz and Armando Marenco; s: Luis Fuentes and Eddy Meléndez; ed: Johnny Henderson, Eduardo Guadamuz and Brian Cotnoir; set design and costumes: Ernesto Cuadra; sp fx: Lilly Montealegre; mus compos: Pablo Buitrago. B/W, 35 mm, 28', 1985.

2. *Qué se rinda tu madre (Nunca nos rendiremos).* d and sc: Fernando Somarriba; asst d: Martha Clarissa Hernández; prod: Brenda Martínez and Danny Pérez; ph: Frank Pineda; s: Moisés Rodríguez; ed: Johnny Henderson; set design and costumes: Ernesto Cuadra; mus: Diego Silva. Color, 16 mm, 36', 1985.

3. *El centerfielder.* d: Ramiro Lacayo; sc: Robert Young, based on story by Sergio Ramírez; ph: Rafael Ruíz; s: Moisés Rodríguez; ed: Eduardo Guadamuz; mus: Pablo Buitrago. B/W, 35 mm, 18', 1985.

4. *Esbozo de Daniel.* d: Mariano Marín; sc: Ramiro Lacayo and Mariano Marín, based on a story by Ramiro Lacayo; asst d: Fernando Somarriba; prod: Danny Pérez; ph: Frank Pineda; s: Eddy Meléndez and Luis Fuentes; ed: Eduardo Guadamuz; set design and costumes: Ernesto Cuadra; mus: Diego Silva (Chamber orchestra of Nicaragua and group "Praxis"). Color, 16 mm, 39', 1985.

5. *Unanse tantos vigores dispersos.* d and sc: Rafael Vargas; prod: Moisés Rodríguez and René Solis; ph: Frank Pineda; s: Guillermo Granera; ed: Jacinto Calero; set design and costumes: Ernesto Cuadra; mus: Julio Cansino. Color, 35 mm, 20', 1986.

6. *Mujeres de la frontera.* d: Iván Argüello; sc: Iván Argüello and Antonio Conte; prod: Lupercio López; ph: Rafael Ruíz and Luis García Mesa; s: José Leon and Guillermo Granera; ed: Eduardo Guadamuz and Justo Vega; mus: Cedrick de la Torre. Color, 35 mm, 55', 1986.

7. *El espectro de la guerra.* d: Ramiro Lacayo; sc: Ramiro Lacayo Deshón and Franco Reggiani; Prod: INCINE, Spanish Television, ICAIC, El Instituto Mexicano de Televisión (INMEVISION); ph: Livio Delgado; s: Luis Fuentes; ed: Michael Bloecher; mus: Randall Watson. 35mm, Color, 84', 1988.

Interviews

María-José Alvarez

    July 23, 1990
    July 26, 1990
    Jan. 15, 1992
    Jan. 10, 1996

Iván Argüello

    April 12, 1990
    Aug. 7, 1991
    Jan. 15, 1992
    July 20, 1994

Alan Bolt

    Aug. 14, 1992

Bolívar González

    Jan. 23, 1992

Johnny Henderson

    June 1991

Felipe Hernández

    Jan. 19, 1996

Martha Clarissa Hernández

    July 26, 1990
    Jan. 13, 1992
    Jan. 15, 1992

    Jan. 25, 1992
    Aug. 7, 1992
    Jan. 11, 1996

Carlos Vicente Ibarra

    Jan. 24, 1991
    Aug. 21, 1991

Iván Jarquín

    Apr. 19, 1990

Ramiro Lacayo

    July 27, 1990
    Aug. 7, 1992
    Aug. 23, 1992
    Jan. 25, 1991
    Jan. 18, 1996

Alberto Legall

    Jan. 16, 1996

Mariano Marín

    July 28, 1990
    Jan. 22, 1991
    Aug. 21, 1992
    Aug. 24, 1994

Brenda Martínez

    Jan. 18, 1996

Frank Pineda

>Aug. 1, 1990
>July 14, 1991
>Jan. 20, 1991
>Aug. 6, 1992
>July 14, 1994
>July 21, 1994
>Jan. 5, 1996

Ronald Porras

>July 28, 1992

Rafael Ruíz

>June 25, 1990

Kathy Sevilla

>Jan. 15, 1996

Fernando Somarriba

>June 8, 1990
>Jan. 25, 1991
>Aug. 2, 1991

>Jan. 12, 1992
>Aug. 21, 1992

Margarita Suzan

>Jan. 17, 1992

Emilia Torres

>Aug. 18, 1992

Julio Torres

>Aug. 11, 1992

Rafael Vargas

>July 18, 1990
>Aug. 25, 1994

Arturo Zamora

>Jan. 19, 1992

Felix Zurita

>July 23, 1990

Notes

Chapter 1

1. Rugama was a young Sandinista poet killed in a Managua safe house by the Guardia Nacional in January 1970.

2. To convey a sense of the type of work done by PRODUCINE, *Cine Cubano* no. 96 reproduced a proposal dated November 6, 1978, sent by owner Felipe Hernández to a car distributor in Managua to produce a 60-second, 35-mm color advertisement for Mercedes Benz.

3. Manuel Pereira, "Prehistoria del Cine Nica," *Cine Cubano,* no. 96 (1980): 3.

4. "Regresar a casa," *Cine Cubano,* no. 96 (1980): 62.

5. *Ibid.,* 64.

6. For a translation of the Declaration, see the appendix. The Declaration was published in *Cine Cubano,* no. 96 (1980): 6–7.

7. The preeminent U.S. scholar of Sandino's thought refers to his philosophy as "bizarre." Donald Hodges, *Sandino's Communism: Spiritual Politics for the Twenty-first Century* (Austin: University of Texas Press, 1992), 186.

8. See Decreto No. 100, "Creación del Instituto Nicaragüense de Cine (INCINE)," in *La gaceta-diario oficial,* September 22, 1979.

9. On at least one occasion, Caldera wrote for *La resistencia.* Year II, no. 3 (A review of *Walker*), January–February 1988. Reprinted in NIREX Collection. (Ed. and distributed by LITTEX, Inc., P. R. Solorgano, compiler), 502–503.

10. Manuel Pereira, "Prehistoria del Cine Nica," 3.

11. Before the term New Latin American Cinema effectively subsumed it, New Cinema was the rubric applied to the films shown at the festivals in Chile. Despite the title of his 1990 book, *Nuevo cine latinoamericano en Viña del Mar* (Santiago: CESOC Ediciones ChileAmérica, 1990), Aldo Francia, the organizer of the festivals, refers to them as the "cradle of New Cinema." (174). Ana López discusses the origins of the term, but while Alfredo Guevara, the head of ICAIC, used the term New Latin American Cinema in a 1967 interview, she cites a resolution from the first Viña del Mar festival called "The Challenge of the New Cinema." "An 'Other' History: The New Latin American Cinema," *Radical History Review* 41 (1988): 116. The first sentence of another resolution from the same festival calls for the creation of a "Latin American

Center of New Cinema." Reprinted in Octavio Getino, *Cine latinoamericano: economías y nuevas tecnologías audiovisuales* (Buenos Aires: Legasa, 1988): 260. See also Zuzana M. Pick, *The New Latin American Cinema: A Continental Project* (Austin: University of Texas Press, 1993), 19–37.

12. Referring to the Havana festival, Julio García Espinosa himself noted, "The festival is not selective . . . the idea is that every Latin American filmmaker may have a forum in which to show his or her work." Julio García Espinosa, "Cuban Cinema," in *Latin American Visions*, ed. Pat Aufderheide (Philadelphia: Neighborhood Film/Video Project of the International House, 1989), 53.

13. The first noticiero was listed at the 1979 festival as *Primer noticiero* INCINE; in 1980, Noticieros 5, 9, 10, and 11 were listed by number only at the 1980 festival. For a catalogue of films shown during the first ten festivals, see Teresa Toledo, *10 años del nuevo cine latinoamericano* (Spain: Verdoux, S.K., Sociedad Estatal Quinto Centenario, and Cinemateca de Cuba, 1990). In fact, most of the first 20 noticieros did not have titles; the titles used in the text for those films are those listed by INCINE in its archives.

14. I am basing this comment about xenophobia on conversations with many Nicaraguans, as well as on the absence of foreigners in the hierarchy of INCINE. For a Nicaraguan account, see interview with Michele Najlis in Margaret Randall, *Sandino's Daughters Revisited: Feminism in Nicaragua* (New Brunswick, N.J.: Rutgers University Press, 1994), 55.

15. "Here in Nicaragua, during the whole period [of my childhood], the cinema was a cinema that was profoundly dominated by the North American films. My cinematic taste was formed by North American films; very few European films came, and many Mexican films, but of very low quality." Interview with author in Managua, July 27, 1990. Commenting on the suggestions of foreigners, Frank Pineda recalled in a 1986 interview, "Sometimes they would look at us and not understand. They had a concept of cinema as perfect cinema, so to speak. Not that we knew about Julio García Espinosa's Imperfect Cinema at the time." "Reconstructing Nicaragua: Creating National Cinema," in *Reviewing Histories: Selections from New Latin American Cinema*, ed. Coco Fusco (Buffalo: Hallwalls, Contemporary Art Center, 1987), 209.

16. Figures are from 1970. Ambrosio Fornet, "Trente ans de cinéma dans la Révolution," in *Le cinéma cubain*, ed. Paolo Antonio Paranagua (Paris: Centre Georges Pompidou, 1990), 101.

17. According to figures cited by Octavio Getino, Nicaraguans have the second highest cinema attendance frequency in Latin America (4.0 films per year), slightly lower than Mexico (4.7), significantly higher than neighboring Costa Rica (3.2), and far higher than Argentina (1.6) and Brazil (0.8). Getino, *Cine latinoamericano: economías y nuevas tecnologías audiovisuales*, 173.

18. See Ley 169, Creación del Instituto Cubano de Arte e Industria Cinematográficos ICAIC, in *Hojas de cine: Testimonios y documentos del nuevo cine latinoamericano*, Volumen III, Centroamérica y el Caribe (México, D.F.: Secretaría de Educación Pública, Universidad Autónoma Metropolitana, Fundación Mexicana de Cineastas, 1988), 13–19.

19. Interview with author in Managua, August 1, 1990.

20. In several recent articles, Rafael Vargas has referred to the "'censorship' or 'ideological monitor' to which our works were submitted." "Rubén Darío y el Cine" (primera parte), *El nuevo diario*, January 15, 2000; "Rubén Darío y el Cine," *El nuevo*

diario, January 22, 2000. However, it may be that the ideologically contested interpretation of Rubén Darío's work influenced the particular case Vargas is writing about, for while other filmmakers did complain to me about changes "suggested" for their films, they could not cite specific examples of political changes. My best guess would be that political considerations figured in these INCINE screening sessions, but they were not clearly distinguished or distinguishable from normal criticisms heard in pre-release screenings of films anywhere, which would certainly include political concerns.

Chapter 2

1. Johnny Henderson, interview with author at Gateshead, June 1991.

2. For sources on the history and problematic of the Atlantic Coast region, see the notes to chapter 9, in which there is an extended discussion of the only INCINE film to examine the topic in depth, *Los hijos del río.*

3. Interview with author in Managua, August 1, 1990.

4. One veteran of INCINE, Martha Clarissa Hernández, has asserted that all of the noticieros were group efforts, and one should not exaggerate the official distribution of credits on the films.

5. The FSLN composed slogans for each year that they were in power. Early slogans included:

> 1979: Year of Liberation
>
> 1980: Year of Literacy
>
> 1981: Year of Defense and Production
>
> 1982: Year of Unity against the Aggression
>
> 1983: Year of Struggle for Peace and Sovereignty

A useful chronology of the seven years following the 1979 victory can be found in Rosa María Torres and José Luis Coraggio, *Transición y crisis en Nicaragua* (San José: Dei, 1987).

6. In the Mobile Cinema print of the film that I saw, one shot of the comandantes on the rostrum had one figure scratched out manually in every frame: Edén Pastora. Pastora had been a military hero of the FSLN before the triumph. Pastora broke with the FSLN in July 1981, eventually taking up arms with contra groups in Costa Rica, presumably the reason for the erasure of his image by a vigilant Mobile Cinema worker. For an unsympathetic account of Pastora's trajectory, see Roberto Bardini, *Edén Pastora, un cero en la historia* (México: Universidad Autónoma de Puebla, 1984).

7. Alfonso Robelo asserted, "The Literacy Campaign is indoctrination. It's an attempt to domesticate the minds of the poor." Valerie Miller, "The Nicaraguan Literacy Campaign," in *Nicaragua in Revolution*, ed. Thomas W. Walker (New York: Praeger, 1982), 244.

8. John Booth, *The End and the Beginning* (Boulder, Colo.: Westview, 1982), 187.

9. As one of the conditions for the release of hostages in both the 1974 and 1978 FSLN raids, the FSLN insisted on the reading of communiqués over the Somoza-controlled media for similar reasons. Sergio Ramírez recounts that the leaders were unknown in the days immediately after the triumph and that they had to wear badges put together with photographs taken with a Polaroid camera found in the Banco Cen-

tral. See *Adiós muchachos: Una memoria de la revolución Sandinista* (México: Aguilar, 1999), 64.

10. Following the practice in Cuba, the first (31) noticieros generally included separate credits for Director and Realizador, with Director referring to the administrative head of the production of noticieros, and Realizador identifying the actual filmmaker, normally called "director" in English.

11. Nacatamales are a Nicaraguan national food, a mixture of pork and vegetables wrapped in tortillas and cooked and sold in banana leaves. Presumably, Ortega means to call elections "cooked" à la Nicaragua under Somoza.

12. Torres and Coraggio, *Transición y crisis en Nicaragua*, 146.

13. According to Johnny Henderson, Legall was a perfectly likeable character, so long as one did not believe a word he said. Interview with author in Gateshead, June 1991. Frank Pineda viewed him as a "political cadre." Interview with author in Mexico City, July 21, 1994.

14. Lacayo recalled that this change "also had a negative effect. For the comandantes, those who had the power to support Nicaraguan cinema . . . also saw themselves presented on the screen and this served as a propaganda organ, but suddenly [when they no longer saw themselves on screen] they began to lose interest in this cinema because it began to be more strictly cultural. . . ." Interview with author in Managua, July 27, 1990.

15. The final syllables, ATA, come from the Miskito phrase "Asla Takanka," meaning "united." See Jorge Jenkins Molieri, *El desafío indígena en Nicaragua: El caso de los miskitos* (Managua: Editorial Vanguardia, 1986), 271.

16. María José Alvarez readily admitted years later, "We didn't know anything about the coast." Interview with author in Managua, July 23, 1990.

17. Some blacks assert that the black/Creole population did not object to the Cuban schoolteachers but wanted to protest the displacement of blacks from posts in the fishing industry by Pacific mestizos and Cubans. See, for example, Edmund T. Gordon, "History, Identity, Consciousness, and Revolution. Afro-Nicaraguans and the Nicaraguan Revolution," in *Ethnic Groups and the Nation State*, ed. CIDCA (Stockholm: Development Study Unit, Department of Social Anthropology, University of Stockholm, 1987) 151–152.

18. For a discussion by one of the Cuban filmmakers, with many illustrations, see Jorge Fraga, "el noticiero ICAIC latinoamericano: función política y lenguaje cinematográfico," *Cine Cubano*, no. 71/72 (n.d.): 24–31.

Chapter 3

1. A salary schedule from 1984 lists the following personnel: Director General (Lacayo); Director of Production (Julio Torres); Executive Producer (Rodolfo Glenton); Assistant Executive Producer (José Martínez); two secretaries; one accountant; six producers; seven directors; four camerapeople; five sound recorders; four editors; two photographers; one laboratory technician; two assistant directors; two assistant camerapeople; two assistant editors; one workshop person; three camera technicians; one lighting person; one equipment restorer; and two drivers.

2. Other examples of distortions are legion. Perhaps the most illustrative is the claim of Jeane Kirkpatrick that the Sandinistas were building concentration camps for "some 250,000 Mestizo Indians" in Nicaragua. Holly Sklar, *Washington's War on*

Nicaragua (Boston: South End Press, 1989), 103. All census figures in Nicaragua are rough estimates, as the last census was taken in 1971, but the estimates used by most scholars for the Miskito population in the early 1980s hover around 80,000. See, for example, Carlos M. Vilas, *State, Class, and Ethnicity in Nicaragua, Capitalist Modernization and Revolutionary Change on the Atlantic Coast,* trans. Susan Norwood (Boulder: Lynne Rienner Publishers, 1989), 2–6.

3. It is likely that Nicaragua helped the FMLN with the delivery of war matériel, but the difficulty of the United States in proving such charges indicates that the amount of aid was minimal. The bulk of FSLN support took the form of logistical support of the FMLN representatives in Nicaragua during the 1980s. Commentary on this issue tends to divide on ideological grounds, for hard evidence is scanty.

4. For more on the relationship between Sandino and Martí, see Donald Hodges, *Intellectual Foundations of the Nicaraguan Revolution* (Austin: University of Texas Press, 1986), 97–99.

5. Regarding Legall's infatuation with the military, Legall told the following story about filming with the army:

> I wanted to film a scene in which the tank passes over the camera. I wanted to show something powerful on the screen. Combined with a musical effect, it works in the noticiero, but to do it, we hadn't rehearsed the scene. It was a fictional scene, because we placed the tank in a location, and the cameraperson, and we experimented. The tank driver was also inexperienced, a kid doing his military service, and then, we tried a dry run. With Rafael [Ruíz, the INCINE cameraperson] already in the hole, over which the tank was going to pass, the Cuban cameraperson says to me, "Hitchcock, look out!" I tell him, no Lupito, can't you see that the kid has tried several times. But he says to me, "No, these scenes have to be carefully rehearsed. Try it without Rafael, do it without Rafita." Okay, we try without Rafita and in fact, the track of the tank passed right over the hole, and at a speed much greater than planned. He tells me, "Jerk! You see." Rafita all upset. The camera had stayed in the hole. After cleaning the dust completely Rafael says to me: "I'm not getting in there. We're not filming this." And I tell him, for me this scene is important for the structure that I've worked out, let's do it. I tell him, we're going to look, to find some technique, man, in fiction film they do this shit, why not us? So the Cuban says—who was not a fiction cameraperson either, just documentary—"Look, what happens is that at a certain point the tank driver can't see the hole. What we have to do is place a stick with a banner in the center, to serve as a guide so that he knows that this is the center and it's the center where you are and it doesn't matter if the stick breaks, but that's where you have to pass." We practiced several times without Rafael to the point that he was convinced that the guy was not going to run him over and it worked. (Interview with author in Managua, January 16, 1996)

6. Marín may be reacting unduly harshly here. In the minutes of a meeting in 1981, Wilma de la Rocha reported that INCINE had been unable to secure the funds to build the lab with the French equipment and proposed returning the equipment to France in hopes of exchanging it for other forms of aid. She called the project "a little premature for INCINE." Minutes of meeting on November 29, 1982, between Francisco Lacayo (Vice-Minister of Culture) and Ramiro Lacayo. INCINE archives. During the summer of 1991, I saw the unopened crates in the storeroom of INCINE.

7. As already noted in the text, I am not trying to exaggerate the importance of this tendency interpretation. Some Sandinistas insist on its significance in explaining many events of the revolution; others, who may have belonged to one or another faction at different times, dismiss any such suggestions. Of INCINE personnel, Frank Pineda subscribes to the tendency interpretation and views INCINE as a tercerista institution. Interview with author in Managua, July 14, 1991. Vicente Ibarra, when specifically asked about it, dismissed the interpretation, claiming that he had been a member of all three tendencies. Interview with author in Managua, August 21, 1991.

8. Henderson, interview with author at Gateshead, June 1991.

9. For an account, see David Whisnant, *Rascally Signs in Sacred Places: The Politics of Culture in Nicaragua* (Chapel Hill: University of North Carolina Press, 1995), 201–204, 241–246; see also John Beverley and Marc Zimmerman, *Literature and Politics in the Central American Revolutions* (Austin: University of Texas Press, 1990), chap. 4; for a more polemical discussion that attacks the reformism of the insurrectional tendency, see Greg Dawes, *Aesthetics and Revolution, Nicaraguan Poetry 1979–1990* (Minneapolis: University of Minnesota Press, 1993), 25–32, 190–195.

10. "Kramer contra mí," *Ventana*, no. 6, January 24, 1981, 13.

11. "El Regreso del Dragón," *Ventana*, no. 7, January 31, 1981, 14.

12. Ramiro Lacayo, "Memoria histórica del pueblo," *Ventana*, no. 8, February 7, 1981, 8–9.

13. There was an attempt to provide a Cine-Forum on television, but it appears to have been short-lived, probably ending sometime in 1980. Alfonso Gumucio Dagrón referred to some of these efforts in "el cine nace en Nicaragua," *formato* 16 (Panama), December 1980, 15–18.

14. "La TV debe ser un proyecto cultural revolucionario" [Television Should Be a Revolutionary Cultural Project], *Ventana*, no. 11, March 1, 1981, 2–3, 15.

15. "Un gran desconocido: el cine latinamericano," *Ventana*, no. 11, March 1, 1981, 11.

16. "Apuntes sobre el Cine Latinamericano," *Ventana*, no. 12, March 7, 1981, 14.

17. "Nicaragua, sede IV Reunión del MECLA," *Ventana*, no. 13, March 14, 1981, 10.

18. "Un Cine Que Expresa la Vida," *Ventana*, no. 15, March 28, 1981, 2–5.

19. Emilio Rodríguez V, "La otra cara del oro," *Ventana*, no. 20, July 18, 1981.

20. Vargas, interview with author in Managua, July 18, 1990. Henderson, interview with author at Gateshead, June 1991.

21. In 1980 Vargas described this as a film "whose story submerges us in a world where dream and reality coexist on the same plane, with human beings debating like puppets over a fate which locks them in the silent language of their fears, anxieties and ancestral yearnings." "Regresar a casa," *Cine Cubano* 96, 2. For a more recent account of the film by Vargas see "¿Cuál cine nacional?" *El nuevo diario: Nuevo amanecer cultural*, November 13, 1999. Vargas notes that "for Nicaraguan cinema, this century

opened with *Señorita* and closed with *Blanco organdí* (1999)." The latter is a film directed by María José Alvarez and Martha Clarissa Hernández; for a review by the author, see *La prensa literaria* (Nicaragua), September 11, 1999. Translated into Spanish by Ramiro Lacayo.

22. Letter in INCINE archives. Though the letter is apparently undated, in a cover note of July 29, 1979, to "Comandante EMILIO," Instituto Nicaragüense de Artes Cinematográficas (i.e., before its name was official), the Junta of National Reconstruction's press secretary, Manuel Espinosa, indicated that Vargas was interested in joining the Institute.

23. Vargas, interview with author, January 14, 1992. In a later article, Vargas claims that he was "'exiled' from noticiero production for lack of 'political clarity.'" "Rubén Darío y el Cine (primera parte)," *El nuevo diario*, January 15, 2000.

24. Interview with author, January 24, 1991, Managua.

25. Henderson, interview with author at Gateshead, June 1991.

26. Ramiro Lacayo Deshón, "Del Aguila al Dragón: Crónicas de una Invasión," *Ventana*, no. 43, October 31, 1981; also *El nuevo diario*, October 22, 1981, 4. The use of the term "águila" (eagle) for the United States derives from Rubén Darío's use of the term in his poetry, as in "Salutación al águila." For a brief discussion, see John Beverley and Marc Zimmerman, *Literature and Politics in the Central American Revolutions*, 58–59.

27. Lacayo, "Del Aguila al Dragón."

28. *Ibid.*

29. Carlos Mohs, "Impresiones Primeras sobre Del Aguila al Dragón," *El Nuevo Diario*, October 22, 1981, 4.

30. Interview with author at Gateshead, June 1991.

31. Letter dated May 10, 1982, INCINE archives.

32. The most commonly cited figure of nearly $2. billion—combining direct material damage of $480 and $1.5 billion in capital flight—comes from CEPAL (Comisión Económica para América Latina): Informe "Nicaragua: el impacto de la mutación política," in *Notas para el estudio económico de América Latina y el Caribe* (México D. F., 1981).

33. "It is immoral and contrary to the education and culture of our people, and thereby prohibited to publish, distribute, circulate, expound, diffuse, exhibit, transmit or sell: Writings, designs, recordings, paintings, books, images, advertisements, emblems, photographs that . . . use women as a sexual or commercial object." Decree No. 48, General Law of the Media of Social Communication, *La gaceta*, August 16, 1979.

Chapter 4

1. Alfonso Gumucio Dagrón, *El cine de los trabajadores* (Managua: Central Sandinista de Trabajadores, 1981), 94. In another publication, Gumucio Dagrón wrote that "the young people who ran INCINE didn't pay much attention to my crazy ideas about Super 8-mm film, internationally looked down upon by the prejudices of the cinema 'professionals.'" "Cine Obrero Sandinista," *Plural*, vol. 11, 2a época, no. 130 (July 1982): 35.

2. Letter from Gumucio Dagrón to Susan Ryan, August 1, 1995, cited in her NYU

Ph.D. dissertation, an invaluable account of the alternative video organizations in Nicaragua during the 1980s. "Popularizing Media: The Politics of Video in the Nicaraguan Revolution" (1996), 208. Arturo Zamora, head of MIDINRA's audiovisual unit, has written an unpublished account of MIDINRA's work, "Movimiento de Video Alternativo. Apuntes para una retrospectiva. Nicaragua 1990. Notas sobre la experiencia del MIDINRA."

3. Lacayo informed Jorge Fraga at ICAIC of Legall's new position as head of Noticiero Production in a letter dated February 23, 1982. INCINE archives.

4. The head of the army's audiovisual unit claimed that the public sees only a small percentage of its work, for "many cannot be shown publicly for reasons of state security and military secrecy." Carlos Powell, "Filming a New Kind of Army," *Barricada International,* April 21, 1988, 14–16.

5. For an account of this episode, see Sklar, *Washington's War on Nicaragua,* 112–113. The captured Nicaraguan, Orlando Tardencilla, wrote an article for *Nicaráuac* in which he described his torture (and the forced witness of the torture of others) by the Salvadoran military and his subsequent adoption by the CIA, which backfired spectacularly. "De las cámaras de tortura al Departamento de Estado," *Nicaráuac* 11 (May 1985): 17–34.

6. For a transcript, see "The Nicaraguan Prisoner," *The MacNeil-Lehrer Report,* March 12, 1982, Transcript #1685.

7. Marín wanted to use this line from Gordillo as the title for the film, "A cien años de distancia, el enemigo es el mismo," but he claims that Lacayo changed it after arguing with Marín about it. Interview with author in Managua, January 22, 1991.

8. The text of this song, "Vivirás Monimbó," among others, was published in *Cantos de la lucha Sandinista* (Managua: Vanguardia/ENIGRAC, 1989), 28–29.

9. Che's discussion of the "foco" can be found in Ernesto Guevara, *Guerilla Warfare* (New York: Monthly Review Press, 1961). Régis Debray elaborated on "foquismo" in two widely read books from the 1960s: *Revolution in the Revolution,* ed. Robin Blackburn, trans. Bobbye Ortiz (New York: Monthly Review Press, 1967), and *Strategy for Revolution,* ed. Robin Blackburn (New York: Monthly Review Press, 1969).

10. For discussions of the "foco" experience of the FSLN, see David Nolan, *The Ideology of the Sandinistas and the Nicaraguan Revolution* (Coral Gables, Fla.: Institute of Interamerican Studies/University of Miami, 1984), 22–24; Donald C. Hodges, *Intellectual Foundations of the Nicaraguan Revolution* (Austin: University of Texas Press, 1986), 221–225.

11. For an account, see George Black, *Triumph of the People: The Sandinista Revolution in Nicaragua* (London: Zed Books, 1981), 87–89. It is interesting that the film does not include the even more spectacular seizing of the National Palace in 1978. On the attack, see pages 124–126. That the leader of that action, Edén Pastora, took up arms against the Sandinistas in 1982 is probably the reason the event was not used. However, one document from August 7, 1979, "Proyectos Immediatos del Instituto," (in this case, Instituto Sandinista de Cine Nicaragüense typed in, with Instituto Nicaragüense del Arte Cinematográfico crossed out) does list for television the "Toma Del Palacio" as one of the four immediate projects. INCINE archives.

12. Translated as Omar Cabezas, *Fire from the Mountain: The Making of a Sandinista,* trans. Kathleen Weaver (New York: New American Library, 1982). Deborah Schaffer directed a film with the same name in 1987. Ruíz wrote an article on the experience of the mountains. "La montaña era como un crisol donde se forjaban los

mejores cuadros." (The mountain was like a crucible where the best cadres were forged.) *Nicaráuac*, no. 1 (May–June 1980): 8–24.

13. Cabezas, *Fire from the Mountain: The Making of a Sandinista*, 132.

14. On this question, see the sober discussion by the political scientist Carlos M. Vilas, "¿Socialismo en Nicaragua?" *Nueva Sociedad*, no. 91 (September–December 1987): 159–175.

15. For Cardenal's description of the festival, see "The Democratization of Culture," in *Hacia una política cultural de la revolución popular Sandinista* (Managua: Ministerio de Cultura, 1982), 250.

16. Regarding this changing conception of the noticieros, one later INCINE report explained that "given the production difficulties and the time it was taking to produce each film, this conception changed and was converted into a short documentary, which reduced considerably the [amount of] production but permitted those films to be relevant for a longer time." "Algunas Consideraciones Generales," May 16, 1985, INCINE archives.

17. Space limitations preclude an account of this struggle, and it is not clear that the battles directly affected INCINE. However, the dissension revolved around both principled and personal disagreements over Sandinista cultural policy, the two factions led by Ernesto Cardenal and Rosario Murillo, wife of Daniel Ortega and founder of an "alternative" Ministry of Culture, the Sandinista Association of Cultural Workers (ASTC). See John Beverley and Marc Zimmerman, *Literature and Politics in the Central American Revolutions* (Austin: University of Texas Press, 1990); David Whisnant, *Rascally Signs in Sacred Places: The Politics of Culture in Nicaragua* (Chapel Hill: University of North Carolina Press, 1995); and especially, the highly partisan and incendiary book by Klaas Wellinga, *Entre la poesía y la pared: Política cultural Sandinista* (Costa Rica: FLASCO, Amsterdam: Thela, 1994). For a retrospective view by Zamora, see Margaret Randall, *Sandino's Daughters Revisited: Feminism in Nicaragua* (New Brunswick, N.J.: Rutgers University Press, 1994), 106, 107.

Chapter 5

1. Carlos Vicente Ibarra, letter to *Barricada*, September 10, 1979.

2. Bolívar González, interview with author in Managua, January 23, 1992.

3. In a later article, Ibarra claimed that the commission screened 92 films in a three-month period.

> The work of the Commission of Classification has been truly difficult. To have evaluated 92 films that entered Nicaragua between January and March has not been, I assure you, an easy task. But there are the results [in an attached table] and the best work of the Commission to succeed in weighing carefully an infinite number of complex factors in favor of the interests of the Revolution.
>
> The banned films represent 22.82% of the total that entered the country. 33.6% were authorized for persons over 18, and 42.3% for those over 12.

Carlos V. Ibarra, "Qué nos vino de Macondo . . . ?" *Ventana*, no. 122, July 2, 1983, 7.

4. Robert D. McFadden, "3 Canadian Films Called 'Propaganda' by U.S.," *New York Times*, February 25, 1983, III 4–5; Stuart Taylor, Jr., "Court Backs 'Propaganda' Label for 3 Canadian Films," *New York Times*, April 29, 1987, A28.

5. In the interview published in *Ventana* in February 1981 (see discussion in chapter 2), Lacayo noted, "We don't say what is going to open, but only what is not going to open." While Lacayo is critical of Hollywood, for their films are "not positive for the education of human beings," he recognizes that there would be no cinema in the theaters without them: "We have to prevent the worst and allow the most inoffensive."

6. A copy of this report is included in the appendix.

7. Some critics go further and read the films as apocalyptic allegories of modern urban subcultures. See, for example, the remarks on *Mad Max* in Danny Peary, *Cult Movies* (New York: Delta, 1981), 215–218.

8. Bulletin No. 2 of the Commission of Classification of Cinema, n.d. (probably end of 1984), INCINE archives.

9. Report dated September 16, 1980, INCINE archives.

10. Report dated December 6, 1979, INCINE archives.

11. Report dated March 1, 1980, INCINE archives.

12. Anteproyecto de exhibición, INCINE archives.

13. In an interview in 1991, Ibarra looked back on these attitudes as "excessive . . . morally conservative and politically damaging. . . . The Commission of Classification says more about the conservative thinking . . . of the Sandinistas than of the society. It says more about the influence the Front wanted to have in the social consciousness, about the values that the Front wanted to reproduce in the society." Interview with author in Managua, August 21, 1991.

14. "Cinematic works bearing the classification of special exhibition will be exhibited exclusively in the National Cinemateca." Article 22, Reglamento de la Comisión de Clasificación de Cine, Ministerial Accord No. 4 of the Ministry of Interior, signed by Tomás Borge, Minister of the Interior, December 30, 1982, printed in *La gaceta-diario oficial*, January 21, 1983. Epoca Revolucionaria.

15. *Anuario estadístico, 1982–1985* (Managua: Oficina ejecutiva de encuestras y censos).

16. "Anteproyecto Para la Creación del Departamento de Exhibición," n.d. (probably late 1979/early 1980), INCINE archives.

17. Ibarra, interview with author in Managua, January 24, 1991.

18. Ambrosio Fornet, "Trente ans de cinéma dans la Revolucion," in Paranagua, *Le cinéma cubain*, 91.

19. Julio García Espinosa, "El cine y la toma del poder," *Plural*, no. 74 (November 1977): 22.

20. "Una imagen recorre el mundo," in *Una imagen recorre el mundo* (Mexico: Filmoteca, UNAM, 1982), 71. In the introduction to the book, Armando Lazo wrote that "in Cuba . . . the decolonization of the screen remains a difficult area" (18).

21. Even Cuban films "are fairly minimally distributed on the continent," according to Paolo Antonio Paranagua, "News From Havana. A Restructuring of Cuban Cinema," *Framework* 35, 1988, 90.

22. Ramiro Lacayo, "Anotaciones a la cultura de resistencia," *Ventana*, no. 30, July 18, 1981, 19.

23. Carlos Vicente Ibarra, "Crónica sobre un verano ardiente. (El cine que nos envían)," *Ventana*, no. 35, August 22, 1981, 13.

24. Carlos Vicente Ibarra, "Crítica Cinematográfica y Sociedad Revolucionaria," *Ventana,* no. 60, February 27, 1982, 14.

25. For a discussion of Brechtian film theory and criticism, see Martin Walsh, *The Brechtian Aspect of Radical Cinema,* ed. Keith M. Griffiths (London: British Film Institute, 1981), and Dana Polan, "A Brechtian Cinema? Towards a Politics of Self-Reflexive Film," in *Movies and Methods,* vol. 2, ed. Bill Nichols (Berkeley and Los Angeles: University of California Press, 1985). For a critical view, see Noël Carroll, *Mystifying Movies* (New York: Columbia University Press, 1988), esp. 90–96.

26. Víctor Martín Borrego, "Un drama sentimental socialista? *Retrato de Teresa,"* *Ventana,* no. 22, May 23, 1981, 13.

27. According to Paranagua, the film "unleashed in all the media an intense debate among psychologists, sociologists, teachers, social workers and spectators of both sexes." *Le cinéma cubain,* 96.

28. Mayra Vilasís, cited in John King, *Magical Reels: A History of Cinema in Latin America* (New York: Verso, 1990), 159.

29. *Nicaragua en cifras* (Managua: Instituto Nacional de Estadísticas y Censos, 1986).

30. From an early INCINE report, probably late 1979, INCINE archives.

31. In the plans for 1983, Mobile Cinema, in coordination with INRA, was "to place special emphasis and attention on the harvest periods, the gathering of coffee and cotton to take advantage of the concentration of workers and to strengthen the work in these zones." "Orientaciones de trabajo para el año 83/cine mobil," INCINE archives.

32. The noticieros were shot and released in 35 mm for the theaters. Cuba normally made 15 copies in 16 mm for use by Mobile Cinema.

33. For comments by some Mobile Cinema workers, see Howard Dratch and Barbara Margolis, "Film and Revolution in Nicaragua. An Interview with INCINE Filmmakers," *Cineaste,* vol. 15, no. 3 (1987): 27–29.

34. Evaluación Semestral Cine Mobil, July 16, 1983, INCINE archives. Julio Torres previously directed Cine Mobil, which had originally been run by his sister, Emilia, who left INCINE to become national director of the Popular Culture Centers. In Ibarra's later view, "Our own sense of political responsibility was reinforced by the interests that the propaganda apparatus of the Frente had toward film; to take an example, the propaganda apparatus of the Frente needed the Mobile Cinema to convoke political mobilizations at times. Our interest was not simply this, but to convert the cinema into a form of national education. . . . We were always subordinated to the political and ideological needs of the medium." Interview with author in Managua, January 24, 1991.

35. In early 1984, directors received 6,000 córdobas/month, while the camera people and sound people received 4,500 córdobas, according to a salary schedule in the INCINE archives. Because of fast-rising inflation, it is often difficult to estimate dollar equivalents of Nicaraguan córdobas. Filmmakers say that their salaries were equivalent to about $50/month. According to one source, 6,000 córdobas in early 1984 would be equivalent to about $43. Geske Dijkstra, *Industrialization in Sandinista Nicaragua: Policy and Practice in a Mixed Economy* (Boulder, Colo.: Westview, 1992), 121.

36. Michele Najlis, *Caminos de la estrella polar* (Managua: Vanguardia, 1990), 14–16.

37. "Exposición de conjunto acerca del Instituto Sandinista de Cine Nicaragüense," August 3, 1979, INCINE archives. According to the administrative flow chart in the

document, the ISCN would be directly below the Political Commission of the Dirección Nacional. For a copy of the flow chart, see the appendix.

38. *Ibid.* At the same time, it was probably Rodríguez who jotted down an early diagram for the proposed administrative structure of the institute, which is included in the appendix.

39. A Cuban journalist, Fernando Pérez Valdés, collected and edited interviews and reminiscences of four of the members of the Leonel Rugama Brigade—Emilio Rodríguez, Ramiro Lacayo, Frank Pineda, and Alvaro Jiménez—in *Corresponsales de guerra* (Havana: Casa de las Américas, 1981).

40. INCINE collaborated with France and Cuba on the coproduction of this 1983 film, directed by the Cuban Octavio Gómez, based on the novel of the same name by the Guatemalan writer Miguel Angel Asturias.

41. Michael Chanan, *The Cuban Image. Cinema and Cultural Politics in Cuba* (London: British Film Institute, 1985), 14–15.

42. As further evidence of Rodríguez's view of the politicized role of INCINE, a 1979 document recommends hiring "militant cadres with experience in communications and the mass organizations, for "it is easier to give technical training to a militant than to politicize [*concientizar*] a technician." Instituto Sandinista de Cine Nicaragüense. "Proyectos Inmediatos del Instituto," August 7, 1979, INCINE archives.

43. "Alsino se debate entre la fantasía y la realidad," *Ventana*, no. 80, July 31, 1982, 2–7, 16.

44. Though Murillo's point about poetry is pertinent, it was also a central complaint in her polemic with the "exteriorism" of Ernesto Cardenal's poetry and the poetry workshops run by the Ministry of Culture. The fullest account of this bitter debate can be found in Klaas Wellinga, *Entre la poesía y la pared* (San José: Flacso; Amsterdam: Thela, 1994). See chapter 4, note 17.

45. These large trucks from East Germany, unknown in Nicaragua before the triumph, were so well known and notorious after the triumph that Nicaraguans always referred to them as IFAs (after the manufacturer's logo on their hoods): "Imposible a frenar al tiempo" (impossible to stop in time).

46. See also interview with Littín, "Alsino y la Realidad Mágica Nicaragüense," *Nicaráuac* año 4, no. 9 (1988): 161–162, and Gabriel García Márquez, "Alsino y el Cóndor," in the same issue, 163–165.

47. In a letter dated August 17, 1982, Lacayo wrote to Alfredo Guevara at ICAIC to report that Ibarra was no longer at INCINE. Regarding *Alsino,* he added, "There are always groups . . . that are unable to understand the search for a richer art more consistent with life." INCINE archives.

48. The official program of the Second Assembly of the ASTC ("segunda asamblea nacional 'fernando gordillo' " asociacíon sandinista de trabajadores de la cultura a.s.t.c. 2 y 3 de febrero, 1982 [Managua]) is explicit on this point. Among the 24 points listed in the "Plan de Lucha," number 8 specifies that the work of the members should be evaluated such that the artistic and literary work "is achieved at levels of quality that our people deserve." And one of the qualifications for membership in the ASTC, included in "Requirements," was "to furnish the documentation required to demonstrate one's artistic and literary trajectory in accord with the rules of the different UNIONS."

As part of the justification for forming the ASTC, one document ("On the Relations between the ASTC and the Ministry of Culture") asserts that individual artists and writers had no formal avenue for expressing their concerns about the work of the Ministry of Culture. Instead, the Ministry "has isolated itself and rejected the artists and writers, who, as individuals, have raised these concerns."

Chapter 6

1. While Marín's claim about his film is reasonable, Lacayo felt similarly about his own recently completed *Viva León*, in which he thought that "the people are talking in a more relaxed manner; before, the people spoke in a more politicized manner, as if delivering a speech. In this noticiero we can sense something more Nica." Interview with author in Managua, January 25, 1991. Lacayo however, was not claiming credit for himself per se, for on another occasion he called Marín "the soul of Nicaraguan cinema." Interview with author in Managua, August 23, 1992. Rather, Lacayo's statement confirms only that the filmmakers themselves saw the films changing at this time. That this new conception of the noticieros had filtered into policy is reflected in an INCINE report from the same time: "significant changes [are] needed to make works of longer relevance, less conjunctural and closer to the focus of the short documentary in the noticieros. This has begun already in 1982 with *Del ejército, El maestro popular,* and *Los innovadores* [the next noticiero]." "Orientaciones de trabajo para el año 83." INCINE archives.

2. Interview with author, January 22, 1991, Managua.

3. Argüello has noted that he had wanted to show that young people could continue to practice their activities and pursue entertainment even during the war. Interview with author, July 1994, Mexico City. Though I don't believe this first noticiero of Argüello succeeds in conveying that idea, the editor Johnny Henderson recalls that Argüello used to refer to the film during the editing as "*My* big lie." Interview with author, June 1991, Gateshead.

4. Interview with author in Managua, April 12, 1990.

5. "We believed that in the formation of our people [FSLN militants], we had to fight caudillismo, to avoid what happened with Sandino, when a whole revolutionary movement fell apart because it was founded exclusively on one person. This is why we promoted the collective leadership [i.e., the Dirección Nacional]." Humberto Ortega, in Gabriele Invernizzi, Francis Pisani, and Jesús Ceberio, *Sandinistas* (Managua: Editorial Vanguardia, 1986, 1987), 87.

6. This formal observance of group leadership solidarity also concealed deep and lasting divisions. First, the most powerful ministerial assignments after the victory went to the most powerful Dirección Nacional members (Defense/Humberto Ortega, Interior/Tomás Borge, Agriculture/Jaime Wheelock), who were leaders of the three factions, and these men surrounded themselves with trusted members of their respective tendencies. Second, the ministries, according to many observers, operated like the leaders' personal fiefdoms, disarticulating the exercise of power instead of consolidating it. In his recent memoir, former Nicaraguan vice-president during the Sandinista period, Sergio Ramírez, who was not a member of the National Directorate during the 1980s, refers to it as "a caudillo with nine heads instead of one." Sergio Ramírez, *Adiós muchachos: Una memoria de la revolución Sandinista* (México, D. F.: Aguilar, 1999), 66.

7. For an excellent discussion of the battle over the legacy and meaning of Darío, see David E. Whisnant, "Rubén Darío as a Focal Cultural Figure in Nicaragua: The Ideological Uses of Cultural Capital," *Latin American Research Review* 27, no. 3 (1992): 7–49.

8. Marín tells the following story behind the use of this version of the International, which for him dates back to the French Commune of 1870; the hymn

> represents more the expression of the workers of 1870 than a Soviet representation. I had seen a [Cuban] film of Enrique Pineda, who has just made *La Bella de la Alhambra*, which is a film about Julio Antonio Mella . . . one of the great leaders of the Cuban Revolution in the time of Machado. He knew Trotsky, Diego Rivera, Siqueiros, Frida Kahlo. . . . I asked one day in Cuba to see it, because I have always been a great admirer of the theories of Julio Antonio Mella. . . . Leo Brouwer did the music for the film . . . so I asked him to lend me the sound track of the film, because he did it and it seemed incredible how he had transformed this [the International]. Because the rhythms that he designed are our agrarian rhythms. The percussion is agrarian, not trendy. So it helps considerably to describe this work that the agrarian workers are doing also, which are in the last shot of the film. (Interview with author in Managua, January 22, 1991)

9. Marín heatedly expressed many times his anger over what happened to the film after he was called for military service:

> Disgracefully, the obtuse mentality of the direction of the Institute says first that it was very long; then that it appeared a little exaggerated; then that they had not authorized a fiction, that they had authorized an allegorized documentary; that there were problems. . . . So they authorized another director to do it. One turned it down; another turned it down. They chose Pallo [Rafael] Vargas. Pallo Vargas said he would do it, because he likes to destroy things also. (Interview with author, January 22, 1991, Managua)

10. Marín referred to the film as "my first short fiction film." Interview with author in Managua, July 8, 1990.

11. Interview with author in Granada, August 24, 1994.

12.
> It's one of the films I hate the most, because here I was making a film showing the efficiency of the security that the police represented. A police highly trained. And while I'm filming some [police] shooting head-on, it really was efficient, because they shot me in the chest, for real. The technical advisor was a Chilean . . . and instead of using blanks he used real bullets. During the last shot of the film I went to get treated in the hospital with a wounded sound person and one of the actors. (Interview with author in Mexico City, July 14, 1994)

13. The title of the film reproduces an expression coined by Tomás Borge to characterize the new Sandinista Police; it is also the title of a book: *Centinelas de la alegría del pueblo* (Managua: Ediciones Raití, 1985).

14. Noticiero 11, *La costa Atlántica,* included the FSLN hymn in Miskito, the only use of the Miskito language in the film.

15. Interview with author in Mexico City, July 20, 1994. In the same discussions, regarding the cultural distance separating the Pacific and Atlantic regions, Argüello observed, "The Atlantic Coast is like Albania."

16. The Department of Propaganda and Political Education published a book with the title *Y se rompió el silencio* in 1981. *Ventana* ran an ad for it on August 9, 1981, describing it as covering a large part "of the period of accumulation of forces in silence until 1974 when the assault took place on the house of José María Castillo, which attained the release from prison of a group of compañeros. This action was converted into a wake up call that would give renewed energy to the Sandinista Front of National Liberation." See also Tomás Borge, *The Patient Impatience,* trans. Russell Bartley, Darwin Flakoll, and Sylvia Yoneda (Willimantic, Conn.: Curbstone Press, 1991).

17. In a sequence not used in the film but included in an early version of the script, a volunteer specifically mentions the lack of extra compensation. "Entrevistas Documental TELCOR," INCINE archives. Note that the document refers to the noticiero as a documentary.

18. The section on the Agrarian Reform, titled "Agrarian Revolution," contains the following introduction, before listing a series of specific measures: "The Popular Sandinista Revolution will formulate an agrarian policy to realize an Authentic Agrarian Reform which will immediately result in the massive redistribution of the land, eliminating the latifundist usurpation to benefit the workers (small producers) who work the land." Two versions of this 1969 document can be found in Dennis Gilbert and David Block, eds., *Sandinistas: Key Documents/Documentos Claves* (Ithaca, N.Y.: Latin American Studies Program, Cornell University, 1990), 30. (All documents in original Spanish version, with the exception of one released in English.)

19. See, for example, Carlos M. Vilas, "El impacto de la guerra de agresión en la revolución Sandinista," *Revista nicaragüense de ciencias sociales* 2, no. 2 (March 1987): 11.

20. Reagan made this charge, for example, in a speech to the joint session of Congress on April 27, 1983: "It has broken its promises to us, to the organization of American States, and most important of all, to the people of Nicaragua." According to Holly Sklar, the charge "refers specifically to a July 12, 1979, letter that the provisional junta sent to the OAS secretary general with its plan to achieve peace and establish the Government of National Reconstruction. The letter was not a formal commitment to the OAS and OAS officers have never treated it as such. It is certainly not a treaty that U.S. officials could legitimately point to as a test of Nicaragua's compliance with treaty agreements." Holly Sklar, *Washington's War on Nicaragua* (Boston: South End Press, 1988), 138, 140.

21. See "A Summary of The Report of The Latin American Studies Association Delegation to Observe the Nicaraguan General Election of November 4, 1984," in Thomas W. Walker, ed., *Nicaragua: The First Five Years* (New York: Praeger, 1985), 523–532.

22. "Generally speaking, in this campaign the FSLN did little more to take advantage of its incumbency than incumbent parties everywhere (including the United

States) routinely do, and considerably *less* than ruling parties in other Latin American countries traditionally have done." Walker, *Nicaragua: The First Five Years*, 531.

23. For Somarriba, the film was just an assignment. The National Electoral Council paid for it and he did what they wanted. Interview with author in Managua, January 25, 1991.

Chapter 7

1. For example, in 1977, a good agricultural year prior to 1979, bananas represented about one percent of total export value, and less than one percent of total agricultural area harvested. See Brizio N. Biondi-Morra, *Hungry Dreams: The Failure of Food Policy in Revolutionary Nicaragua, 1979-1990* (Ithaca and London: Cornell University Press, 1993), 50, 53–54. For a discussion of the banana industry during the 1980s, see James Pfeiffer, "*Bananeras:* Workers, Peasants, and Democracy on a Nicaraguan State Farm," *International Journal of Political Economy* 20 (Fall 1990): 69–80.

2. Pfeiffer, "*Bananeras,*" 74.

3. Pfeiffer, "*Bananeras,*" 74.

4. Pfeiffer, "*Bananeras,*" 74.

5. "It seems to me now that it was more important, or perhaps now it is more important, to have brought to the attention of the FSLN leadership certain aspects of the society which perhaps the society was not examining, blinded, because we believed that we were having a revolution." Interview with author in Managua, July 27, 1990.

6. For a discussion of the enclave economy, see Carlos M. Vilas, *State, Class, and Ethnicity in Nicaragua: Capitalist Modernization and Revolutionary Change on the Atlantic Coast* (Boulder, Colo.: Lynne Reinner, 1989), 8–12.

7. In an interview with the author in Managua on August 7, 1994, Lacayo kept repeating, "What debate? What debate?" when asked about the debates over UNAG and the Agrarian Reform, among others.

8. Interview with author in Managua, January 25, 1991. When I asked Lacayo about this letter, Lacayo did not remember it, but said that he probably threw it in the trash.

9. "Compared to what I knew about film, and editing, he was the person who really guided us, gave us options. He was directing along with us when we were editing." Interview with author in Managua, July 23, 1990.

10. Alvarez has spoken angrily on several occasions of the work discipline imposed by some INCINE administrators, such as not permitting Alvarez to leave INCINE premises to visit her home less than five minutes away. She cites one particularly rigid FSLN cadre as the reason for her leaving INCINE, though she has also admitted on other occasions that personal reasons pulled her away from INCINE, for her future husband lived and worked on the Atlantic Coast.

11. A translation of the letter can be found in Robert Edgar Conrad, ed. and trans., *Sandino: The Testimony of a Nicaraguan Patriot, 1921-1934* (Princeton: Princeton University Press, 1990), 239–242. For the letter in Spanish, see *Augusto C. Sandino: El pensamiento vivo*, vol. 1, ed. Sergio Ramírez (Managua: Editorial Nueva Nicaragua, 1981), 324–328.

12. The line comes from a poem by Joachín Pasos, "Desocupación pronta, y si es necesario violenta" ("Prompt, and if necessary, violent, withdrawal"). Cited in Whisnant, *Rascally Signs in Sacred Places*, 358. For discussion of Pasos, see Greg Dawes,

Aesthetics and Revolution: Nicaraguan Poetry 1979-1990 (Minneapolis: Minnesota University Press, 1993), 39–43.

13. Fernando Birri admired *Pan y dignidad*, for he also directed a "carta" in Nicaragua, and he paid homage to the film in an article on New Latin American Cinema, "which came from a particular time, something in the air, in the history of people awakening with great strength to the consciousness of occupying their place in history, a place denied us for so many years, a place which once and for all, as the title of the beautiful Nicaraguan film has it, is a place of bread and dignity." Fernando Birri, "For a Nationalist, Realist, Critical and Popular Cinema," *Screen* 27, no. 3–4 (May–Aug. 1986): 89. For the text in Spanish, see Fernando Birri, "Por un cine nacional, realista, crítico y popular," *Areíto*, vol. X, no. 37 (1984): 6–7. For the text of Birri's film, *Rte: Nicaragua (Carta al mundo)*, produced by INCINE and the Laboratorio Ambulante de Poéticas Cinematográficas de Fernando Birri, see Fernando Birri, *El alquimista poético-político por un nuevo cine latinamericano, 1956-1991* (Madrid: Catedral Filmoteca Española, 1996), 295–303.

14. According to Martha Clarissa Hernández, who worked in various capacities at INCINE since the end of 1979, "INCINE was part of the Ministry of Culture, but it was always absolutely autonomous. Furthermore, it had its own premises, apart, so they were two distinct entities." Interview with author in Managua, January 11, 1996.

15. In a generally sympathetic brief account of INCINE, Dee Dee Halleck described INCINE as "the most chaotic of the media groups that I visited." See Dee Dee Halleck, "Nicaraguan Video: 'Live from the Revolution,'" in *Communicating in Popular Nicaragua*, ed. Armand Mattelart (New York: International General, 1986), 119. The original article appeared in *The Independent*, November 1984, 2–3; Lacayo wrote a somewhat petulant response in the December 1985 issue, accompanied by a comment from Dee Dee Halleck. Many people, inside and outside of INCINE, have told me of the impressive disorder found at INCINE. Alan Bolt, an outspoken critic of FSLN rigidity, recalled his visit once to INCINE as "total, total chaos, disorder." Interview with author in Managua, August 14, 1992. Mariano Marín claimed, "We at INCINE had a reputation throughout the state institutions of being total anarchists. It's where all the whores, the fags, the libertines . . . were. And it wasn't only here that we had this reputation. In Cuba, ICAIC had the same image of us. They saw us as crazies, hippies, dope smokers, everything." Interview with author in Granada, August 24, 1994.

16. Carlos M. Vilas, "Family Affairs: Class, Lineage and Politics in Contemporary Nicaragua," *Journal of Latin American Studies* 24 (1992): 328.

17. According to Mariano Marín, Rossana Lacayo was supposed to direct *Nuestra Reforma Agraria*, for she was, at the time, the girlfriend of Bayardo Arce, propaganda head of the FSLN. But Jaime Wheelock was infatuated with her, so "there was some complication with the heart, the skirt and the photography," and Rafael Vargas ended up directing it. Interview with author in Grenada, August 24, 1994.

18. In his retrospective account, Jaime Wheelock noted the following: "What was the model of the agrarian reform? In principle, we reject the idea of copying. This was very important." Jaime Wheelock Román, *La Reforma Agraria* (Managua: Vanguardia, 1990), 64.

19. See, for example, Nolan and Hodges, who view the FSLN as Leninist; for less label-obsessed commentaries, see, among many others, Dunkerley, Booth, and the many works of Vilas.

20. Eduardo Baumeister, "The Structure of Nicaraguan Agriculture and the Sandi-

nista Agrarian Reform." in Richard L. Harris and Carlos M. Vilas, eds., *Nicaragua: A Revolution Under Siege* (London: Zed Books, 1985), 19.

21. John Weeks, *The Economies of Central America* (New York: Holmes and Meier, 1985), 160.

22. There has been considerable debate on the peasant work force during the revolution and its relation to the Agrarian Reform. See Carlos M. Vilas, "Reforma Agraria, agroexportación y empleo rural en Nicaragua," *Canadian Journal of Latin American and Caribbean Studies* 18 (1984); Michael Zalkin, "Agrarian Class Structure in Nicaragua in 1980. A New Interpretation and Some Implications," *Journal of Peasant Studies*, vol. 16, no. 4 (July 1989); various articles by Baumeister listed in the bibliographic essay.

23. Many commentators have noted this bias. To cite one example, "When, by the late 1970s, the revolutionary struggle assumed a national dimension, it was the urban rather than the rural masses that actively engaged in the armed struggle to overthrow the Somoza dictatorship." Peter Utting, *Economic Reform and Third-World Socialism* (Houndsmill: Macmillan: United Nations Research Institute for Social Development, 1992), 228.

24. See Marvin Ortega, "The State, the Peasantry and the Sandinista Revolution," *Journal of Development Studies* (July 1990) 122–142; Carmen Diana Deere, Peter Marchetti, and Nola Reinhardt. "The Peasantry and the Development of the Sandinista Agrarian Policy," *Latin American Research Review* XX(3) (1985), 88, and Eduardo Baumeister, "Farmers' Organizations and Agrarian Transformation," in *The New Politics of Survival: Grassroots Movements in Central America*, ed. Minor Sinclair (New York: Monthly Review Press, 1995), 239–249.

25. According to one estimate, 82 percent of the land distributed from the state to peasants was conditioned on the formation of production cooperatives. "This policy was opposed by peasants." Elizabeth Dore, "The Great Grain Dilemma: Peasants and State Policy in Revolutionary Nicaragua," *Peasant Studies*, vol. 19. no. 2 (Winter 1990): 116.

26. Baumeister noted that "unlike agrarian reform laws in other parts of Latin America, [the Nicaraguan Agrarian Reform Laws of 1981 and 1986] did not penalize the landowner for the size of her/his land; rather, they confiscated land that was inadequately or not used. In this way the reform did not destroy the modern productive largeholder sector." Eduardo Baumeister, "Agrarian Reform," in *Revolution and Counterrevolution in Nicaragua*, ed. Thomas W. Walker (Boulder, Colo.: Westview, 1991), 237.

27. Scholars of the Agrarian Reform often divide the process into other phases according to more technical criteria than the very crude yardstick provided by the dates of the three legal decrees cited in the text. Martinez, for example, lists six periods. Philip R. Martinez, "Peasant policy within the Nicaraguan agrarian reform, 1979–1989." *World Development*, vol. 21, no. 3 (March 1993): 479–481. Of the period during which *Nuestra Reforma Agraria* was made, one scholar has claimed, "There was 'serious debate' over agricultural strategy. The focus of debate was sometimes obscure and was changing a great deal." Elizabeth Dore, "La respuesta campesina a las políticas agrarias y commerciales en Nicaragua: 1979–1988," *Estudios sociales centroamericanos*, vol. 49 (January–April 1989): 33.

28. "Rather than a 'transition to socialism,' the Sandinista revolution is entangled in a difficult 'transition to development.'" Carlos M. Vilas, *The Sandinista Revolu-*

tion: National Liberation and Social Revolution in Central America, trans. Judy Butler (New York: Monthly Review Press, 1986), 268. Two years later (*The Sandinista Revolution* appeared originally in Spanish in 1984), Vilas offered an even less ambitious assessment: "It would be difficult to affirm that the Sandinista Revolution is (in its current stage) anticapitalist. . . . What it is fundamentally is a 'transition from underdevelopment,' toward levels of greater justice, social welfare, development and national self-determination, more than proletarian or socialist." Carlos M. Vilas, "El impacto de la transición revolutionaria en las clases populares: la clase obrera en la revolución Sandinista," *Cuadernos políticos,* no. 48 (October/December 1986): 92.

29. According to Frank Pineda, Wheelock saw a first cut of the film, which included some criticism of cooperatives, that they needed more support, and Vargas recut it. Interview with author in Mexico City, July 21, 1994.

30. Orlando Núñez, "The Third Social Force in National Liberation Movements," *Latin American Perspectives,* vol. 8, no. 2 (Spring 1981) 5–21, translated from "La tercera fuerza en los movimientos de liberación nacional." *Estudios sociales centroamericanos* 27 (September/October 1980): 141–157.

31. "There were diverse elements at play upon the formation [of UNAG]. On one side, and perhaps most important, was the creation of a corporate alternative to the business organizations grouped within The Consejo Superior de la Empresa Privada (COSEP) and growing increasingly alienated from the revolution." Eduardo Baumeister and Oscar Neira, "La Conformación de una Economía Mixta: Estructura de Clases y Política Estatal en la Transición Nicaragüense," in *La Transición difícil: La autodeterminación de los pequeños países periféricos,* Coordinadores José Luis Coraggio and Carmen Diana Deere (Mexico: siglo veintiuno, 1986), 299.

32. Thus, though 68 percent of the land distributed to cooperatives by 1982 went to production cooperatives (Cooperativa Agrícola Sandinista, or CAS), the most collectivized form, only 11.5 percent of the cooperative population belonged to CAS. Deere, Marchetti, and Reinhardt, "The Peasantry and the Development of the Sandinista Agrarian Policy," 97. Whether they joined cooperatives or not, many resented the pressures to join.

33. According to the assistant director, Martha Clarissa Hernández, Vargas was responsible for the baseball uniforms, and her comments indicate that Vargas was consistently intervening in the material he was filming:

> Everything [in the film] is constructed. It's exactly like this.
> What he wanted to be seen in the film [my interpretation, for
> example, of the function of the baseball uniforms] is exactly
> what you have seen. He got there and they were there, and then
> he showed the baseball. But all of this is constructed. He told
> them to put the uniforms on, "Put them on and work like this,"
> and then the sequence of baseball. In this sense I disagree with
> him—as documentary filmmaker that I am—I would not have
> done it like that. I would have done it like that if it had occurred
> like that in real life, but not construct it. . . . I see the film and it
> looks false. (Interview with author in Managua, January 11, 1996)

34. Interview with author in Mexico City, July 20, 1994.

35. As noted in the introduction, this book examines INCINE's films which deal

more or less directly with political matters. Space considerations, thematic margin-ality, and inaccessibility of prints precluded discussion of films devoted to literary topics: *Un secreto para mi sóla, Escuchemos a las mujeres, Más es mío el alba de oro, Unanse tantos vigores dispersos,* and *Una canción de amor para el otoño;* other non-literary films include *Managua de sol a sol, Más claro no canta un gallo,* and *Estos sí pasarán.*

Chapter 8

1. When discussing the production of his noticiero *La ceiba,* Marín explained it in the following way:

> What happens is that when I get there, the people, the things they do, they don't do them when it's light outside, when we have electric power, there isn't any . . . with difficulty I carry batteries, already charged for the length of time we're going to shoot. Then, I have to do everything. Then, everything that gets filmed is re-enacted—you follow me?—set up for shooting [puesto-en-escena]: the meeting, the people, the object they hit, the men running around, I had to do all that with them because I had very little time, because the batteries would not last long, there is no electric power and the closest place is about thirty miles away by boat. It was very dangerous, it was the boundary with Honduras. So I preferred to do it like this and I set up [montar] everything. Set it up, set it up—you follow me? That is, grab the people and "You, sit over here, you, you say this." Yes, it's true that they speak, but instead of having them say it in that way—because the Nicaraguans say a lot but little is understood. They talk and talk but their sentences get lost and in the countryside it's even worse. There were thousands of feet of film and I was thinking about all of this, of saving money, and it couldn't go on like that. So what did I do? I grabbed the film that we had . . . "We're going to rehearse," I would tell them; then we tried a run through and when I saw that it was going well I said to Armando (Marenco, the cameraperson) "Start the camera." We had a signal to start the camera and then film, like this, because if I started the camera right away, they would change everything. It's terrible! The camera is terrible! I don't like to be filmed. We preferred to do this and we pulled it off; we spent about ten days there with them. Incredible!" (Interview with Mariano Marín in Granada, August 24, 1994)

2. Interview with author in Managua, July 14, 1991. Lacayo also noted that Francisco Lacayo did not want fiction, for he had been Vice-Minister of Adult Education before coming to the Ministry of Culture. Interview with author in Managua, January 18, 1996.

3. Interview with author in Managua, June 25, 1990.

4. Interview with author in Managua, July 14, 1991.

5. Interview with author in Managua, January 16, 1996.

6. Interview with author in Managua, August 21, 1991.

7. "Algunas Consideraciones Generales," May 16, 1985, INCINE archives. Fernando Somarriba claimed that Cine RAP passed to the control of INCINE on March 8, 1985. Interview with author in Managua (in Cine RAP office, which Somarriba headed for a short period in 1991), January 25, 1991.

8. Interview with author in Granada, August 24, 1994.

9. Marín maintains that people didn't like the orientation of his proposal, so it was changed and "fell into the hands of a director who didn't have such a drastic, provocative concept of what the issue was; for him it was more about 'what's most important for the revolution.' So I said, 'Forget it, I'm not doing it,' something like that. So he ended up making *Manuel*, which is a basically oneiric and hedonistic concept of a kid in the military. I see it as a world apart from the reality." Interview with author in Granada, August 24, 1994. Alberto Legall, head of Production at the time, recalls that there were many discussions both over the military draft and the move to fiction. He disagreed with the decision to concentrate on fiction, one of his reasons for leaving INCINE. "As head of Production, I always supported the documentary idea, to the point that I had certain differences with Ramiro . . . but in the end, after a lot of friction and discussions, it [*Manuel*] was converted into fiction. Ramiro had the final word as Director of INCINE." Interview with author, January 16, 1996. In a recent article about the film, Vargas sheds little light on the production history, though his comments do center on the war: "The war that we were living and the proximity of death produced in my mind obsessive and paranoid ideas." "CINENICACENTROACARIBE," *El nuevo diario*, November 9, 1999.

10. On the school, see Birri, *El alquimista poético-político*, 229–235. For more on Fernando Birri as the "pope" of the New Latin American Cinema, see chapter 10.

11. Interview with author in Managua, July 18, 1990.

12. Interview with author in Managua, January 16, 1996.

13. Interview with author in Managua, January 18, 1996.

14. Mimicking the delivery of Vargas, Hernández recalled, "I didn't make a sound, I didn't do anything to make them [Lacayo and Vargas] chase me away. I didn't want to move, nor make any sound so they would not realize I was there and say "Get out!" now that we're talking of something else. That's how we got to see *Manuel*." Interview with author in Managua, January 11, 1996.

15. Though Frank Pineda recognized the talent of Vargas, he could not tolerate working with him: "In the middle of shooting he started meditating. Everyone was waiting, and I said, 'Have we come to film or do yoga? If you're going to do yoga, find someone else. I'm leaving.' And I left." Interview with author in Mexico City, July 21, 1994.

16. Memorandum from Brenda Martínez to Alberto Legall, July 1, 1983, INCINE archives.

17. Letter from Alberto Legall to Rafael Vargas, November 3, 1983, INCINE archives.

18. Letter from Rafael Vargas to Julio Torres, March 8, 1984, INCINE archives.

19. Informe de mes de mayo de 1984, Dirección de Producción, June 13, 1984, INCINE archives.

20. Memo from Julio Torres to Ramiro Lacayo, April 16, 1985, INCINE archives.

21. Vargas, "CINENICACENTROACARIBE," *El Nuevo Diario*, November 9, 1999.

22. Vargas has commented, "In the 1960s the influences of Bergman and Buñuel were determinant, the profundity of Bergman, the surrealism of Buñuel and the Latin American novelists who created Magical Realism, which is a translation of surrealism in a variation of Latin American baroque." Interview with author in Managua, July 18, 1990.

23. The quote is from a mural commemorating his death. See David Kunzle, *The Revolutionary Murals of Revolutionary Nicaragua* (Berkeley and Los Angeles: University of California Press, 1995), 96.

24. Memo from Vargas to Legall, August 16, 1983, INCINE archives. For the most part, I have refrained from referring to budget figures for INCINE. Financial figures are extremely difficult to estimate for the work of INCINE for various reasons. Inflation wreaked havoc with budgets. Apart from the noticieros, most films did develop budgets, in both córdobas (for domestic goods and services) and dollars (for imported goods and services, principally film and sound stock and processing), but virtually all films depended heavily on services in kind, both in Nicaragua and in Cuba for postproduction, so the written numbers probably bore little relation to real costs. In one budget request for 1984, the document lists 24,581,702 córdobas, though INCINE received only 12 million. For that same year, a list of salaries for all INCINE personnel, not including Cine Mobil, indicated that current salaries were 228,250/month for 48 people, or 2,967,250 for the year (including the normal "thirteenth month" salary for everyone). In September 1984, the official exchange rate was 10 córdobas to the dollar, and the black market brought 250 córdobas per dollar. Four months later, in February, the official rate rose to 28, and the black-market rate reached 500. INCINE's budget was paid, of course, in córdobas, so the institution did not have access to dollars at the black-market rate. With government food programs, salaries could cover food and other expenses, but for any foreign goods, such as spare parts, the córdobas at the official rate had little buying power. Nonetheless, to give a sense of what the INCINE numbers were, Vargas's memo of August 16, 1983, includes a budget for *Manuel, Daniel,* and *Gabriel* (the original name of *Noel*):

	Córdobas	Dollars
Manuel	73,354	4,007
Daniel	150,507	5,807
Gabriel	150,507	5,907

25. Memo from Vargas to Legall, August 16, 1983, INCINE archives.

26. The title is a famous sentence used by Julio Buitrago while single-handedly holding off the Guardia Nacional for four hours before succumbing. Omar Cabezas provides an account of the battle, which he claims "every last person in Nicaragua with a TV set saw," in *Fire from the Mountain,* 21–23.

27. See for example, Carlos M. Vilas, *Transición desde el subdesarrollo: Revolución y reforma en la periferia* (Caracas: Editorial Nueva Sociedad, 1989), 210; Holly Sklar, *Washington's War on Nicaragua,* 117–118.

28. Somarriba complained bitterly about the postproduction work of the laboratory in Cuba. For their 16-mm productions, INCINE worked with the Cuban television lab at the ICRT (Instituto Cubano de Radio y Televisión), apparently a less professional lab, with poor quality control. In various memos, Somarriba objected to the dissolves, the color, and the sound, and Ramiro Lacayo at one point wrote to Third Horizon Films

in Holland requesting financial support to find another lab capable of finishing the film properly.

29. Review of *Que se rinda tu madre.* November 1985. Typescript.

30. Ramiro Lacayo Deshón, "El Esbozo de Daniel," *Ventana*, no. 86, September 11, 1982. Reprinted in Ramiro Lacayo Deshón, *Nadie de importancia* (Managua: Editorial Nueva Nicaragua, 1986), 23–30.

31. Interview with author in Managua, January 22, 1991.

32. Memo dated February 2, 1985, INCINE archives.

33. In the best account of the war—cowritten by one of the policy makers of the Agrarian Reform, Orlando Núñez—the authors emphasize on several occasions the dissatisfaction with the revolution among the peasantry. For example:

> The war in Nicaragua was provoked by two fundamental factors. On the one hand it is the negative reaction of the local bourgeoisie and the government of the United State to the very existence of the revolution, and its alignment with the Soviet bloc. On the other hand, it is the rejection by the middle peasantry of the policy of mercantile control of the revolution: material and ideological hostility to private property, promoting collective forms in an individualist culture, administration of prices and the market. . . . Only once the war was well underway (1985) did the FSLN recognize that there existed a significant campesino participation in the ranks of the counterrevolution. (Nuñez et al., *La Guerra en Nicaragua* [Managua: CIPRES, 1991], 79, 85)

34. "There's a moment when it can't be just a teacher-student relation. There's a gay relationship here. It could be a confused love, a lost love, a love misinterpreted, but it is in some way 'queer.' It's like *Death in Venice.*" Interview with author in Granada, August 24, 1994.

35. The young actress, Maritza Castillo, had played a more spectacular role in a real-life mise-en-scène dreamed up by the Ministry of the Interior as a propaganda coup to embarrass the Catholic Church. Castillo played the role of lover of a Catholic priest, Father Bismarck Carballo, spokesperson of Archbishop Obando. The script called for her "husband" to return home to surprise the couple in bed. When the naked priest rushed out of the house, photographers from the Sandinista press were waiting to record the event for an exposé of a "classic triangle of passion," according to *Barricada*, August 13, 1982. Cited in Dennis Gilbert, *The Sandinistas* (Cambridge: Basil Blackwell, 1988), 141. Gilbert wryly comments that this was "uncharacteristically florid language" for *Barricada*, as the FSLN organ was popularly viewed as written in aggressively dry and serious partyspeak.

36. See Beverley and Zimmerman, *Literature and Politics in the Central American Revolutions*, 72–73, and Whisnant, *Rascally Signs*, 165–168.

37. Fornet refers to "its way of inserting itself in a creative manner in a process of affirmation of the national consciousness." He describes the other characteristic as "its tendency to suppress the boundaries between documentary and fiction." Ambrosio Fornet, "Trente ans de cinéma dans la Révolution," in *Le cinéma cubain*, ed. Paolo Antonio Paranagua (Paris: Centre Georges Pompidou, 1990), 87.

38. For one now-classic account of severing one's ties to a former life, see Omar Cabezas, *Fire from the Mountain*, 203. For example, he describes the psychological effects of this isolation in the following passage:

> As things continue to get lost or ruined, the objects that reaffirm your present are disappearing, the objects that confirm your identity, your consciousness of your own existence, your sense that you are not just living on the surface, but have a history.
>
> So, when you lose all your things, it's as if many pieces of your present have broken off from you. It's so extreme that for a moment you don't know if you'll ever go back, if you'll ever return, and each thing that you lose is like a paring away, a whittling down, a falling off of piece after piece of your persona. And in time—unforgiving, unrelenting time that flows on, unchanging—you lose everything, even your mind.

39. Douglas Carcache, "Filman primera obra literaria nicaragüense," *El Nuevo Diario*, September 13, 1984.

40. "'El centerfielder' no es tan fácil como aparenta," *Barricada*, September 15, 1984, 12.

41. Review of *Esbozo de Daniel*. August 1985. Typescript.

Chapter 9

1. Somarriba claimed that the idea came to him after seeing *Rompiendo el silencio*. Conversation with author.

2. According to one estimate, by 1983, nearly 80 percent of state institutions on the coast were run by Pacific or Atlantic Coast mestizos, though the source is not provided. P. Sollis, "The Atlantic Coast of Nicaragua: Development and Autonomy," *Journal of Latin American Studies*, vol. 21 (1987): 499.

3. According to one U.S. anthropologist who lived on the coast, Charles Hale, "a near-adoration for white North Americans was and is common in Miskitu popular perception." From "Institutional Struggle, Conflict and Reconciliation: Miskitu Indians and the Nicaraguan State (1979–1985)" in CIDCA/Development Studies Unit, *Ethnic Groups and the Nation State*, 106 (Stockholm: Univ. of Stockholm, 1987).

4. *Cultural Survival Quarterly*, based in Cambridge, has served as a forum for discussions of indigenous rights and Fourth World Theory. For a detailed, and sometimes fantastic, analysis of the Miskito situation in Nicaragua from such a perspective, see Bernard Nietschmann, *The Unknown War: The Miskito Nation, Nicaragua and the United States* (New York: Freedom House, 1989).

5. Letter from Somarriba to Julio Torres, May 14, 1986, INCINE archives.

6. Letter from Ramiro Lacayo to Bayardo Arce, June 11, 1985, INCINE archives.

7. For a discussion of population figures, see Roxanne Dunbar Ortiz, *The Miskito Indians of Nicaragua* (London: Minority Rights Group, 1988).

8. The organization excluded Creoles. See Carlos M. Vilas, *State, Class and Ethnicity in Nicaragua: Capitalist Modernization and Revolutionary Change on the Atlantic Coast*, trans. Susan Norwood (Boulder, Colo.: Lynne Rienner, 1991), 125.

9. According to the memoir of one Miskito military leader, "Brooklyn Rivera had

been released from jail and had gone to Honduras to work with Fagoth. They struggled over power, and Fagoth had Brooklyn put in jail for about fifteen days. Under pressure from several of the Indian officers, Fagoth released him but, assisted by the Honduran military, planned his assassination. So Brooklyn fled to Costa Rica." Reynaldo Reyes and J. K. Wilson, *Ráfaga: The Life Story of a Nicaraguan Miskito Comandante* (Norman: University of Oklahoma Press, 1992), 44.

10. "Though it criticized the conduct of the Atlantic Coast relocation, Americas Watch found that it was not unreasonable for the Nicaraguan government to relocate civilians away from a border area to facilitate the defense of the country's territorial integrity. The IACHR [Inter-American Commission on Human Rights] concurred." Sklar, *Washington's War on Nicaragua*, 104.

11. Roxanne Dunbar Ortiz, *The Miskito Indians of Nicaragua*, Minority Rights Group, Report No. 79 (London: Minority Rights Group, 1988).

12. The proposal probably dates from early 1985, for the proposal estimates the projected production schedule from April 1985 to April 1986, INCINE archives.

13. *Ibid.*

14. Contract between INCINE and Instituto Mexicano de Cinematografía, signed and dated August 9, 1985, INCINE archives.

15. Letter from Fernando Somarriba to Julio Torres, August 28, 1985, INCINE archives.

16. Letter from Fernando Somarriba to Josefina Rivas, Director Administrativo, Gobierno Regional, Zona Especial I, January 6, 1986, INCINE archives.

17. Letter from Fernando Somarriba to Julio Torres, May 12, 1986, INCINE archives.

18. As late as August 11, 1986, Somarriba wrote an angry note to Julio Torres with a list of complaints. Torres jotted a note on the letter: "This seems an outrage to me after the support he has been given." INCINE archives.

19. Vilas, *State, Class and Ethnicity in Nicaragua*, 34–35.

20. For a helpful chart through the acronym maze of the Atlantic Coast conflict, see Charles R. Hale, *Resistance and Contradiction: Miskitu Indians and the Nicaraguan State, 1894–1987* (Stanford: Stanford University Press, 1994), 240–241.

21. As one example, Lacayo recalled that MINT personnel objected to showing three burned Moravian churches, for it implied that all Moravian churches had been burned. Interview with author in Managua, August 23, 1992.

22. Interview with author in Managua, August 21, 1992.

23. The interviews that have been cut are those with Rafael Oliver, Centuriano Knight, Juan Salgado, Armando Rojas, Victor Ordóñez, and Rufino Lucas, in addition to the clips of the speech by Luis Carrión.

24. While the Consejo Directivo included the heads of the various INCINE departments, one set of minutes from a meeting of May 7, 1984, indicates that Iván Argüello attended as the Political Secretary of the FSLN. INCINE archives. Argüello had a more philosophical explanation: "The metaphysics were in my favor." Interview with author in Mexico City, July 20, 1994.

25. The INCINE budget lists the following figures (in Córdobas):

INCINE contribution:	7,829,410
UNAG	3,565,000
AMNLAE	6,005,334
Total:	17,399,744

26. Interview with author in Managua, January 20, 1992.

27. According to Lacayo, in the first cut, to take one example of the incoherence, when the captain warns the women not to proceed without permission, a bombardment follows, implying that the military was bombing the women. Interview with author in Managua, July 27, 1990.

28. Felix Navarrete, "*El espectro de la guerra*. Un homenaje cinematográfico a la juventud nicaragüense," *El nuevo diario*, November 28, 1987.

29. Both Mariano Marín and Fernando Somarriba often expressed their resentment at this preferential treatment given by Lacayo to himself as director of INCINE. They cited a number of precedents even before *El espectro*, such as his shooting in 35 mm when they had to shoot in 16 mm, his use of Robert Young as screenwriter for *El centerfielder*, and so on. The credits on the films lend credence to these charges.

30. Felix Navarrete, "*El espectro de la guerra*. Un homenaje cinematográfico a la juventud nicaragüense," *El nuevo diario*, November 28, 1987, 4–5.

31. "Don Teófilo y la 'Tour Eiffel,'" *Ventana*, May 20, 1989.

32. Peter Schumann has written quite critically of the style of Solás, with "his tendency toward preciosity, his taste for the perfectionism of the image and his weakness for an empty and gratuitous aestheticism." *Historia del cine latinoamericano* (Buenos Aires: Legasa, 1987), 175–176. See also Paolo Antonio Paranagua, "News From Havana. A Restructuring of Cuban Cinema," *Framework* 35 (1988): 99.

33. Navarrete, *El espectro de la guerra.*

34. "Don Teófilo y la 'Tour Eiffel'." The person who played the role of the peasant, Carlos Aleman Ocampo, responded to these criticisms two weeks later, tongue in cheek. He wrote and signed the response in the name of the character he played, Teófilo Ayerdis Ortéz, with an accompanying picture of him bearing the caption "Typical Nicaraguan campesino." Teófilo Ayerdis Ortez, "Don Teófil ataca de nuevo," *Ventana*, June 3, 1989.

35. As John King put it: "a glossy musical which becomes a lacrimose melodrama as a lively break-dancer is crippled by the Contras." (164). Later, he added that "it proved impossible to graft a 'Travolta-style' sophomoric love story on to the daily reality of the community at war." John King, *Magical Reels*, 241. In all fairness, Lacayo was not satisfied with the film. He claims that he was unable to use almost 30 minutes of the film, which explains the resultant dominance of the musical passages. Interview with author in Managua, June 25, 1991.

36. Interview with author in Managua, June 25, 1990.

37. Two groups of INCINE personnel, with some overlap, formed around this time. Lacayo set up an independent production company, ENCI (Empresa Nicaragüense de Cine), and several others, including Fernando Somarriba and Mariano Marín, established ANCI (Asociación Nicaragüense de Cine). The organizations made several films, working in association with INCINE, but the films were not part of the former INCINE structure.

Chapter 10

1. "Cinema and Underdevelopment" in *Twenty-five Years of the New Latin American Cinema*, ed. Michael Chanan (London: British Film Institute, 1983), 12.

2. In the view of Octavio Getino, always sympathetic to Birri's work, "The films of Birri did not reach taking on the world of the proletariat—fundamental protago-

nist of the history of the country beginning with the decade of the 1940s—limiting themselves to the limited universe of the 'poor' and marginals." Octavio Getino, *Cine y dependencia: El cine en la Argentina* (Buenos Aires: Puntosur Editores, 1990), 61.

3. In the same article, in a discussion of Argentine cinema during the postwar period, Birri asserts that Argentine cinema "prostituted itself under Peronism," suggesting that he was no supporter of Peronism, the movement that Getino and Solanas enthusiastically supported in their work several years later.

4. Paolo Antonio Paranagua, "Brésil," in *Les cinémas de l'Amérique latine*, ed. Guy Hennebelle and Alfonso Gumucio Dagrón (Paris: CinémAction/Lherminier, 1981), 145. Writing in 1970, Rocha stated quite clearly the political goals of cinema novo: "The program: conquer the market and maintain economic independence in order to sustain freedom of production." "From the Drought to the Palm Trees," Randal Johnson and Robert Stam, eds., *Brazilian Cinema*, Expanded Edition (New York: Columbia University Press, 1995), 88.

5. *Brazilian Cinema*, 33.

6. *Brazilian Cinema*, 38.

7. "For an Imperfect Cinema," in *Twenty-five Years*, ed. Michael Chanan, 33.

8. García Espinosa specifically denied that his manifesto was a call to embrace the lack of technical means. See "Theory and Practice of Film and Popular Culture in Cuba" in *Cinema and Social Change in Latin America*, ed. Julianne Burton (Austin: University of Texas Press, 1986), 24.

9. In Michael Chanan, *Chilean Cinema* (London: British Film Institute, 1976), 83–84. According to Mouesca, Littín claimed to have edited the manifesto. Jacqueline Mouesca, *Plano secuencia de la memoria de Chile: Veinticinco años de cine chileno (1960-1985)* (Madrid: Ediciones Michay, 1988), 54; see also Jean Verdejo, Zuzana Mirjam Pick, and Gaston Ancelovici, "Chili," in *Les cinémas de l'Amérique latine*, 210.

10. Hennebelle and Gumucio Dagrón, *Les cinémas de l'Amérique latine*, 206.

11. In my consideration of the theoretical statements, I have excluded the work of Jorge Sanjinés. Sanjinés certainly adopted an articulate militant stance in his writing, but he committed himself to working with the large indigenous population in Bolivia, an important issue to be sure, but one not applicable to the situations under consideration in the text. See Jorge Sanjinés, *Theory and Practice of a Cinema with People* (Willamantic, Conn.: Curbstone Press, 1989).

12. Interview with Ruíz in *Araucaria de Chile*, no. 11 (1980) (Madrid). Cited in Mouesca, *Plano secuencia*, 32.

13. *Tricontinental* 1 (English) (July/August 1967). Havana.

14. Many of the writings are collected in Octavio Getino and Fernando Solanas, *Cine, cultura y descolonización* (Mexico: Siglo Veintiuno, 1973). For a retrospective view, see Octavio Getino, *A diez años de "hacia un tercer cine"* (Mexico, D.F.: Filmoteca UNAM, 1982).

Later relevant material can be found in Octavio Getino, *Cine y dependencia. El cine en la Argentina* (Buenos Aires: Puntosur Editores, 1990); Octavio Getino, *Notas sobre cine argentino y latinoamericano* (Mexico: Edimedios, 1984).

15. Jim Pines and Paul Willemen, eds., *Questions of Third Cinema* (London: British Film Institute, 1989). Zuzanna Pick notes that Latin American filmmakers criticized her use of the term "third cinema" for the title of a book she edited in 1978: "During my first visit to Cuba in 1979, filmmakers and critics pointed out that the title of

my recently published anthology—*Latin American Film Makers and Third Cinema* was misleading in that not all of the New Latin American Cinema should be defined as "third cinema." *The New Latin American Cinema: A Continental Project* (Austin: University of Texas Press, 1993), 200–201. Getino specifies that the first use of the term "third cinema" appeared in *Cine Cubano*, nos. 56/57 (March 1969). See also "Algunas observaciones sobre el concepto del 'Tercer Cine,'" reprinted in *Notas sobre cine argentino y latinoamericano*, 116.

16. "The fact that still today [1982] it is difficult to separate the concept of Third Cinema from the film *Hour of the Furnaces* once again proves the intimate dependence of the theoretical elaboration on concrete practice." "Algunas observaciones sobre el concepto del 'Tercer Cine,'" Getino, *Notas sobre cine argentino y latinoamericano*, 116.

17. Pines and Willemen, *Questions of Third Cinema.*

18. I have revised the standard English translation here. The most common English translation was done by Julianne Burton, published originally in *Cineaste*, and reproduced and revised by Burton and Chanan in *Twenty-five years of New Latin American Cinema.* See also my comments in "A Closer Look at Third Cinema," *Historical Journal of Film, Radio and Television*, vol. 21, no. 2 (June 2001) 153–166.

19. Walter Benjamin, "The Work of Art in the Age of Mechanical Reproduction," in *Illuminations*, Hannah Arendt, ed. (New York: Shocken, 1969).

20. "Fernando E. Solanas y Octavio Getino responden a cine cubano," *Cine Cubano* 56/57 (March 1969): 33. Commenting specifically on *La hora de los hornos*, Solanas elaborated on this idea of the elimination of "the spectator": "He ceases to be a spectator and becomes the protagonist and actor passing from the screen to the projection room and from the projection room to the screen." Interview with Louis Marcorelles, *Cahiers du cinéma*, no. 210 (March 1969): 62.

21. "El cine como parte de los proyectos de liberación" in *A diez años de "hacia un tercer cine,"* 34.

22. Fernando Solanas and Octavio Getino, "Towards a Third Cinema" in *Twenty-five Years*, ed. Michael Chanan, 26.

23. *Ibid.*, 27.

24. See, for example, Robert Stam, "*The Hour of the Furnaces* and the Two Avant-Gardes" in *The Social Documentary in Latin America*, ed. Julianne Burton (Pittsburgh: University of Pittsburgh Press, 1990), 264.

25. John King viewed the film's endorsement of Perón as "pathetically misplaced." *Magical Reels*, 88.

26. See "El cine como hecho político," in *Cine, cultura y descolonización*, 141. Before the publication of the manifesto, Solanas provided the fullest explication of their position on Peronism in an interview with Solanas by Louis Marcorelles in *Cahiers du cinéma*, 60. In a later interview, after the death of Perón, Solanas expressed his annoyance at the European left's criticism of Perón in *Framework* no. 10 (Spring 1979): 35–38.

27. "El cine como hecho politico," *Cine, cultura y descolonización*, 144.

28. *Ibid.*, 129. "The category of militant can be determined only on the basis of the work and practice realized within organic militant formations" (143).

29. In a recent discussion, Getino refers to an internal document distributed by Cine Liberation to popular organizations, "Recomendaciones para la difusión de cine militante," which stated, "In each projection of militant cinema, what is most important is not the film(s), but the participants and the political work which can be accom-

plished with them." According to Getino, a fragment of this document was published in *Cine y liberación* no. 1 (September 1972). See Getino, *Cine argentino entre lo posible y lo deseable* (Buenos Aires: CICCUS, 1998): 59.

30. "Cine militante. Una categoría interna del tercer cine" (March 1971) in *Cine, cultura y descolonización*, 121–123.

31. "Cine militante," 122–123. In an article published in 1980, Getino wrote that the article on militant cinema was meant to clarify certain "imprecisions" in the formulation of "third cinema."

32. "El cine como hecho político," *Cine, cultura y descolonización*, 134, 143.

33. "Apuntes para un juicio crítico descolonizado," *Cine, cultura y descolonización*, 116.

34. "El cine como hecho político," *Cine, cultura y descolonización*, 131.

35. *Ibid.*, 133.

36. "Apuntes para un juicio," 117.

37. "Algunas observaciones," Getino, *Notas*, 123.

38. "El cine como hecho político," *Cine, cultura y descolonización*, 147, 162. Solanas repeated this formulation 25 years later: "The documentary . . . is an irrefutable truth." "La hora de los hornos." in Fernando Ferreira, *Luces, cámara . . . memoria: Una historia social del cine argentino* (Buenos Aires: Corregidor, 1995), 298.

39. "L'Influence du 'Troisième Cinéma' dans le monde," Dossier réuni par *CinémAction, Revue Tiers Monde* vol. XX, no. 79 (July–September 1979): 617–618.

40. Alfonso Gumucio Dagrón. "El cine militante en américa latina desde 1969," *Plural*, vol. 9, no. 98 (November 1979): 53.

41. Emilia Torres, first head of Cine Mobil and later national director of the Popular Houses of Culture, repeatedly used this expression in a 1992 interview in Managua with the author, August 18, 1992.

42. Julio García Espinosa, "El Nuevo Cine Latinoamericano en el Mundo de Hoy" in *El nuevo cine latinoamericano en el mundo de hoy* (México: Universidad Nacional Autónoma de México, 1988), 137. Getino, *Cine latinoamericano: economías y nuevas tecnologías audiovisuales* (Buenos Aires: Legasa, 1988).

43. In addition to Getino's figures, I have used figures from *VII festival del nuevo cine latinoamericano* (Mexico: Coordinación Cultural/Dirección de Cinematografía, 1986); Tim Barnard, "After the Military: Film in the Southern Cone Today," *Review: Latin American Literature and Arts*, no. 46 (Fall 1992): 29–36.

44. *Cuba en cifras* (La Habaña: Comité Estatal de Estadísticas, 1989), 116.

45. Figures from Randal Johnson, "The Rise and Fall of Brazilian Cinema, 1960–1990," *Iris*, no. 13 (Summer 1991); Michael Chanan, ed., *Chilean Cinema* (London: British Film Institute, 1976); *VII festival del nuevo cine latinoamericano* (Mexico: Coordinación Cultural/Dirección de Cinematografía, 1986).

46. Figures from Getino, *Cine latinoamericano.*

47. Getino, *Cine latinoamericano*, 137–138.

48. Randal Johnson, "The Rise and Fall of Brazilian Cinema, 1960-1990," 110.

49. Robert Farias, former head of Embrafilme, complained that Brazilian television, because it is private, cannot be forced to show Brazilian films. María de la Luz Hurtado, ed., *La Industria cinematográfica chilena: desafíos y realidad* (Santiago: CENECA, 1986), 26.

50. Getino, *Cine latinoamericano*, 225.

51. *Ibid.*, 78.

52. Néstor García Canclini, "La cultura visual en la época del posnacionalismo.

¿Quién nos va a contar la identidad?" *Nueva sociedad,* no. 127 (September–October 1993): 29.

53. Nor is this phenomenon limited to Latin America. Getino cites similar trends in audience figures in developed countries. "El cine: entre la extinción y el cambio," *Plural,* no. 188 (May 1987): 38.

54. "El cine y la toma del poder," *Plural* (Mexico), no. 74 (November 1977): 25.

55. "La experiencia de la historia," *El nuevo cine latinoamericano en el mundo de hoy,* 107. Ana López criticized Michael Chanan in her discussion of more recent Cuban documentaries in noting the "traumatic creative decline of the late 1970s *not* mentioned by Chanan." "Revolution and Dreams," *Studies in Latin American Popular Culture,* vol. 11 (1992): 47. As for fiction films from the late 1970s, Agustín Mahieu commented that "In certain recent films, the discussion of ideological or material problems dramatized as fictional stories has fallen back a bit into a Manichaean schematization of certain films of the Soviet cinema during the Stalin epoch." Agustín Mahieu, "El cine cubano," *Cuadernos hispanoamericanos,* no. 348 (June 1979): 646.

56. John Beverley, Review of *The Cuban Image, Cuban Studies,* vol. 20 (1990): 207.

57. However, one should not necessarily jump to conclusions about the distribution of Latin American telenovelas within Latin America. According to one recent account, a 1997 study of audiovisual trade flows based on industry-supplied data indicates that "for all the regional trade in television programmes, the major traded product being the *telenovela,* only 6 per cent of total audiovisual imports came from within the region itself, . . . with the overwhelming majority of 86 per cent coming from the U.S." John Sinclair, *Latin American Television: A Global View* (New York: Oxford University Press, 1999), 156.

58. In the view of one veteran observer, this cinema has already appeared, though he does not applaud it: "The superficial aesthetic and the internal narrative structure are so similar, so interchangeable, so internationalized, that the Latin American cinema today, from North to South, is marked by the same aesthetic boredom." Peter Schumann, "La Experiencia de la Historia," in *El nuevo cine latinoamericano en el mundo de hoy,* 198.

59. *Statistical Yearbook (Unesco)* (Paris: Unesco, 1999), IV-217.

60. In 1970 García Espinosa underlined the centrality of that assertion: "This simple statement was meant to serve as a catalyst, to establish a fundamental question of principles. . . . One sentence summed it up: 'The Cinema is an Art.'" Alfredo Guevara, "Un cine de combate," *Pensamiento crítico,* no. 42 (1970): 12.

61. Such criticism is not limited to Solanas's Peronism of the 1970s. In a scathing critique, Kathleen Newman has attacked the "Peronist nationalist allegory" in his 1987 film *Sur.* See Kathleen Newman, "National Cinema after Globalization: Fernando E. Solanas' *Sur* and the Exiled Nation," *Quarterly Review of Film and Video,* vol. 14, no. 3 (1993): 69–83.

62. There are surprisingly few reports on the number of members of the FSLN. According to one estimate, "all three FSLN tendencies combined probably numbered between five hundred and a thousand armed regulars in mid-1978." John Booth, *The End of the Beginning: The Nicaraguan Revolution,* 145. For a report on the numbers of FSLN members, see María Molero, *Nicaragua Sandinista: Del sueño a la realidad* (Managua: CRIES y IEPALA, 1988), 39.

63. For a retrospective assessment, see Luis Serra, "The Grass-Roots Organizations," in *Revolution and Counterrevolution in Nicaragua,* ed. Thomas W. Walker (Boulder, Colo.: Westview, 1991), 49–75.

64. For one post-defeat discussion, see the harsh treatment of Elizabeth Dore and John Weeks, *The Red and the Black: The Sandinistas and the Nicaraguan Revolution* (London: Institute of Latin American Studies, 1992).

65. In a recent account, Phil Ryan describes Wheelock's success in marginalizing the Ministry of Planning headed by Henry Ruíz. He refers to Wheelock's belief that technology was the answer to the agrarian problem as "techno-utopianism." Though the Ministry of Planning was replaced by the Secretariat for Planning and Budgeting, its demotion in status "led to the departure from the SPP of many MIPLAN veterans who felt that 'planning should be planning'. . . ." Phil Ryan, *The Fall and Rise of the Market in Sandinista Nicaragua* (Montreal: McGill-Queens University Press, 1995), 132–140; 165.

66. According to Ramiro Lacayo, the audiovisual units of the other ministries worked in video. "When they wanted to make something with a little more quality, more developed, they called INCINE." Interview with author in Managua, January 18, 1996.

67. Interview with author in Managua, July 14, 1991.

68. In their 1985 discussion of Chile, Edgardo Pallero, Bebé Kamín, and Manuel Martínez Carrill assert, "With the lack of buying power of most of the population, most of the theaters in the popular neighborhoods have closed. The cinema has become a luxury good and even within this category it has to compete with television and video." "La industria del cine en Argentina, Chile y Uruguay" in *VII festival internacional del nuevo cine latinoamericano* (Mexico, D.F.: Coordinación de Difusión Cultural, Dirección de Cinematografía, 1986, in Cuadernos de cine, no. 30 [n.d.?]: 97).

69. Randal Johnson, "In the Belly of the Ogre," in *Mediating Two Worlds*, ed. John King, Ana López, and Manuel Alvarado (London: British Film Institute, 1993), 206. The title of the article refers to the expression "philanthropic ogre" coined by Octavio Paz to characterize the state in Latin America.

70. In an attempt to grapple with the slippery concept of national cinema, Stephen Crofts includes third cinema as one of the "seven varieties of 'national cinema.'" "Reconceptualizing National Cinema/s," *Quarterly Review of Film and Video*, vol. 14, no. 3 (1993): 50. Certainly in terms of the "Towards a Third Cinema" manifesto, it is difficult to think of third cinema as a national cinema. However, to the extent that a particular political formation identifies itself with a national project and succeeds in taking power, one might consider the cinema that participates in and/or articulates such a project a "national cinema," but I prefer to use the term "national cinema project," for that expression tries to preserve the aspiration toward hegemony in competing national discourses.

71. For an excellent account of these developments, see Pat Aufderheide, "Latin American Cinema and the Rhetoric of Cultural Nationalism: Controversies at Havana in 1987 and 1989," *Quarterly Review of Film and Video*, vol. 12, no. 4 (1991): 70. See also Jorge Fraga's comments specifically about Cuba in King, *Magical Reels*, 162, and R. Ruby Rich, "An/Other View of New Latin American Cinema," *Iris*, no. 13 (Summer 1991) 5–28.

72. Carlos M. Vilas, "Nicaragua: A Revolution that Fell from the Grace of the People," in *Socialist Register: Communist Regimes—The Aftermath* (London: Merlin Press, 1991) 302–321.

73. Interview with author in Mexico City, July 20, 1994.

74. King, *Magical Reels*, 146.

Bibliographic Essay

General

The geopolitical significance of the Sandinista revolution as a Marxist-inspired national liberation movement supported by Cuba and the Soviet Union led to an explosion of writing about Nicaragua in the 1980s, which then tapered off after the election loss of the Sandinistas in 1990. Thomas W. Walker edited the following series of books that surveyed the revolution, offering a broad, sympathetic overview and serving as a useful introduction to many of the central issues: *Nicaragua in Revolution* (New York: Praeger, 1982); *Nicaragua: The First Five Years* (New York: Praeger, 1985); *Reagan versus the Sandinistas: The Undeclared War on Nicaragua* (Boulder: Westview, 1987); *Revolution and Counterrevolution in Nicaragua* (Boulder: Westview, 1991); and *Nicaragua without Illusions* (Wilmington, Del.: Scholarly Resources, 1997). John Booth's *The End of the Beginning: The Nicaraguan Revolution* (Boulder: Westview, 1982) provides a useful one-volume early overview; for a collection of articles and documents, see Peter Rosset and John Vandermeer, eds., *Nicaragua: The Unfinished Revolution* (New York: Grove Press, 1986); see also Rosa María Torres and José Luis Coraggio, *Transición y crisis en Nicaragua* (San José: DEI, 1987), which includes a useful detailed chronology.

FSLN and the Sandinista Revolution

Donald Hodges has examined the thought of Sandino, though Hodges is critical of the FSLN's Marxist filtering of Sandino's highly idiosyncratic ideas, in the following two books: *Intellectual Foundations of the Nicaraguan Revolution* (Austin: Univ. of Texas Press, 1986) and *Sandino's Communism: Spiritual Politics for the Twenty-first Century* (Austin: Univ. of Texas Press, 1992). For a translated collection of Sandino's writings, see Robert Edgar (editor and translator), *Sandino: The Testimony of a Nicaraguan Patriot, 1921–1934* (Princeton: Princeton Univ. Press, 1990). David Nolan presents the FSLN as a Leninist party in *The Ideology of the Sandinistas and the Nicaraguan Revolution* (Coral Gables, Fla.: Institute of Interamerican Studies/Univ. of Miami, 1984).

Two early leftist interpretations contain detailed political accounts of the FSLN and the victory of the revolution and its immediate aftermath. They are George Black's *Triumph of the People: The Sandinista Revolution in Nicaragua* (London: Zed Books, 1981) and Henri Weber's *Nicaragua: The Sandinista Revolution* (translated by Patrick Camiller; London: Verso, 1981). Orlando Nuñez wrote an early influential article on the singularity of the FSLN: "La tercera fuerza en los movimientos de liberación nacional," *Estudios sociales centroamericanos* 27 (Sept./Oct. 1980): 141–157. The Marxist Argentinean scholar, Carlos Vilas, has written penetrating analyses of a whole range of topics during the Sandinista years, some of which can be found below. His *The Sandinista Revolution: National Liberation and Social Transformation in Central America* (New York: Monthly Review Press, 1986), a translation of the 1984 Spanish edition, is essential. For a discussion of the FSLN, see Dennis Gilbert, *Sandinistas* (Cambridge, Mass.: Basil Blackwell, 1988); for a collection of Sandinista documents, see Dennis Gilbert and David Block, eds., *Sandinistas: Key Documents = Documentos Claves* (Ithaca, N.Y.: Latin American Studies Program, Cornell Univ., 1990). For a collection of speeches by FSLN leaders, see Bruce Marcus, ed., *Sandinistas Speak* (New York: Pathfinder, 1982). For retrospective accounts by FSLN leaders, see Omar Cabezas, *Fire from the Mountain: The Making of a Sandinista,* translated by Kathleen Weaver (New York: New American Library, 1986); Tomás Borge, *The Patient Impatience* (Willamantic, Conn.: Curbstone Press, 1992); Giocondo Belli, *The Country under My Skin: A Memoir of Love and War,* translated by Kristina Cordero and the author (New York: Knopf, 2002); and especially Sergio Ramírez (who has broken with the FSLN), *Adiós muchachos: Una memoria de la revolución sandinista* (Mexico: Aguilar, 1999).

One of the founders of the FSLN, Carlos Fonseca, was the central figure in resurrecting the memory of Sandino's thought and struggle as the inspiration for the formation of the FSLN. In an excellent article, Steven Palmer shows how Fonseca shaped the interpretation of Sandino for the FSLN's contemporary purposes: "Fonseca, Carlos and the Construction of Sandinismo in Nicaragua," *Latin American Research Review* 23, no. 1 (1988): 91–109. A recent biography of Fonseca—Matilde Zimmerman's *Sandinista: Carlos Fonseca and the Nicaraguan Revolution* (Durham: Duke, 2000)—tries to trace how the FSLN, after Fonseca's death in 1976, tamped the radicalism of Fonseca's life and thought. For a collection of Fonseca's writings, see *Obras: Bajo la bandera del sandinismo,* Vol. 1 and *Viva Sandino,* Vol. 2 (Managua: Editorial Nueva Nicaragua, 1982).

FSLN in Power

A number of edited works, most written by sympathetic foreign academics, concentrate on the economic challenges faced by the revolutionary government. These include Carlos Vilas and Richard Harris, eds., *Nicaragua: A Revolution Under Siege* (London: Zed Books, 1985); Rose Spalding, ed., *The Political Economy of Revolutionary Nicaragua* (Winchester, Mass.: Allen and Unwin, 1987); Richard R. Fagen, José Luis Coraggio, and Carmen Diana Deere, eds., *Transition and Development: Problems of Third World Socialism* (New York: Monthly Review Press, 1986); José Luis Coraggio and Carmen Diana Deere, eds., *La Transición difícil: La autodetermincación de los pequeños países periféricos* (México: Siglo veintiuno editores, 1986); and Michael E. Conroy, ed., *Nicaragua: Profiles of the Revolutionary Public Sector* (Boulder and London: Westview Press, 1987). Carlos Vilas covers a range of topics in *Transición desde el subdesarrollo: Revolución y reforma en la periferia* (Caracas: Nueva Sociedad, 1989).

For a masterful condensed account, see James Dunkerley, *Power in the Isthmus: A Political History of Modern Central America* (London and New York: Verso, 1988).

Many authors lived in and wrote on Nicaragua during the 1980s and subsequently published books in the 1990s based on their field research, often as FSLN advisers, after the fall from power of the FSLN. Most of them acknowledge failures of the FSLN; some are sympathetic, others critical. For sympathetic accounts, see Rose Spalding, *Capitalists and Revolution in Nicaragua: Opposition and Accommodation, 1979–1993* (Chapel Hill: Univ. of North Carolina Press, 1994); Laura Enríquez, *Harvesting Change: Labor and Agrarian Reform in Nicaragua, 1979–1990* (Chapel Hill: Univ. of North Carolina Press, 1991) and *Agrarian Reform and Class Consciousness in Nicaragua* (Gainesville: Univ. Press of Florida, 1997); and Ilja Luciak, *The Sandinista Legacy: Lessons from a Political Economy in Transition* (Gainesville: Univ. Press of Florida, 1995). For a highly critical view, see Forest Colburn, *Managing the Commanding Heights* (Berkeley and Los Angeles: Univ. of California Press, 1990).

The importance of the contra war is reflected in virtually all discussions of the Sandinista years. The best treatment of the war can be found in this collective work by FSLN militants: Orlando Nuñez et al., *La guerra en Nicaragua* (Managua: CIPRES, 1991). In English, see Holly Sklar, *Washington's War on Nicaragua* (Boston: South End, 1989) and Stephen Kinzer, *Blood of Brothers* (New York: Putnam's, 1991).

Aside from the contra war, perhaps the most ambitious and challenging transformation attempted by the FSLN in power was the Agrarian Reform, and that complex process has attracted considerable attention. Two early articles outlined some of the basic problems; they are James Austin, Jonathan Fox, and Walter Kruger, "The Role of the Revolutionary State in the Nicaraguan Food System," *World Development* 13, no. 1. (1985): 15–40, and Carmen Diana Deere, Peter Marchetti, and Nola Reinhardt, "The Peasantry and the Development of the Sandinista Agrarian Policy," *Latin American Research Review* 20(3) (1985): pp. 75–109.

Once the basic contours of the situation began to emerge with greater clarity, the debate over agricultural policy revolved around the role and power of the state versus the autonomy and independence of the campesinos. With a large non-proletarian peasant population, FSLN policies favoring high-tech investment projects ran up against significant peasant resistance. At the policy level, analysts often referred eventually to the tension as a debate between developmentalists and campesinistas. Two U.S. researchers, David Kaimowitz and Michael Zalkin, in a number of articles, helped reorient the discussion by reexamining earlier studies and assumptions; see, for example, David Kaimowitz, "Nicaraguan Debates on Agrarian Structure and Their Implication for Agricultural Policy and the Rural Poor," *Journal of Peasant Studies* 14, no. 1 (Oct. 1986): 100–117, and Michael Zalkin, "Agrarian Class Structure in Nicaragua in 1980: A New Interpretation and Some Implications," *Journal of Peasant Studies* 16, no. 4 (July 1989): 575–605. For the perspective of one of the leading campesinista proponents, see Eduardo Baumeister, *Estructura y Reforma Agraria en Nicaragua (1979–1989)* (Managua: Ediciones CDA—ULA, 1998); for a shorter discussion in English by the same author, see "Farmers' Organizations and Agrarian Transformation in Nicaragua" in *The New Politics of Survival*, edited by Minor Sinclair (New York: Monthly Review Press, 1995): 239–263. For another pro-campesinista writer, see Marvin Ortega, "The State, the Peasantry and the Sandinista Revolution," *Journal of Development Studies* 26, no. 4 (July 1990): 122–142. Brizio Nico Biondi-Morra presents a caustic critique of state policy in *Hungry Dreams: The Failure of Food Policy in Revolutionary Nicara-*

gua, 1979–1990 (Ithaca: Cornell Univ. Press, 1993). Toward the end of the Agrarian Reform process, some of the key researchers participated in a conference in 1988 devoted to the debate; the papers were published in Raul Rubén and Jan P. De Groot, coordinadores, *El debate sobre la Reforma Agraria en Nicaragua: Transformación agraria y atención al campesinado en nueve años de Reforma Agraria (1979–1988)* (Managua: INIES, 1989). For a less academic, but informed, approach, see Joseph Collins, *Nicaragua: What Difference Could a Revolution Make?* (San Francisco: Institute for Food and Development Policy, 1985). For the official retrospective view of the FSLN comandante in charge of the Agrarian Reform after he declared it completed in 1989, see Jaime Wheelock, *La Reforma Agraria Sandinista* (Managua: Vanguardia, 1990) and *La Reforma Agraria en Nicaragua, 1979–1989,* Vol. I. Estrategia y políticas (Managua: CIERA, 1989).

Supporters of the FSLN, and the FSLN itself, described the revolution as one based on participatory democracy. That description depended in large part on the formation of grassroots organizations, known as mass organizations, intended as a source of both ideological support and popular creativity. As with the Agrarian Reform, a debate surfaced over the degree to which the mass organizations in fact became executors of the "orientations" of the FSLN. Luis Serra, an Argentinean political exile who lived in Nicaragua throughout the period, contributed several articles to the Walker anthologies listed above. He ultimately published a dissertation on the mass organizations, *Movimiento cooperativo campesino: Su participación política durante la revolución Sandinista, 1979–1989* (Managua: Universidad Centroamericana, 1991). Gary Ruchwarger, an American who lived and worked in Nicaragua during the period, wrote two valuable, sympathetic grassroots accounts in *People in Power: Forging a Grassroots Democracy* (South Hadley, Mass.: Bergin and Garvey, 1987) and *Struggling for Survival: Workers, Women, and Class on a Nicaraguan State Farm* (Boulder: Westview, 1989). For a vivid sense of the tension attached to this debate on the left, see Carlos Vilas, "The Mass Organizations in Nicaragua: The Current Problematic and Perspectives for the Future," *Monthly Review* 38, no. 6 (November 1986): 20–31; the attack on Vilas by Kent Norsworthy and William I. Robinson in December (44–47); and the response by Vilas in March 1987 (49–51).

If the Agrarian Reform provoked sharp polemics within Nicaragua, the policies on the Atlantic coast drew international attention for what critics viewed as the harsh treatment of the indigenous Indian population. A variety of factors resulted in armed resistance to the FSLN government on the coast by the Miskitos, opening another front in the contra war. With the rising prominence of indigenous rights organizations at the time, war with the Miskitos, combined with forced population transfers, was a public relations disaster for the FSLN. Several early articles by anthropologists supplied relevant historical background without taking sides in the developing polemic. See, for example, Philippe Bourgois, "Las minorías étnicas en la revolución Nicaragüense," *Estudios sociales centroamericanos,* no. 39 (1984): 13–31. By the middle of the decade, the FSLN attempted to defuse the situation and initiated a long Autonomy process for the coast. The FSLN established a study center, CIDCA, devoted to the coast, and CIDCA, around 1985, published a booklet on the coast, *Trabil Nani: Historical Background and Current Situation of the Atlantic Coast of Nicaragua* (Managua: CIDCA, n.d.); see also CIDCA/Development Study Unit, ed., *Ethnic Groups and the Nation State* (Stockholm: Akademitryck AB, 1987). As part of a series of pamphlets devoted to indigenous peoples throughout the world, the Minority Rights Group published *The Mis-*

kito Indians of Nicaragua (London: Minority Rights Group, 1988), written by Roxanne Dunbar Ortiz, a longtime indigenous-rights activist. For an extremely detailed historical account through the mid-1980s, see Jorge Jenkins Molieri, El desafío indígena en Nicaragua: El caso de los mískitos (Managua: Vanguardia, 1986). After not mentioning the Atlantic coast once in his book on the Sandinista revolution in 1984, Carlos Vilas turned his attention to it in the second half of the 1980s and wrote a stimulating study of the coast, brought out in English as State, Class, and Ethnicity in Nicaragua: Capitalist Modernization and Revolutionary Change on the Atlantic Coast (Boulder: Lynne Rienner, 1989). Vilas tries to demonstrate that the U.S. Protestant ideology of the Moravian Church contributed to the overreaction of the Miskitos. Two American anthropologists who lived on the coast during the 1980s published studies based on their field research: Charles Hale, Resistance and Contradiction: Miskitu Indians and the Nicaraguan State (Stanford: Stanford Univ. Press, 1994), and Edmundo Gordon, Disparate Diasporas: Creole Politics and the Sandinista Revolution (Austin: Univ. of Texas Press, 1998); see also Peter Sollis, "The Atlantic Coast of Nicaragua: Development and Autonomy," Journal of Latin American Studies 21 (October 1989): 481–520. The leading international authority on the Miskitos, Bernard Nietschmann—a Berkeley geographer—became an adviser to the Miskitos during the period and published a hyperbolic attack on the Sandinistas, accusing them of wanting to use the sea lanes from Cuba to launch a communist attack from the Caribbean. It is The Unknown War: The Miskito Nation, Nicaragua, and the United States (New York: Freedom House, 1989). He also enlisted the support of the Cambridge-based journal Cultural Survival Quarterly to pursue his campaign against the FSLN in the theoretical context of Fourth World Theory; see his "The Third World War," where the opening lines set the tone: "The Third World War has already begun. It began when new states tried to take over old nations" (Cultural Survival Quarterly 11, no. 3 (1987): 1–16.

The fall of the FSLN in 1990 led to postmortems of the Sandinista years and analyses of the electoral defeat. Carlos Vilas has written one of the most balanced analyses, addressing mistakes of the FSLN as well as, above all, the changed international conjuncture following the end of the Cold War and the evaporation of crucial external aid from Cuba and the European Socialist countries; this analysis, "Nicaragua: A Revolution that Fell from the Grace of the People" is found in Ralph Miliband and Leo Panitch, eds., Socialist Register: Communist Regimes—The Aftermath (London: Merlin Press, 1991: 302–321). Other commentators on the left faulted the ambiguity of the FSLN class identity; see, for example, Elizabeth Dore and John Weeks, The Red and the Black: The Sandinistas and the Nicaraguan Revolution (London: Institute of Latin American Studies, Univ. of London, 1992; Research Paper no. 28). For a liberal critique, see Paul Berman, "Why the Sandinistas Lost: Eleven Years of Nicaraguan Revolution," Dissent vol. 37, no. 3 (Summer 1990): 307–314.

Cultural Politics

For a sense of the official discourse at the intersection of culture and politics, see the Ministry of Culture publication Hacia una política cultural de la revolución popular Sandinista (Managua: Ministerio de Cultura, 1982).

Within the Ministry of Culture, Rosario Murillo, the wife of comandante (and later president) Daniel Ortega, established an alternative power center through the journal Ventana, distributed weekly with the official FSLN organ Barricada (available on microfilm). Murillo gathered the FSLN's most prominent writers and intellectuals at *Ventana* and soon founded an independent organization for established artists, the ASTC (Asociación Sandinista de trabajadores de la cultura); see *Segunda asamblea nacional "fernando gordillo,"* 1982.

For obvious economic reasons, literature is the easiest cultural product to export, so commentaries on literature have tended to dominate the publishing scene. American literary scholars Marc Zimmerman and John Beverley published a book on Central American literature, just after the 1990 electoral loss, in which they discussed the literary works and the bureaucratic literary politics: *Literature and Politics in the Central American Revolutions* (Austin: Univ. of Texas Press, 1990). In 1995 David Whisnant published a magisterial study of the cultural efflorescence, and tensions, across the arts—unleashed and fomented by the Sandinista revolution; it is *Rascally Signs in Sacred Places: The Politics of Culture in Nicaragua* (Chapel Hill: Univ. of North Carolina Press, 1995). Whisnant surveys a very broad range of artistic production, including cinema, and is sensitive to the ideological stresses in the cultural infrastructure. In the hard-to-find *Entre la poesía y la pared: política cultural Sandinista, 1979-1990* (Costa Rica: FLASCO, and Amsterdam: Thela, 1994), Klaas Wellinga presents an extremely detailed analysis of Sandinista cultural policy, including lengthy commentaries on the bitter ideological and personal battle between the head of the Ministry of Culture, Ernesto Cardenal, and Rosario Murillo.

Cinema

Nicaraguan cinema would probably not have existed without the extensive support of Cuba, through the Cuban Institute of Cinema, ICAIC. Michael Chanan has written the best history of Cuban cinema, *The Cuban Image: Cinema and Cultural Politics in Cuba* (London: British Film Institute, 1985), though it ends in 1980. For an excellent complement, see Paulo Antonio Paranagua, ed., *Le Cinéma Cubain* (Paris: Centre Georges Pompidou, 1990); see also Julianne Burton, "Film and Revolution in Cuba: The First 25 Years" in *Cuba: 25 Years of Revolution,* edited by John M. Kirk and Sandor Halebsky (New York: Praeger, 1985): 134–153.

As Cuban cinema offers the most sustained model of film production in a socialist country in the Western hemisphere, readers can also consult issues of the official ICAIC journal, *Cine cubano,* and a number of anthologies published in Cuba, including Ambrosio Fornet, *Cine, literatura, sociedad* (Havana: Editorial Letras Cubanas, 1982) and Julio García Espinosa, *Una imagen recorre el mundo* (Ciudad de la Habana, Cuba: Editorial Letras Cubanas, 1979).

Since 1979 Cuba has hosted the annual Festival of New Latin American Cinema in Havana. Teresa Toledo has compiled a catalog of all films shown during the first years of the festival in *10 años del nuevo cine latinoamericano* (Spain: Verdoux, S. L., Sociedad Estatal Quinto Centenario, and Cinemateca de Cuba, 1990). Several collections of papers from the festival have been published, including the important tenth anniversary publication *El nuevo cine latinoamericano en el mundo de hoy* (Mexico: Universidad Nacional Autónoma de Mexico, 1988). U.S. scholars have written two perceptive discussions of recent Latin American cinema, each trying to relate contemporary filmmaking to the more militant production of the past. They are Pat Aufderheide, "Latin American Cinema and the Rhetoric of Cultural Nationalism: Controversies at Havana in 1987 and 1989" in *Quarterly Review of Film and Video* 12, no. 4 (1991): 61–76 and

R. Ruby Rich, "An/Other View of New Latin American Cinema," *Iris* no. 13 (Summer 1991): 5–27.

The triumph of the Cuban revolution and the successes of Cuban filmmakers inspired political filmmaking throughout Latin America, a creative achievement often referred to, somewhat loosely, as the New Latin American Cinema. For the best history of cinema in Latin America, see John King's *Magical Reels: A History of Cinema in Latin America*, 2d. ed. (New York: Verso, 2000). Peter Schumann covers similar ground, from a more politicized point of view, in *Historia del cine latinoamericano* (Buenos Aires: Legasa, 1987). For histories of film in individual countries, written (in most cases) by scholars and critics from the respective countries, see Guy Hennebelle and Alfonso Gumucio Dagrón, eds., *Les Cinémas de l'Amérique Latine* (Paris: CinémAction/Lherminier, 1981). The dean of Latin American film studies in the United States, Julianne Burton, has written a critical overview of the central period of political filmmaking in Latin America: "The Camera as 'Gun': Two Decades of Film Culture and Resistance in Latin America," *Latin American Perspectives* 5, no. 1. Issue 16 (Winter 1978) 49–76. In addition, readers can look at these anthologies edited by Burton: *Cinema and Social Change in Latin America* (Austin: Univ. of Texas Press, 1986); *The Social Documentary in Latin America* (Pittsburgh: Univ. of Pittsburgh Press, 1990); and *The New Latin American Cinema: An Annotated Bibliography of Sources in English, Spanish, and Portuguese, 1960–1980* (New York: Smyrna Press, 1983); see also Coco Fusco, ed., *Reviewing Histories: Selection from the New Latin American Cinema* (Buffalo, N.Y.: Hallwalls, Contemporary Arts Center, 1987). Zuzana Pick has written a less inclusive, more interpretive discussion in Zuzana Pick, *The New Latin American Cinema: A Continental Project* (Austin: Univ. of Texas Press, 1993).

On the historiography of Latin American Cinema, see these articles by Ana Lopez: "A Short History of Latin American Film Histories" in *Journal of Film and Video* 37, no. 1 (1985) 55–99; "An 'Other' History: The New Latin American Cinema" in *Radical History Review* no. 41 (April 1988): 93–116; and "Setting Up the Stage: A Decade of Latin American Film Scholarship" in *Quarterly Review of Film and Video* 13, nos. 1–3 (1991): 239–260.

For a wonderful cornucopia of documents, see *Hojas de cine: Testimonios y documentos del nuevo cine latinoamericano* (Mexico, D.F.: Universidad Autónoma Metropolitana, 1988), especially Volume I (Central America and the Caribbean) and Volume III (Central and South America). Michael Martin has gathered, in English, many of the most important statements and manifestos in *New Latin American Cinema*, Volumes I and II (Detroit: Wayne Univ. Press, 1996).

For various reasons, the rubric of "third cinema" has emerged and persisted as the most prominent label from the rich and varied practice of political filmmaking, known originally as the New Cinema of Latin America. Unfortunately, with the exception of "Towards a Third Cinema," most of the complementary articles and interviews by the authors of "Towards a Third Cinema" are not available in English. For the most important texts, consult Fernando E. Solanas and Octavio Getino, *Cine, cultura y descolonización* (Buenos Aires: Siglo XXI, 1973), and Octavio Getino, *A diez años de "hacia un tercer cine"* (Mexico D. F.: Filmoteca UNAM, 1982). As Solanas has continued to make films, Getino has continued to write, particularly about the implications of the changing technologies in image making. In a sense, while no longer promoting third cinema, per se, Getino has retained an interest in popular communication and for more than ten years has tried to adapt that interest to the radically transformed audiovisual landscape. He has concentrated on the political economy of modern communication in Latin America, specifically widened to include television and video; see, most pertinently, *Cine latinoamericano: economías y nuevas tecnologías audiovisuales* (Buenos Aires: Legasa, 1988) and *La tercera mirada: panorama del audiovisual latinoamericano* (Buenos Aires: Paidós, 1996).

Interest in "third cinema" resurfaced in English in the 1980s, though in adulterated form. See Paul Willemen and Jim Pines, eds., *Questions of Third Cinema* (London: BFI, 1989) and Teshome Gabriel, *Third Cinema in the Third World* (Ann Arbor: UMI, 1982). "CinémAction" published a dossier of responses by critics and filmmakers on "L'influence du 'Troisième Cinéma' dans le Monde," *Revue tiers monde* xx, no. 79 (July–September 1979): 615–645.

For Nicaraguan filmmaking, the best sources are the materials collected in *Cine cubano* 96 (1980) and articles published during the 1980s in *Ventana* by Ramiro Lacayo and Carlos Vicente Ibarra, among others. For oral autobiographical portraits by several of the founders of INCINE, see Fernando Pérez Valdés, *Corresponsales de guerra* (Habana: Casas de la Americas, 1981). Armand Mattelart edited *Communicating in Popular Nicaragua* (New York and Bagnolet: International General, 1986), reprinting an interview with Ramiro Lacayo and a report on video by Dee Dee Halleck. A New York University dissertation by Susan Ryan (*Popularizing Media: The Politics of Video in the Nicaraguan Revolution*, 1996) is well worth looking at for grassroots video production. Recently, Rafael Vargas has published several articles in *El nuevo diario* (Managua): "Rubén Darío y el cine," January 22, 2000; "Rubén Darío y el cine," January 15, 2000; "¿Cuál cine nacional?," November 13, 1999; "CINENICACENTROACARIBE," November 9, 1999; and "Campocontracampo," September 4, 1999.

The following journals have reported on political filmmaking in Latin America: *Cineaste, Jump Cut, Iris, Framework, Afterimage, Screen, Jeune cinéma,* and *Cinéma politique.*

Index

Page numbers in italics indicate photographs.

Area of People's Property (APP), 244
Argentina, cinema attendance in, 237
Argüello, Iván, 149, 248; background of, 125. Films: *Bienaventurados los que luchan por la paz*, 129; *Esta tierra es ese hombre*, 127–128, 176; *La gran equivocación*, 125–127; *Mujeres de la frontera*, 175, 213–216, *215*, 217, 221, 247, 249, 295n. 25; *Rompiendo el silencio*, 137–142, 178, 198, 285n. 15; *Teotecacinte*, 170–174, 199
Argüello, Javier, 2
Association of Nicaraguan Cinematography (ANCINE), 63–64
Association of Nicaraguan Women "Luisa Amanda Espinosa" (AMNLAE), 20, 221; in *Acto del primero de mayo*, 27; in *Generosos en la victoria*, 133; and *Mujeres de la frontera*, 214, 216; in *Pan y dignidad: Carta abierta de Nicaragua*, 156–157
Association of Rural Workers (ATC), 151; in *The Agrarian Reform*, 30; in *Generosos en la victoria*, 133; in *1979: Año de la liberación*, 18; in *Nuestra Reforma Agraria*, 157, 165, 170
Association of Women Confronting the National Problematic (AMPRONAC), 100, 156–157. *See also* AMNLAE
ASTC. *See* Sandinista Association of Cultural Workers
ATC. *See* Association of Rural Workers
Atlantic Coast, 74–75, 247; and *La costa Atlántica*, 37–44; in *El espectro de la guerra*, 217–220; in *Los hijos del río*, 198–213; as inspiration for the slogan "Giant Awakens," 18, 200, 211; and Literacy Campaign, 39–40, 43; and modernization, 43; in *Nacionalización de las minas*, 15; in *1979: Año de la liberación*, 18; in *Nuestra Reforma Agraria*, 167–168; in *La otra cara del oro*, 65–69; in *Rompiendo el silencio*, 137–142
Aufderheide, Pat, 272n. 12
auteurs, 247

Bananeras, 118, 150–154, *152*
Barricada, 4, 12, 18, 20, 47, 55, 64, 76, 180, 220
basic grains: in *Economic Plan of 1980*, 21; in *Nuestra Reforma Agraria*, 167–168

Battle of Algiers (Pontecorvo), and third cinema, 124
Bazin, André, 235
Beatles, 66, 130
Belli, Gioconda, 59, 60, 61, 118, 120
Benjamin, Walter, 229–230
Beverley, John, on ICAIC, 238–239
Bienaventurados los que luchan por la paz, 129
Birri, Fernando, 105, 224, 230, 247, 296n. 2; and *Pan y dignidad: Carta abierta de Nicaragua*, 287n. 13; on Peronism, 297n. 3; and talleres, 178
Bishop, Maurice, 31
Blanco Organdí, 277n. 21
Bloecher, Michael, 217
Blood of the Condor (Sanjinés), 226
Bolivia, 110
Bolt, Alan, 82
Borge, Tomás, 45, 54, 96, 137; in *La defensa militar*, 49; in *Del ejército defensor de la soberanía nacional al ejército popular Sandinista*, 86–87, 89; in *Los hijos del río*, 206, 208, 210, 211, 212, 213; in *1979: Año de la liberación*, 18; and *Primer aniversario de la revolucion popular Sandinista*, 31, 32
Borrego, Victor Martín, 108–109
Brazil, cinema attendance in, 237
Brecht, Bertolt, 230, 249
Buitrago, Julio, 96; in *Del ejército defensor de la soberanía nacional al ejército popular Sandinista*, 87, 88, 90; and *Qué se rinda tu madre*, 292n. 26
Buñuel, Luis, 72; influence of, on Rafael Vargas, 182

Cabezas, Omar, 83, 196
Caldera, Franklin, 4, 45, 63, 97, 99
Calero, Adolfo, in *La Democracia*, 35
"camera is a gun," 1
Campbell, Lumberto, 44
campesinos, 21, 28, 30–31, 247; and *The Agrarian Reform*, 30–31; and *La ceiba*, 142–145; and Literacy Campaign, 34; in *Nuestra Reforma Agraria*, 157–170; in *Río San Juan, a este lado de la puerta*, 146–147
canción de amor para el otoño, Una, 289n. 35
Carballo, Father Bismarck, 293n. 35
Cardenal, Ernesto, 3, 24, 26, 92, 143, 168,

173; in *La Cultura,* 94–95, 154; in *1979: Año de la liberación,* 18; and poetry workshops, 55; and Rosario Murillo, 121–122, 222, 243–244, 276n. 9, 279n. 17, 282n. 44; as tercerista, 53; in *Wiwilí sendero a una victoria,* 127

Cardenal, Fernando, 26, 45, 173; in *Clausura de la cruzada nacional de alfabetización,* 33; in *Inicio cruzada de alfabetización,* 24

Carmen Meza, José del, in *Nacionalización de la minas,* 13, 15, 17

Carrión, Luis, in *Los hijos del río,* 206, 208, 211, 212

Carter administration, in *La Democracia,* 36–37

Casas Populares de Cultura, in *La Cultura,* 94

Castillo, José María ("Chema"), 88, 90, 140, 141, 278n. 11

Castillo, Maritza, and *Esbozo de Daniel,* 293n. 35

Castro, Fidel, 7, 74, 228, 240; and ICAIC, 45, 223; in *Primer aniversario de la revolución popular Sandinista,* 31

Catholic Church, 247, 293n. 35; in *Teotecacinte,* 172–173

caudillismo, 128, 283n. 5, 283n. 6

Cecilia (Solás), 219

ceiba autodefensa, La, 142–145, 146, 219, 290n. 1

censorship, 10; pre-revolutionary, 7–8; within INCINE, 154. *See also* Commission of Classification

centerfielder, El, 194–197

centinelas de la alegría del pueblo, Los, 134–137, *136,* 137, 149, 177

Chacal de Nahueltoro, El (Littín), 195

Chanan, Michael, 117

Chávez, Lisandro, 118, 119

Chile, 110; cinema attendance in, 237; cinema of, 226–227; lesson of, 242

Chile Films, 227

Chomarro, Violeta Barrios, 26–27, 77

Cine Cubano, 2

Cine Liberación, 5, 230

cinema, in pre-revolutionary Nicaragua, 7, 272nn. 15, 17

Cinema Company of Nicaragua (ENCI), 296n. 37

cinema criticism, 56, 107–108. See also *Ventana*

Cinema Novo, 5, 8, 224–225

Cinemateca, 104

Cine RAP, 9, 178, 236, 240, 244

Clausura de la cruzada nacional de alfabetización, 32–34, 35

COCULTURA. *See* Cultural Corporation of the People

COIP. *See* Industrial Corporation of the People

comandantes: in *Economic Plan of 1980,* 21; and INCINE, 274n. 14

Comintern, 48

Comites de Defensa Sandinista (CDSs), 18, 111; in *La defensa política,* 54

Commission of Classification, 99–104, 107, 109, 117, 279n. 3, 280n. 14; criteria for, 125

Compadrazgo, 143

Consejo Directivo (INCINE), 46–47

contrarevolución, La, 47, 81, 247

contra war, 20, 80, 86, 129, 197, 199, 241, 244, 248, 293n. 33; and Atlantic Coast, 211; in *La ceiba,* 143–144; in *Esbozo de Daniel,* 190–191; in *El espectro de la guerra,* 217; in *Los hijos del río,* 198–213; in *Qué se rinda tu madre,* 186–189; in *Teotecacinte,* 171–174. See also *Manuel; Mujeres de la frontera*

cooperatives, 29, 31, 76, 160, 166, 192, 288n. 25, 289n. 32; in *The Agrarian Reform,* 30, 31; in *La ceiba,* 143–145; credit and service, 163

coproductions, 176, 198, 244

Coraje del pueblo, El (Sanjinés), 195

Corazo, Odio, 34

Cortázar, Octavio, 117

costa Atlántica, La, 37–44, *39, 41, 42,* 45, 74, 75, 198, 274n. 16

Council of State, 20, 147, 148, 151; in *Acto del primero de mayo,* 27; in *La democracia,* 35; in *Nicaragua ganó,* and military draft, 178; in *Primer aniversario de la revolucion popular Sandinista,* 32

Creoles: in *La costa Atlántica,* 40, 42; and *El espectro de la guerra,* 219–220; in *The Iván Dixon Cultural Brigade,* 73–75; in *Nacionalización de la minas,* 15

Cruz, Arturo, 147, 148

CST. *See* Sandinista Central of Workers

Cuba, 28, 37; advisors from, 20; and Atlantic Coast, 44, 201; and *El centerfielder,* 195–196; commitment to cinema in, 245; economic crisis in, 236; exhibition in, 105, 280n. 21; and INCINE, 65, 97, 236; influence of, 7; and Mobile Cinema, 109, 110; newsreels of, 129; support of FSLN by, 8; and *Teotecacinte*, 214. *See also* Cuban cinema

Cuban cinema, 11, 195, 225–226, 246

Cuban Institute of Cinematographic Art and Industry (ICAIC), 5–6, 7, 11, 238–239, 248; autonomy of, 240; change in status of, 245; founding of, 8–9, 223, 272n. 18; and INCINE, 8, 44, 46, 123, 245; influence of, 8, 45; and *Mujeres de la frontera*, 214; and newsreels, 274n. 18

Cuban Institute of Radio and Television (ICRT), 194; Somarriba on, 292n. 28

Cultura, La, 94–95, *95*, 154

Cultural Corporation of the People (COCULTURA), 9, 244

culture, 94–95; in *La Cultura*, 94–95; coverage of, 12

Cunningham, Mirna, in *Los hijos del río*, 209, 210

Daniel. See Esbozo de Daniel

Darío, Rubén, 284n. 7; in *Bienaventurados los que luchan por la paz*, 129; in *La Cultura*, 95; in *Manuel*, 183; and *Qué se rinda tu madre*, 189

Davis, Peter. See *Hearts and Minds*

De Asis, Francisco, 59, 62, 118, 119, 120

decisión, La, 81

Declaration of Principles, 2–3, 247, 258, 259

Deerhunter, The (Cimino), 102–103

defensa económica, La, 47, 50–51, *53*

defensa militar, La, 47, 49–50, *50*

defensa política, La, 47, 51–54, 62, 137

Delgado, Livio, 21, 217

democracia, La, 34–37, *36*, 48

DeNiro, Robert, in *Deerhunter*, 102

Department of Propaganda and Political Education (DEPEP), 4, 57, 60; and Commission of Classification, 100

DEPEP. *See* Department of Propaganda and Political Education

Días de crisis, 14

Diegues, Carlos, 247

Dirección Nacional (FSLN), 28, 49, 128, 200, 247; in *Clausura de la cruzada nacional de alfabetización*, 33, 45; and

fiction, 189; and mass organizations, 242; in *1979: Año de la liberación*, 17, 20, 28; in *Primer aniversario de la revolución popular Sandinista*, 31

Dispuestos a todo por la paz, 83–84

Distribution, 4, 9, 96, 236, 241, 244. *See also* ENIDIEC

Doce, Los, 46, 195

documentaries, 44, 46–47, 62, 70, 77, 150, 174, 241

Duarte, José Napoleon, 48

Economic Plan of 1980, 20–22, 45, 130

Eisenstein, Sergei, 72, 110, 131

ejército defensor de la soberanía nacional al ejército popular Sandinista, Del, 85–90

El Salvador, 81, 120

ENABAS. *See* Nicaraguan Company of Basic Foods

ENCI. *See* Cinema Company of Nicaragua

enclave economy, 67–68, 286n. 6

Engels, Friedrich, 27

ENIDIEC. *See* Nicaraguan Company of Cinematic Distribution and Exhibition

Esbozo de Daniel, 185, 189–194, 195, 197, 221; budget of, 292n. 24; Ibarra on, 197; original story of, 189–190; and writing credit, 191

Escuchemos a las mujeres, 289n. 35

espectro de la guerra, El, 175, 198, 216–222, *218*, 245–246

Espinosa, Leonel, 118

Esta tierra es ese hombre, 127–128, 176

Estos sí pasarán, 289n. 35

exhibition, 4, 98, 104–105, 236, 241, 244. *See also* Cine RAP

Exodus (Preminger), 102

export crops: in *El abastecimiento*, 132; in *The Agrarian Reform*, 31; in *Economic Plan of 1980*, 21; in *Nuestra Reforma Agraria*, 158–170

Fagoth, Steadman, 44, 200, 201, 294n. 9; in *Los hijos del rio*, 205–206, 208, 209, 211

Fanon, Franz, 228

Farabundo Martí Front for National Liberation (El Salvador) (FMLN), 47, 48, 49

115, 124, 125, 126, 140; and Alfonso Robelo, 26–27; and Atlantic Coast, 38, 43, 199, 206; and *Clausura de la cruzada nacional de alfabetización,* 32–34; and *La Cultura,* 94; and *Esbozo de Daniel,* 191–192, 193; and *Inicio cruzada de alfabetización,* 22–24; and *Pan y dignidad: Carta abierta de Nicaragua,* 156; and UNESCO prize, 22

Littín, Miguel, 5, 99, 195, 226, 227, 247; and *Alsino y el cóndor,* 117–122, 219; in *La Cultura,* 94–95; in *Ventana,* 59–60

Lopez, Ana, 271n. 11

López Pérez, Rigoberto, 86, 88, 90; in *Viva León,* 96

Lorentz, Pare, 68–69

Lucia (Solás), 111, 195

MacNeil/Lehrer Report, 81

Mad Max (Miller), 101

maestro popular, El, 123–125, 126, 129, 145, 193, 220

Managua de sol a sol, 289n. 35

Mandel, Ernest, 88

Manifestos: "Cinema and Underdevelopment," 224; Filmmakers Manifesto (Chile), 226–227; Imperfect Cinema, 225–226; Rocha, 224–225; "Towards a Third Cinema," 227–236, 247, 248

Manley, Michael, 31

Manuel, 137, 177, 178–185, 189, 193, 203, 221, 291n. 9, 291n. 14; and talleres, 178; budget of, 292n. 24

Mao Tse-tung, 228

Marín, Mariano, 49, 149; background of, 82; and fiction, 134, 137, 176, 177, 284n. 9; and *Manuel,* 178, 284n. 9, 291n. 9; on *Nuestra Reforma Agraria,* 287n. 17; on Ramiro Lacayo, 296n. 29; and super-8mm filmmaking, 52, 276n. 6. Films: *La ceiba,* 142–145, 146, 290n. 1; *Los centinelas de la alegría del pueblo,* 134–137, 177, 284n. 9; *La defensa política,* 51–54, 137; *Esbozo de Daniel,* 185, 189–194, 195, 197; *Generosos en la victoria,* 133–134, 137; *Homage to the Heroes and Martyrs of Monimbó,* 84–85, 137; *Los innovadores,* 129–131, 145; *Jornada anti-intervencionista,* 81–82, 84, 137; *El maestro popular,* 123–125, 145, 193, 220

Marker, Chris, 235

Martí, Frabundo, and Sandino, 48, 275n. 4

Martínez, Brenda, 46; and *Manuel,* 179

Marx, Karl, 27, 91

Marxism and worker-peasant alliance: in *Los innovadores,* 129–131, *131;* in *Nacionalización de la minas,* 15; in *Los trabajadores,* 91–93

Más claro no canta un gallo, 194

Más es mio el alba de oro, 289n. 35

mass organizations, 18, 242, 247; AMNLAE, 20, 27, 133, 156–157; AMPRONAC, 156–157; ATC, 18–20, 133, 151, 159, 166; CDS, 18, 50, 135, 157, 159; CST, 18, 94, 133, 151; INCINE, 80, 242–243, 245; UNAG, 142–145, 159, 165–166

MDN. *See* Nicaraguan Democratic Movement (MDN), in *Acto del primero de mayo*

mechanization, in *Economic Plan of 1980,* 21

media, transformation of, 11, 236–238

Mejía Godoy, Carlos, 85

Meléndez, Eddy, 222

Memories of Underdevelopment (Alea), 111

Mercado Nuevo Cine Latinoamericano (MECLA), 57–59

Mercado Oriental: in *El abastecimiento,* 132–133; in *Acto del primero de mayo,* 26, 28; in *País pobre, ciudadano pobre,* 76

mestizos, 15; on Atlantic Coast, 37

Mexican films, influence of, 10

Mexico, 110; and Mobile Cinema, 109; support of, for Nicaragua, 54; U.S. films in, 238

Miami Vice, 134, 136, 177

MICOIN. *See* Ministry of Interior Commerce

MIDINRA. *See* Ministry of Agricultural Development and Agrarian Reform

militant cinema, 11, 223–224, 231–234, 241, 242, 247–248

militarization: of society, 15, 83–84, 94; of youth, 15

military draft: in *El espectro de la guerra,* 217, 219–220; in *Manuel,* 178

Miller, Glenn, 71

mimados, Los, 95–96

Ministry of Agricultural Development

and Agrarian Reform (MIDINRA), 160, 170

Ministry of Agriculture, 11; and media projects, 243

Ministry of Culture, 3–4, 9, 57, 60, 94, 99, 149, 180, 194; closing of, 222, 236–237, 246; and Commission of Classification, 99–100; creation of, 8, 12; and INCINE, 240–241, 257; and Rosario Murillo and ASTC, 121–122, 243–244

Ministry of Defense, 11, 135; and media projects, 243

Ministry of Interior, 11, 100, 135, 137

Ministry of Interior Commerce (MICOIN), 9, 244

Ministry of Justice, 135–136

Miskitos, 38, 74, 247; attitude of, toward North Americans, 294n. 3; and *La costa Atlántica*, 40–44; in *Los hijos del río*, 198–213; and Mobile Cinema, 112, 117; and *Nacionalización de la minas*, 15; and *La otra cara del oro*, 67; population figures for, 274n. 2; and *Rompiendo el silencio*, 138–142; and Sandino, 42

Miskitos, Sumos, Ramas (MISURA), 201, 204, 209

Miskitos, Sumos, Ramas, Sandinistas Together (MISURASATA), 39, 43–44, 200, 201, 205–206, 209, 274n. 15, 294n. 8

Missing (Costa-Gavras), 191

MISURA. *See* Miskitos, Sumos, Ramas

MISURASATA. *See* Miskitos, Sumos, Ramas, Sandinistas Together

Mobile Cinema (INCINE), 9, 12, 47, 56, 99, 109–117, 129, 273n. 6; and Cuba, 7; and *History of a Committed Cinema*, 112–117; Ibarra on, 109–110, 281n. 34; Michele Najlis on, 112

modernism, 247

Mohs, Carlos, 63; on *Acts of Marusia*, 108; on *Del águila al dragón*, 72–73; and ANCINE, 109

Monimbó, 84

Moravian Church, 43–44, 199–200; and *Los hijos del río*, 205, 211

Morrison, Jim, 126

Mother (Pudovkin), 191

Mujeres de la frontera, 175, 213–216, 215, 217, 219, 220, 221, 247, 249; budget of, 295n. 25

Murillo, Rosario: and debate on *Alsino y el cóndor*, 118–122; and Ernesto Cardenal, 121–122, 222, 243–244, 276n. 9, 279n. 17, 282n. 44; and *Ventana*, 55, 60–61

Nacionalización de la minas, 13–17, 16, 69

Najlis, Michele, 112

national cinemas, 237, 243; viability of, 245–247

National Film Board of Canada, 203

nationalization: of land, 9; of mines, 13–17, 69; of theaters, 9

National Liberal Party, in *La democracia*, 35

National Opposition Union (UNO), 222

National Union of Farmers and Cattlemen (UNAG), 111; and *La ceiba*, 142–145; formation of, 289n. 31; and *Mujeres de la frontera*, 214, 216; and *Nuestra Reforma Agraria*, 165

neo-realism (Italian), 7, 58, 124, 225

New Cinema, 5–6, 7, 108, 111, 178, 271n. 11

New Latin American Cinema, 5–6, 7, 271n. 11; in *Ventana*, 58

New Latin American Cinema, Festival of, 6, 238; and *Mujeres de la frontera*, 214; and video, 11

Nicaragua ganó, 147–149, 286n. 23

Nicaraguan Association of Cinema (ANCI), 296n. 37

Nicaraguan Company of Basic Foods (ENABAS), 132–133

Nicaraguan Company of Cinematic Distribution and Exhibition (ENIDIEC), 9, 104, 109, 178, 236, 240, 244

Nicaraguan Democratic Movement (MDN), in *Acto del primero de mayo*, 27

Nicaraguan Institute of Cinema (INCINE), 2, 6, 7, 247; budget figures of, 292n. 24; closing of, 221–222, 236–237, 240–249, 262; and Consejo Directivo, 46–47; coproductions of, 114, 133; and Cubans, 239–240; disorganization in, 287n. 15; documentaries by, 44, 46–47, 62, 70, 77, 150, 174, 241; early name change of, 2, 28, 57, 64, 248; failure of, to explore sensitive issues, 247, 286n. 5; and fiction, 78, 84–85, 127, 128, 134, 174–

ejército popular Sandinista, 85–90;
in *Mujeres de la frontera*, 214–215; in
Teotecacinte, 174
Sandinista Association of Cultural
Workers (ASTC), 121–122, 282n. 48
Sandinista Central of Workers (CST), 18,
94; in *Generosos en la victoria*, 133;
and super-8mm workshop, 79–80
Sandinista Front for National Liberation
(FSLN), 1, 3, 6, 10, 17, 21–22, 54; and
"accumulation of forces in silence,"
196, 285n. 16; in *Acto del primero de
mayo*, 28; and *The Agrarian Reform*,
30–31; and Atlantic Coast, 38–44, 74,
140, 198–213; bureaucratic feudalism
of, 11, 65; and Council of State, 20;
and democracy, 34, 35; developmental
strategy of, 151; early perception of,
22; in *Economic Plan of 1980*, 21; in
*Del ejército defensor de la soberanía
nacional al ejército popular Sandinista*, 85–90; and elections, 32, 34, 37;
and electoral defeat, 236, 247; flow
charts of, 253–257; and foco theory,
87, 278n. 10; founding of, 3, 8, 96; Historical Program of, 285n. 18; history
of, 52–53; hymn of, 39; ideological
strategy of, 28, 58; and INCINE, 10, 37,
64–65; in *Inicio cruzada de alfabetización*, 23–24; interest of, in cinema, 8,
10, 241; and land, 40–41; and Marxism
(Leninism), 92; and mass organizations, 18–20; and *Nacionalización de
la minas*, 15; and nationalizations, 9;
number of members in, 28, 300n. 62;
and panfletario films, 56; and policy
conflicts, 245; and public awareness
of, 273n. 9; and religion, 172–173;
and socialism, 92, 288n. 28; urban
profile of, 159, 288n. 23; as vanguard
organization, 242; and video, 11
Sandinista Institute of Nicaraguan
Cinema, 2, 28, 57, 64, 113, 247, 248,
281n. 37, 283n. 42
Sandinista Police, 13, 28; in *Los centinelas de la alegría del pueblo*, 134–137;
in *1979: Año de la liberación*, 18, 28
Sandinista Revolution, in *The Agrarian
Reform*, 30
Sandinista Television System (SSTV), 4;
relation to INCINE, 13, 57, 65
Sandino, Augusto César, 3, 17, 82, 92,

106, 271n. 7; and *Acto del primero
de mayo*, 27; and Atlantic Coast, 37–
38, 39, 42; and *La defensa militar*, 49;
and *Esta tierra es ese hombre*, 127–
128; and Farabundo Martí, 48; and
Nacionalización de las minas, 13, 15;
and *Nuestra Reforma Agraria*, 161;
and *Pan y dignidad: Carta abierta
de Nicaragua*, 155; and *Patriotic Day
of Sandino*, 22; and *Qué se rinda tu
madre*, 189; as theoretical guide, 158;
and *Wiwilí, sendero a una victoria*,
90
Sanjinés, Jorge, 5, 111, 195, 247; and third
cinema, 233, 235
Santana, Carlos, 127
Schumann, Peter: on Cuban cinema,
238; on Humberto Solás, 296n. 32
Secreto para mí sola, Un, 289n. 35
*Segundo aniversario de la revolución
popular Sandinista*, 54
Señorita, 63, 276n. 21
Señor Presidente, El (Gómez), 114, 244,
282n. 40
Shaw, Art, 71
Shogreen, Andy, in *Los hijos del río*, 208,
210
Siuna, 13, 15, 139
Solanas, Fernando, 5, 6, 247, 248, 249;
and third cinema, 227–236, 241–242,
246; and Peronism, 231, 298n. 26,
300n. 61
Solás, Humberto, 5, 217, 219, 296n. 32
Solentiname, 168
Somarriba, Fernando, 90, 96, 109; on
ICRT, 292n. 28; on Ramiro Lacayo,
296n. 29. Films: *La Cultura*, 94–95,
154; *Dispuestos a todo por la paz*, 83;
Los hijos del río, 198–213; *Managua
de sol a sol*, 289n. 35; *Los mimados*,
96; *Nicaragua ganó*, 147–149; *Qué se
rinda tu madre*, 185–189, 193, 195; *Río
San Juan, a este lado de la puerta*,
145–147, 198
Somocismo, 17, 33, 133; and Atlantic
Coast, 200
Somocismo without Somoza, 17
Somoza Debayle, Anastasio, 1, 84; and
1979: Año de la revolución, 17; and
*Pan y dignidad: Carta abierta de
Nicaragua*, 155–156
Somoza family, 9, 12, 64, 135, 152; and

Viña del Mar, festival of, 5, 7, 226
Viva León Jodido, 96–97, 176
Vivas, René, and *Nacionalización de la minas,* 13–15

Walker (Cox), 244
Walker, William, 82, 106
Wayne, John, 102
Wheelock, Jaime, 29, 45, 54, 75, 143, 160; in *The Agrarian Reform,* 30; and agricultural policy, 29; in *La costa Atlántica,* 41, 43; in *Economic Plan of 1980,* 21–22; in *Del ejército defensor de la soberanía nacional al ejército popular Sandinista,* 89; in *1979: Año de la revolución,* 18; in *Nuestra Reforma Agraria,* 163, 165; and proletarian tendency, 160
White, Robert, 48
Wild Geese (Margheriti), 102

Willemen, Paul, 229, 232
Wiwilí, sendero a una victoria, 90, 92, 127, 176–177
women: and *Bananeras,* 151–152; and *Pan y dignidad: Carta abierta de Nicaragua,* 155–157. *See also* AMNLAE
worker-peasant alliance: in *Nacionalización de la minas,* 15; in *1979: Año de la liberación,* 18
working class, 9, 15, 21, 28, 51, 91, 92–94

Xiloa, in *El espectro de la guerra,* 220–221

Yelín, Saúl (prize), 6
Young, Robert, 195

Zeledón, Benjamin, 82
Zamora, Daisy, 97